Public Value

REAL TIME NETWORK PROTECTION

Fortinet delivers unified threat management
and specialized security solutions.
Our consolidated architecture integrates critical
security technologies, delivering increased
performance and protection while reducing TCO.

Fortinet
St Clements House
27 - 28 Clements Lane
London EC4N 7AE
United Kingdom
Mobile: 07765 686135
Email: gburgess@fortinet.com
Web: www.fortinet.com

George W. Burgess
Major Account Manager
Public Sector

Public Value
Theory and Practice

Edited by
John Benington
and
Mark H. Moore

© Editorial matter and selection © John Benington and Mark H. Moore 2011

Individual chapters (in order) © John Benington and Mark H. Moore, John Benington, Colin Crouch, Noel Whiteside, Mark Swilling, Louise Horner and Will Hutton, Robin Wensley and Mark H. Moore, John Alford, Jonathan Q. Tritter, Jean Hartley, Guy Stuart, Richard Norman, Geoff Mulgan, Bob Fryer, David Winkley, Mark H. Moore and John Benington 2011

All rights reserved. No reproduction, copy or transmission of this publication may be made without written permission.

No portion of this publication may be reproduced, copied or transmitted save with written permission or in accordance with the provisions of the Copyright, Designs and Patents Act 1988, or under the terms of any licence permitting limited copying issued by the Copyright Licensing Agency, Saffron House, 6–10 Kirby Street, London EC1N 8TS.

Any person who does any unauthorized act in relation to this publication may be liable to criminal prosecution and civil claims for damages.

The authors have asserted their rights to be identified as the authors of this work in accordance with the Copyright, Designs and Patents Act 1988.

First published 2011 by
PALGRAVE MACMILLAN

Palgrave Macmillan in the UK is an imprint of Macmillan Publishers Limited, registered in England, company number 785998, of Houndmills, Basingstoke, Hampshire RG21 6XS.

Palgrave Macmillan in the US is a division of St Martin's Press LLC, 175 Fifth Avenue, New York, NY 10010.

Palgrave Macmillan is the global academic imprint of the above companies and has companies and representatives throughout the world.

Palgrave® and Macmillan® are registered trademarks in the United States, the United Kingdom, Europe and other countries

ISBN 978-0-230-24903-5   hardback
ISBN 978-0-230-24904-2   paperback

This book is printed on paper suitable for recycling and made from fully managed and sustained forest sources. Logging, pulping and manufacturing processes are expected to conform to the environmental regulations of the country of origin.

A catalogue record for this book is available from the British Library.

A catalog record for this book is available from the Library of Congress.

10 9 8 7 6 5 4 3 2 1
19 18 17 16 15 14 13 12 11 10

Printed and bound in Great Britain
by the MPG Books group, Bodmin and King's Lynn

Dedication (JB)

To my sister, Pauline Benington, who has courageously maintained her commitment to public service and to the creation of public value at the frontline of her neighbourhood community, over many years and in spite of many pressures and hardships.

Dedication (MM)

To the public managers who seek to create public value for their citizens every day of their working lives, and who have contributed so much to my understanding of the nature of the work they do, and its enduring importance.

Contents

List of Tables and Figures

Tables

Figures

Preface and Acknowledgements

We first met at an international conference in Dublin in 1997, shortly after Mark had published his pioneering book *Creating Public Value*. This started a lively conversation, and a warm friendship between us which has grown and flourished for well over a decade, and which shows signs of continuing for the rest of our lifetimes. Our debate has developed in seminar rooms at Harvard and at Warwick Universities; in conference halls, government offices, masterclasses and executive development programmes in the USA, Australia, England, Wales, Scotland and Northern Ireland. It has also often intruded in family holiday visits and long walks on Cape Cod and in the Cotswolds and the West of Scotland.

Over the past decade we have also worked together in dozens of forums in which public value ideas could be presented, discussed, and improved, in dialogue with fellow academics, public policymakers and public managers. In the course of this process we have developed many intellectual debts to others which we are very happy to acknowledge here. These include:

Our co-contributors to this book. The genesis of the book lies in a seminar at Warwick University's Institute of Governance and Public Management (IGPM) in which many of the authors were able to meet together over two days to question basic assumptions, to develop some shared ideas and to discuss draft chapters. This helped us to identify some differences in perspective, and to develop some common themes which hopefully have resulted in a clearer and more critical narrative about public value.

Our academic colleagues and doctoral students at Harvard and Warwick Universities who have contributed generously to critical discussion of the ideas over the years, and commented helpfully on seminar papers and draft chapters.

Richard Neustadt and Graham T. Allison who, as the architects of the Kennedy School of Government at Harvard, first put Moore to the task of developing a theory that could be the foundation of a new approach to public management that responded to the important intellectual developments and significant institutional changes that had occurred in the world since the original concepts of public administration in democratic polities had been developed in the early twentieth century.

Mark's academic colleagues at the Kennedy School who joined him in this effort, including in particular Philip Heymann, Joseph Bower, Robert Reich, Roger Porter, Herman 'Dutch' Leonard, Michael O'Hare, Stephen Hitchner, Ronald Heifetz, James Sebenius, Robert Leone, Michael Barzelay, John Donahue and Linda Kaboolian; and a group of practitioners who provided extensive advice and guidance along the way, including Mannie Carballo, Gordon Chase, Hale Champion, Richard Haas and Peter Zimmerman.

John's academic colleagues at Birmingham and Warwick Universities and elsewhere who have fanned the flames of his interest in the public sphere, civil society, community development, democratic politics, and public leadership and management – especially Colin Crouch, Nick Deakin, Jonathan Davies, David Donnison, Mike Geddes, Jean Hartley, Steve Leach, Kevin Morrell, Robin Murray, Stewart Ranson, Chris Skelcher, John Stewart, Gerry Stoker, Mark Swilling, Jonathan Tritter, Robin Wensley, Noel Whiteside and David Winkley.

Literally thousands of public policymakers and managers from the public and voluntary sectors who have taken part in our masters and diploma programmes, executive programmes, short courses and seminars, in the UK, Europe, the USA, Australia and New Zealand, South Africa, Southern Sudan and many other countries, and who have helped to shape the ideas both in discussion and in their essays and dissertations.

Sir John Harman, who as chair of the Advisory Board for Warwick's Institute of Governance and Public Management supported and contributed to the identification and development of public value as one of the core themes of IGPM's work and for several of our IGPM conferences.

Geoff Mulgan, who when he was the head of the UK Prime Minister's Strategy Unit organized several joint seminars with us, and commissioned his Cabinet Office colleagues Gavin Kelly and Stephen Muers to read and critique *Creating Public Value*. The resulting document helped to stimulate wide discussion among UK government ministers, permanent secretaries and senior civil servants in Westminster and Whitehall.

We are grateful particularly for the personal interest and support in developing and applying the ideas of public value shown us by Sir Gus O'Donnell, cabinet secretary and head of the UK civil service, Sir John Elvidge, permanent secretary of the Scottish Assembly Government, Sir Jon Shortridge, permanent secretary of the Welsh Assembly Government, Sir Nigel Hamilton, permanent secretary of the Northern Ireland civil service; David Spencer, Rod Clark, Cary Cooper and Sue Richards and colleagues from the UK's National School of Government (formerly the Civil Service College), and the Sunningdale Institute which forms part of the National School.

Our ideas have received an equally enthusiastic reception from UK local government political leaders and chief executives who have debated these ideas widely both in individual local authorities and through their professional associations and peak organizations (the Audit Commission, the Chartered Institute of Public Finance and Accountancy, the Local Government Association, the Improvement and Development Agency, the Leadership Centre, the National Policing Improvement Agency and the Society of Local Authority Chief Executives)

In the UK's National Health Service, Dame Yve Buckland and Bernard Crump at the NHS Institute for Innovation and Improvement initiated a joint project with Warwick University on public value outcomes in the health service, and

Julian Denney, Diane Ketley, Heather Shearer and Iestyn Williams formed the project team for this joint work.

Will Hutton and others at the Work Foundation commissioned a major programme on the application of Public Value thinking to the BBC, the Further Education sector and other public services.

Professors Alan Fels and John Alford at the Australian and New Zealand School of Government (ANZSOG) gave these ideas a place of honour in the ambitious programmes they have developed for senior public officials in these two countries.

Professors Rod Rhodes and John Wanna from the Australia National University (ANU) sparked off a lively and widespread academic debate through their frontal critique of Mark Moore's formulation of public value, in the journal *Public Administration* and the *Australian Journal of Public Administration*. And Professor John Alford from Melbourne University who responded robustly to their critique.

Steven Kennedy at Palgrave Macmillan and Gerry Stoker who have helped to shape the ideas, structure and balance of the book.

Kwaku Dako, Gill Devine, Yvonne Field, Kam Johal and Jane Miller who all contributed at various times to the production of successive drafts of this book, and especially Esme Farrington, who helped compile the bibliography and index, and who brought the whole project to completion with great efficiency.

The interest shown by these and other individuals and organizations have helped the ideas of public value to get a small purchase on academic scholarship in public management, but more importantly, a larger purchase on the thinking and practices of public managers, particularly in Great Britain and the Commonwealth countries. We trust that this book will both reflect this depth and breadth of thinking, and also move the debate about the theory and practice of public value substantially further forward.

JOHN BENINGTON
MARK H. MOORE

Notes on the Contributors

John Alford is Professor of Public Sector Management at Melbourne Business School, University of Melbourne, Australia, and also at the Australia and New Zealand School of Government. His research and publications are on organization–client relationships, public sector strategy and inter-organizational collaboration. His most recent book is *Engaging Public Sector Clients: From Service Delivery to Co-Production* (Palgrave Macmillan 2009) .

John Benington is Emeritus Professor of Public Policy and Management, University of Warwick, where for over 20 years he led Warwick Business School's research, development and teaching work in the fields of public policy and management, including the setting-up of the Institute of Governance and Public Management (IGPM), the Local Government Research Centre, the Warwick MPA (the public sector MBA) and the Masters and Diploma Programmes in Public Leadership and Management. John also has 20 years' prior experience of senior management in the public and voluntary sectors. He has been an adviser to the governments of the UK, South Africa, Sierra Leone, and Southern Sudan. He is a non-executive member of the board of the UK's National School of Government (formerly the Civil Service College), and a member of the Sunningdale Institute which forms part of the National School. He is national chair of the UK Local Authorities and Research Councils Initiative (LARCI), and is on the editorial boards of the journal *Leadership*, and of the *International Journal of Public Administration*. His research and publications are on community and economic development, networked governance, public value and civic leadership.

Colin Crouch is Professor of Governance and Public Management at Warwick Business School, the University of Warwick. He is also the External Scientific member of the Max-Planck-Institute for Social Research at Cologne. He previously taught sociology at the LSE, and was Fellow and Tutor in politics at Trinity College, Oxford, and Professor of Sociology at the University of Oxford. Until December 2004 he was Professor of Sociology at the European University Institute, Florence. He has published within the fields of comparative European sociology and industrial relations, on economic sociology, and on contemporary issues in British and European politics.

Bob Fryer CBE was until 2008 Chief Learning Adviser and National Director for Widening Participation in Learning at the UK's Department of Health, and is currently an Honorary Professor at Warwick University. Prior to this he was Chief Executive of the NHS University, Assistant Vice-Chancellor at the University of Southampton, and Principal of Northern College for Residential Adult Education.

Jean Hartley is Professor of Organisational Analysis at Warwick University and Head of the Institute of Governance and Public Management within Warwick Business School. Her research and publications are on organizational and cultural change, innovation and improvement, public leadership and learning, and leading with political awareness. Her most recent book, with John Benington, is *Leadership for Healthcare* (Policy Press, 2010).

Louise Horner joined the Work Foundation from the Cabinet Office Strategy Unit, where she developed research and policy on leadership in the public sector, and on workforce development and skills. At the Work Foundation she was a Senior Research Fellow managing research projects ranging from performance and productivity to public value. She has authored or co-authored several Work Foundation publications and case-studies on public value, with Will Hutton and other colleagues.

Will Hutton is a political economist, and a writer, columnist and former editor-in-chief for *The Observer*. He is currently Executive Vice-Chair of the Work Foundation having been Chief Executive from 2000 to 2008. He is a Governor of the London School of Economics, a Visiting Professor at Bristol and Manchester Universities and a Visiting Fellow at Mansfield College Oxford. His books include *The State We're In* (Cape, 1995), *The World We're In* (Little, Brown, 2002), *The Writing on the Wall* (Little, Brown, 2007) about the rise of China, and *Them and Us: Politics, Greed and Inequality* (Little, Brown, 2010).

Mark H. Moore is the Hauser Professor of Nonprofit Organizations at Harvard's Kennedy School of Government, and Faculty Chair of the Hauser Center for Nonprofit Organizations. He was the Founding Chairman of the Kennedy School's Committee on Executive Programs, and served in that role for over a decade. From 1979 to 2004 he was the Guggenheim Professor of Criminal Justice Policy and Management and Faculty Chairman of the Program Criminal Justice Policy and Management at the Kennedy School. His research interests are public management and leadership, civil society and community mobilization, and criminal justice policy and management. His publications include *Creating Public Value: Strategic Management in Government* (Harvard University Press, 1995).

Geoff Mulgan is Director of the Young Foundation. Between 1997 and 2004 he worked in the UK Government in a variety of roles including Director of the Strategy Unit and Head of Policy in the Prime Minister's Office. Before that he was the Founding Director of the think-tank Demos. He is a Visiting Professor at LSE, UCL and Melbourne University. His latest book is *The Art of Public Strategy: Mobilizing Power and Knowledge for the Common Good* (Oxford University Press, 2009).

Richard Norman is Senior Lecturer in Human Resource Management and Industrial Relations at Victoria Management School, University of Wellington, New Zealand. He is the author of *Obedient Servants: Management Freedoms and Accountabilities in the New Zealand Public Sector* (Victoria University Press, 2004) and of many articles on performance management.

Guy Stuart is a Lecturer in Public Policy at Harvard's Kennedy School of Government. He received his PhD from the University of Chicago in 1994 and then worked for four years in Chicago in the field of community economic development. During this time he served as the Director of the FaithCorp Fund, a non-profit community loan fund. At the Kennedy School he teaches courses on management and microfinance. His book *Discriminating Risk: The U.S. Mortgage Lending Industry in the Twentieth Century* traces the historical origins of today's mortgage loan underwriting criteria in the United States and examines current underwriting practices. He is currently conducting research on microfinance, using participatory methods and financial diaries in East Africa and South Asia.

Mark Swilling is a Professor in the School of Public Management and Planning at the University of Stellenbosch, South Africa, and is responsible for the coordination of the Masters Programme in Sustainable Development. He is also Academic Director of the Sustainability Institute, an international living and learning centre located in the Lynedoch Eco Village. He has a long history of activism in the NGO sector and co-founded the Graduate School of Public and Development Management at the University of the Witwatersrand in 1992 where he later became Director and Professor until 1997. He has written extensively on democratization, management development, local economies, cities, local government and civil society.

Jonathan Q. Tritter is a Professorial Fellow at Warwick University Business School. He graduated from the University of Chicago and then completed a DPhil at Nuffield College, Oxford University. Before joining the University of Warwick he was a Research Fellow at the Social Sciences Research Centre at South Bank University. His main research interest has been in the nature and relevance of patient and carer experience for service development, service evaluation and improving the patient experience. His current preoccupation is patient and public involvement both in the UK and internationally, and the implications of the tensions between consumerism and choice and collective and community engagement for policy and practice.

Robin Wensley is Professor of Policy and Marketing at the Warwick Business School and was Chair of the School from 1989 to 1994, Chair of the Faculty of Social Studies from 1997 to 1999 and Deputy Dean from 2000 to 2004. He is also Director of the ESRC/EPSRC Advanced Institute of Management Research. His research interests include marketing strategy and evolutionary processes in competitive markets, investment decision-making, the assessment of competitive advantage and the nature of choice processes and user engagement in public services. He was Chair of the Council of the Tavistock Institute of Human Relations from 1998 to 2003, having been a member since 1992. He was co-editor of the *Journal of Management Studies* from 1998 to 2002. He has published a number of articles in the *Harvard Business Review*, the *Journal of Marketing* and the *Strategic Management Journal* and has twice won the annual Alpha Kappa Psi award for the most influential article in the US *Journal of Marketing*.

Noel Whiteside is Professor of Comparative Public Policy at the University of Warwick and a historian whose main research agenda concerns labour markets, trade union organization and labour market policies in historical and comparative (European) perspective. Within this framework, she works largely on classifications of social dependency, systems of governance and developments in social security; and in UK governance – specifically, the use of state regulation of market mechanisms to achieve policy objectives. Her current projects include: governance and regulation of pensions in major EU economies (particularly Britain and France); labour market activation policies in selected European cities in the late nineteenth century; and comparative developments in European social insurance schemes in the inter-war years.

Sir David Winkley was a founder-member of the Centre for Contemporary Studies at the University of Birmingham. He has an MA in English Literature from Cambridge, and a DPhil in Philosophy from the University of Oxford. He has been a Fellow of Nuffield College, Oxford, and is an Honorary Fellow of Wadham College, Oxford. He was head of Grove School, Handsworth, for some 24 years – an inner-city primary school of more than 700 children. The school became nationally famous for its innovations and achievements, and its story has been fully described in the book *Handsworth Revolution*. He has taught children and students from ages 3 to 21 at various times and still teaches philosophy to inner-city youngsters once a week. David has been on various Government advisory committees, including the Standard Task Force, and the PM's Education Advisory group. He has founded a number of national projects, including the Children's University, 6s and 7s (a national mental health programme for disadvantaged children) and most recently the Health Exchange. He is currently Vice-Chair of Heart of Birmingham NHS Teaching Trust. David has published numerous articles on education, philosophy and management including three full-length books. He is currently an Honorary Professor at the University of Warwick. He was knighted in 1999, the last knight of the twentieth century.

Chapter 1

Public Value in Complex and Changing Times

JOHN BENINGTON AND MARK H. MOORE

Public value and related concepts like the public good, the public interest, and the public realm have been actively debated within political philosophy since the time of the ancient Greeks. However, the stimulus for the current debate about public value within the field of public management was Mark Moore's seminal book *Creating Public Value: Strategic Management in Government* (Moore 1995). Thinking about public value has since moved well beyond its origins in neo-liberal American discourse of the 1990s, and is now at the forefront of cross-national discussion about the changing roles of the public, private, and voluntary sectors in a period of profound political economic, ecological, and social change. This chapter traces that intellectual journey, mapping out the key ideas and debates surrounding the concept of public value, and suggesting ways in which it may provide a compass bearing and a clearer sense of direction for strategic thinking and action by public policymakers and managers, under conditions of complexity and austerity.

Moore's initial aim in 1995 was to build a conceptual framework for public sector managers to help them to make sense of the strategic challenges and complex choices they faced, in a similar way to which notions of private value had provided strategic purpose for private sector managers. He developed this framework through years of engagement with public managers from the USA and around the world who took part in executive programmes at Harvard's John F. Kennedy School of Government. One of his goals was to develop a conceptual framework that would be practically useful to public managers doing their jobs, and to encourage strategic thinking and entrepreneurial action to tackle complex problems in the community.

This book, published 15 years later, aims to develop and to sharpen both the theory and the practice of 'public value' in a very changed context from the one in which *Creating Public Value* was written – a new climate in which there is a widespread sense of political economic

1

ecological and social crisis. Over the intervening years public value has emerged as an increasingly powerful idea in both academic and policy circles, internationally (especially in the UK, Europe, the USA, Australia and New Zealand, and more recently in South and sub-Saharan Africa). There is a growing sense that it is an idea whose time has come – that public value thinking and action may help to make sense of the very complex changes and tough challenges now facing governments and communities in a period of profound political economic and social restructuring.

The idea of public value has attracted particularly high-level attention in the public policymaking and practitioner communities, often as part of wider debates about public service reform and improvement (Benington 2007). It has been discussed and used by literally thousands of managers from the public and voluntary sectors on courses at Harvard, Melbourne and Warwick Universities, at the Australia and New Zealand School of Government, and at the UK's National School of Government. Public value frameworks have also been tested and applied in practice by many public sector organisations. For example, in the UK, 'public value' has been used by the British Broadcasting Corporation as a core argument for renewal of its charter as a public body funded by licence fee, and in its assessment of the value of specific radio and TV programmes, by the UK chancellor of the exchequer in his 2008 budget speech; by the National Health Service Institute of Innovation and Improvement in its search for measures of health outcomes; by the Department of Culture Media and Sport, as part of the evaluation framework for their policies and programmes; and in a wide range of policy reports and discussions within the Audit Commission, the Further Education service, the Scottish government, the Welsh Assembly government, and the Trades Union Congress.

The debate about public value within the academic community has been emerging more slowly, but has now erupted vigorously and controversially in several academic conferences and journals (notably in the *Australian Journal of Public Administration*, in *Public Administration*, and in a special issue of the *International Journal of Public Administration*). Critique and development of public value theory is emerging from the points of view of ecology (Swilling 2007), economics (Hutton *et al.* 2007), philosophy (Morrell 2009), political science (Stoker 2005; Rhodes and Wanna 2007; Gains and Stoker 2009), and public administration and public management (Alford and Hughes 2008; Benington 2007, 2009; Kelly *et al.* 2002; Mulgan 2009; Talbot 2009).

This book aims both to contribute to and to shape this burgeoning academic and policy debate by providing:

- First, critical analysis and further development of the theory surrounding public value, and its relationship to related theories of public policymaking and strategic management.
- Second, the testing of this conceptual framework in its application to key policy issues and complex cross-cutting problems facing policymakers and managers in the public and voluntary sectors.

The book aims both to open up the theoretical debates and critiques surrounding public value, and also to explore and test out the ideas in their application to a number of specific policy themes and service areas.

This first chapter introduces the debate in five main ways:

- Summarizing the core ideas associated with Mark Moore's book *Creating Public Value*.
- Reviewing the history and the neo-liberal context in which public value ideas were first developed in the 1990s.
- Analysing the very different political economic and social context, and the more complex challenges facing governments and communities, in the first decades of the twenty-first century, and the ways in which public value concepts may help to make sense of them.
- Reviewing the main academic debates surrounding public value.
- Highlighting the ways this book will move both the theory and the practice of public value forward.

Each of these 5 issues will now be explored in turn.

The core ideas associated with Moore's Creating Public Value

The ideas developed by Mark Moore in *Creating Public Value* in the USA in the 1990s challenged the then orthodox thinking about three key issues:

- The role of government in society – seen by Moore not just as a rule-setter, service-provider and social safety net, but potentially as a creator of public value and a pro-active shaper of the public sphere (politically, economically, socially and culturally)
- The roles of government managers – seen by Moore not just as inward-looking bureaucratic clerks, and passive servants to their political masters, but as stewards of public assets with 'restless value-seeking imaginations', who have important roles to play in helping governments to discover what could be done with the

assets entrusted to their offices, as well as ensuring responsive services to users and citizens.

- The techniques needed by public managers – seen by Moore not just as procedures to assure consistency and reliability of routines in government organizations (important as these can be), but also as the means to help governments to become more adaptable to changing material and social conditions, and to changing needs and political aspirations. *Creating Public Value* drew attention to the role of public managers in orchestrating the processes of public policy development, often in partnership with other actors and stakeholders, in ways which try to ensure that good choices are made in the public interest, and which legitimate, animate, and guide the subsequent implementation, in order to improve outcomes for the public.

It is arguable that *Creating Public Value* spent less time defining public value in theoretical terms than in operationalizing it in practical terms. (The current volume aims to reverse this imbalance and to tackle the questions of both theory and practice more fully.) Three of the key ideas developed by Moore (partly in the book and more fully in his executive teaching) to conceptualize and operationalize public value are the strategic triangle, the authorizing environment, and the use of state authority. Each will be summarized and discussed briefly.

The strategic triangle

The strategic triangle is a framework for aligning three distinct but inter-dependent processes which are seen to be necessary for the creation of public value:

- Defining public value – clarifying and specifying the strategic goals and public value outcomes which are aimed for in a given situation
- Authorization – creating the 'authorizing environment' necessary to achieve the desired public value outcomes – building and sustaining a coalition of stakeholders from the public, private and third sectors (including but not restricted to elected politicians and appointed overseers) whose support is required to sustain the necessary strategic action
- Building operational capacity – harnessing and mobilizing the operational resources (finance, staff, skills, technology), both inside and outside the organization, which are necessary to achieve the desired public value outcomes

The strategic triangle thus suggests that strategies to create public value must satisfy three tests. First, they must aim convincingly at creating publicly valuable outcomes (see below for a fuller definition of what this might mean). Second, they must mobilize sufficient authorization and be politically sustainable – that is, gain ongoing support from key political and other stakeholders. Third, they must be operationally and administratively feasible – that is, supported by the necessary finance, technology, staff skills and organizational capabilities needed to create and deliver the desired public value outcomes (Moore 1995:71). This is shown in Figure 1.1.

Each of these three factors is strategically important, but of course, they are rarely in alignment, and public managers have to strive constantly to bring them in to alignment and to negotiate workable trade-offs between them:

> Thus, if the most valuable thing to do is out of alignment with what the key players in the authorizing environment will find acceptable, the manager can either seek to persuade the key players to move their position, or revise the value-proposition so that it is more in line with their wishes, or some combination of the two. Similarly, if a more valuable purpose is not achievable with the currently available operational capabilities, then the manager has to tailor the purpose accordingly. This entails more than just a resigned acceptance of political or operational constraints. (Alford and O'Flynn 2009)

Figure 1.1   *The strategic triangle of public value*

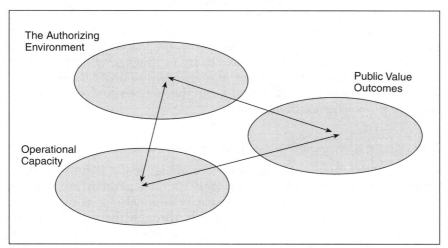

The Authorizing
Environment

Public Value
Outcomes

Operational
Capacity

The authorizing environment for the creation of public value

Public managers clearly need a strong mandate from elected politicians and from their line managers, in order to do their job. This mandate can come from the legislation and/or the policies that the agency has been set up to implement; or from the roles the public manager has been appointed to perform; or from the job description which they have been given to carry out. However, while these formal mandates from above are necessary, they may not be sufficient to achieve the desired public value outcomes. In order to achieve those goals it may also be necessary to win the support of other individuals, organizations and stakeholders, and to create a broader-based authorizing environment. Public policymaker and manager may have to create a network of partners and stakeholders, and to negotiate a coalition of different interests and agencies (from across the public, private, voluntary and informal community sectors) to support them in achieving their goals. This has to mobilize sufficient authorization to achieve the desired public value outcomes, but does not necessarily imply a complete consensus by all parties. Indeed the creation of public value does not require support from all agencies ('just enough' support to achieve the desired outcomes is sufficient). It will also sometimes involve conflict with other organizations with other interests and priorities, or with those that are wedded to the status quo.

The authorizing environment is therefore conceptualized as a place of contestation where many different views and values struggle for acceptance and hegemony. Conflicts of ideology, interest and emphasis are often not fully resolved by elected politicians within the formal democratic process, but may be passed on unresolved for public managers to do the best they can, to resolve the ambiguities in practice at the front line (Hoggett 2006). In this kind of situation, the knowledge and judgement of professional public managers may be courted by the public as legitimating assets in addition to the mandate of politicians. Public managers may therefore have to try to bring several parts of the authorizing environment together in a coalition in order to strengthen the overall legitimacy and support for the policies and programmes they are proposing or administering.

The use of state authority in the creation of public value

Creating Public Value also included a reminder that a defining feature of government is that it has a monopoly on the legitimate use of force in a society, and that it uses this capacity routinely in its operations. Government makes things happen partly through the use of government money and legislation, and partly through the use of government authority. The fact that government authority is often engaged has huge implications for government activity. On the one hand, it changes the basic normative framework that can be used to evaluate government operations; once government authority is engaged, we have to be concerned about the fairness with which the authority is used, as well as its efficiency and effectiveness. On the other hand, when government authority is used in encounters with individual citizens, it changes the nature of the encounters in a profound way. A citizen who is stopped by the police, or required to pay taxes, or to pay a fine for polluting a river, cannot easily be seen as a customer. The point of this kind of encounter is not to please or delight the client in the transaction! And it is not to hope for more encounters of the same type – public managers don't aim for 'repeat business' of this kind, but for less business!

This is a very different kind of encounter and different kind of relationship with the public from that typical in the private market. Instead of receiving services, the client gets an obligation. Instead of trying to satisfy the client, the goal is to encourage compliance with the obligation, and in doing so, to be sure that rights are protected and duties imposed in a just and fair way. This use of state authority means that the creation of public value clearly has some very distinctive and different features from the creation of private value.

Having summarized some of the key ideas in Mark Moore's original book *Creating Public Value* we now turn to critically examine the context of neo-liberal ideas within which it was written in America in the early 1990s.

The neo-liberal context in which 'Creating Public Value' was initially conceived

Creating Public Value was written in the USA in the early 1990s at a time when powerful political, economic and social forces were bearing down on governments in advanced industrial societies, and challenging their standing as important, value-creating social institutions. Far from being seen as institutions essential for the safeguarding of individual and collective wellbeing and the assurance of social justice, governments were increasingly portrayed (particularly in the USA and UK) as obstacles to economic and social progress – an unproductive sector feeding parasitically off the value supposedly being created largely in the private sector. Ronald Reagan famously alleged that 'government is not the solution; government is the problem.' The Reaganite/ Thatcherite solution, then, was to shrink government.

Along with the diminution of government as an institution went the diminution of the collective as an idea. The effort to liberate individuals from oppressive political, social and economic conditions was seen to have reached its apotheosis in the triumph of political liberalism on the one hand, and market-guided capitalism on the other. The idea that individuals were ultimately the most important arbiters of value was celebrated and institutionalized in the commitment to representative democracy on the one hand, and to private markets guided by individual consumer choices on the other. The difficulties of making collective choices through democratic political processes – long understood to be time-consuming and frustrating at best, and prone to various kinds of corruption at worst – were argued to be theoretically problematic as well. If it was not easy for a collective to make a decision that could produce the public good efficiently then would not it make sense to minimize the number of choices that had to be made by the collective? In short, many in the West lost confidence in democratic politics as a device for forging a coherent 'we' from a diversity of individual interests. Many lost confidence in government's ability to advance public purposes, without corruption or self-serving motives blunting both the efficiency and effectiveness, and the justice and fairness, of governmental operations.

As confidence in the public sphere as a definer and producer of public value was challenged, confidence grew in the importance of market mechanisms as devices for meeting individual choices and social needs. Neo-liberals tried to expand the domain of individual choice – partly by shrinking the size and scope of government, so that more choices about how to use resources would be guided by individuals acting through markets rather than by collectives acting through government, but also by trying to give more room to individual choices in activities that were financed by government. Governments were to encourage competition among providers of government financed services. All this was in accord with Margaret Thatcher's stated belief that 'there is no such thing as society', and that individual and family interests are primary.

While the attack on government as an institution, and on collective decision-making, shrank the public sphere, these efforts could not, in the end, do away with government completely. There remained important production, service delivery and regulatory functions that government still had to perform to promote economic prosperity, maintain social cohesion, and to advance the cause of justice as it was encoded in constitutions and laws. Public managers still had to make decisions about how to spend the collectively owned assets that had been entrusted to them, and there were strong pressures to improve the core managerial processes of government. Again, because of increased confidence in all things private, many thought that improved public management could be achieved by importing techniques from the private sector into the public sector. Thus, government agencies were encouraged to adopt a customer focus in delivering services to individuals defined as consumers. They were also encouraged to improve the measurement of their results, and to adopt 'pay for performance' methods to motivate both frontline workers and higher-level managers to work harder and smarter, and to be more accountable to users of their services.

Creating Public Value was written at least in part as a response to these pressures for changes in the ways that people thought about government and its relationship to the wider society, and also about what constituted effective public management. The argument in *Creating Public Value* included the idea that citizens could debate the role of government in society, and contribute to deciding which individual circumstances and social conditions they wanted to treat as a collective public responsibility to be managed by government, and which they wanted to treat as a private responsibility to be managed by individuals through market relationships. *Creating Public Value* did not start with any fixed idea about the substantive content of government's responsibilities. It accepted the claim that government needed to improve its operations; and that this could include not only changing the size and scope of government as described above but also shifting the model to one in which government could pay for things to be produced, but not necessarily produce them itself. It also emphasized the potentially important role of innovation as a way of increasing the efficiency, effectiveness and responsiveness of government organizations. Thus, it accepted the criticism that government had been insufficiently flexible, innovative or creative, either in responding to changing citizens' aspirations about what they wanted from government or in finding ways to produce the results that citizens wanted in a more efficient and effective way.

Creating Public Value also accepted the idea that there was much to be learned from the private sector about how to manage large production organizations successfully. It gave particular attention to corporate strategy, and the idea that large organizations had to continually re-position themselves in the complex, dynamic, changing environments in which they found themselves. Just as the private sector executive had to keep an eye focused on changing market conditions, so the public sector executive had to keep their eye on changing political, economic and social conditions that might create new or different political demands. Just as a private sector executive had to be searching continuously for new technological breakthroughs which they could use to improve the performance of their organization, so a public sector manager had to be searching continuously for innovative ways to accomplish their objectives efficiently and effectively.

In all these ways, the argument of *Creating Public Value* went with the flow of ideas which we now associate with 'the new public management' (Hood 1991) – looking for a more responsive, more innovative, more effective government. But there were other ways the book stood firm with tradition against the claims of the new public management.

The most important of these was the commitment to the idea that the proper arbiter of public value is society as a whole acting as best as it can through the imperfect processes of representative government. What makes something publicly valuable is partly that a public values it. And a public is something different from the simple aggregation of individual consumer interests. Furthermore, it might even be a bit different from the views of the 'government of the day' – although the views of elected and appointed officials will always carry the most weight in defining the public value to be pursued by government. *Creating Public Value* thus did not yield to the idea that individuals are the only arbiters of value. It took direct issue with Margaret Thatcher's dismissal of the idea of a society that could become articulate about its interests as a collective.

Creating Public Value also gave a lot of attention to the structures and processes that called public managers to account for their actions. It developed the concept of an 'authorizing environment' that is as important to public managers as a 'market environment' is to private managers. Just as customers within the private market are ultimately the ones who call private sector managers to account, by deciding whether or not to buy the particular product or service offered for sale, so stakeholders in the political authorizing environment (primarily, but not only, democratically elected representatives) are ultimately the ones who call public managers to account, by deciding whether or not to continue to support their efforts to produce a particular public service and/or conception of public value.

At one level, there was nothing particularly new in these observations about the importance of politics and public engagement in public administration and public management. Woodrow Wilson had tried to define the proper relationship between political representation and authorization on the one hand, and efficient public administration on the other (by making a distinction between policymaking and administration, and by giving politicians principal authority in the domain of policymaking, and public administrators principal authority in the domain of administration). However this distinction proved to be intellectually incoherent and practically unsustainable. But no one had taken the next difficult step of developing a set of ideas about how we could understand and improve the relationship between politics and administration, and between politicians and administrators, if it was neither accurate nor realistic to think of these as two completely distinct and separate arenas.

Creating Public Value plunged into this confused debate by focusing the attention of both policymakers and public managers on the normative and practical importance first of defining the value outcomes to be achieved for the public, and second of building 'legitimacy and support' for governmental action. In many ways, this was the opposite side of the coin of 'accountability.' One could say that public managers should be accountable for their actions to the public as well as to elected politicians. But one could also say that increased accountability also gave them increased legitimacy and support. And that they would be more effective in creating valuable outcomes for the public if they found ways to build stronger legitimacy and wider support from the public and other stakeholders for what they were doing.

Creating Public Value explored some of the important sources of legitimation for public managers. Political mandate is one important kind. But so is the law. And so is professional knowledge and technical expertise. And there might even on some occasions be a kind of moral legitimacy created by public managers and professionals reminding society and its representatives of important values that are being put at risk by actions that are politically supported, have legal sanction, and would likely work technically, but fail to protect or promote foundational moral values.

So *Creating Public Value* addressed questions associated both with traditional public administration (for example the relationship between policymaking and administration, and the sources of authorization for public managers), and also with the new public management (for example entrepreneurship, innovation and the need to focus outwards on users and communities as well as upwards on elected politicians and government). *Creating Public Value* problematized these issues in a way which responded to the complexities they posed in practice for public managers, and offered a number of concepts to help make sense of and manage the dilemmas – for example, the strategic triangle, the authorizing environment, and the use of state authority (discussed earlier in this chapter).

The increased relevance of public value for public managers facing an age of austerity and systemic change

In this section we recognize and analyse the profound changes in the political economic and social context which have been taking place since *Creating Public Value* was written over 15 years ago. We argue that public value thinking and action is now even more relevant in helping to make sense of the new complexities and tough challenges facing governments and communities, and public policymakers and managers.

Changes in the context for public services

The profound structural changes taking place in the ecological, political, economic, technological and social context pose major questions for governments and public managers.

The global economic and financial crisis of 2009 acted as a catalyst for a radical review of government roles and responsibilities. The pressure to be 'doing more with less' has become stronger as public sector spending comes under intense scrutiny and is expected to decline sharply in real terms over the next few years. In this context more effective leadership across the whole public service system is increasingly seen as one of the most powerful ways of reducing transaction costs between stand-alone organizations, and of improving efficiency, performance and productivity through collaboration across the whole public sector. Part of that leadership may include re- framing the questions not just in terms of financial inputs and operational outputs but in terms of public value outcomes which add benefit for users, citizens and communities (Benington and Hartley 2009).

Previous experience, in both the private and the public sectors, of managing periods of economic recession and financial cutback suggests that this is also an opportunity to review all activities and processes within the public value chain, and to identify those points at which value is being added, where it is being destroyed and where it is stagnating. The concept of the public value chain (developed more fully in Chapter 2) is useful in identifying the activities and processes of production and co-production of public service, and in focusing on how to add public value at various stages in the process. This can lead to some radical conclusions – in some cases redistributing resources to the front line of the organization (for example school classrooms, hospital wards and neighbourhood communities) where public value is often co-created between public professionals (for example teachers, nurses, police) and users, families, communities, partner organizations and other stakeholders.

However, the benefits of public value thinking and action do not derive solely from the current economic crisis, far-reaching though this is in its implications for governance and public management. Human society is in the throes of an even more fundamental restructuring of the global ecological, political-economic, technological and social context. This includes climate change and an impending peak in the oil supply; rapid exponential growth in information and communication technologies; the emergence of an electronically networked society; globalization of the economy, of financial markets and of culture; a gradual shift of political and economic power away from the USA and the Anglo-Saxon North, towards China, India and Latin America in the South; a decline in the manufacturing base in northern countries; a rise in importance of the service sector (which now provides over two-thirds of GDP in the UK for example); the consequent shrinking of the traditional industrial working class, and the rise of the middle and professional classes; a dramatic increase in population and in the number of households; the ageing of the population, with people in the North living much longer, and fewer people of working age and in work to support them; greater diversity of needs, a rise in expectations, a decline in deference to hierarchy and authority, and the emergence of the 'critical consumer/ citizen'.

The scope and scale of these structural, system-wide changes arguably requires a Copernican revolution in our basic paradigms for governance and public service. Benington suggests in Chapter 2 that public value can help to interpret and shape those new paradigms. Whereas traditional public administration assumes a context of relative political economic and social stability, and whereas new public management trusts the logic of free market competition, public value recognizes the complexity, volatility and uncertainty in the environment. While the landscape and contours of government and public management are changing, and the maps are no longer as accurate or useful, public value may offer a compass to provide a sense of direction and destination to take us through the surrounding fog.

In this changing context, citizens and communities are increasingly confronted by a whole series of complex cross-cutting problems (for example ageing and community care; child protection; climate change; crime and the fear of crime), for which there are no simple technical solutions – and indeed where there is no clear or settled agreement about either the causes of the problems or the best ways to address them. These complex, cross-cutting and often contested issues have been described by John Stewart as 'wicked' problems, and by Ron Heifetz as 'adaptive' problems – 'wicked' or 'adaptive' problems of this kind being seen increasingly to require a kind of response from governments qualitatively different from that which they extend to 'tame' or 'technical' problems (Heifetz 1994; Stewart 2001; Grint 2005).

Traditional public administration assumes that the needs and problems to be addressed by governments are fairly straightforward, and that the solutions are known and understood. New public management assumes that needs and wants will be expressed and satisfied through the mechanism of market choice. The public value framework, however, starts from a recognition that the needs and problems now facing citizens, communities and governments are complex rather than simple, 'wicked' rather than 'tame', and diverse rather than homogeneous. And while previous patterns of governmental intervention have not been notably successful in resolving these problems, better solutions and responses are not yet known or understood. Governmental policies and programmes have therefore to be developed in a more provisional and reflexive way – often involving extensive dialogue between government and the public and other stakeholders about both the nature of the problems to be addressed and the strategies to tackle them.

The rise in people's aspirations and expectations, and their desire for services that are customized to meet their needs, means that the public are increasingly vociferous about what they want and do not want. Interactive information and communication technologies open up greater access to knowledge and information and to the opportunity to influence decision-making through electronic networks. There is less deference towards authority and towards top-down solutions offered by the paternalistic state, which is associated with traditional public administration.

There is also a growing recognition that the individual consumer choices offered through new public management (NPM) and its competitive markets do not and cannot provide adequate responses for complex cross-cutting problems like care for an ageing population, or violence in the home and on the streets. The public value framework encourages managers to move beyond the language of market 'wants' into the more difficult question of what the public most 'values', and what adds value to the public sphere – including challenging the public to make painful choices and trade-offs between competing priorities (Kelly *et al.* 2002).

Traditional public administration assumes that the state will be the main provider of public services, and new public management assumes that the market will be the provider of first choice, with the state as a safety net of last resort. On the other hand, Benington's 'networked community governance' framework (outlined in Chapter 2) recognizes that the interdependencies between the state and the market mean that watertight distinctions between the two are no longer accurate or realistic. Benington also argues in Chapter 2 that in addition to the state and the market, civil society is an important and often neglected third sphere of activity and source of public value creation. Indeed the most valuable outcomes for the public can often best be achieved by harnessing the commitment and resources of all three spheres, state, market and civil society, jointly behind specific shared 'public value' goals.

The need for new paradigms

The above changes in the political economic and social context, and the complex cross-cutting problems now facing citizens and communities, require governments and public managers to develop new paradigms to make sense of the new context, and to guide strategic thinking and action. The new paradigms may include thinking about government and public services less as machines or structures and more as 'complex adaptive systems' (for example the language of cultures and organisms rather than of levers and cogs).

Public value thinking and action includes the capacity to analyse and understand the interconnections, interdependencies and interactions between complex issues, and across multiple boundaries:

- Between different sectors (public, private, voluntary and informal community).
- Between different levels of government (local, regional, national, supranational).
- Between different services (for example education, health, housing, policing, social security).
- Between different professions involved in tackling a common problem.
- Between political and managerial and civic leaderships and processes
- Between strategic management, operational management and frontline delivery.
- Between producers and users of services (in new patterns of 'co-creation' between producers, users and other stakeholders outside the governmental system).

Public value concepts and tools like the strategic triangle, the authorizing environment and the public value chain help to make sense of this complex new pattern of polycentric networked governance (see Chapter 2 by Benington; Benington 2006a), and to strengthen the capabilities necessary to think and to act effectively along several different dimensions, often simultaneously:

- Horizontally – between different sectors, organizations, disciplines, professions stakeholders, and partners.
- Vertically – along all the links in the value chain, from policy design in Westminster and Whitehall right through to service 'delivery' or engagement at the front line in local neighbourhood communities – with movement in both directions, from top to bottom, bottom to top, and middle upwards and downwards.
- Diagonally – across the decision-making networks, linking together political leaderships, strategic managers, operational managers, frontline delivery staff, users and communities.

This requires a radically different approach to policy development and public management, with a need to link policy to implementation, and strategy to operations, in an end-to-end process which can deliver greater public value – through practical action on the ground at the front line with communities.

The complex cross-cutting problems facing citizens, communities and governments also require different patterns of leadership to create public value outcomes – leadership which can address the interconnections between issues, negotiate coalitions between different stakeholders, orchestrate inter-organizational networks and partnerships, harness disparate resources behind a common purpose, and achieve visible and measurable outcomes with and for citizens, communities and other stakeholders. This involves the exercise of leadership outside and beyond the organization, often through influence rather than through formal authority, in addition to leadership of and inside the organization (Benington and Hartley 2009).

Leadership of this kind has to resist the pressure from followers to act as a god or guru who can provide magical solutions to complex problems, and instead has to persuade stakeholders to accept that they themselves are part of the whole system, and therefore part of the problem, and to engage in the painful process of grasping difficult nettles, working though problems, and adapting thinking and behaviour (Heifetz 1994; Benington and Turbitt 2007).

Public value concepts like the strategic triangle, the authorizing environment, the public value chain and the focus on outcomes for the public sphere can all help public managers to make sense of these issues, and to reframe problems more clearly so that they can act more decisively and effectively.

The academic debates surrounding public value

Mark Moore's book, the full title of which is *Creating Public Value: Strategic Management in Government,* was written mainly as a contribution to public management theory and practice. Indeed the ideas were initially developed not primarily from academic theory or desk research, but out of a long process of interactive teaching and engagement with public managers. Once the book was published the ideas were tested and developed further, mainly through debate and practical application by public managers in their workplaces, and by teachers on courses for public managers, for example at Harvard, Melbourne and Warwick Universities.

As with so many theories of management, the academic debate about public value has lagged well behind the emerging practice. Apart from a few lone voices most academics appear to have been seduced by the apparent dominance of neo-liberal ideology during the 1990s, and have remained fixated on retrospective interpretations of the new public management – failing to notice that practitioners were already not only grappling with a much more complex set of problems than

NPM could explain or resolve, and but also searching for new frameworks of explanation and action.

Very belatedly, academic debate has finally begun to catch up with the frontiers of practice, and academic interest in public value (as an alternative both to traditional public administration and to new public management paradigms) is now mushrooming. Some of this is frankly little more than the following of fashion (Talbot 2009) , but there are also signs of serious analysis of public value from the point of view of several different disciplines (philosophy, psychology, political science, ecology and management science), and of different countries, traditions and cultures (Anglo-Saxon; Australia/New Zealand; continental Europe and Africa).

One important critique comes from philosophy, and focuses on traditional though contested questions about virtue, the public good and the source of values. The main writers on this theme at present are from the USA and continental Europe and one of their preoccupations is with defining and categorizing public service values (notice the plural) and exploring public value failures (cases where public service values have been breached). Some of this literature is concerned with establishing hierarchies of public values or constellations of competing values (Bozeman 1987; Bozeman 2002, 2007; Kernaghan 2003; Bozeman and Sarewitz 2005; Jørgensen and Bozeman 2007) This literature on public values (in the plural) seems to have originated quite independently of the debate about public value (in the singular), but there is now some cross-referencing between the two previously separate literatures (for example, Davis and West 2008; Van der Wal and Van Hout 2009). Critical accounts of public value are emerging from the perspective of philosophical theories of virtue and the public good, linked to political-economic questions of governance, power and control (Morrell 2009), and also from philosophy linked to social theory, particularly Latour's actor-network theory and the 'new pragmatism' associated with Boltanski and Thevenot 1999 (West and Davis 2010). Both schools argue, in different ways, the importance of seeing questions of value not in abstract terms but in their embodiment and enactment in material situations and technologies, and in political and daily practices.

Another stream of commentary on public value is based in psychology. For example, Meynhardt (2009) argues for a notion of the public as

> a necessary fiction. *The public is inside.* The 'public' – psychologically speaking – is an individually formed abstraction generated on the basis of experiences made in daily practices, analytical insight, and all sorts of projections as to complex phenomena.

Similarly, Meynhardt argues:

> if we cannot assume the derivation of values from some objective
> basis (for example natural right) and further do not restrict values
> to a normative constitution or the like (such as a religious text) ...
> one promising candidate is basic needs theory in psychology ... In
> this view we gain a structure for value content that is closely linked
> to psychological theory building. (p. 204)

The most robust and critical debate about public value, however, has
erupted within political science, and is focused around a series of articles in the *Australian Journal of Public Administration*. Rhodes and
Wanna (2007) mount a frontal attack on Moore's *Creating Public
Value*, asserting that it is confused or wrong about seven sets of issues.
They argue, first, that it is unclear whether public value ideas are based
on normative or empirical reasoning; second, that it embraces too
broad and loose a definition of the public manager; third, that it is not
applicable to Westminster-style democracies, where there is a sharper
distinction between the roles of elected politicians and appointed managers, than in the US and other systems; fourth, that it assumes too
benign a view of public managers and public organizations – and
ignores the 'dark side' of the state's regulatory activity, and the asym-
metrical power relations between state officials, clients, citizens and
other interest groups; fifth, that it gives a dangerous primacy to entrepreneurial public managers in shaping the content of policies and programmes, at the expense of elected politicians and political parties;
sixth, that it defers too much to private sector models of management
and fails to acknowledge the very different goals and accountabilities
of public management within a democratic political framework; and
seventh, that it downgrades the importance of party politics, and raises
public managers to the status of Platonic guardians and arbiters of the
public interest, instead of recognizing that public value is highly contested territory, in which competing and conflicting interests can only
be negotiated between elected politicians through the democratic political process (Rhodes and Wanna 2007).

John Alford responds to Rhodes and Wanna's critique with an
equally sharp rejoinder (Alford 2008). He accuses Rhodes and Wanna,
first, of wilfully misrepresenting Moore's arguments, and uses detailed
quotations from *Creating Public Value* to support this; second, of
holding on to outdated and discredited textbook theories of the separation between politics and administration; and third, of misunder-
standing the complex interplay between politicians and public
managers in generating policy and in developing innovative programmes to respond to changing public needs, and to create public
value (Alford 2008).

Finally, Rhodes and Wanna respond to Alford's criticisms in two further astringent articles in the same journal (Rhodes and Wanna 2008; 2009). In the first, they start by reiterating that Mark Moore's conception of public value does not transplant from American government to Westminster parliamentary government:

> the hierarchy of a strong executive with disciplined political parties and neutral public officials is markedly different from the divided executive, weak party system, and elected or partisan public officials of the USA. Cabinet ministers are visible and interventionist. They are not just one among many competing actors. They are the pre-eminent actor. So, to urge officials to build coalitions inside and outside government to legitimise 'their' initiatives on public value may well be understandable in the pluralist, fragmented American government but it is dangerous in [Westminster-style and] Australian parliamentary government. (pp. 367–70)

Leading on from this, their second argument is a reassertion of the primacy of politics over administration, and of politicians over public managers, in governance. Their third argument is that public value is a utopian concept and ignores the dark side of government – including at times spying, unlawful imprisonment, interrogation and torture. The second rejoinder repeats some of the above arguments but adds a series of case-studies of this dark side, to illustrate their contention that Moore's concept of public value is based upon an overly benign view of governmental organizations and of the role of public servants as 'platonic guardians' (Rhodes and Wanna 2009).

The Rhodes, Wanna, Alford debate raises an important set of questions which are addressed fully in the chapters which follow. At this stage it should just be noted that some British political scientists have engaged with public value thinking in an equally questioning but less polarized and simplistic way. For example Stoker explores the potential of public value as a framework to make conceptual and practical sense of the new patterns of networked governance (Stoker 2006; Gains and Stoker 2009) and as an alternative paradigm to new public management.

However, the most fundamental critique of current conceptions of public value come from ecology. In Chapter 5, Swilling asks whether and how the public value approach can face up to the challenge of sustainable resource use, and can it be greened? His conclusion is that a public value approach can potentially offer a new paradigm for sustainable governance and public management if it can move beyond the 'triple bottom line' approach, which essentially sees sustainable development as a point where the economic, social and environmental spheres (often depicted as interlocking circles) overlap. Swilling argues that this approach locks one into a language of trade-offs, with each sphere retaining its own respective logic (an economy driven by markets, society glued together by welfarism, and the environment protected by conservationism). A systems approach offers an alternative perspective that essentially sees these spheres as embedded within each other. Following the logic of institutional economics, the economy is embedded within the social-cultural system, and, following ecological economics, both are embedded within the wider system of ecosystem services and natural resources. The result, Swilling argues, is a way of thinking about sustainability as the organizing principle for an expanded 'complex systems' conception of public value that encompasses all three spheres.

Thus the academic debate about public value has moved well beyond the fields of public administration and strategic management where it originated, and is now at the centre of lively interdisciplinary debates about the purposes and roles of government within a rapidly changing ecological, political-economic and social context; about the changing relationships between state, market, civil society and the ecosphere, and about the nature of the contract being renegotiated between citizens, communities and governments.

How will this book move the public value debate forward?

This book is being published at a critical conjuncture in the above developments, and aims to move the debate about public value substantially forward in both the academic and policy communities.

We aim, in the following chapters:

- To sharpen the definition of public value (which is currently in danger of being used like an aerosol, sprayed around widely but hazily, with misty meanings which can indicate different things to different people).
- To expose the public value concept to critical questioning, with contributions from sceptical as well as neutral and committed points of view, and providing a forum for debate and contest.
- To draw on perspectives from practitioners (politicians and policy advisers and public managers), as well as academics.
- To analyse public value from several different disciplinary perspectives (for example ecology, economics, history, management, philosophy, political science, organizational psychology, social policy, sociology).
- To highlight and elaborate the political, economic, social, and ecological dimensions of public value.

- To encompass perspectives from a range of different countries, contexts, continents and cultures (for example the UK, Europe, USA, Australia and New Zealand and Africa).
- To test the application of the public value concept in relation to key policy arenas (including education, health, pensions, the built environment).
- To grapple with the question of how to assess or measure public value.

We build on and extend the initial definition of public value offered in *Creating Public Value* (Moore 1995), as a framework for thinking about strategic management in the public sector. We aim to address the following key questions, among others:

- What is the difference between public and private value?
- How does public value relate to other concepts such as the public sphere, the public interest, the public good, or public goods?
- What do we mean by value and how do we judge it?
- How and where and by whom is public value created?
- How would we recognize it and assess it?
- What are the implications of differing political, economic, social and cultural contexts for public value creation?
- What contribution to public value creation is made variously by the state, market and civil society?
- How do power and politics shape the contested discourses about public value?
- How far are competition and/or collaboration necessary or useful for public value creation?
- What are the conditions for co- creation of public value?
- How does public value relate to other management frameworks like 'best value', 'value for money', 'value management'?
- Under what conditions can innovation and improvement in public services add to public value?
- How can public value be measured or evaluated?

The chapters within this book aim to progress both the theory and the practice of public value, in the following ways:

In Chapter 2, John Benington builds on Mark Moore's ideas in *Creating Public Value*, but transposes them into an alternative framework which starts with the public and the collective as the primary units of analysis, rather than with the private and the individual. As noted earlier in this chapter, Moore's ideas were developed initially in the USA in the early to mid 1990s, at the height of the dominance of neo-liberal ideology. Neo-liberal perspectives promoted and privileged conceptual models based on individual consumers within a private competitive market (where the state is seen as an encroachment upon, and threat to, individual liberty), over models based on communal citizens within a public democratic state (within which individual liberties have to be protected). Benington argues that public value can best be understood and achieved within the notion of the 'public sphere' – a democratic space which includes, but is not coterminous with, the state, within which citizens address their collective concerns, and where individual liberties have to be protected. This leads him to define public value not just in terms of 'what does the public most value?' but also 'what adds value to the public sphere?' The tension between these two perspectives (the first emphasizing dialogue and engagement with current users, citizens, and communities; and the second emphasizing the longer term public interest and future generations of citizens yet unborn) is explored further in Chapter 2.

Benington argues that this reformulation of public value – as part of a deliberative process, embedded within a democratic public sphere within which competing interest and contested values can be debated and negotiated – provides a strong conceptual framework to guide a newly emerging paradigm of 'networked community governance' (NCG) – similar to the ways theories of public goods provided the rationale for 'traditional public administration' (TPA), and public (rational) choice theory provided the conceptual framework for 'new public management' (NPM). This also helps to address some of the concerns expressed by Rhodes and Wanna about the interrelationships, in public value creation, between political, managerial and civic processes.

In Chapter 3, Colin Crouch examines the question of the public sphere further by developing a historical, philosophical and sociological perspective on the complex interchanging meanings of public and private over time. He analyses three different meanings of private and five different meanings of public, and argues that private and public should be seen as end points on a continuum rather than as alternatives. Crouch argues that states within the polity should not be equated solely with the public, and firms within the market should not be equated solely with the private, but that each should be seen as a particular combination of both the public and the private. Most importantly, he develops a typology to explore three realms in which public and private are linked (the state, the firm and religious organizations) and he identifies the last of these three as the key arena within which crucial value questions are formulated and articulated.

In Chapter 4, Noel Whiteside challenges the currently dominant neoliberal market paradigm in which the public good is identified as a collective consequence of the pursuit of personal interest. Whiteside offers instead a model to underpin public value, drawing on the French theory of 'the convention'. She argues that in both private and public sectors, and in the relationships between state and market, collective coordination mechanisms are needed to enable individuals and societies to make choices that secure their objectives. Such mechanisms must command universal respect; they are embedded in conventions of economic action that form the foundations of public value. However, for coordination to be effective, its mechanisms need to be internalized by all social actors. Efficiency depends not just on external 'top-down' regulation by government, but on careful negotiation with key participants, allowing deliberations that both explain mechanisms and identify possible future problems. Here, negotiation acts not merely to create compromise, but as the means whereby new systems can be absorbed and understood by all, removing or reducing the uncertainties that prevent participation. She thus argues that public value creation depends less upon market competition, or state command and control, than upon efficient coordination – and highlights the role played by confidence and trust in securing this and, conversely, the damage done by uncertainty. Uncertainty may provoke distrust and non-participation, sometimes leading to the breakdown of economic systems.

In Chapter 5, Mark Swilling starts by agreeing with John Benington (see Chapter 2) that neither traditional public administration (TPA) nor neo-liberal new public management (NPM) are adequate frameworks to make conceptual or practical sense of the complex challenges facing societies and governments now and in the future. Swilling also highlights a third governance model (the strong, interventionist 'developmental state' espoused by several rapidly developing countries like Singapore), but criticizes all three models for their failure to comprehend that unsustainable development poses the greatest threat to the processes of both private and public value creation that we as a human species face:

> Traditional Keynesian economics and so-called 'developmental states' in developing countries have ignored ecological realities. Neo-liberal philosophies have allowed market forces to ransack global resources for the benefit of the billion or so people who make up the global middle and upper class that enjoys an ecological footprint that is far greater than their fair share of global resources.

Swilling attempts to synthesize insights from the new institutional economics, ecological economics and a public value approach to governance, in order to arrive at a tentative conception of 'sustainable public value'.

In Chapter 6, Louise Horner and Will Hutton discuss two key issues where public value perspectives may help policymakers and managers to address and resolve current dilemmas in public services – the 'democratic deficit' and the 'delivery paradox'. Tackling the democratic deficit depends upon recognizing the user of public services not only as a consumer who seeks what is good for her/himself, but also potentially as a citizen who seeks what is good for the wider society. Horner and Hutton offer several case-studies of public participation in public services (for example, citizens' juries, citizens' panels) and active user involvement in service design and delivery, as examples of 'inclusive management,' in which public managers not only exercise professional judgment but also seek to maximize public participation. Here, accountability is not only to elected politicians, but also to the public, to local communities, to service-users and other stakeholders. In this way, public value perspectives encourage public managers to understand the plurality of the publics they serve, and the public outcomes they are employed to achieve, as well as to fulfil the wishes of elected governments.

Horner and Hutton also discuss the 'delivery paradox', whereby the quality of public services is improving in many ways but measures of public satisfaction are declining. They question the usefulness of 'satisfaction' as the primary criterion for measuring the value of public services and explore the feasibility of developing practical measures of performance that go beyond economic outputs or value for money, and also take into account wider public value outcomes like equity and security. Horner and Hutton then discuss each of the three processes highlighted by Mark Moore's strategic triangle – recasting them slightly as authorization, creation and measurement of public value.

In Chapter 7 Robin Wensley and Mark Moore analyse the conceptual and practical dilemmas surrounding notions of marketing, customers and choice in the public sector. They explore the ways in which even where individual choice seems to be offered in the public sector there is almost always also a concern not just with satisfaction of the individual's needs as a 'customer' but also with promotion or regulation of the individual's responsibilities as a 'citizen', and also with the benefits and costs to the citizenry in general – the value added or subtracted to the public sphere. They also discuss the role played both by private firms and by governments in shaping individual choices and behaviours – and the boundary between responsible social marketing, and intrusive, even subliminal, manipulation.

In Chapter 8, John Alford focuses on the concept of co-production which is a key feature in value-creation in public and voluntary services. Alford focuses on a specific type of co-producer; the client of a government organization. Whereas contractors, community organizations, other government agencies and volunteers are more analogous to suppliers of services to a public sector organization, clients appear to be more like consumers, who receive services from it. The idea that they are also suppliers of co-productive effort is therefore counterintuitive at first sight. Alford notes that clients of public organizations differ from their private sector counterparts in that they are sometimes non-fee-paying beneficiaries of state services (for example welfare), and sometimes unwilling clients or 'obligatees'. Sometimes they are required to pay not with money but with changed behaviours. Alford then looks in some detail at what may induce clients to co-produce public value; a combination of willingness and ability. Willingness can be encouraged by incentives, material rewards, and non-material rewards. Ability to co-produce can be influenced by two types of initiative – by the producer, to simplify their systems for working with their clients, and by the user, to increase their knowledge and capabilities to engage with the organization. Alford examines several case-studies of co-production with clients, which suggest that in some cases (for example: services for the long-term unemployed; completing tax returns) public and voluntary organizations are completely dependent upon their clients to co-produce the service. Public value creation is therefore a relational concept, in which the value chain is highly dependent upon creating productive relationships with actors (for example clients) who are outside the boundaries and outside the control of the organization itself.

In Chapter 9, Jonathan Tritter also explores the concept of co-production of public value, but extends this beyond individual clients (health service patients in this case) to include the wider 'public' and other organizations and stakeholders with an interest in improving health outcomes. Tritter uses Moore's public value 'strategic triangle' to look at the ways clarification of a clear public value mission can be used as a basis not only to negotiate authorization of the mission by a wide range of partner organizations, but also to unlock their resources and to harness these behind that mission. Thus the lead organization is given the opportunity to access resources from other organizations that share a common value mission. This differentiation between leadership of the value mission and the provision of resources provides the basis for a distinctive form of collaboration between different organizations and actors.

In Chapter 10, Jean Hartley examines why, how and under what conditions innovation and improvement in public and voluntary services may add to, or subtract from, value in the public sphere. Her chapter aims to contribute to the understanding of public value in two ways – first, by examining how innovation and improvement may contribute to the achievement of public value; and second, by using the prism of innovation and improvement to illuminate some aspects of the theory and practice of public value. Hartley distinguishes conceptually between incremental improvement and step-change innovation, and explores in some detail the varied relationships which may occur between innovation and improvement outcomes – improvement combined with innovation; improvement without innovation; innovation with no improvement; neither innovation or improvement. She uses each of these four scenarios to analyse the conditions under which public value may be added or subtracted, and argues that a key factor is alignment, and active engagement, between the organization or interorganizational network and its external environment, including users, citizens and communities – one test of fitness for public purpose. Hartley concludes that public value has to be created without the benefit of hindsight, and it sometimes requires political and managerial judgement as to whether a particular policy or strategy will achieve the sought-after outcomes. Therefore, the question, 'How can public value be measured for any innovation or improvement?' can never be finally answered, but requires continuous review and commitment over time.

In Chapter 11, Guy Stuart tests the relevance of a public value perspective, and the usefulness of the strategic triangle in particular, to addressing the dilemmas surrounding microfinance. He argues that the public value framework provides a useful way of understanding the hotly debated question over whether microfinance institutions (MFIs) should focus on financial sustainability, defined as revenue from customers exceeding the costs of service provision, or make their primary goal efforts to broaden their outreach to serve the poorest of the poor. He concludes that the public value framework makes two distinct but related contributions to this debate. One is to broaden the definition of sustainability to encompass revenues and benefits not generated through direct service provision. The framework makes this contribution via the concept of public value in and of itself – that there is a legitimate collectivity for whom an MFI manager can produce value. The second contribution is to place the debate about whether MFIs should be in the business of creating public value, in particular fulfilling a mandate to serve the poorest of the poor and not just the poor, in the context of the strategic questions facing MFI managers. It gives us a 'manager's eye view' of a thorny public policy question. In addition the public value framework helps to encompass the social relations of microfinance as well as the financial flows. Fairness and accountability in the processes and relationships of microfinance can be seen to promote the effective production of public value, as well as give it legitimacy in the eyes of the authorizing environment. The case-study of microfinance thus helps to extend the public value framework by linking the production process more closely to the legitimation process – MFIs gain competitive advantage through their adherence to fairness and accountability in delivering financial services.

In Chapter 12, Richard Norman draws on the New Zealand government's experience since 1986 to discuss another of the key concepts within the public value management framework – a focus on outcomes which add value for the public, and for the public sphere. Norman shows that there was a deep scepticism about outcome measures in the radical redesign of the New Zealand public sector in the late 1980s, which was carried forward under both the Labour government of 1986–90, and the National government of 1990–1999. In contrast to the major effort involved in specifying outputs and creating cost systems to track them, outcome goals and targets were left as the responsibility of politicians to articulate in rather general utopian terms.

However, concerns about the impact of a single-minded focus on outputs accumulated during the 1990s. The reliance on contracts and output measures had led to a checklist mentality where managers delivered only those things that were specified in the formal performance measurement system; and public sector managers were increasingly uneasy about the undue emphasis on measurable and auditable results. Effectively, the focus on outputs benefited those public services where the final output is also an outcome – productivity gains were more easily reported in areas like tax administration, passports, land titles, employment placements and company registration, while services which involved long-term processes such as health, social welfare and education struggled to demonstrate measurable increases in outputs, at least in the short term. These concerns prompted the incoming 1999 Labour-led government to review the performance management system, and to introduce 'strategic intent', organizational capability and outcomes, as a focus for public service work. Although problematic both in terms of conception and implementation, managing for outcomes is envisaged as a cycle of continuous improvement, a self-assessment tool – not solely an accountability mechanism – for direction-setting, planning, implementation and delivery, and review.

In Chapter 13, Geoff Mulgan grapples with similar dilemmas in the measurement of public value outcomes. He acknowledges that better metrics do not by themselves deliver better outcomes. He reviews the various methods which try to monetize public value, some of them based either on what people say they would pay for a service or outcome ('stated preference methods'), or else on the choices people have made in related fields ('revealed preference'). Other monetizing methods he examines try to adjust the cost of public services with reference to quality, or to compare public policy actions by estimating the extra income people would need to achieve an equivalent gain in life satisfaction. Mulgan argues however that paying too much attention to monetary equivalence can lead to bad decisions. The different methods used to assess value can generate wildly different numbers; they often miss out what people turn out to value most, and can thus be unreliable.

Mulgan aims to develop a more sophisticated approach to thinking about value by analysing what really matters to the public. He reviews a range of methods for trying to make sense of value in this wider social dimension, including cost–benefit analysis; welfare economics; environmental economics; social accounting (including quality adjusted life years); 'value added' measures in education; and social impact assessment methods, which try to capture direct and indirect impacts of an intervention, and which can be used to justify preventive actions now that will save money on remedial action later.

Mulgan argues, however, that all measurements of complex effects are inherently difficult. Social science is not robust enough to make hard predictions about what causes will lead to what effects. An even more fundamental problem is that these analytic methods presume that everyone agrees on what counts as valuable. But in many of the most important fields for government action – like childcare, crime prevention or schooling – the public are divided over values as well as value. This is why the economic models for thinking about public goods and externalities, though informative, are often inadequate to the real choices faced by policymakers and out of sync with public attitudes and politics.

He outlines an alternative approach based on the assumption that something should be considered valuable only if citizens – either individually or collectively – are willing to give something up in return for it. Sacrifices can be monetary (that is, paying taxes or charges); they can involve granting coercive powers to the state (for example in return for security), disclosing private information (for example in return for more personalized services), and/or giving time (for example as a school governor) or other personal resources (for example donating blood). Some idea of 'opportunity cost' is essential for judging public value. He describes how value arises from the interaction of supply and demand for public goods and services and sets out the principles underpinning a set of tools now being used in the UK health service to guide investment decisions.

In Chapter 14, Bob Fryer investigates the relationship between the 'personal troubles' and 'public issues' of learning and its capacity to furnish people with the wherewithal to survive and/or thrive, in today's complex and turbulent 'risk society'. Drawing on sociological research and thought, Fryer focuses particularly on the persistent and distorting influences of social class in Britain on learners' opportunities to engage equitably in learning and to succeed, especially for those people from family and neighbourhood backgrounds most threatened by economic and social turbulence. He makes the case for adopting an 'enhanced' public value frame of reference so as to assess learning from a broader and deeper perspective than can readily be provided by conventional indicators of successful learning. He suggests that this needs to grasp the subtle and pervasive ways learning opportunities are influenced (and often distorted), and learners' potential shaped (and often constrained), by the contexts and cultures in which learning is embedded, both immediate and global. Such a framework has to show how public value can be better realized, by giving a clear and critical voice to learners, to potential learners and to those striving professionally and organizationally to serve them better. Finally, a full approach to public value must recognize the key role that learning can play, in the lives of both individuals and communities, in holding out the promise not just of personal improvement and progression, but also of social emancipation and participation in change.

Chapter 15 is an extended case-study by David Winkley, of an attempt to generate public value in one primary school in a disadvantaged inner-city area of Birmingham in the UK, over a period of more than 20 years. Winkley's practice as head-teacher embodies and enacts many of the themes we have been exploring in previous chapters, bringing them alive as public value praxis. He sees the school as a living organism, made up of teachers, pupils, parents and families, closely networked with a wide range of other agencies and actors in the neighbourhood, and embedded within the diverse cultures of the multiracial local community. He sees the job of the school to engage critically with those cultures, to challenge and to shape thinking and behaviour both within the school and within the local community, and actively and continuously to promote questioning, learning, self-reflection and improvement.

Winkley generated within the school a strong focus on public value outcomes, and a culture of personal, organizational and community development and measurable improvement over a 20-year period. This unusual concern with both processes and outcomes (inspiration and challenge combined with measurement and impact) is reflected in his chapter. Winkley thus brings public value theory alive, both as an innovative way of thinking and as a challenging form of praxis, for public managers at the front line.

Moore's *Creating Public Value*, published in 1995, begins with a discussion of the challenges facing the local librarian in a prosperous suburb of Boston in the USA. This book, published 15 years later, closes with a discussion of the challenges facing a school head teacher in a disadvantaged inner city area of Birmingham in the UK. What these two public managers have in common is a commitment to using their position as public managers not only to look upwards to the government organizations which employ and mandate them, and not only to look inwards to the organizations they manage, but also to look outwards to the local communities they serve. The American librarian and the British head-teacher both search for ways to add value not only for their immediate public, in the short term, but also to add value to the wider public sphere, in the longer term.

Finally, in Chapter 16, Mark Moore and John Benington weave some of the threads of the book together, and look forward to the future. They begin by addressing two key concerns that will continue to challenge theorists and practitioners of public value.

First, to what extent are the principles of public value still relevant to the world we now inhabit and seek to improve?

Second, what are the important conceptual and practical difficulties that continue to frustrate those who would like to apply the principles of public value creation to particular concrete tasks?

They highlight a number of incipient trends and themes which have been addressed in the previous chapters of this book, including:

- The revival of a recognition of government as a value-creating institution.
- The re-emergence of a consciousness of interdependence within society.
- The necessity of social institutions to constrain individuals and individualism.
- The recognition that public value can often only be co-created between producers and users of services, and with other partners and stakeholders.
- The specific challenges of 'calling a public into existence' in order to create public value.

In attempting to grapple with these wider questions we clearly move well beyond the roles envisaged for public managers within the framework of either traditional public administration or new public management. Public value aims to provide both a conceptual framework to interpret the complex new patterns of networked governance and to shape a new paradigm for public management, and also a managerial framework to help practitioners to make sense of the new challenges they face and to find clearer ways to lead and manage through the contradictions.

All this leads us to conclude that public value, in theory and in practice, is likely to have an enduring value for both academics and practitioners, in helping both to make sense of the complexity of a fast-moving and volatile world, and to guide more effective action in changing and uncertain times.

Chapter 2

From Private Choice to Public Value?

JOHN BENINGTON

Introduction

This chapter will build on Mark Moore's foundational ideas in *Creating Public Value* (Moore 1995), but transposes them into an alternative framework which starts with the public and the collective as the primary units of analysis, rather than with the private and the individual. Moore's ideas were developed initially in the USA in the early to mid 1990s, at the height of the dominance of neo-liberal ideology which emphasized models based on individual consumers within a private competitive market (where the state is seen as an encroachment upon, and potential threat to, individual liberty), over models based on communal citizenship within a public democratic state (within which individual liberties then have to be protected).

I will argue that public value can best be understood and achieved within the notion of the 'public sphere' – a democratic space which includes, but is not coterminous with, the state within which citizens address their collective concerns, and through which individual liberties have to be protected. This leads to a redefinition of public value not just in terms of 'What does the public most value?' but also in terms of 'What adds value to the public sphere?' There is a clear tension between these two perspectives (the first emphasizing dialogue and engagement with current users, citizens, and communities; and the second emphasizing the longer-term public interest and future generations of citizens yet unborn). Among other things, this chapter will explore how to balance and manage these contradictions in both theory and practice.

I will also argue that this reformulation of public value (as part of a deliberative process, embedded within a democratic public sphere within which competing interest and contested values can be debated and negotiated) provides a strong conceptual framework to guide the newly emerging paradigm of networked community governance

(NCG), similar to the ways in which theories of public goods provide the rationale for traditional public administration (TPA), and public (rational) choice theory provides the conceptual framework for new public management (NPM).

From private choice to public value?

There is a growing literature arguing that we live in an era of deep systemic change – ecological, technological, political, economic and social (for example Beck *et al.* 1994; Castells 1996). This is seen as posing individuals, households and communities with the challenge of how to adapt, survive and thrive in what Ulrich Beck has called a 'risk society' (Beck 1992). This context of continuous change, complexity and uncertainty can offer rich opportunities for innovation, learning and creativity for those who have the knowledge, experience, capability, disposition and confidence to cope. However these changes are also felt to have undermined many of the traditional beliefs, structures and support networks which helped people to manage and make sense of their lives in the past. Christopher Lasch describes this as the dilemma of 'psychic survival in troubled times . . . [when] people have lost confidence in the future' (Lasch 1984).

This experience of atomization at personal and small group level has been reinforced at the societal level by the widespread adoption since the 1980s of neo-liberal ideologies, with a privileging of models of the private market over the public sphere, the individual over the community, the consumer over the citizen, the economic over the social, competition over collaboration, passive commodity consumption over active social participation, and personal choice over communal responsibility (Hoggett 2000; Sennett 1977; Marquand 2004; Cooper and Lousada 2005).

Governments at both national and local levels have tried to counter some of these forces of fragmentation by improving public support services for individuals and households. Considerable strides have been made in the UK, for example, in improving basic standards in education (for example literacy and numeracy); employment (for example the minimum wage); health (for example reducing waiting times in hospitals); housing (for example improving the quantity and quality of social housing); criminal justice (for example tackling antisocial behaviour and violence).

However these improvements in basic services to individuals and to households will be undermined if they remain purely at the personal and family level. They cannot be sustained or consolidated unless public infrastructure and communal services and values are also strengthened. For example education standards cannot be maintained if the culture surrounding schools is one of 'dumbing down', and unless families and peer groups actively support serious learning as well as mass entertainment. The gains in health services for individual users (for example heart disease) cannot be consolidated and embedded in society unless the causes also are tackled through public health measures, and changes in behaviours and lifestyles. Changes in the social context and public culture relating to smoking, alcohol, exercise, sport and nutrition are needed to secure for future generations the health improvements achieved for current individuals.

The challenges facing governments and public services therefore include how to complement improvement of basic services for individuals, with strategies also to improve the context and culture within which individuals live and work; to strengthen longer-term preventive measures as well as short-term remedial services; to create the preconditions for the development of communal and shared responses to needs; and to support and promote the development of citizenship, 'the community' and the public sphere.

Alongside greater 'personalization' of public services, the UK Government, for example, is therefore also now exploring fresh approaches to 'place-making' and the strengthening of neighbourhood communities, city regions, cultural spaces and other aspects of civil society (Department for Communities and Local Government 2006; Lyons 2007; Blond 2010).

These include attempts to move beyond the mass-production of separate policies and standardized services by different professions and organizations, and to develop more 'joined-up' strategies and 'people-centred' approaches, in which different levels of government work together in closer partnership with other public, private, voluntary and informal community organizations, in trying to promote 'community wellbeing' and satisfaction, more devolved 'self-sustaining systems of improvement', and under the Coalition Government of 2010 the notion of a Big Society and a smaller state.

We are therefore seeing the emergence of new patterns of governance and public service, which cut across the traditional boundaries and divisions between:

- different sectors (the state, the market and civil society);
- different levels of government (local, regional, national and supra-national);
- different services (for example, education, health, housing, policing);
- and (most significantly) producers and users of services, in various forms of 'co-production' between public service workers and their clients and communities – for example the growth in 'patient and public involvement' in the UK National Health Service.

In its commitment to more citizen-centred services and more devolved 'self-sustaining systems of improvement' (Benington 2007) the UK government seems to be moving towards a new model which differs quite radically both from the traditional model of public administration associated with the postwar welfare state and from the so-called new public management (NPM) associated with the neo-liberal state. I have called this newly emerging model networked community governance (NCG). Table 2.1 highlights some of its differences from both traditional public administration (TPA) and new public management (NPM), along several dimensions. The second section of this chapter, 'Networked Community Governance', will explore these differences and then the third, 'Public Goods, Public Choice and Public Value', will develop the notion of public value as a conceptual framework to make sense of these new patterns of governance.

Networked community governance

Table 2.1 suggests that the emerging paradigm of networked community governance is associated with a shift in the centre of gravity of governance from state and market towards civil society; from regula-

Table 2.1   *Public value and networked community governance*

	Traditional public administration	*New public management*	*Networked community governance*
Context	Stable	Competitive	Continuously changing
Population	Homogeneous	Atomised	Diverse
Needs/problems	Straightforward; defined by professionals	Wants, expressed through the market	Complex, volatile and prone to risk
Strategy	State- and producer-centred	Market- and customer-centred	Shaped by civil society
Governance through	Hierarchies	Markets	Networks and partnerships
Regulation by:	Voice	Exit	Loyalty
Actors	Public servants	Purchasers and providers Clients and contractors	Civic leaders
Theory	Public goods	Public choice	Public value

tion by exit and voice towards regulation by loyalty; and from coordination by hierarchies and markets towards coordination through networks. These three aspects will be explored in turn.

State, market – and civil society

The neo-liberal model of new public management (NPM) has focused attention primarily on the relationships between the state and the private market, and the consumer. However, the emerging patterns of networked community governance (NCG) shift the focus on to the relationships between the state and civil society, and the citizen (see Figure 2.1). For example, the UK government's strategy for public service reform, based on more devolved self-sustaining systems of improvement and more substantial engagement with neighbourhoods and local communities, reflects a redrawing and rebalancing of the relationships between the state, the citizen and civil society (Benington 2007).

A useful working definition of civil society is

> a sphere of social interaction between economy and state, composed above all of the intimate sphere (especially the family), the sphere of associations (especially voluntary associations), social movements, and forms of public communication. (Cohen and Arato 1992)

This places civil society at the heart of debates about deliberative democracy and the public sphere (Habermas 1962; Gramsci 1971).

The role of civil society in governance is much less thoroughly debated than the private market or the state, partly because up until the 1980s there had been less recent theorization and research on civil

Figure 2.1 *Three nodes of networked governance*

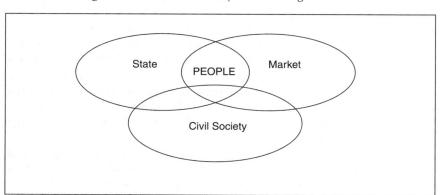

society (in the West at least), and partly because in the postwar period the political parties have focused many of their ideological and positional differences around the relative roles of the state and the market (the left calling for public regulation of the private economy, and the right calling for privatization or marketization of the public sector). In this bipolar contest between state and market, the third sphere, civil society, has been relatively neglected.

However, since the late 1980s, the powerful influence of civil society upon the state has been increasingly demonstrated by the popular mass movements for democratization in Eastern Europe, South Africa and Latin America. This has stimulated fresh interest in civil society among both theorists and policymakers (Keane 1988; Cohen and Arato 1992; Deakin 2001).

A potential tension for governments, in their attempt to increase legitimation by engaging more directly with civil society, lies in the possibility that more active participation by individual citizens, neighbourhood groups and voluntary associations will result in more vocal challenge to government policies and programmes. The emergence of new patterns of networked community governance reflects and implies a shift in the centre of gravity of governance away from the state and towards civil society, and some consequent loss of control by government policymakers and managers. The government's traditional sources of leverage through the use of legislation and taxation clearly remain in the hands of the state. However, the policy initiative (the definition of goals and priorities, the generation of policy ideas and options, the assessment of alternatives, the design of programmes, the forms of organization and implementation) is increasingly shared with informal networks of users, neighbourhood associations, community groups and minority ethnic organizations, as well as with more formal partners from the public, private and voluntary sectors.

This more active engagement with civil society, in which much public service is 'co-produced' with a range of formal and informal partners rather than by the state alone, implies a need for governments to discover new ways of indirect influence on the thinking and activity of other organizations and actors, in addition to direct use of 'state assets' and 'state authority' to achieve its ends (Moore 1995). One of the biggest challenges facing governments in a networked, multilevel, polycentric society is how to 'lead' not only in partnership with other levels of government and with organizations from other sectors, but also with active involvement from informal associations, community groups and individual citizens.

The role of government in this kind of situation is increasingly being seen not simply as to act as referee between competing interest groups, but also to work proactively to try to develop some kind of shared vision or common purpose out of the diversity of perspectives, and to

Table 2.2   *Some differences between state, market and civil society*

Sphere	Primary form of regulation	Primary form of coordination
State	Voice	Command and control hierarchies
Market	Exit	Competitive markets
Civil society	Loyalty	Collaborative networks

negotiate and mobilize coalitions of interest to achieve communal aims. Public policymakers and managers thus increasingly have to work across the boundaries between state, market and civil society in order to deliver public services. Public value provides a conceptual framework to help shape both thinking and action across these boundaries, within a pattern of networked community governance.

However, it is important to recognize that state, market and civil society are very different from each other in terms of their regulation and coordination, and that engaging with civil society in particular poses very new challenges for government – in terms of a shift from regulation by voice and exit to regulation through loyalty; and a shift from coordination by hierarchies and markets to coordination through networks (Table 2.2). These three dimensions will be discussed in turn in the following paragraphs.

Exit, voice – and loyalty

In terms of ideal theoretical types, whereas the state is regulated primarily through its citizens' 'voice' (for example, through voting and pressure group activity) and the private market is regulated primarily through consumer 'choice' or exit (for example, by taking their custom to another supplier), civil society is regulated primarily by loyalty and trust (Hirschman 1970).

Loyalty, trust and reciprocity provide the social glue that binds civil society together – including members of neighbourhood associations, community groups, civic organizations, churches, choirs, clubs and other kinds of voluntary activity (and also the dark side of civil society – for example the mafia, street gangs). Robert Putnam and others have written widely about the importance of this kind of 'social capital' to the effective functioning of societies (Putnam 1993, 2000) and others have written about the importance of socially embedded networks within economic relationships (Granovetter 1985). However, less has been written about how governments can mobilize trust and loyalty within organizations and local communities, in order to create public value (Benington 1997, 1998).

The current fascination with the concepts of trust and loyalty in both the public and the private sectors may be because voice and exit are increasingly recognized to be forms of regulation which are too crude and inflexible to respond adequately to the continuous fluctuations in the ecological, political, economic, social and technological context – and particularly to the uncertainties of 'risk society' (Beck 1992). The public bureaucratic state and the private competitive market are both being found to be inadequate instruments for responding to many of the complex changes in patterns of need within society. The law of requisite variety (Ashby 1956 and 1958) would suggest that more complex and variegated forms of organization are needed, and that these may be found, in ideal type terms at least, in the trust-based networks and loyalty-based associations supposedly characteristic of civil society.

In times of major disasters (for example, the Buncefield oil explosion, the Lockerbie air disaster, the Hillsborough football stadium crisis, the Dunblane massacre, the Manchester bombings, 9/11, and, earlier, Coventry after the wartime blitz) people have often turned to the public authorities – not only to respond to the crisis, but also for support in their fears and uncertainties; to express their latent desire to belong to a community governed by trust rather than by distrust; and to restore a sense of belonging and public purpose and value. In these circumstances the creation of public value requires 'place shielding' as well as 'place shaping' (Lyons 2007).

The official report of the local authority's role in the aftermath of the Lockerbie disaster gives a glimpse of a local government fully embedded in civil society, albeit at a moment of extreme crisis. Immediately after he was notified of the crash the chief executive visited the disaster area, and quickly moved his whole office there to personally operate this as a 24-hour point of coordination both for the emergency services, and direct services such as social work, bereavement and counselling services, and as a focal point for the local community and the families of those who had died in the crash. In a similar way, Stirling Council in Scotland became a focal point for both the local and the worldwide community in the wake of the Dunblane massacre – not only in the immediate period of shock, anger and grieving, but also in the longer-term process of coming to terms with the trauma and loss, and in the ensuing campaign to ban handguns. Similarly close relationships between the local authority and its people can also be established at times of success and celebration (for example, when Coventry City won the FA Cup in 1987, against the odds).

The reason why public authorities (and particularly local councils) seem to carry and to embody these latent hopes on behalf of people at risk is partly because of their unique role as the only organization with an elected democratic mandate to represent the interests of the whole community, rather than just a fraction or subset of the whole. They can also represent future generations as well as current customers or voters, regardless of personal or political beliefs. In practical terms they can also rapidly mobilize a network of trusted public and voluntary services.

Disasters, emergencies and celebrations are of course situations in which people are likely to be less aware of their divisions and more united with each other and with the authorities. The bigger challenge for public authorities in more everyday situations is, first, how to rebuild trust within communities which are disunited, divided and demoralized, and second, how to develop confidence, trust and loyalty between the people and the public authorities. Co-creation of public value jointly between civil society and the state offers a framework for conceptualizing such goals.

Hierarchies, markets – and networks

Similarly, in theoretical terms, whereas the state is coordinated mainly through hierarchies, and the private market through competition, civil society is co-ordinated mainly through networks (Frances *et al.* 1991).

Government programmes of public service reform have made substantial use of both command and control hierarchies and competitive markets, but the complex, cross-cutting problems now facing governments seem to require, in addition, more effective use of collaborative networks. Networks and inter-organizational partnerships offer greater flexibility and adaptability of response than hierarchies, and greater scope for sharing of risks and rewards than competitive markets – particularly when the context is complex and fast-changing. (Though networks also introduce major problems of steering and accountability – see below, and Benington 2001.)

We are therefore seeing the emergence of innovative new patterns of networked community governance and public service, which cut across the traditional boundaries and divisions between different spheres (the state, the market and civil society), different levels of government (local, regional, national and supranational), and different services (for example education, health, housing, policing). These networked patterns of governance also cut across the boundaries between producers and users of services, in various forms of co-production between public service workers and their clients and communities (Alford 2009).

Intersectoral and inter-organizational networks can be seen to help governments to resolve (or to reconfigure) three sets of dilemmas and contradictions (Benington 2001):

- Political legitimation – networks can provide opportunities to coopt a wider range of potentially conflicting or competing interests into shared responsibility for governance and management of the complex cross-cutting problems facing society, and an alternative form of legitimation for the actions and the interventions of the state given the erosion of confidence in elected representative government.

- Economic innovation – networks can provide opportunities for spreading the risks and the rewards of innovation between a number of partners, who in isolation would find the costs prohibitive. The hierarchies of the state have sometimes been found too rigid and inflexible to act as catalysts for rapid innovation, while the private competitive market by itself is rarely able to provide the context of trust and collaboration necessary for high-risk innovation. Joint ventures, strategic alliances and other inter-organizational partnerships may help to create the collaborative conditions to foster innovation which none of the individual organizations could provide on its own.

- Social problem-solving – networks can provide opportunities for the state to grapple with some of the complex cross-cutting social problems which face governments, citizens and communities. The hierarchical structures of public bureaucracies were very effective in the mass-production of standardized basic public services in the postwar period, but are often now found to be too rigid to respond rapidly to the fast-changing and increasingly diverse patterns of need in today's multicultural communities, being disconnected from the front line where needs and problems are first identified and where tailor-made solutions have to be developed and tested. Competitive markets are very successful in proliferating commodities to satisfy changing desires for personal consumption, but are increasingly found to be less capable of catering for more complex, profound and enduring social needs – for example care for older or mentally ill people.

Networks have greater potential than either hierarchies or markets to function as complex adaptive systems, with capabilities for coordination between many different actors and organizations, and the organizational flexibility to respond to continuous change. The new information and communication technologies are opening up opportunities for new forms of networked governance and public service to provide more frequent democratic dialogue, engagement and consultation with users, citizens and communities; more integrated tailor-made services to diverse groups of citizens and local communities; and upstream involvement as co-producers in the design and development of services. However, while the strength of partnerships and networks is their flexibility and adaptability their limitation is their instability and volatility. They are better adapted to change than to continuity, and they also present major challenges in terms of both steering (how to sustain clear strategic direction) and accountability (how to account to multiple stakeholders, with very different mandates).

Public goods, public choice and public value

The traditional public administration characteristic of the postwar welfare state was informed by Fabian political economy and theories of public goods (which are distinguished from private goods by being non-excludable and having low rivalry of consumption – Samuelson 1954). The so-called new public management (NPM) which has dominated academic and practitioner debate over the past two decades has been informed by neo-liberal political economy, and theories of rational or public choice (where individuals are seen as the primary unit of analysis, and the maximization of self-interest as the main determinant of both economic and social behaviour).

In contrast, the new patterns of networked community governance which are now emerging have lacked the support of a distinctive economic and social theory, apart from rather generalized notions of a 'third way' which combines a competitive market with a redistributive state, and balances economic innovation with social justice (Giddens 1998, 2000). The 'third way' philosophy provided a broad rationale and vision for change, and stressed the need to link individual and social strategies, but it did not provide a clear enough theory or strategy to focus reform at the institutional and organizational level. Roberto Unger (Unger 1998) argues that to be effective radical reforms need to be based upon intermediate-level theories that address questions of institutional and organizational change rather than just provide broad ideological narratives. In the absence of a clear overall theory of change of this kind to provide coherent logic and clear strategic direction, public service reforms can easily add up to little more than a plethora of pilot programmes and a relentless succession of piecemeal initiatives, which contribute little to an overall sense of public purpose or direction.

The competing theories of 'public goods' and of 'public choice' were each effective not just in terms of driving political economic strategies, but also in providing a clear logic and focus for policy development, institutional reform, and organizational and cultural change, by the governments which espoused them. The new patterns of networked community governance are potentially high on innovation, but are still lacking a theory to provide a clear conceptual framework and overall strategic purpose, and criteria by which to judge the value of the outcomes.

The concept of public value has been attracting growing interest among public policymakers and managers in the UK, Europe, Australia and New Zealand, and in several developing countries, over the past 10 to 15 years, and more recently among academics in these countries too. However, there is a danger in the UK, at least, of public value getting used loosely, as a broad portmanteau phrase expressing ideals and aspirations about public service, but also capable of meaning many different things to different people. There has been less rigorous development of the definition and of the theoretical assumptions behind the notion of public value, and less testing of the concept through the lens of different academic disciplines and policy contexts. This section of the chapter aims to contribute both to the process of theoretical development of public value, and also to its application in practice.

What is public value?

Public value can be thought of in two main ways:

- First, what the public values
- Second, what adds value to the public sphere

These two aspects are often in tension and sometimes in conflict with each other, but it is necessary to link both dimensions if the theory is to be robust.

The question of 'what the public values' can be seen as a counterbalance to previous traditions in public administration in which 'producers' defined and determined the value of public services – for example through political goal-setting, expert policy analysis and professional standards and regulation.

A growing body of both neo-liberal and social-democratic thinkers (Hayek 1960; Le Grand 2003) argue for a shift away from producer-led to consumer-led models of government and public service. This raises a number of interrelated questions:

- What are the differences, in terms of judging value, between products and services? (In the case of services 'the process' may itself be 'the product'; for example bereavement counselling, where the value depends upon a subjective judgement about the quality of a relationship rather than an objective evaluation of a product.)
- What are the differences between private services and public services? In the former the unit of analysis, and the target of the service, is often an individual consumer, whereas in the latter it is sometimes a group or community.
- How does the notion of what the public values differ from what the public needs, wants or desires? Much current discussion of public service tends to focus on notions of client or public satisfac-

tion, but in order to establish more robust measures of public value it may be necessary for the public to be asked to make trade-offs between competing sources of satisfaction. The Cabinet Office report on public value (Kelly *et al.* 2002) argues that what the public values is meaningful only when linked to questions of what it is willing to give up in exchange for any benefit – establishing public value therefore includes trade-offs.

- Finally, what does public value mean in those cases where public service may be of a regulatory kind (for example, police or public health enforcement), and when it may take the form of an 'obligation encounter' imposed on an unwilling user, who has not requested and may not want the service (Moore 1995)?

What adds value to the public sphere?

The second dimension of my definition of public value is 'what adds value to the public sphere'. This counterbalances the first part of the definition ('what the public values') by focusing attention not just on individual interests but also on the wider public interest, and not just on the needs of current users but also on the longer-term public good, including the needs of generations to come.

Again this raises a number of inter-related questions:

- First, what is the public sphere? The public sphere can be thought of as the web of values, places, organizations, rules, knowledge, and other cultural resources held in common by people through their everyday commitments and behaviours, and held in trust by government and public institutions. It is what provides a society with some sense of belonging, meaning, purpose and continuity, and which enables people to thrive and to strive amid uncertainty (Sennett 1977; Bentley and Wilsden 2003; Marquand 2004).

- Second, who and what is 'the public'? It is arguable that the public is not given but made – it has to be continuously created and constructed. Part of the role of government is to take the lead in shaping and responding to people's ideas and experiences of the public, of who we are, and what we collectively value – what it means to be part of, and a participant in, the public sphere, at this moment in time and in this place/space, and what adds to public value and what detracts from it. This involves a constant battle of ideas and values, because the public sphere is heavily contested territory, and there are many competing interests and ideologies in play. The 'public realm' is under current challenge from tendencies which undermine the sense of interdependence within a multicultural society – for example, racism, sexism, fascism, fundamentalism, brutalization and consumerism, which fragment the notion of what we have in common as a public (Marquand 2004; Sennett 1977).

- Third, what constitutes value in the public sphere, and who decides? This goes right to the heart of classical debates about the good society from Plato and Aristotle onwards, and raises many questions about absolute and relative values (Doyal and Gough 1991). Public value is a necessarily contested concept, and, like cultural or artistic value, it is often established through a continuing process of dialogue. This is similar to the process of democratic dialogue which Habermas envisages as part of the process of creating and sustaining the public sphere (Habermas 1989). It also echoes the dialectical process of literary criticism which T.S. Eliot calls the 'common pursuit of true judgment' (Eliot 1923), and which FR Leavis describes as 'a consciously collaborative enterprise – a sustained effort to promote the co-operative labour of criticism' (Leavis 1952).

What do we mean by value?

Value has been debated within disciplines like philosophy, politics, economics, religion and literature over a long period of time, and we cannot summarize this vast body of thinking here. However, in claiming that public value may be able to offer the public sector an equivalent concept to private value in the private sector, Mark Moore implicitly accepts the challenge of considering the economic dimensions of public value, among other definitions (Moore 1995).

Classical economics distinguishes between:

- Exchange value (which reflects an item's price on the open market).
- Labour value (which reflects the amount of human effort invested in its production).
- Use value (which reflects how useful an item is to a given person or situation.

Neo-liberal economic approaches to value (including rational/public choice theory) which have dominated public thought in the West for over 25 years have concentrated on the measurement of exchange value, at the expense of both use value and labour value.

In the late 1970s and early 1980s the notion of use value was resurrected by a group of practitioners concerned with developing alternative economic strategies both for specific industrial sectors (for example aerospace, auto, coal, steel) and for regional and local economies (Cooley 1982; Benington 1986). This involved innovative ideas for socially useful production, and for planned production for social needs which had not been met through the private market (for example the production of combined heat and power from the recycling of waste; the design of hybrid road/rail vehicles to reduce traffic congestion and pollution; the development of all-in shower units with wheelchair access for disabled people).

The relevance of this for our discussion of public value lies in the identification of social needs which have not been satisfied either by the private competitive market (because individual needs could not be translated into effective demand or commodified within the market, without the state providing the risk investment and bulk purchasing on behalf of individuals who lack sufficient purchasing power of their own) or by the state (because the needs fell outside the category of traditional public goods – non excludable, low-rival). In these examples value is being added to the public sphere, not through arm's-length market demand and supply, but through closer linking of users and producers in creative joint development of products and services tailor-made to meet unmet human need – co-creation of public value.

The concept of labour value is also useful in defining public value, in that it focuses attention on the value of the human effort and skill invested in the production of public service. Rational/public choice and other neo-liberal perspectives tend to emphasize the self-interest of public sector practitioners and professionals, and the dangers of producer interests dominating over those of users and consumers (Le Grand 2003). Keynesian and public goods perspectives also tend to downplay the creative skill and effort of the public servant, seeing him or her instead as a bureaucratic cog within an organizational machine. In contrast, the public value perspective recognizes the importance of the labour (both by hand and by brain) of public professionals and managers in the co-creation of public service, through the interaction between producers and users and other stakeholders, for example in education, health and criminal justice (see below).

The notion of public value, therefore, extends beyond market economic considerations, and can also encompass social, political, cultural and environmental dimensions of value:

- Economic value – adding value to the public realm through the generation of economic activity, enterprise, and employment.
- Social and cultural value – adding value to the public realm by contributing to social capital, social cohesion, social relationships, social meaning and cultural identity, individual and community wellbeing.
- Political value – adding value to the public realm by stimulating and supporting democratic dialogue and active public participation and citizen engagement.

- Ecological value – adding value to the public realm by actively promoting sustainable development and reducing public 'bads' like pollution, waste, global warming.

Who creates public value?

Public value is not created by the public sector alone. Public value outcomes can be generated by the private sector, the voluntary sector and informal community organizations, as well as by governments. One of the potential roles of government is to harness the powers and resources of all three sectors (the state, the market and civil society) behind a common purpose and strategic priorities, in the pursuit of public value goals.

The UK Cabinet Office-led programme of 'Better Government for Older People' is a good example of joint working between central and local government, health authorities, the private sector, employers' organizations and trades unions, the voluntary sector and pensioner action groups, to achieve a clear goal, namely better services and quality of life for older people (Hayden and Boaz 2000). By focusing on the value added to the public sphere it is possible to orchestrate the contributions of many different stakeholders behind common goals.

How is public value created?

Public value can be created in many different ways, given the diversity of activities covered by the public service sector. For example, the processes of value creation in mass-production services like street lighting, housing repairs, or water and sewerage, are very different from those in 'small-batch' production services like health, or child care, or policing. In some cases we first need to clarify the nature of the production process involved, and then to think through the ways public value can be added (or can be increased) at various stages in the value chain. In other areas we need to start with the group of people concerned and engage them in the discussion and definition of how they can both contribute to and benefit from the creation of public value.

In key services like education, health and policing we need to take account of the complex processes of co-creation between producers and users of the service within which value is created. The focal point for the production of public value in education, for example, lies in the interrelationships between teachers, pupils and parents. This challenges the traditional distinction between producers and consumers, and clients and contractors, trading at arm's length from each other within a competitive market place, and instead focuses on the quality of the interrelationships established in a collaborative process of value creation (Alford 2009).

Where is public value created?

The prime arenas for the creation of public value are therefore often found at the front line of public service organizations, where there is the most direct interaction between public service workers and users, citizens and communities. The adding of public value through education, health and social care, and policing therefore depends crucially upon the calibre, the capabilities and the commitment of these frontline staff – in school classrooms, hospital wards, neighbourhood communities.

Many upstream policies and contextual factors influence the quality, effectiveness and productivity of these frontline relationships and processes, including the national and local policy context, organizational culture, resource base, levels of knowledge generation and transfer, training and development. For example, medical staff and patients cannot generate a context and culture of healing and health in hospitals and in communities unless the staff are backed up with relevant training, support and advice, good buildings and equipment, and unless the patients have proper information, housing, sanitation, nutrition, and loving care from family, friends and neighbours.

How is public value measured?

The concept of public value highlights the importance of focusing on processes and outcomes ('what value is being added to the public sphere, by whom and how?') not just on inputs and outputs, or on input/output ratios and productivity. For example, public value perspectives in the health service will focus on improvements in public health and in preventive strategies, and on the respect with which patients are treated, as well as on reductions in hospital waiting lists and times. Public value outcomes in education will take into account the cultivation of a life-long thirst for learning, questioning and reflection as well as the achievement of high test scores in annual exams.

Public value creation can be pictured in terms of an open system in which inputs are converted, through activities and processes, into outputs and outcomes, with the active help of co-producers and partner organizations (see Figure 2.2).

Analysis of the public value stream can be used to clarify the specific public value outcomes desired for specific groups of citizens, communities or services. It can then help to focus on three key questions:

- At what stages in the process is public value clearly being added? Where is a positive contribution to the desired public value goals and outcomes being made? These are the stages/processes in the public value stream which need supporting and strengthening and resourcing.

Figure 2.2   *The public value stream*

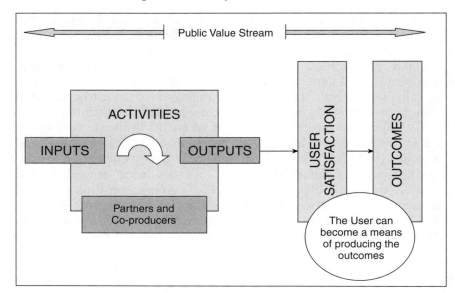

- At what stages in the process is public value being subtracted or destroyed? What activities are not actively contributing to the achievement of the desired public value goals and outcomes? Can they be realigned and reharnessed behind the desired public value goals and outcomes? If not, how can these activities be removed or stopped?
- What parts of the public value stream are lying idle or stagnant? Where is there little or no movement, either forward or back, towards achieving the desired public value outcomes? What can be done to unblock the situation and mobilize new flow, energy and actively to achieve the goals?

The assessment of value includes aspects of public satisfaction, but also goes beyond this, as public value outcomes are measured in terms of economic, social, political and ecological value added to the public sphere. Public value outcomes may therefore include factors which are not easily registered in public satisfaction surveys (for example, investment in the maintenance of clean water supplies, or the repair of sewerage systems, which may not be visible or apparent to the individual service-user). Public value outcomes may also include factors that some sections of the public experience as negative constraints (for example, control of drug-dealing, under-age drinking, or child pornography).

Public value outcomes are therefore complex and contested, and frequently involve trade-offs not only between 'goods' and 'bads', but also between competing priorities (Kelly *et al.* 2002). Nevertheless, the concept of public value helps to focus attention on the processes by which it is created or co-created, and the outcomes for whom and with whom. Public value can therefore be used not only as a conceptual tool for strategic planning, but also as a heuristic device to stimulate debate between competing interests and perspectives, and to generate dialogue about how to improve services, about who gains and who loses, and about relative benefits and costs. (See Chapters 12 and 13 by Norman and Mulgan.)

When is public value created?

Because of the focus on outcomes, public value focuses attention on, and is measured over, the medium to longer term. For example, high-quality primary education can have long-term impacts in raising aspirations and achievements which will only become apparent over a 5- to 10-year period, or indeed when the pupils go on to further or higher education, or have children themselves. These longer-term measures of the value added to the public sphere by investment in an educated population are as important as the shorter-term measurement of results in annual exams and tests (Winkley 2002). Governments, dictated by electoral cycles, inevitably tend to focus on the shorter term, but public managers also have a responsibility to focus on the longer-term public interest, and to act as guardians of the public sphere in the interest of future generations yet unborn, who lack a voice in current decision-making. This may include drawing on decision support tools like scenario planning, future search, Delphi techniques, cost–benefit analysis, quality-of life indicators, and so on. However, it is helpful to set these management techniques in the context of an overall concept of what adds value to the public sphere.

Conclusion

Public value has the potential to develop as an alternative to both rational/public choice theory and theories of public goods, in providing a conceptual framework to inform and inspire reform and improvement of public services. Public value thinking can help to define, clarify and operationalize the notion of adding value to the public sphere, in the same way that the concept of added value within the private market provides a benchmark for private sector activity. Public value focuses attention both on what the public values and on what strengthens the public sphere. Public value highlights the processes of value creation, and the longer-term outcomes for the public sphere, not just short-term activities and outputs. Public value highlights the processes of co-creation, which are necessary for the production of public value in much of the public service sector, including the education, health and criminal-justice services. Public value provides a conceptual framework within which competing values and interests can be expressed and debated, in a deliberative democratic process, by which the question of what constitutes value is established dialectically. The concept of public value allows for contest, and for diversities of values and identities, within a negotiated understanding of what it means to be part of the wider public sphere, at that time and place. Public value perspectives can also help to contribute to the development of a common purpose and direction for public service organizations, elected politicians and managers. Governments cannot create the public value or the public realm on their own – it depends on a wider network of institutions, actors and cultures – but it cannot be achieved without government and political leadership. This can include political, economic, and social and community development roles.

The political development role in searching for public value can draw upon the authority of the government, derived from its mandate as the only representative, democratically elected body, with a remit and a responsibility to act on behalf of the whole community (young and old; black and white; women and men; poor and rich; employed and unemployed; indigenous and immigrant), and including future generations yet unborn. However, the authorization to create public value comes not just from electoral mandates, but has to be won and constantly replenished from a wide variety of different stakeholders, from different levels of government, and from different parts of the public, private, voluntary and informal community sectors.

Political development roles to create and sustain public value include shaping ideas, and generating public debate about public value and the public realm; creating a 'holding environment' (challenging but safe spaces) within which nettles can be grasped, and difficult issues can be grappled with (Heifetz 1994); legitimating certain kinds of cultural values and activity (and de-legitimating others) by government recognition, celebration, and awards and rewards for excellence; stimulating civic knowledge, learning and capabilities for individuals, communities and organizations (public, private and voluntary); establishing regulatory frameworks, promoting ethical and civic values, and good standards of public and political behaviour.

Economic development roles to promote public value can draw upon the leverage and resources of the government as a major employer, purchaser, investor, property owner and developer, and might range from investing in the long-term public health of the nation; developing, recognizing, and validating civic knowledge and skills and enabling them to be developed through training and employment; promoting equity in the availability of resources, opportunities for employment and improvement of local infrastructure; supporting declining or changing local economies and helping localities to diversify their economic and employment bases; and providing a framework for stimulating and evaluating innovation in both the public, private and voluntary sectors.

Social and community development to promote public value can draw upon the roles and responsibilities of governments to promote social justice, fairness and equity, access for all, and opportunities for participation in the public sphere; promoting community development and active engagement in public and political life through a wide range of community organizations; orchestrating the work of a wide group of partner organizations and stakeholders in the public, private, voluntary and informal community sector; acting as a catalyst for innovation and creative forms of engagement with political, civic and community networks; protecting and promoting diversities of culture, especially within minority communities; creating innovative intermediary organizations and networks to help individuals, groups and informal community organizations to link up with the more formal structures of the public, private and voluntary sectors; assuring equality of access and seeking to limit inequalities of outcome.

One of the risks with the concept of public value is that it will be adopted as a fashionable new idea, and will be used loosely and uncritically. To be useful in the longer term we need to define and analyse public value more tightly in theoretical terms and apply and test it more rigorously in practice in particular service areas. Hopefully this book and this chapter make a contribution to this process.

Chapter 3

Privates, Publics and Values

COLIN CROUCH

'Public' and 'value' are concepts with multiple meanings which change over time. Public is problematic when set alongside its usual antagonist, 'private'. Value is difficult because our language is unable to distinguish between a monetary estimation (exchange value) and the idea of something above and beyond calculation (ultimate and moral value). In this chapter I want to explore these problems, taking a long historical perspective on the public/ private contrast, and putting value in a particular context. The main objective is to challenge certain taken-for-granted assumptions about how these terms are used; and to propose that contestation over the meanings that might be given to the idea of 'public value' constitutes a lively and fruitful field for political debate.

Returning to simple, 'state-of-nature' first principles enables us to clear away a large number of distortions and misperceptions that prevent us from getting beyond the polarization of private and public, and obscure the concept of value. By the end I hope to have established a theoretically rooted approach to understanding public value, providing a vantage-point for appraising Mark Moore's concept from the perspectives of history, political philosophy and sociology.

The Hobbesian concept of state of nature pictures the lonely, vulnerable human person in a hostile environment. That person constitutes the simplest, most irreducible concept of the private. It will here be called 'Private1' (see Table 3.1). For that person to progress at all in their journey through the social contract, they have to be equipped with a rational, calculating mind and to be treated as an individual. Both these are problematic. First, with just how much rationality, and with what kind of rationality, must the human person be endowed to enable it to operate before they have had any opportunity for training of a kind that cannot be found in the state of nature? This leads us to the issue of the fundamental role of concepts and values which will concern us further below.

Second, how are we to cope with the fact that, since the individual with which all social philosophy is concerned is human (and not, say,

Table 3.1 *Different meanings of private and public*

Private1	The lonely, vulnerable human
Private2	Private1, plus family
Private3	Private1 and 2, extended to include property appropriated through the use of public means
Public1	The open, the wild
Public2	Unbounded aggregates of human persons
Public3	Distinct, bounded aggregates of human persons, formed by organizations in one or more of the three realms (polity, market, value)
Public4	As Public3, but with the persons included having some citizenship rights over how the collectivity should act
Public5	Aggregates of persons neglected by rent-seeking within Public3 institutions

an insect or a fish), we have to imagine someone incapable of surviving for themselves for at least their early years? This raises the question of the relationship of individual to family, about which most social theories are highly equivocal, and which will appear at a number of points below. The family being necessary to the initial survival of the human, it should be seen as part of the private sphere of the individual rather than as a public or even semi-public institution, and so it has been seen in most social philosophy since ancient times. The individual in her or his family context, including the inheritance of property within the family, therefore constitutes a second meaning of private, 'Private2'.

To find an initial meaning of public, we turn first to the complete opposite of Private1 – the full range of that which is 'out there', external to the individual and potentially hostile to him or her. There are two interpretations of this in the state of nature, both of which can be held to represent primeval concepts of the public. The first comprises everything, including the physical, that is not owned or controlled. This is the public as the 'open', even the 'wild'. Something open is also the understanding of public embodied in the concept of a 'public good' in economic theory: that which cannot be appropriated, and access to which is non-rival.[1] This sense of public will here be called 'Public1'.

However, an important component of this openness comprises other human persons (and families), which gives us a second, social meaning of public as the mass of other private persons external to the original individual, seen as a boundless, undifferentiated aggregate – also therefore as a kind of openness.[2] This second sense of public will be called 'Public2'. For sparse populations living amid largely untamed environments, Public1 looms larger; among thickly populated and particularly urban groups living in a domesticated nature, Public2 is the more important.

Linking private and public

Survival for any one human individual depends on them being able to rely on controls being exercised over both nature and other human individuals (Public1 and Public2) so that they sustain rather than threaten the individual's life. The private human cannot thrive or even survive without bridging the gap between self and the public. As noted, in the first instance this might be achieved through the family, Private2. To go beyond its limited capabilities requires the use of one or more of three fundamental means, found in three institutional realms that construct the private–public links that are necessary for human survival and development:

- Coercion over others – leading, when stabilized, to the exercise of rule over them to enforce collaboration with collective tasks, and hence to the establishment of a *political realm*.
- The development of shared normative perceptions and cognitions – leading to the creation of identities that distinguish insiders (to whom obligations and trust are owed, making collaboration possible) from outsiders, who continue to constitute Public2; ultimately, construction of a *realm of values*.
- The establishment of exchanges with others – in order to build up networks of collaborative obligations: the *realm of markets*.

In the first instance the mechanisms behind these three realms constitute sporadic actions: episodes of coercion, attempts at the assertion of moral obligation, and offers of exchange. But those using them successfully seek to go beyond the sporadic and to construct organizations to sustain and develop elements of the activities embodied in the respective realm. To use modern parlance, those working at the polity try to construct states; those in the realm of value construct religious or other moral organizations[3]; and those in the market construct firms (see Table 3.2).

It is common to speak of 'state and market' as constituting a kind of opposition or pair of alternatives, but this is to confuse an organization with an institution. The appropriate comparator with the state within the realm of market exchange is the firm, as both are organizations; the appropriate comparator with the market within the political realm is the polity. One should therefore speak of state and firm or polity and market. The importance of this distinction for our present purposes is that these two pairs of entities have different relations to

Table 3.2 *Basic terminology for institutions and organizations*

	Realms of the private–public link		
Type of action	Coercion	Normative appeal	Exchange
Institution	Polity	Values	Market
Characteristic organization	State	Church	Firm

public and private. As we shall see below, both polity and market (and values) are means and as such cannot be appropriated; they always exist primarily in the public sphere. The organizations that people form in order to make use of these means (states, firms, churches) can be privately appropriated, though in practice may not be. Their relationship to the public/private distinction is therefore ambiguous and changing.

In the process of organizational formation, a complex logic of interests develops within each realm. It is in the interests of dominant entrepreneurial individuals or families and their closest associates who take the initiative in fashioning or reforming organizations to make them primarily as extensions of their private selves, their property, using others as instruments of that purpose, even if tasks for a wider collectivity may also be performed by the organization. This gives us a third meaning of private (Private3): the extension of the reach of Private1 and Private 2 through acquisition of elements of Public1 or Public2 as private property. This is the use of 'private' most commonly intended in political debate and in contemporary contrasts between public and private. Other persons within the organization also benefit from the exploitation of Public1 and 2 that result from the organization's activities, but cannot claim it as part of the scope of their private. It must be noted that, unlike Private1 and Private 2, Private3 is not a 'pure' private, as it uses the public resources of coercive capacity, normative cognition or exchange in order to achieve its extension.

The polity

At least in post-Roman European history, this process of organizational formation proceeded very differently in each of the three realms. It was first seen most clearly in the case of the polity. The various concentrations of coercive power that gradually coalesced and institutionalized to form states began unequivocally as instances of Private3. Individual strong men (only very rarely women) and their close supporters secured control over weaker or less-well-equipped people in order to make them work for them, offering in exchange a remission from violence and a stabilization of life that made possible various collaborative tasks for taming nature. They usually tried to make the political organizations they formed in doing this inheritable – the main confirmation of the private status of these organizations, Private2 rather than Private1 being the main form taken by the private in societies with generally thin institutional resources.

In the long term, it frequently became necessary to the interests of the ruling group to present its pursuit of this private interest as being in the interests of all those involved in its domains. Institutionalized as states, the resulting structures were deemed to constitute the whole collectivity (parts of Public2) encompassed by their power as well as the natural world or wild (Public1) contained within the geographical territories they controlled. Private3 could then be claimed to constitute a public zone (Public3), and indeed gradually became the dominant meaning given to the adjective 'public', especially in confrontation with the private as Private3. Just as the latter is a most impure private, so Public3 is a very partial public, standing at a relationship of 180 degrees to that of Public1, the economist's sense of the public, or to Public2 as the unbounded generality of persons. While Publics1 and 2 signify openness, Public3 marks a state of clear closure and definition of both territory and persons, eventually marked by patrolled borders, badges of membership (such as passports), and definitions of insider and outsider.

During the course of modern history there has been considerable indeterminacy over where certain institutions ceased to be primarily Private3 (the private purview of the ruling family and its entourage) and became Public3. Louis XIV famously tried to resolve the problem with the phrase '*L'État, c'est moi.*' The Austrian Empire, though it extended over many different peoples across central and southern Europe, never ceased to take the form of being the private demesne of the Hapsburg family. Much of the nomenclature of the British state continues to refer to the private possessions of the monarch: 'Her Majesty's Government'.

This long and halting journey of Public3 from being the by-product of successful coercion by a dominant family or families to being the constitutional state, with the abolition of heredity as a principle for determining office-holding, government itself being subject to the rule of law and subject to periodic election, led eventually to a fourth sense of public (Public4). This is now a noun and denotes a universal adult citizenry who, rather than any one family or group of families, 'own' the state. This is still a more restricted concept of public than in Public2, as it is still only a part of the public that is included. It is a rather private kind of public. The rise of modern citizenship has often been described and cannot be repeated here. We need to note only: (i) the dual interests served by Public3, (ii) its relationship to Public1 and

Public2, (iii) the possibility of the emergence of Public4, and (iv), the continued interdependence and inter-relationship between public and private.

The realm of values

Instead of coercion, private persons might try to solve the problem of taming nature and each other by collaboration made possible through a sense of being together in the face of the dangers of the wild, and of other humans beyond the range of the potentially collaborating group. This may happen to such an extent that they regard each other as part of a 'we', a first-person plural. The roots of this possibility lie in the inevitability of this approach within the family, and the fact that in a state of nature with limited travel possibilities, persons will be linked to most people they encounter through some family relationship. Further development of these senses of obligation and trust will depend, as does the development of coercion into an instrument for achieving collective tasks, on persons who make it their concern, as part of their project for advancing their own personal interests, to develop mechanisms for shaping ideas and values concerning who should be counted as within the collaborating group and who is an outsider and therefore part of the potentially hostile. Again a dual interest system is constructed: the virtuosi in identity and value development, the value-controllers, are able to pursue a private interest; the rest of the collectivity gains from being defined as insiders.

The controllers of values have been at their most successful when they have linked their authority to powers beyond the scope of human life, in an unseen world of gods and spirits, to whom the value controllers have special channels of access. They become priests rather than rulers and establish religions rather than states. As such, unless they can secure an intervention by the gods in everyday life, they are potentially vulnerable in a conflict with those who wield worldly coercion. In many cases therefore priests and rulers are one and the same, but it is remarkable how often in human history they have been at least partly separate. They have then often developed an interdependence, whereby the priests declare that the gods support the worldly rulers and the latter protect the priests. On the other hand, there have been remarkable instances of conflict and confrontation between the two. How these patterns play out has differed considerably across societies and over time. For example, some, though not all, forms of Islam do not recognize the distinction between faith and state at all. We shall here therefore remain with post-Roman European history.

The separation between state and religion that became such a distinctive feature of that history was a somewhat chance result of the ability of the church to maintain some kind of sway over the

European territories of the Roman Empire when the reach of the polity had crumbled into various small, warring groups. During the Roman Empire itself the emperor had also served as *pontifex maximus*, head of the state religion, whether that was the original paganism or later Christianity. It was as Christians dealt with the fall of their secular arm while the spiritual thrived that a theoretical and institutional divide was made between, in Augustine's words, the City of God and the City of Man, and the institutions of polity and of religion were clearly divided.

For several centuries (very broadly, until the sixteenth) it was the Western Church that could make the stronger claim to have linked private and public, embracing the most extensive meanings of Public1 and Public2. Its concept of the whole, the universe, extended further than anything subsequently achieved by any other institution, going further even than the economists' sense of the public good. It also claimed the loyalty of the subjects of a wide range of constantly changing polities – though it was usually dependent on the rulers of those polities to deliver 'converts' to it. Also, and profoundly important, whether by accident or design, the rule of celibacy separated the holding of office in the church from the claims of individual families – exactly the opposite of what occurred in the state.

Political power during these centuries could make little claim to make much of a link to the public sphere at all, serving primarily to extend the scope of Private2 for ruling families and their leading supporters. Most rulers therefore found it useful to make alliances with the church, from Charlemagne's symbolic request to be anointed by the pope in 800 onwards; political power had very few direct links to the population, most of what we would today regard as 'public services', if they existed at all, being seen as part of the City of God. On the other hand, the church was in turn anxious for the support of whatever secular rulers emerged, if only to ensure the protection of the secular arm for church property, and the suppression of ideological challenge from rival interpretations of faith.

Exchange

While economists and economic philosophers (for example Hayek 1963) tend to see market exchange as the main form of interaction to which human persons will have recourse provided nothing interferes with their so doing, other social scientists have been more sceptical. Political and legal theorists point to the role of law in sustaining and guaranteeing not just markets but the idea of property ownership itself. This requires the prior development of something like a state, a taming and channelling of the monopoly of coercion so that it operates through predictable and fairly stable rules. In practice, medieval monarchs often did interfere with property rights, and so long as they did so the development of capitalism was inhibited (North 1990).

Economists point to such developments as the medieval lex mercatoria, which seemed to operate without legal support, or much more recently to the use of private arbitration over contracts in some parts of the US economy. However, for the great volume of transactions, large and small, contract enforcement relies on law; currencies are backed by governments; and property rights are protected by police forces. Medieval institutions of exchange were weakly developed, as the polity was not in a position to provide much of the public institutional infrastructure that they needed; indeed, monarchs were the people most likely to show disrespect for the obligations of contract. What material economic infrastructure there was, again was provided primarily through the church and its monasteries.

More profoundly, sociologists (principally Durkheim (1897) and Parsons (1949)) have argued that before people can make contracts they need to have the idea of a contract and its obligations, and that requires the prior development of some social values. It therefore seems reasonable to regard the development of the third means whereby individuals extend the reach of their private selves to tame and exploit the Public1 and Public2, exchange on the basis of property rights, as being derivative from the other two.

A more important point is to note how market transactions are used, as are political measures, to extend the reach and meaning of the private from the human person or family (Private1 or 2) to a network of other persons and things that can be regarded as private property and embraced by the first person possessive ('mine', or 'ours') (Private3). As in the political realm, this sense of private, which is the main one used in economics and in concepts like 'private property' and 'private sector', is in fact an amalgam of private and public, because the private person (Private1) can only extend itself to become Private3 by the use of public means. The law is, clearly, a public institution (even when it is private law); but so also is the market. Individual markets (such as a city's stock exchange, or a market hall) can be privately owned, but 'the' market in the sense of the Walrasian abstraction to which economic theory refers is a public good (Walras 1874). All exchanges that take place occur within it; there is universal access to it for anyone who has the means to buy and sell; it is not appropriable and it is non-rival.

Private3 arrived at through the market is therefore as much a mix of public and private as when achieved in the polity. In complex economies this becomes even more evident through the concept of the 'public' or 'publicly quoted' company, identifying a company whose shares can be traded within the public institution of the stock exchange. Such firms are distinguished from the 'private' company, though both are found within the 'private' sector of the economy. In the case of a public company, a 'general public' (in theory but not in practice something approximating to Public2) is invited to buy shares with limited liability in a firm. It then ceases to be the purely private possession of its owner and becomes subject to a whole new legal regime designed to safeguard the interests of both present and potential shareholders. When a firm 'goes public' it loses some of its private character.

It is for reasons such as these that some legal authors have written of the privilege of property ownership rather than its 'natural' state as perceived by Hayek and others (for example, Solomon and Collins 1987). It is only through the intervention of public phenomena that private property can exist. This was perceived by Adam Smith, who, writing before the days of the modern welfare state, wrote that it was only just that private property was taxed, as much of the expenditure of the state was devoted to its protection (Smith A. 1759; 1776).

Strange though it seems from a nineteenth- to twenty-first-century perspective, in the medieval and early modern period economic institutions made more successful bridges between public and private than the nascent state, even if over small geographical areas and not so much in their predominant modern form of the individual firm. Crafts and merchant activities (today's secondary and tertiary sectors) developed within towns,[4] while a militarized aristocracy (together with monasteries) ruled primarily over agricultural territory. The close living conditions of towns and the dependence of both craft and merchant activities on rules (of apprenticeship, of trade, of contract, and so on) required a more extensive development of Public3 than purely political power at that time provided. This sense of public was rooted firmly in Private2 – leading merchant families dominated both the economic and the political life of the cities, intriguing with and against each other, sometimes violently, in order to hold advantage. But it was these nascent capitalists who constructed the first examples of what we would today regard as urban public services and infrastructure, far more than the monarchies that are normally seen as the forerunners of the modern state. Often acting alongside the church, but sometimes alone, many of the merchant cities of Flanders, some parts of Germany and northern Italy in particular established institutions for the care of the sick, orphans and other deprived persons under the general names of 'hospitals'. The various guilds established social security institutions for their members and, after the deaths, their widows and orphans. Rudimentary traffic regulations and noise control were often enforced, and even some cleaning services. (Black 1984 has described how much of the history of this activity was suppressed after the various monarchies suppressed urban autonomy itself, a fate which Flanders, parts of Germany and northern Italy escaped longer than most.)

Relationships among the realms; implications for the private/public distinction

Some fundamental points need to be noticed with respect to all three of these basic means of linking private to public.

First, in each case there is a mix of private and public. None of them can be allocated unambiguously to either realm, though at different historical moments the balance between private and public contained in each has varied.

Second, within each there are several grades of beneficiary. Their ranking is a function of the extent to which they are able to make the public nature of the organization's activities synonymous with their private interests. We can identify at least three such grades:

- *Controllers*, for whom the instrument for linking public and private primarily serves the purpose of enabling them to move to major Private3 acquisitions: emperors, kings and princes; heads of priesthoods; owners and directors of firms.
- *Followers*, or insiders of the organization, who hope to gain some minor advantages from the control over fractions of the public that the organization makes possible: officials, or other public employees; priests and loyal congregations; managers and other employees.
- A more general *public* (in the sense of Public4) who are able to gain some Private1 benefit from their relationship to the organization: citizens and subjects; believers; customers.

Third, there will also always be losers, whose Private1 and possibilities of achieving Private3 have been diminished or expropriated by the success of the organization concerned: rulers and citizens in polities threatened with or defeated in war by a particular polity; priests and believers of religious minorities deemed heretical by a dominant religion; owners and employees, just possibly customers, of firms defeated in competition by a successful corporation.

These three basic realms of engagement between private and public appear repeatedly in the record of social organization. There were, for example, the three estates of medieval Europe: nobility (rulers), clergy (priests), bourgeoisie (traders); and the three orders of the Indian caste system as rationalized in the Moghul period: Brahmin (priests), Rajput (rulers), Kshastriya (merchants) – interestingly, priests ranked above rulers here. (In both cases the merchant trading classes shade off into the ordinary population: these ranking schemes were often produced by alliances of priests and rulers, partly in defence against the growing power of the bourgeoisie.) The architectonic structure of the Greek, Roman, and medieval European city typically featured a centre comprising a temple or church, a seat of urban government, and a market-place. The houses of priests, nobility and (less officially) leading merchants were also clearly marked, with the last tailing off into the nondescript and often temporary homes of the poor.

There are certain similarities in the organization of the modern social sciences: economics, political science, philosophy, with sociology usually providing the residual, the intellectual equivalent of 'the often temporary homes of the poor'. Some of the most powerful individual conceptual schemes within the social sciences follow a similar trinity: Weber's class (derived from market relations), status (value) and party (political) (1925); Hirschman's exit (economic), voice (political) and loyalty (values) (1970).

From a contemporary perspective we are likely to make a different set of associations, linking the private to the firm, the public to the state, and the realm of values to the voluntary sector. This might then lead us to identify public value as taking place at some intersection between the state and religion. This last conclusion is not entirely false, but that way of arriving at it is quite wrong, and we need to trace another path.

As we have seen above, all three realms are means for relating private and public. We have already seen with our brief glance at early post-Roman European history how their balance in this respect has changed considerably over time, as have their relationships with each other.

In the medieval period, relations among the three realms acquired an intertwining complexity that has never subsequently been equalled. Although the church retained its separation from (and was from time to time at war with) the empire, its interdependence with secular authorities grew more intense as the latter strengthened their hold and developed stable monarchies and duchies across much of the European land mass. At the same time, church leaders often also became political rulers: the Holy See itself became a typical geographically extended Italian city state, and prince-bishops ruled in such cities as Cologne and Liège. Although the celibacy rule survived, some families managed to get control over particular bishoprics and other appointments, the Borgia and Medici families even temporarily annexing the papacy itself. While the church started to lose its public character, political rulers gradually extended the scope of Public3, establishing the public goods of lawcourts and providing something approaching a rule of law for their subjects, though not to which they would subject themselves as under a true rule of law. And, as we have seen above, in the towns it was infant capitalism, linked to urban political forms, rather than the state that was associated with characteristically modern public services.

A highly significant break in the relationship among the realms occurred when the emerging states began to claim sovereignty over the articulation of values, bringing the church under their control and strengthening their claim to 'public' status, the realm of value being able to make so much more successful a claim to that than the polity. This could not happen so easily in Catholic lands, as the seat of religious authority remained a territorially based power in its own right – though the century-long exile of the popes in Avignon, under the watch of the French kings, was an early sign of what was to come. But to the north and to the east, for quite different reasons, there was a major nationalization of religion from the turn of the fifteenth to sixteenth centuries. In the East the occasion was the fall of Constantinople to Islamic power, and the consequent dependence on local political authorities for protection of authority for religious leaders in various parts of the Greek and Russian world. In the North West the occasion was the Reformation, the first successful revolt against the authority of the Vatican. Secular authorities loyal to the church (in France, Italy, Spain, Portugal, Poland, and the lands ruled from Vienna by the Empire) ensured the elimination of heresy, but in the Nordic lands, the British Isles, and large parts of Germany and eventually the northern Low Countries, secular authorities protected the reformers, in exchange for their subsequently supporting them in their claims to rule their territories in the name of God and attract the loyalty of their peoples. This was most extreme in the English case, where the motives of Henry VIII in sponsoring a Reformation were more political than religious, and where the church took the name of the country. But even the more transnational Lutheran and Calvinist faiths, in the absence of any centre as powerful as the Vatican, adopted primarily nation-state identities.

These realigned political and religious institutions (modern states) then continued on their paths of simultaneously serving the private interests of their leaders and certain public interests, still with a division of labour between them, but with the polity more clearly in the ascendancy. The land-based polities of monarchy (particularly the French one) also embarked, either peacefully or violently, on a programme of bringing the towns and the urban economy under their control, though until the nineteenth century this did not extend to much of the main city belt running from the Netherlands, through most of Germany into northern Italy. Where monarchs took control of urban trade they did so by selling monopolies, a particular fusion of political and economic, public and private power.

Where the monarchies dominated, by the end of the seventeenth century the state had taken major steps towards achieving its claim to being the primary link between private and public that is familiar to twentieth- and twenty-first-century perspectives; the church was increasingly sharing its public role with the state, and bourgeois economic institutions were losing their way as the power of cities declined.

The massive implications of the major changes wrought in the late eighteenth and early nineteenth centuries in economy (by English industrialism) and polity (by the French Revolution) are well known. For present purposes we need only examine briefly their vast consequences for the division among the three realms and for the balance between public and private within them.

The theory of the free market preceded the rise of industrialism, but it was the latter that gave that theory revolutionary importance, as industrialism opened so many new possibilities for markets and the expansion of capital. Among the many radical breaks with past thinking wrought by free-market theory, the one that interests us here was a fundamental reworking of the relationship between public and private. Until this point, attempts to orient private action to public concerns had taken the form of either moral persuasion or the imposition of obligations (principally contributed by church and state respectively, or together). Classical economic theory proposed that, provided selfish privately oriented actors could be required to operate through a free and pure market, the pursuit of private selfishness would automatically have benign public consequences. This led in practice to a change in the relationship between private economic property and the public realm, from the civic duties of commercial bourgeois classes to the maximization of profit within a market context. It is essential to note that the concept of public good as such was not lost. The market itself, as we have noted, is a public institution; and the justification of private profit was that its maximization served a public end.[5]

The changes and ideas surrounding the French Revolution and its prolonged aftermath had two implications. First, the state, which had previously formally presented itself as the protector of the church (whether Catholic or Protestant), which was in turn the guardian of values, now itself directly assumed the role as their promulgator and champion. Second, the state changed from being presented and legitimated as the private property of a monarch, who then accepted public obligations, to being presented and legitimated as the possession of all, a res publica, a 'public thing', ultimately as a democracy. The state was proposed as the perfect embodiment of Public3. This fundamental concept was developed in various ways. An important step was Hegel's (1821) conception of the state (though not a democratic one) as the institution through which mankind could realize its highest and most noble aspirations, something which he considered that the humdrum exchanges of 'Manchester' commerce and economics were not equipped to achieve. We arrive eventually at the twentieth century's three great innovations in the role of the state: state socialism, fascism, and (very different from the other two) the British and Scandinavian concept of the democratic welfare state. Each of these owed something to Hegel. State socialism claimed to derive its ideology from Karl

Marx, who had thoroughly absorbed Hegel, even if he had turned him on his head. Nazism (though not, strictly speaking, southern European fascism) was a perversion of the Prussian concept of the state. And a kind of 'welfare Hegelianism' was explicitly important among British and Scandinavian welfare state advocates.

It should be noted that, from the French Revolution onwards, the distinctively 'modern' state has presented its claims as those of rational universalism, implying the unboundedness of Public2, while in practice it has remained with Public3, a 'universe' bounded by the essentially irrational boundaries of the nation-state.

By the mid twentieth century the relationship between the three realms, and the distinction between public and private in those parts of the world proclaimed by their political, religious and economic elites to be liberal democracies, can be summarized as follows:

- The state, as the central organization within the polity, fully in public ownership and detached from being the personal, inheritable property of rulers, and claiming control of the realm of value as well as that of polity, made the central claim to represent the public. However, as with the medieval church, families have from time to time tried to secure a hold over public office, nepotism is always at large, and individuals use it as their claim to a grasp on private wealth and privilege; in addition, the 'public' status of the state is always limited to Public3.
- The firm, legitimated as being an organization in the public interest because it has to operate through the public instrument of the market and the associated state-directed forms of regulation that accompany that status, was thereby permitted to be a pure Private3 organization, with the proceeds of its activities fully appropriable by individuals, and with heredity an unchallenged principle of property transmission;
- The church, challenged in its heartland of values by the state and by (a process beyond our scope here) growing disbelief in its eschatological claims, tried to cling to remnants of its historic position.

In reality, relations among these three forces are more complex than this. Resources being convertible among the three spheres, it is possible, for example, to use those accumulated through market activity in order to achieve political influence. This not only enables wealthy interests to distort the operation of the polity in their favour, but can also be used to distort markets: the state is responsible for the law, which in turn defines the rules of the market. Firms might also use their organizational power to develop moral agendas, whether expressed through the backing of various causes or through corporate social responsibility programmes.

Towards public value

While discussion of public and private concentrates normally and for good reasons on the antagonism between state and market, the primary exhibitors of these opposed forces, our present focus is on public value. We will therefore now concentrate on the place, within (or despite) the dichotomy, of the third realm, the fragmented world of value.

At some points and in some places this remains just as it always was – strong, formal religious organizations claim to stand for an eternal and infinite sense of the public. They derive their continuing force because many people believe that they convey a truth going far beyond any mundane truths. Today, this is particularly the case in the USA, parts of Africa and in the Islamic world;[7] far less so in Europe, Latin America, China and Japan; India stands somewhere in between. But in all liberal democracies religion has been required not to challenge the claim of the democratic state to interpret the values that will predominate within it. However, being liberal democracies, these states do not demand an authoritarian control over the articulation of values. Elements of the pursuit of value did not flow unequivocally into the state when religion's monopoly over that realm was broken. (The same was not true of totalitarian secular states, which did try to capture all components of the realm of values.) Two subsidiary streams can in particular be identified; two different institutional forms that can be taken by an orientation to a value interpretation of public ends: 'voluntary' activities and the 'professions'.

The voluntary or charitable sector

An alternative name for the voluntary sector is 'charity', which is still the legal designation in use for it in several countries (including the UK). The word in its current meaning has absolutely Christian origins, signifying as the Latin *caritas* the idea of universal love, both divine and human. It is a vastly more extensive term than the nineteenth-century concept of charity, but it can easily include that. It was in fact developed to have that meaning by Thomas Aquinas in the thirteenth century, leading to a major renewal of interest in Aquinas's work as European Catholics confronted the crises of poverty and social dislocation associated with the early years of the industrial revolution (Van Kersbergen 1995:199–205). Being universal in its scope, caritas, unlike other forms of love, can be directed towards strangers, and is unconditional, requiring no reciprocity. As such it has long been used by the church to describe not only God's love but also the benevolent activities that it undertakes itself and which it commends to its followers. In the centuries before states accepted any welfare role, the distribution of welfare was part of the domain of the City of God, not that of Man, and was the business of the Church.[8] The contemporary concept of charitable activity descends directly and immediately from these ideas. Within the Catholic world the organization Caritas remains the principal organizer of voluntary welfare activity, with its partner organization Misericordia.[9]

The contemporary understanding of secularized charity follows the following logic. A publicly oriented activity can be understood in one (or more) of only three ways. It might rest in the polity, either as part of a drive for political power or as an activity mandated, funded and organized by the state; or it might rest in the economy, either as part of a drive for private gain, or as an activity mandated, funded and organized by a firm. If it is neither of these, then it must rest in the realm of value, carried out for neither power nor material gain. It might, as with Caritas, be carried out within the framework of a religious organization, but it might also be part of a fragmented secular set of organizations and informal groups.

Charitable or voluntary activities are never found purely in the realm of value, but must share in the other realms: they employ staff and hold assets that require participation in the capitalist economy; they are regulated by law that issues from the state; individuals working for charities may well have motives of private and personal advancement. All other organizations are similarly mixed: the state, too, uses the labour and property markets to carry out its activities, and calls on commitments of value and loyalty; firms need a legal base and try to generate loyalty among their employees. But charitable activities are distinguished by the value component playing a particularly large, indeed dominant, part. In this way they belong in the realm previously dominated by religion, even when fully secularized; and in societies where the state claims the dominant role in the definition of value, they represent a potential alternative, possibly even a rival.

All value-oriented activity is 'public', but (forgetting for the moment activities aimed at Public1) are they aimed at Public2 or Public3? The scope of caritas being universal, it can be and is argued that charitable activity has no bounds. However, as noted at the outset, the original and always a major historical use of value has been to define a community of identity, distinguishing insiders from outsiders, and it can be argued that the bounds of the scope of the charitable universe are set by the group who share the identity (whether this is defined by race or creed). This debate is a very old one, and certainly cannot be resolved here. We must however note that this is the same ambiguity between Public2 and Public3 that we find in the public as defined by the modern state.

What then is the legitimacy of charitable or voluntary activity? If it is rooted in a religion, it claims the legitimacy of that faith. If it denotes a particular community of identity, it is claiming the legitimacy of that identity and the right or obligation of persons having that identity to do things for other members of it without political or economic motivation: the sheer claim of shared identity. Other claims, as noted, seek to identify Public2 or even Public1 and claim the moral superiority of the truly universal. It is a difficult claim to make heard, but it is one towards which a good deal of charitable activity devotes itself. It involves constant discourse and dialogue in which fragments of religious values, appeals to a sense of common human identity, and Kantian concepts of rational universalism are deployed. It is a discourse without hope of final resolution, agreement or resting place; but as it continues a good deal of activity takes place, governed at least in large part by the drive for a value-oriented (rather than politically or market driven) means of connecting individual private persons to Public2.

In very recent decades, when risks of environmental damage have begun to threaten the planet itself and its climate, there has even been a return to prominence of Public1 – the public conceived as the natural world and the wild, taken for granted for so many centuries as civilization looked to an urban and social expression.

Professions and callings

The concept of a profession, at least in the Christian world, also derives from religion. The concepts of 'calling', 'vocation', the German '*Beruf*', all have the concept of being 'called' to pursue a particular path. The original use of this is in the idea of hearing a call from God to take up the religious life. The idea spread to certain secular occupations in the early modern period, keeping (as with misericordia) the aura of the religious idea that this is not simply a form of work, but a particular kind of work, to which the practitioner makes a moral commitment, to pursue beyond the extent of a private, material interest. The concept may become humbug in many individual cases, as it did within the church itself. Indeed, such moral claims may serve as a concealment and protection from suspicion, behind which even unscrupulous activities may be conducted. However, the important point at the heart of the concept of the 'calling' is that work activity may acquire a public meaning via the realm of values, and not just because it is mandated by the state or responding to the market. Persons who pursue that concept of their role may come into conflict with the claims of the state and the firm, depending on who is engaging their services. The state will claim a democratic legitimacy to decide how and for what purpose work tasks should be conducted; the firm will claim that its board's or senior managers' interpretation of shareholders' interests must prevail over employees' sense of their own professional responsibilities. It can be difficult to avoid value struggles.

Also associated with the professions, including the manual crafts, is the concept of 'mystery'. With the exception of the usually humorously intended phrase 'the mysteries of the craft', this has completely lost its meaning in the English language. The everyday French (*métier*) and Italian (*mestiere*) words for any skilled occupation that a person tends to practise as a long-term career retain the link with the idea of specialized and arcane knowledge.[10] The Christian church applied the idea of mysterium to the inaccessible knowledge of divine matters that humans could not understand, taking upon itself the role of guardian and interpreter of such knowledge. Thence the term became associated with knowledge that was difficult to access. The secularization of this idea enabled it to be taken over by the skilled trades and professions, retaining the sense that knowledge must be protected from interference by 'lay' (another term carried over from religion) outsiders. This interpretation implies a form of appropriation, of building up Private3, and has rendered claims to professional knowledge vulnerable to criticism by agents of state and firm.

Pluralism in the realm of values

The claims of both the volunteer and of the professional are potentially dangerous.[11] Those who claim the right unselfishly (because acting as volunteers) to define an ethnically bounded community of right are likely to be intolerant towards all others. But even those who stake their claim on universalism may be dangerous when they claim the right to interpret the meaning of the universal (as the Catholic Church, the French Revolution, and communism all did in their turn). Professionals insisting on the arcane nature of their knowledge are in a position to fool the public or at least to engage in rent-seeking behaviour (extracting high fees) because customers cannot exercise intelligent market choice where, by definition, they do not share the knowledge that is needed to help them make a choice.

But note that these dangers occur when the volunteer and the professional mix the pure pursuit of value with political or economic motive. In the case of the volunteer the more likely corruption is that from the addition of political means to those of the values of the cause. Professions are more likely to exploit monopolistic market positions. It is significant that the rules that govern charities usually proscribe political involvement, while professions are often regulated to limit their exploitation of labour market monopoly.

What remains is contestation over the definition of value. However much we may despair at normlessness and value confusion, societies with complete value certainty have not been appealing ones – or at least they do not appeal to late twentieth- or early twenty-first-century westerners. When churches and states make an effective claim to value monopoly, there is a good deal of intolerance. Intolerance of a different kind occurs when the pursuit of value is defined as monetary value and made coterminous with the maximization of shareholder value.

To return to one of the problems set out earlier in this chapter: all attempts at constructing links to the public realm include components of the construction of Private3 on behalf of organizational leaders and their closest followers. Different techniques are deployed to prevent this from completely corrupting the public components of the activity. In the case of the state, this has mainly taken the form of trying to ban private appropriation of state property. In the case of the firm, appropriation is explicitly permitted, but should be routed through the market, which is supposed to safeguard a public interest. Specialists in the world of value – whether religious leaders, voluntary sector leaders or practitioners of professions – are expected to subject themselves to a transparent ethic of conduct and practice. All are vulnerable to corruption and rent-seeking, and at any particular moment it is relevant to examine in which realm the supposed safeguards are functioning most effectively. A further way of securing some protection against exploitation is to ensure that no one realm can dominate all the others, and that those dominating one realm cannot easily extend their control over another. At the present time this means challenging the claim of states to be the primary definers of value, and of firms to be the organization to which public tasks should be entrusted.[12]

Civil society

This brings us to a further troublesome concept: civil society, which, as properly understood, deals with this question of balance.[13] It is troublesome because its meaning has stood on its head at least twice in its long history. The Greek term of Aristotle, 'κοινονια πολιτικέ', eventually translated into Latin by Leonardo Bruni in Florence in 1416 as '*societas civilis*', gives us this concept (Hallberg and Wittrock 2006). For Aristotle it signified all areas of public life, using 'public' in the sense of Public3 (not a universal public): the ordered life of the city state where free male citizens dealt with matters concerning their life together. This included all three institutions discussed above that enabled people to transcend the private: the polity, religion, the market (αγορα) – those central topographical features of the ancient and mediæval European city. The market, note, is again part of the public. This public was contrasted with the private, but in the sense of Private2 (the individual and the immediate family or household (οικοζ).[14] Polity, religion, and market are all found within the *societas civilis*, held in a certain balance.

Over the centuries that followed the translation of Aristotle into Latin, the city state became overwhelmed – as it had before, during

Rome's Imperial period – by states that stood outside and over the rest of society. Aristocratic and monarchic elites monopolized control of the state within their family groupings, and weakened the towns which preserved something of the public unity of market, polity, and religion. The state became at best detached from the rest of Public3, at worst a part of the household of the ruler, and part of Private3. Therefore, when the concept of 'civil society' began to be used again, in the nineteenth century, it usually excluded the state: paradoxically, the seat of the polity was no longer part of the πολιτεια. The concept had been stood on its head. For Marx (though perhaps not for Hegel) civil society became the market, relationships of exchange that alienate man from his species life.

The concept of civil society was returned again to prominence in the late twentieth century, by thinkers (initially in central Europe and Latin America) trying to identify a realm of dialogue and human exchange excluded by polity and market alike. So Marx's account itself had now been stood on its head. Today, not only in social philosophy but in common parlance, 'civil society' is usually used to denote those organizations and informal groupings that concern themselves with public affairs, but which operate without the power of either state or firm. (Significantly, they have become generally known today by the nonsensical name 'non-governmental organizations' (NGOs).) Whether civil society now includes religious organizations is left ambiguous – they are usually included when they have lost their power, which reinforces the idea of civil society as 'the power of the powerless'. (This phrase itself was coined by Vaclav Havel (1985) in the 1980s to refer to the civil society outside the party-state that was being rediscovered in the then Czechoslovakia and elsewhere in central Europe.) Civil society certainly includes, though extends further than, the voluntary sector. It therefore constitutes a kind of Public5, defined as all those extensions of the scope of human action beyond Private1 that lack recourse to the primary contemporary means of exercising power: the state and the firm.

This is a rather gloomy concept, as almost by definition anything that succeeds has to be excluded from it. Or it is a concept whose advocates have turned their backs on the actual world and seek to act out a better but unreal one. It is erroneous to mock such behaviour as futile, as there have been dark times in human history when the best that anyone could do was privately or even secretly to preserve the knowledge and practice of certain values until better times might come – one thinks of Irish monks protecting knowledge of Christianity, or of various underground activities in the Soviet period. In terms of the ideas being used in this chapter, this is an odd case of public values being preserved by extremely private action. This is normally possible only when the individuals concerned have some means of relating the extreme private to the extreme public with virtually no intermediary institutions, a kind of activity that comes easiest to a religious attitude that enables the private person to feel in communication with or at one with the infinite.

In less extreme times, however, the practitioner of such 'escapist', private interpretations of the public is vulnerable to the challenge that if state, market and/or religion have not been completely captured by rent-seeking and self-referential power, should you not at least try to use those parts of them that are organized around public purposes to realize some of your values in the here and now?

This offers us a continuum of civil society and its relationship to the institutions of power, as follows:

- At one extreme, where one or other, or perhaps all, of these institutions is totally dominant and self-referential, there is no civil society; all that remains is the private preservation of value.
- Along the continuum, where one or other or all of the institutions is dominant, but accessible, or where there is some conflict among the interests represented by state, market, and religion, those in pursuit of public value will have to develop their own life primarily detached from them, but will be able to secure some victories by working through them, or even setting them against each other.
- At the other extreme, where none of these institutions is dominant, and all are highly responsive, those in pursuit of public value can make use of them as part of their normal activities.

In other words, civil society is stronger, the more that state, firm, and church can be incorporated within it (with voluntary organizations, the professions, and other participants in the fragmented world of value) in a dialogistic and pluralist world of non-dominating institutions. In Western societies today we live somewhere near the midpoint of the continuum. States and firms do dominate. The realm of value has become fragmented with the decline of churches. As a result it is there, in that fragmented realm, that challenges to domination can be made, and concepts of public goals explored and turned into practical projects. Against the state's claim to monopoly of the legitimate interpretation of public value, and against the firm's claim that the conversion of value into the maximization of shareholders' interests is as good as life can get, the proponents of challenge (whether governed by religious or secular motives) must claim some combination of personal altruism and disinterested professional knowledge. Like the inhabitants of the realms of politics and market, they will sometimes betray these ideals with rent-seeking and attempts at appropriation – they are, like everyone else, ultimately preoccupied with their personal situation as

Private1 or 2. But the struggle to clarify the means whereby human beings can build links from the private to the public must continue.

Finally, it is essential for that struggle to remember that:

1. Public and private should not be used to denote the respective realms of states and firms; these are both particular combinations of public and private, serving and excluding different aggregations of private interests in terms of both participation rights and substantive benefits.
2. Public and private should be used as end points on a continuum, not as alternatives.
3. In particular the partial nature of the public (usually Public3), the public nature of the extended private (Private3), and the reducibility of most publics to aggregations of privates need to be recognized.
4. Whenever we analyse the operation of an organization in any of these sectors we should identify and distinguish between controllers, followers (or secondary beneficiaries), the excluded and the deprived.
5. Climate change, environmental damage and globalization finally confront us again with the primæval sense of the public (Public1), in the face of which all our other concepts of public appear as extended privates.

Chapter 4

Creating Public Value: The Theory of the Convention

NOEL WHITESIDE

Introduction

Over the past 20 years, the view that competition and choice provide the foundations for better public services has dominated government policy. This strategy assumes that the private sector is more efficient than the public. Concomitantly, the civil service has been reformed and restructured, to promote the adaptation of business management to the public sector. Governments all over Europe have sought to follow suit, by placing service delivery in the hands of private (not-for-profit and commercial) agencies. In the UK in particular, the introduction of league tables and benchmarking has measured achievement; state regulations and regulators have proliferated to monitor performance. The multiplication of public–private partnerships and agencies of varied form and power have raised issues of public accountability and reset the borders of state responsibility. Sustained by logics of public choice and an apparent conviction that private provision is more responsive to consumer demand, UK governments have shifted from competitive tendering, to measuring outcomes, to specifying targets, in an effort to secure improvement. Whether services have improved as a result remains an open question (Institute of Public Policy Research 2001; Timmins 2001). The lack of an alternative blueprint led New Labour towards a 'what works' agenda for the modernization of government. The problem lies in determining what this means.

The Blair government's dilemmas stemmed from widespread uncertainty about whether reforms had produced promised improvements. Does consumer choice raise the quality of public services and offer better public value? This chapter addresses this issue by focusing on the relationship between markets and the state. The coordination of all social and economic activity is necessary for effective choice and collective welfare. Collective coordination mechanisms enable individuals to make choices that secure their objectives. Such mechanisms must

74

command universal respect: they are embedded in conventions of economic action that form the foundations of public value. This argument will be illustrated by examining different frameworks of pension provision in key economies, demonstrating how diverse forms of coordination work to promote trust and ensure public participation under various systems that involve state intervention at different points. However, for coordination to be effective, its mechanisms need to be internalized by all social actors. Efficiency depends not just on 'top-down' regulation by government, but also on careful negotiation with key participants, allowing deliberations that both explain mechanisms and identify possible future problems. Here, negotiation acts not merely to create compromise but also as the means whereby new systems can be absorbed and understood by all, removing or reducing the uncertainties that prevent participation.

Recent pension debates have focused less on issues of governance than on those of finance: on the sustainability of present schemes in the light of problems posed by rising pension obligations. In response to pressures to reduce public expenditure, European states have restructured state pensions and, under a range of initiatives, have sought to promote private saving to sustain old age income. Such reductions in public provision follow a neo-liberal economic logic. Markets offer consumers a range of personal savings schemes: state intervention distorts market signals while driving up costs. At the extreme, we could conclude that states should not provide pensions at all (Blinder 1988). This position contrasts with that adopted after World War Two, when state protection for all elderly and infirm was considered a fundamental social obligation. The recent pursuit of private solutions to pension problems, however, has belied many assumptions about the virtues of market provision. Far from allowing the market free rein, recent British governments have become increasingly enmeshed in regulating both providers and purchasers in an effort to secure trust and increase participation. An explanation of this apparent conundrum is found if we view the creation of public value from a different perspective and to this aspect of the analysis we now turn.

The theory of the convention and the creation of public value

The virtues of market systems rest primarily on neo-liberal tenets of political economy based on principles governing individual action. Within this paradigm, rational individuals, left to their own devices, act to optimize personal interest, seeking out and utilizing perfect information to secure this end. The public good (and hence public value) is thereby identified as a collective consequence of the pursuit of personal interest. Within this framework, public sector interventions should be minimal and confined to residual provision for those who, through no fault of their own, are unable to exercise this responsibility. State-sponsored alternatives supposedly make markets less efficient: high taxation (to fund state services) distorts price signals and the belief that government will offer universal protection against risk breeds social dependency. At best, market provision offers choice, and market competition guarantees that these choices are available at optimally efficient prices. Within an ordered analytical logic, collective choice thus facilitates innovation and growth in the provision of optimally efficient services. Within this analysis, the role of the state is minimal: it becomes a residual agency rescuing market casualties. This crude analysis of how market behaviours can and should be allowed to shape collective development is based on a rational utility-maximizing model combining private provision, commercial interest and personal wellbeing.

Sociologists and economists working within the theory of 'the convention' offer an alternative explanation by focusing on issues of efficient coordination: the role played by confidence and trust in securing this and, conversely, on the damage done by uncertainty. Instead of understanding each individual as an independent agent, social and economic actors are seen as interdependent. The chief problem for individuals is to anticipate how others might respond to their initiatives: this generates uncertainty over outcomes. Uncertainty provokes distrust and non-participation, leading to the breakdown of economic systems. For uncertainty implies no basis for understanding the consequences of action: if I hand over money on the promised future delivery of goods or services, can I be assured of their receipt? Or if I hand over goods or services on the promise of payment, can I guarantee that correct payment will be forthcoming? In the absence of conventions that serve as a basis for economic coordination, I cannot act. No transaction will take place if uncertainty is too strong. Successful economic action depends essentially on close coordination between actors: on collective trust and mutual expectation that all will know and respect the conventions of exchange surrounding the transaction. As all individuals need to anticipate the response of others, so coordination emerges as the cornerstone of social and economic efficiency, rather than competition *tout court*.

The term 'uncertainty' is here employed to define a world where outcomes of action are unknowable; it should be distinguished from risk or hazard, the phenomena that form part of the insurance world. In the latter case, possible adverse outcomes are identifiable and, with the aid of expert diagnosis, a probable consequence of action is predictable and risk can be measured. Actuarial evaluation shapes the calculation of premiums in an insurance environment that offers compensation in the event of action or accident producing a collectively recognized but undesired result – but such an outcome is identifiable in advance. Protection against acknowledged risk establishes the confidence necessary for full participation in entrepreneurial activity. In the world of economic action, risk (multiple but identifiable, possibly predictable) lies at one end of the spectrum, and uncertainty (infinite and unknowable) at the other. In short, taking a risk implies previous knowledge about (even awareness concerning the likelihood of) adverse outcomes of action, while uncertainty denies the actor any basis for reaching a judgement about the effects of action, if any (Knight 1921). From this perspective, the exercise of choice depends, fundamentally, more on the reduction of uncertainty than on the containment of risk.

Risk may be insured individually or collectively. Classical mechanisms of social insurance, the foundation of state pension schemes, allow low-risk cases to compensate for the high-risk ones. These systems have long protected working people against conventionally defined 'risks' that threaten their livelihood, covering illness, unemployment and invalidity as well as old age. In different countries and contexts, protection against some or all of such risks is assumed to be a personal, not a collective, responsibility – current renegotiations over pension provision demonstrate how this balance can change. Further, close examination of how such risks are defined (whether permanent invalidity, retirement from work, the achievement of a pre-specified age, or any combination of these, is required for receipt of a pension) reveals variation in terms of place, occupation and time. In these instances, moreover, we can observe how the achievement of a particular personal state justifies receipt of a pension. In other words, it is collectively accepted that physical breakdown and/or the withdrawal from the labour market and/or the achievement of an age collectively recognized as the end of a working life or occupation – legitimates the receipt of an indemnity (of whatever sort). The factors that secure identification (of potential recipients) and legitimacy (of offering a pension) are constantly being reshaped. This fluidity, however, remains hidden behind the 'convention' that the risk of a dependent old age exists – and that collective agencies (commercial, mutual, state-sponsored) are in place to offer compensation. The identity of the risk and the nature of the compensation themselves reflect expectations about behaviours proper to public or private, collective or individual action. Expectations shape the conventions sustaining trust and define remits of welfare provision. In this way, the 'right' to a pension does not depend solely on financial questions (how long the person has contributed or worked in a specified job) but also necessarily incorporates issues of social justice.

There is considerable variation in what is collectively considered to be the right and proper way of doing things. In the need to justify our actions publicly, to offer explanation or to resolve dispute, different conventions (that act as collectively accepted systems of coordination) stand revealed (Boltanski and Thevenot 1991, 1999). At points of breakdown or conflict, when people may be called upon to explain their actions in order to create or sustain public acceptance, these conventions become pivotal points of reference. The 'rights' and 'wrongs' of particular actions are tested in open debate. In this way, public justifications rely on reference to accepted values to explain and locate actions within established collective implicit or explicit understandings that underpin acceptable behaviour. The agent necessarily has to anticipate the actions of others to secure desired objectives: in so doing, she makes necessary reference to commonly held values and assumptions concerning the remit of valid action. This reference to different value frameworks that serve, formally or informally, to coordinate collective action gives rise to moral judgements that reflect specific evaluations (or hierarchies) of worth. These evaluations are the building-blocks of collective understanding and trust – and form the foundation stones of public value.

Different evaluations of worth – or ways of assessing value – pertain to different given objects and the actions that involve them. Within plural frameworks of social ordering, market-based systems, reliant on competition and dependent on signals of quality and price, offer one form of coordination. There are others. Standardized forms of measurement provide the basis for technical knowledge: these coordinate collective evaluations in construction, medicine and other professions – including actuarial expertise. This 'industrial' world displays the permanent value of certain types of knowledge and analysis frequently labelled 'scientific': the foundations for planning and for the coordination of future developments. While physical measurement and market price appear to offer us a hard currency through which to ascertain public value, we must recognize that other hierarchies of worth also demarcate collectively held values that shape our socio-political worlds. They legitimate the public exercise of authority and distinguish civic virtues from antisocial behaviours that merit collective condemnation. This civic world includes varying bases of moral-political evaluations, to identify legitimate forms of decision-making that help to determine not only varying spheres of state power but also the reasons why different governments in different countries intervene at different points in economic activity in order to secure similar goals. In the first place, democratic processes of public deliberation are generally regarded as a morally superior and more legitimate basis for determining state policy and creating new laws than any other form of government. In the second, taken an effective democratic polity, collective conventions of public behaviour are not externally imposed (not, at least, without considerable difficulty) but rather reflect multiple compromises between traditional communal behaviours that have evolved over time to manage local affairs.

Not all forms of collective coordination that endow objects and persons with specific merit are underwritten in law. Many (concerning, for example, religious observance or the status endowed to celebrities) delineate the domestic or familial world in households or local communities, where the bonds of love and the desire for intimacy foster compliance and conformity with different social practices. As Thevenot argues (2001), such hierarchies are neither permanent nor stable (as exemplified by the recent emergence of an environmental or 'green' order of worth). All are grounded in historical precedent and all are constantly modified in the course of action. All offer different foundations for rational action: while all coexist, none can be used to denigrate or disqualify any other, as all operate within their own terms of reference. In this way, plural coordinating reference points based on different hierarchies of worth form frameworks for individual choice, thereby demonstrating multiple identities and differing values endowed to objects and persons in accordance with their location in different hierarchies of worth. In the words of Thevenot:

> objects might qualify as efficient tools, or commodities appropriate for marketing, or regulatory devices enforcing civic equality in terms of health or safety in particular, or patrimonial assets that relate to the past and anchor trust. Other qualifications relating to different orders of worth are signs supporting fame or creative innovations which testify to inspiration. Persons qualify jointly as: professionals or experts; dealers and customers; equal citizens; trustworthy and authoritative people; celebrities, creators. The format of relevant information is always conventional. (Thevenot 2001: 411)

Social frameworks (collectively respected conventions) are necessary for market activity, so individual choices are made within complex situations. To secure specified outcomes, individuals make decisions based on their expectations concerning the consequences of their actions and the relationship of these to their desired goals. This implies the pre-existence of a collective understanding about right and proper behaviour; to act, each person requires the common knowledge embedded in conventions shaping different environments (Dupuy 1989). Hierarchies of worth reflect worlds of moral judgement, which identify respectable behaviour, accepted duties and civil codes. Here, public value is found: not a side-product of the collective pursuit of personal interest, but embedded in conventions accepted by all as a proper basis for coordinating social and economic action – including the means by which they are defined and enforced. Even as these conventions identify the 'good' and 'bad' (behaviours, transactions, attitudes, assessments, measurements and so on) so they address issues of value. As they are collective, they are also public and as they are public, the state becomes involved in brokering the means to guarantee their observation. Equally, from this perspective, firms and other agencies now no longer appear as anomalies in individualized market competition, but instead represent formalized compromises between different hierarchies of worth (Thevenot 2001).

Far from relying solely on product quality and price, real-life markets depend on the development of trust between seller and buyer. The very term 'marketing' denotes the ambition of creating consumer confidence: the 'Find, Mind, Bind, Grind' of the management consultancy manuals stresses how customer relations are based on care to foster trust and confidence as necessary preconditions to the extraction of profit. All markets, including pension markets, are thus compromises between different hierarchies of value. When choosing between complex goods and services, for instance, consumers turn to friends, work colleagues and family for advice – and will be happier using domestic orders of worth to choose the 'good enough' product ratified by intimates, than one that appears to offer better value for money (for a historical example see Whiteside 1997).

To achieve coordination, all markets rely on collectively recognized codes of conduct, some of which are ratified in law. There exist (implicitly or explicitly) moral orders that reflect collective perceptions of social justice, or the 'proper' way of doing things. The rules of competition and contract, of agency and its just remuneration, have to be known and accepted for market economies to function. Institutional arrangements ensure that rules are observed. The state, solely sovereign in such matters, acts as coordinator of last resort: guaranteeing social justice, identifying undesirable behaviours and protecting the polity from external threat or the sudden alien imposition of new rules (Salais 1998). In all market-based economies, regulation is present; should markets wobble or threaten to fail, the public turns to government for more legislative protection, not less. From this angle, the division between 'state' and 'market', common in neo-liberal discussion, becomes hard to sustain, for the state (through the law) remains charged with underwriting market operations to secure the confidence and trust necessary for participation. The process of thereby creating public value goes well beyond a simple evaluation of comparative costs (after all, the public regulation of private markets is considerably more expensive in terms of collective costs than any publicly provided alternative). It necessarily invokes both technical expertise and civic virtue to arrive at effective conclusions that are accepted and understood by all concerned.

As economists have noted, contractual relations, the governing institutions that enforce them and their underpinning conventions vary widely – between nations, between products and over time (for example Storper and Salais 1997; Dore 2000; Hall and Soskice 2001). All governments, however, are involved in making moral judgements concerning acceptable market behaviour. There is no simple distinction between public and private systems. Problems arise, however, when market activities stretch beyond local communities or nation-states, creating confrontations between different forms of market behaviour. This belies political rhetoric that refers to 'the market', as if this were a single entity rather than a range of social constructions specific to particular goods, services or places that have evolved over time. As the conclusions to this chapter will argue, using the pensions example, the globalization of financial services and products has revealed the problems endemic in situations where differently constructed markets, the product of different compromises between technical, civic and market worlds, come into confrontation with each other – requiring a major readjustment of established conventions with new circumstances, but now in the absence of any overarching authority capable of enforcing new compromises or codes of conduct.

From this perspective, governments have established or sustained very diverse typologies of pension provision, requiring different points of state intervention reliant on varied direct and indirect controls. The reorientation of complex arrangements towards commercial systems has required the internalization of new forms of confidence and trust – and new spheres of action. An examination of developments in pension policy illustrates this point.

Securing retirement income: public value and pension reform[1]

In Europe, state-funded pensions formed part of a postwar settlement characterized by a standardized working week and faith in state welfare. These varied schemes were less an economic than a political product: a compromise reached between industrial, labour and national economic interests underwritten by collective agreements and social legislation (Whiteside and Salais 1998). Postwar labour shortages encouraged firms to develop company pensions to foster employee loyalty, a development equally evident in the professional protections established in fast-expanding public sectors. This drive to rationalize labour distribution and to secure worker cooperation for an agenda based on a specific vision of the future represented an apogee in state-sponsored security (Salais and Whiteside 1998). As postwar living standards rose, so demand increased for the socially dependent – particularly pensioners – to share in rising prosperity. To protect public expenditure from future burdens, some European governments, such as the UK, the Netherlands and France, promoted industry-based, earnings-related provision, turning to the extension of occupational schemes to meet rising expectations. Others, such as Germany, transformed basic state provision to incorporate an earnings-related component, with rights still based on contributions. In all continental schemes, the governance of both public and occupational schemes required the participation of both employers and employed. Pensions were essentially deferred wages and hence the property of the contributors. In the UK this civic perspective remained unrecognized: until the 1990s, company schemes remained under corporate control with minimal regulatory interference from the central state.

Through collective agreement and legislative obligation, major continental economies consolidated and extended established occupational earnings-related pension schemes to guarantee coverage for all. The object was to guarantee pension security while promoting labour mobility and economic investment: collective provision protected acquired pension rights. In Sweden, the Netherlands and even France, accumulating pension contributions, invested largely in government securities, were initially used for state-sponsored programmes of modernization – reflecting the public equivalent of what German corporate book reserve pensions continued to offer the private firm. This formed one foundation, reinforcing technical and industrial values, of the European social model. Concordance between public and private was not, however, so visible in Anglo-Saxon economies. Debates over pension reform in the UK illustrate a different political trajectory, privileging market-oriented hierarchies of worth and different conceptions both of public value and of the role that the state should play in its creation. As welfare expenditure reached crisis proportions and governments sought to reduce their pension obligations in the early 1990s, the British system was held up as an exemplar for others to follow (World Bank 1994). From a purely financial point of view, the British system seemed to work rather well. The growth of global financial markets following the removal of capital transfer controls and the information technology revolution of the 1980s had encouraged a huge expansion of private pension funds (Clark 2000:27–30). In the 1990s, this trust in markets appeared vindicated: funded schemes with balanced portfolios in bonds and equities were reaping rich rewards. By contrast, high labour on-costs, the consequence of rising unemployment and growing social security contributions, were burdening continental European economies – notably in Germany, where the situation was exacerbated by the high price paid for reunification (Schmahl 1992). The commitment to the single European currency added further pressures in Europe to contain state pension budgets. Collectively, these factors stimulated a plethora of official inquiries on public pension expenditure with the view to its restriction.

Continental problems vindicated British pension policy and a market-based appraisal of public value; UK policy initiatives proceeded to push further down the market road. The Thatcher government promoted personal pension plans invested in commercial markets (Bonoli 2000:ch. 5); this created a scandal as insurance company agents persuaded many contributors to sound occupational schemes to opt out. Government intervention was required to secure compensation. This proved to be the thin end of the regulatory wedge. The *Mirror* scandal (the diversion of company pension funds for other purposes), the Equitable Life crisis, the Enron saga (Blackburn 2002:188–97, 328–30) and the downturn in global financial markets (2000–3) have created pension fund deficits and the collapse or closure of company final salary pensions, which currently seem to be in terminal decline (Clark 2006). In consequence, the public regulation of private pensions has turned into a growth industry. The specification of marketing procedures, the promotion of state-approved products (stakeholder pensions), state subsidies for small savers (pension credit), the official inspection of commercial practices by the Financial Services Authority, the partial compensation for fund failure – all tried to create confidence and trust and promote personal savings.

They have done nothing of the sort. Far from creating the stability necessary to foster participation, the constant meddling by UK governments has created constant change and instability. This has increased complexity, obliterating signals of quality and price, the hallmark of market systems. Potential consumers, particularly the poorer ones, have wisely steered clear, preferring the certainty of a means-tested pension to the uncertainty of a market-based one that requires present financial sacrifice. The proportion of working people in the UK with no or inadequate pension cover has risen steadily over the past 40 years, in spite of every official attempt to promote personal savings. We might conclude that it is high time to stop flogging this distinctly dead horse.

In some respects at least, the reports of the Pensions Commission (2005–6) promised to do just that. Its recommendations included the creation of a basic citizen's pension for all, paid for by raising the retirement age, supplemented by a National Pension Savings Scheme (NPSS), which would consist of joint-funded, centrally collected, quasi-compulsory personal accounts, to be invested in bonds and equities and managed by a permanent Pension Commission charged with securing continuity. Such recommendations break with market-based orthodoxy and incorporate a more civically respectable form of pension governance (Clark 2006). They also provoked predictable opposition from the pensions industry and the Treasury. Careful reading of the White Paper (2006) reveals a reluctance to abandon old perspectives. Some concessions will reduce the elderly population reliant on means tests from over 40 percent (where it stands today) to around 33 per cent by 2050: hardly a revolutionary improvement. The fate of NPSS has been placed with the private sector – signifying a reaffirmation of market principles and the virtues of public choice that offers the British public yet another version of the failed stakeholder pension. Most importantly, the proposed Permanent Commission, charged with guaranteeing pension security for all NPSS savers, has been scrapped. The Treasury, in short, refuses to give up its position of ringmaster in the pension circus.

Continental and Scandinavian systems have also undergone reappraisal and reform, but – thanks to the different principles guiding policymaking and shaping public value – with rather different results (see, for example, Natali and Rhodes 2008). Further, thanks to their historical development, their real problem was to reduce state pension liability rather than reappraise its imbalances. This is not to argue that the reform process has been uncontroversial. The participation of the social partners in pension policy administration has required modification and accommodation to public demand. In France in particular, civil disruption and strikes paralysed the country in 1995–6, in 2004, in 2008 and again in 2010 as pension cuts were forced through in the teeth of considerable public opposition. In Germany and Italy, the need to accommodate similar opposition initially forced established plans off course, with the result that the whole question has been revisited repeatedly over recent years (Fererra 2006; Hinrichs 2006). However, this has not removed controversy. First and foremost, the recent financial crisis – far from removing faith in financial markets as a source of pension security – has reinforced it. Public subsidies have converted private debt into public liability; renewed budget austerity makes any revival of publicly funded pensions impossible. European state pensions in general will represent by 2030 a lower proportion of previous earnings than previously, while the UK will retain its privileged position of offering the lowest public pension in the developed Western world. In the absence of any international agreement on the management of financial markets (sporadically under discussion at the time of writing), the outlook for future generations of pensioners looks bleak.

The main lesson for our purposes from such comparisons concerns less the policy outcomes than the process by which decisions are made and solutions introduced. Here modes of justification come to the fore. More open methods of policymaking in Germany have required continuous negotiation with the political opposition, using concessions and amendments to secure political consensus but breaking up the technical actuarial calculations on which original proposals were grounded, thus requiring the situation to be continuously revisited. This respect for civic convention was not found in France, where the uproar surrounding pension debates has been caused by the tendency of right-wing governments to impose (rather than negotiate) solutions: technical competence is protected at the price of civic disruption. From this perspective, Swedish and Dutch policymaking has been almost exemplary. In Sweden, the pension problem was, by common consent, removed from the arena of party politics in the early 1990s. Whether or not reform was required was subject to extensive collective deliberation and, once agreement was reached, a committee of technically informed experts worked for 4 years to sort out the details. Their proposed scheme effectively revolutionized earlier principles of Swedish pension policy by injecting a large market-based component into the calculations – including the creation of personal accounts. This solution was put in place under a single piece of legislation in 1998, just in time for every Swede to lose heavily as global financial markets took a turn for the worse in 2000–3. The consequences of the 2008–9 crisis have inflicted further and more dramatic damage. There has been little protest: as civic processes of creating public awareness and acceptance had been completed, there has been no just cause for complaint. The contrast with UK pension policymaking, determined by a small group of economic experts in the Treasury in consultation with a handful of specialists from leading finance firms, and unilaterally imposed on an uninformed public, could not be more marked.

Conclusion

Historically, we witness how a common strategy (the promotion of earnings-related pensions) was originally put in place to solve common problems (pensioner poverty, wage restraint, funding for inward investment) in postwar Western Europe under widely differing combinations of private and public responsibility. All countries aimed to secure public value yet, thanks to differing conventions of state intervention in industrial relations and social welfare, all earnings-related pension schemes involved governments at different points of the process. From the roots of a common strategy emerges a history of divergent political trajectories generating multiple public–private productions of old age security. Varied pathways were taken towards a common goal. Distinctions between 'public' and 'private' provision, common in neo-liberal discourse, are ill suited to describing these developments. Both Dutch and French occupational systems, for example, were established by legislative enactment, but were initially understood as private concerns in terms of their ownership, funding and management. Nor is the state entirely absent from any of these systems: even in the UK, tax advantages subsidize companies providing occupational pensions. Hybrid compromises serve varied political purposes, linking old-age security to strategies of modernization and growth, with official agencies performing their coordinating role in a variety of ways. When employing a conventionalist approach, we can see how, in each situation, particular compromises primarily between market, industrial and civic hierarchies of value created public trust and hence shaped the viability of new systems.

With the re-emergence of pension problems at the end of the twentieth century, old settlements have been drawn into question. The creation of immense wealth through the mechanisms of global financial markets forced the debate in all countries towards the promise that pension reform might offer. Market-based systems, as found in Britain, became the model and when that model itself started to display weaknesses and inconsistencies, the assumption was (and largely remains) that the solution is to be found through the creation of more market competition, not less. However, real-world markets are themselves compromises between different orders of worth: all actors must respect both the rules under which they operate and the authority of those who shape such rules – be they elected politicians or technical experts. In France, the lack of civic legitimacy (due to the lack of consultative processes assumed proper to republican politics) became reflected in sporadic disruption and protest. In Germany, a technically sound settlement was compromised by the need to guarantee proper democratic processes in securing change. In both countries, the civic order of worth (to allow a public voice to enter policy debate) has been a central issue. In Britain, an obsession with market values promotes the domination of technical competencies, grounded in principles of market behaviour as understood by a handful of experts within Whitehall, with minimal attempt to address civic orders of worth to enable the public to engage and comprehend. In Sweden, where public consent was won before technical details were put in place, a comparatively stable balance between the different hierarchies of collective value was achieved.

This is not to argue that the Swedish model can or should be adopted at all costs: on the contrary, history demonstrates how state interventions that are acceptable in some countries and contexts are less so in others. In postwar Britain there was little evidence that major trade unions would have welcomed the limitations on free collective bargaining that a state-sponsored system of earnings-related pensions would have entailed. In this, their attitude contrasts strongly with the Swedish trade unions, who pushed strongly for precisely this measure. However, policy processes that represent effective compromises between all orders of worth offer the only means to establish public confidence and trust. The situation in Britain is currently seriously unbalanced: far too much faith is placed in the creation of market mechanisms as the sole solution to a range of policy problems with predictable results: low collective confidence, distrust and non-compliance. While this chapter has focused on pensions, a similar analysis might be applied to education policy and health policy. In both areas, New Labour's policy initiatives failed to take root; established technical and professional competencies (newly interpreted as special interests) and civic requirements are pushed to one side, as all major political parties endorse the virtues of the markets and turn to so-called 'market experts' for direction and advice.

This approach has generated two key weaknesses. First, mechanisms for deliberation and consultation have been destroyed: the recent use of YouGov or public-opinion polling cannot generate coherent responses that elected assemblies (trade unions, local authorities) may achieve. Sources of organized opposition dissolve but lines of two-way communication are cut; government is left isolated, with political debate confined to the Westminster village and public opinion erratically whipped up by a largely hostile commercial press. Second, the primacy of market orders of worth based on neo-liberal tenets bodes ill for the authority of government. Such market systems, based on the virtues of unfettered competition, reject state intervention as counterproductive. They endorse the rampant individualism that currently blocks any collective conception of public value and weakens the voice of government as co-ordinator of last resort. As argued above, in the real world all markets require rules. Public justification appeals to commonly accepted principles of social justice that are central to economic efficiency and sustain collective public support, thereby reducing the need to 'police' economic systems. This is a hallmark of public value.

We can extend this last point from the national to the international stage. The growth of global markets and current assumptions about the benefits of market-based systems explain recent compulsions to reduce state budgets and the translation of the state from welfare provider to welfare guarantor. However, recent adaptations of commercial solutions have, in the light of the recent crisis, stimulated demand for new regulation beyond national boundaries. The expansion of global financial markets and the drive to privatize pensions (Orenstein 2008) have encouraged even the most neo-liberal administrations to promote international agreement on collective rules to foster confidence in their operation. The slow, painful (and still incomplete) birth of a single market for European financial services has required extensive negotiation and elaboration of its remit to determine the identification of legal and illegal practices (The Lamfalussy process, a four-level regulatory approach for the enforcement of measures designed to promote the integration of European financial services and reliant on the harmonisation of national regulatory authorities within the European Union, is highly technocratic and not notably efficient.) The negotiation of international accounting standards (FRS 17), rules on disclosure, investment regulations and so on reflect collective attempts to guarantee coordination by making international markets user-friendly, in order to foster confidence and trust in their activities and enable the uninitiated to participate. Thus are new conventions established and institutional hybrids born.

  For this is the new challenge for those seeking to create public value. As economies spread beyond and without national borders, so new agreement and convention must be created to enable participation in economic and social action. As market systems replace state provision, so the rules of the game to co-ordinate action must be put in place: the boundaries of competition, the identification of fraudulent practice, the designations of personal responsibility – all must be collectively negotiated and clearly understood, at local, national and international levels. Far from allowing the state to withdraw, therefore, the resort to markets has enmeshed it in a quagmire of new duties and obligations, creating expensive administrative complexities that destroy the very market signals that were the supposed advantage of new systems. And far from being established by administrative fiat, history demonstrates the central role played by the civic virtues of deliberation and negotiation for the successful creation of new systems.

Chapter 5

Greening Public Value:
The Sustainability Challenge

MARK SWILLING

Introduction

The public value approach to governance and public management coincides with the emergence of a scientific consensus that the future of human development is being undermined by the rapid depletion of the natural resources and ecosystem services that societies depend on for their survival and ongoing prosperity. Is this just a coincidence, or is there a causal relationship between the challenge of sustainable development and the search for new modes of governance that transcend traditional Keynesian approaches, contemporary neo-liberalism and developmental statism?

This chapter will argue that there is a relationship, but it has yet to be fully recognized and conceptualized. The public value approach offers a way forward, but only if it manages to transcend the kind of anthropocentrism that prevents social scientists from comprehending that unsustainable development poses the greatest threat to the processes of private and public value creation that we as a species face. Traditional Keynesian economics and so-called 'developmental states' in developing countries have ignored ecological realities. Neo-liberal philosophies have allowed market forces to ransack global resources for the benefit of the billion or so people who make up the global middle and upper class that enjoys an ecological footprint that is far greater than their fair share of global resources (World Wildlife Fund *et al.* 2006). How can the public value approach face up to the challenge of sustainable resource use, and can it be greened? This chapter will attempt to answer this question.

Unsustainable development refers to patterns of socio-economic development that consume non-renewable natural resources (for example fossil fuels, metals and minerals) and destroy vital renewable ecosystem services (for example air quality, soils, fisheries, climate regulation, water resources such as rivers, aquifers and wetlands, and the families of micro-organisms and insects from bees to earthworms that keep biological systems going) in ways that generate negative feedback loops that slowly but surely undermine the strategic goals of our socio-economic development policies. This is what the massive and rapidly growing 'sustainability science' literature is all about.

Remarkably, most of those who write about democratic governance, public management and public value ignore this literature and the realities of unsustainable development. Equally remarkably, most of those who write about sustainability repeatedly call on governments to face up to the sustainability challenges, but there are few within this community who have paid attention to how state systems work. Why have governments been so oblivious to the severe threats to their citizens, economies and environments which natural scientists have articulated since at least the early 1970s? Underpinning this dialogue of the deaf is a disciplinary divide – sustainability science is dominated by natural scientists and environmentalists, while the social, policy and management sciences dominate the field of public policy and management. It is high time that the sustainability community entered into a dialogue with the public management community. Hopefully this chapter contributes to this dialogue by proposing ways of thinking about ecologically sustainable public value that could help to expand the boundaries of the public sphere to include rather than exclude the modalities of the ecosphere.

This chapter starts by suggesting that a traditional discipline-based epistemology undermines our capacity to understand the sustainability challenges. A summary overview of these global sustainability challenges follows, focusing in particular on global inequality and the implications of unsustainable development in an urbanizing world. This leads into a discussion of the developmental state and why governance for development within a developing country context has hitherto ignored ecological sustainability. This provides the basis for proposing an approach to sustainable public value as an organizing framework for rethinking the future of global development and governance.

Beyond disciplinary apartheid

Although this chapter has an ontological focus, there are deep-seated epistemological causes for this disjuncture between public management and sustainability science. C. P. Snow's famous 1959 Rede Lecture in the Senate House at Cambridge University marked a decisive moment in the debate about the nature of the relationship between the natural and social sciences, at a time when Keynesian economics and welfare state politics seemed unassailably dominant in Europe and North America (Snow 1993). Unfortunately, what Snow worried about then remains a worry today : 'So the great edifice of modern physics goes up, and the majority of the cleverest people in the western world have about as much insight into it as their Neolithic ancestors would have had' (Snow 1993:15). Replace 'physics' with 'ecosystem science' and you have an apt summary of the effects of contemporary disciplinary apartheid.

The French complexity theorist Edgar Morin has blamed the failure to address our complex problems on disciplinary reductionism:

> Intelligence that is fragmented, compartmentalized, mechanistic, disjunctive, and reductionistic breaks the complexity of the world into disjointed pieces, splits up problems, separates that which is linked together, and renders unidimensional the multidimensional. It is an intelligence that is at once myopic, colour blind, and without perspective; more often than not it ends up blind. It nips in the bud all opportunities for comprehension and reflection, eliminating at the same time all chances for a corrective judgement or a long-term view. Thus, the more problems become multidimensional, the less chance there is to grasp their multidimensionality. The more things reach crisis proportions, the less chance there is to grasp the crisis. The more problems become planetary, the more unthinkable they become. Incapable of seeing the planetary context in all its complexity, blind intelligence fosters unconsciousness and irresponsibility. (Morin 1999: ch. 7)

Seeing the way that political, economic and social systems are embedded within this wider 'planetary context' involves a systems approach to sustainable development. Following most of those who write about sustainability, a theory of complex adaptive systems underpins the argument elaborated in this chapter (see Capra 1996; Morin 1992; Morin 1999; Berkes and Folke 2000; Nicolescu 2002; Gallopin 2003; Hirsch-Hadorn *et al.* 2006).

Given the magnitude and implications of the multiple interlocking sustainability crises referred to in the next section, it is baffling that Morin's strident warnings – together with those of others who share his concerns (see Erhlich 2002; Nicolescu 2002) – have failed for some decades now to dislodge the disciplinary reductionism and specialization that prevents a transdisciplinary understanding of what Morin has called the 'poly-crisis' (Morin 1999:73). What Beck describes as the 'risk society' is in fact a society wracked by multiple crises that cannot be comprehended in the old ways (Beck 1992). Instead, we suffer from what Castells has described as a condition of 'informed bewilderment' (Castells 1997).

Despite the fact that by the middle of the twentieth century governments had expanded their analytical capacities to include surveillance of natural resource reserves (for example geological survey) and ecosystem performance (environmental pollution), this kind of 'hard science' was at most background noise for a policymaking community obsessed with economic growth at all costs. This is why it is still possible for those writing about public management to ignore the consequences of this expanded public knowledge about underlying natural resource and ecosystem vulnerabilities. Indeed, Mark Moore's definition of public value falls into this trap:

> I argued that government was a value creating sector that used the collectively owned assets of the state to improve the quality of individual and collective life. It was a key ingredient in advancing the material prosperity and security of its citizens, the sociability of the society at large, and the justice its citizens could claim and enjoy.

The notion that the state has a responsibility to at least protect natural resources and ecosystem services for the benefit of its citizens (following an anthropocentric perspective) was either simply taken for granted and collapsed into the notion of 'advancing material prosperity', or else totally ignored by the public management community. Obviously, under these circumstances, there would be no point in expecting a more ecocentric perspective, namely that we have a duty to protect nature for its own sake and in the interests of all human and non-human species (see Brinkerhoo and Jacob 1999).

Reflecting a more general awareness within public policy circles of environmental problems, Benington in Chapter 2 proposes that public value goes beyond market-determined values to include 'social value' and 'environmental value', that latter defined as 'adding value to the public realm by actively promoting sustainable development and reducing public 'bads' like pollution, waste, global warming'. In this conception, 'environmental value' is placed alongside and equated to all the other 'values', namely economic, social and cultural, and political value. This approach is widespread and is found in virtually every statement on sustainable development found in business circles, the mainstream multilateral institutions (UN, UNEP, World Bank, EU, among others), and most of the large environmental NGOs (for example, the IUCN and the WWF). It is best referred to as the 'triple bottom line' approach which essentially sees sustainable development as a point where the three spheres (economic, social and environmental – often depicted as interlocking circles) overlap. Following Hattingh (Hattingh 2001), this approach locks one into a language of trade-offs, with each sphere retaining its own respective logic (an economy driven by markets, society glued together by welfarism, and the environment protected by conservationism). A systems approach offers an alternative perspective that essentially sees these spheres as embedded within each other. Following the logic of institutional economics (see below), the economy is embedded within the social-cultural system, and, following ecological economics, both are embedded within the wider system of ecosystem services and natural resources. The result is a way of thinking about sustainability as the organizing principle for an expanded 'complex-systems' conception of public value that encompasses all three spheres. An elegant definition of sustainability that captures this process-oriented systems perspective emerged from the US-based National Science Foundation Workshop on Urban Sustainability that took place in 1998, with its report published in 2000:

> In light of ... countervailing definitions based on conflicting eco-nomic and political agendas, we propose a definition of sustain-ability that focuses on sustainable lives and livelihoods rather than the question of sustaining development. By 'sustainable livelihoods' we refer to processes of social and ecological reproduction situated within diverse spatial contexts. We understand processes of social and ecological reproduction to be non-linear, indeterminate, con-textually specific, and attainable through multiple pathways. (Centre for Urban Policy Research 2000)

There are obvious conceptual overlaps between this approach (albeit in a different language) and Benington's approach to public value, in Chapter 2: 'what the public values' is to know that the conditions for ongoing wellbeing can be sustained, and 'what adds value to the public sphere' is making sure these conditions are not destroyed by production and consumption patterns that run contrary to this foundational com-mitment. The results, however, are highly contested emergent outcomes that cannot be predicted but can be circumscribed by a knowable range of probabilities. What is widely agreed is that it if nothing changes, it is highly probable that the conditions for human life as we know it will fall away within 30 to 50 years (depending on who is making the pre-dictions). Unsurprisingly, how we create sustainable public value is rapidly becoming the unifying challenge of our generation.

Sustainability challenges – an overview

In 1987 the World Commission on Environment and Development (WCED) published a report entitled *Our Common Future* (World Commission on Environment and Development 1987). More com-monly known as the Brundtland Commission after its leader Gro Harlem Brundtland, this report attempted to reconcile the ecological limits to growth articulated by the Northern green movement since the early 1970s, and the need for growth to eliminate poverty as articulated by Southern developing country governments, quite a number of whom had recently broken free from colonial control. The Commission catapulted the term 'sustainable development' into global public discourse because it was able to capture – and for the optimists transcend – the tension between the opposing interests of Northern anti-growth movements and Southern governments committed to poverty eradication via growth. The most-quoted definition of sustainable development originated in this report: 'Sustainable development is development that meets the needs of the present without compromising the ability of future generations to meet their own needs.' Significantly, the report argued that sustainable development was possible, and that the only limitations were technology and social organization. A fixed stock of natural capital was not regarded by the Brundtland Report as a constraint for future development strategies. Nearly 20 years later, we now know more about the consequences of ignoring the fact that there is a finite stock of natural capital, in particular fossil fuels. According to Jared Diamond, throughout human history civilizations have fallen due to their failure to replenish natural capital – he also pointed out that most did not recognize these causes, and, if they did, it was often too late to avoid disaster. He used this history to suggest ways beyond the current limits of unsustainable industrial societies (Diamond 2005). For the researchers at the Institute for Social Ecology in Vienna, the history of development is incomprehensible without understanding the 'transitions' from one 'socio-ecological regime' to the next. It follows that a transition to a 'sustainable socio-ecological regime' will mean recognizing that the 'industrial socio-ecological regime' that depends on fossil fuels will come to an end as fossil fuel supplies cease to be available at the prices that have made 300 years of industrialization possible (Fischer-Kowalski and Haberl 2007).

Nevertheless, the Brundtland Report was extremely influential and provided the strategic foundation for the 1992 Earth Summit in Rio, the World Summit on Sustainable Development (WSSD) in Johannesburg in 2002, and numerous international sectoral policy conferences over the 30 years 1972–2002 (UNDP 2004). Leading up to, but more significantly since, the Brundtland Report, a massive literature on sustainable development has emerged across all the major disciplines (for examples of overviews of this literature see Pezzoli 1997; Mebratu 1998; Dresner 2002; Sneddon *et al.* 2006). Since the publication of *Our Common Future* we have learnt a lot more about the challenges we face: numerous crises that were predicted – but little done to avoid them – are starting to be felt and noticed by many nations across the world (Sneddon *et al.* 2006; World Wildlife Fund *et al.* 2006).

Seven globally significant mainstream documents, plus a key website, will in one way or another shape the way we understand the nested clusters of sustainability challenges. They are as follows:

- Ecosystem degradation – the United Nations Millennium Ecosystem Assessment compiled by 1360 scientists from 95 countries and released in 2005 (with virtually no impact beyond the environmental sciences) has confirmed for the first time that 60% of the ecosystems that human systems depend on for survival are degraded and that the damage is largely irreversible (United Nations 2005).
- Global warming – the broadly accepted reports of the Intergovernmental Panel on Climate Change (IPCC) confirm that global warming is taking place, due to release into the atmosphere of greenhouse gases caused by among other things the burning of fossil fuels, and that this is going to lead to major socio-economic changes that will affect the poorest countries first and the most, although they have contributed least to this global threat (Intergovernmental Panel on Climate Change 2007).
- Oil peak – although there is still some dispute over whether we have hit peak oil production or not, even the major oil companies now agree and mount public campaigns to say that oil prices are going to rise and alternatives to oil must be found sooner rather than later. Our cities and global economy are designed for systems that depend on cheap oil and changing them will mean fundamentally rethinking the assumptions underpinning nearly a century of urban planning (see www.peakoil.net).
- Inequality – according to the United Nations Human Development Report for 1998, 20% of the global population who live in the richest countries account for 86% of total private consumption expenditure, whereas the poorest 20% account for only 1.3% (United Nations Development Programme 1998) –inequality is increasingly seen as a driver of many threats to social cohesion and a decent quality of life for all.
- Urban majority – according to UN population statistics, the majority (that is, just over 50%) of the world's population is now officially living in urban areas (United Nations 2004) – whatever our future is, for a growing majority it will be an urban one.
- Planet of slums – according to the UN Habitat Report *The Challenge of Slums*, 1 billion of the 6 billion people who live on the planet live in slums, or put differently one third of the world's total urban population (rising to over 75 per cent in the least developed countries) live in slums (United Nations Human Settlements Programme 2003);
- Food insecurity – according to the recently released International Assessment of Agricultural Science and Technology for Development (IAASTD) (Watson *et al.* 2008) – the most thorough global assessment of agriculture systems and knowledge – food prices are rising as agricultural production fails to keep up with

demand, food crops get redirected into biofuels and as ecosystem services break down due to global warming and over-exploitation. '23% of all used land is degraded to some degree' (Watson *et al.* 2008:ch. 1, p. 73) and this is the primary source of the food that is supposed to feed a population that will grow from 6 billion in 2005 to 8 billion by 2030.

Assembled together, the above trends combine to conjure up a picture of a highly unequal urbanized world dependent on rapidly degrading ecosystem services, with looming threats triggered by climate change, high oil prices and declining agricultural yields. This is what the mainstream literature on unsustainable development is worried about. This is the growing dark shadow of modernity that has been denied for so long.

After all is said and done, the key challenge of sustainable development in the current global conjuncture is about eradicating poverty once and for all, and doing this in a way that rebuilds the ecosystems and natural resources that we depend on for our collective survival as a species. Very little is known about how this will be achieved, and pessimists tend to be highly influential (for example Lovelock 2006). If *Time* magazine (3 April 2006) wants us to 'worry' about the future of classical modernity, then its call to 'be very worried' reflects a yearning to salvage the modernist aspiration to make progress. The same aspiration lies at the centre of Al Gore's climate change message, no doubt legitimized by the fact that he won the Nobel Peace Prize in 2007 (shared with the IPPC).

In practice, however, the challenge of sustainability will be faced in the mushrooming cities of the developing world where the realities of daily life and urban governance are profoundly different from the realities that most of the readers of *Time* magazine are familiar with. Indeed, modernist conceptions of progress within an institutionalized public sphere are to all intents and purposes nonexistent within these developing environments. Progress under these conditions is about surviving from one day to the next, and this is best done via a combination of extreme flexibility and sustained opportunism that simultaneously depends entirely on networks of mutually reinforcing loyalties. Without institutionalization, the public sphere in developing country cities is an ever-changing, unstable, contested set of emergent outcomes held together by networks rather than formal institutions.

Cities may well provide the spatial context for imagining and institutionalizing new cultural frameworks for more sustainable living. This may sound simple and logical (though some might well disagree), but in reality it will entail a profound transformation of our understanding of development, which in turn directly challenges the existing structures of political and economic power. Sustainability challenges the way the city is imagined by the design professions and it also challenges the existing circuits of capital that drive the production and operation of the urban system (from the way the built environment is constructed, through to the way it is spatially distributed, traded, lived and travelled). Even within the less-formalized, de-institutionalized developing country cities, sustainability creates surprising opportunities – community-based waste collection and recycling systems, for example, fit nicely into the way these informal worlds already work. For example, the waste in the city of Cairo is collected by the well-organized Coptic Christians who feed discarded food to their pigs – a forbidden farming practice for the Muslim majority; they live among the rubbish dumps, and sell other waste materials into the market.

The tension between ecological limits and the modernist aspiration to progress means that poverty cannot be eradicated via a development strategy that promises everyone that they can all live like the (city-based) global middle class, which comprises approximately 20 per cent of the population (about 1 billion people) but consumes over 80 per cent of extracted and manufactured resources; there will simply not be sufficient resources available to make this happen. (This statement is a generalized interpretation of the figures referred to at the outset of the chapter from the *Human Development Report 1998*.) Human needs have expanded while the ecosystems we depend on have remained formally finite and are in the process of being substantively eroded.

The only way poverty eradication can be achieved is if we radically decouple our production and consumption systems from rising levels of resource use (Gallopin 2003; Bringezu *et al.* 2004; Dobereiner 2006; Fischer-Kowalski and Haberl 2007). This is what is referred to as 'dematerialization' or, in more popular terms, reduction in the size of our 'ecological footprint' (Wackernagle and Rees 2004). It is now technically possible for entire communities to meet all their material needs by reusing all their solid and liquid wastes, using renewable energy instead of burning fossil fuels to meet at least 50 per cent of their energy requirements (Monbiot 2006), renewing rather than degrading soils for food production (Badgley and Perfecto 2007), cleaning rather than polluting the air, preserving instead of cutting down forests and natural vegetation, under- and not over-exploiting water supplies, and conserving biodiversity instead of killing off other living species (in particular marine species).

If it is technically possible, what's left is to make the necessary policy and financial decisions that will, of course, change living and behavioural patterns. However, it would be naive to ignore the fact that this will cut across the way most production and consumption systems are currently configured. This, in turn, means that sustainability – and footprint reduction in particular – will more than likely be opposed by some of the most powerful economic stakeholders obsessed with short-term financial gains. But as Cuba after the collapse of the Soviet Union demonstrated, adjustment is possible that can lead, ultimately, to strengthening of the economy and greater livelihood security.

The socio-economic consequences of non- or underdevelopment in many parts of the developing world are well known: three-fifths lack basic sanitation; a third have no access to clean water; a quarter have inadequate housing; a fifth have no access to modern health services; a fifth do not get enough protein; and worldwide 2 billion people are anaemic. What is not so well known is that these indicators of poverty are directly related to increasingly unequal access to the world's primary natural resources, most of which, as argued earlier, are reaching their ecological limits. As the *Human Development Report 1998* demonstrates, the richest fifth of the world's population consumes 45 per cent of all meat and fish, the poorest fifth 5 per cent; 58 per cent of total energy, the poorest fifth less than 4 per cent; 74 per cent of all telephone lines, the poorest fifth 1.5 per cent; 84 per cent of all paper, the poorest fifth 1.1 per cent; and unsurprisingly 84 per cent of the world's vehicles (made mainly from metals and polymers made from oil), the poorest fifth less than 1 per cent (United Nations Development Programme 1998:2).

Without denying that rising consumption is essential for human development (defined as the enlargement of capabilities and opportunities), the *Human Development Report 1998* articulated a clarion call for sustainability as follows:

> Today's consumption is undermining the environmental resource base. It is exacerbating inequalities. And the dynamics of the consumption–poverty–inequality–environment nexus are accelerating. If the trends continue without change – not redistributing from high-income to low-income consumers, not shifting from polluting to cleaner goods and production technologies, not promoting goods that empower poor producers, not shifting priority from consumption for conspicuous display to meeting basic needs – today's problems of consumption and human development will worsen. (United Nations Development Programme 1998:1)

Can we really afford to subsidize inefficient and unsustainable systems and simultaneously generate the funds required to eradicate poverty? Contrary to what most development economists think, the depleted resource base is such that we can no longer first eradicate poverty and then 'clean up the environment'. This was a key finding of the *Millennium Ecosystem Assessment* (United Nations 2005) and the subject of serious academic criticism (Fischer-Kowalski and Amann 2001).

Nor is there much sense in the neo-liberal resource economics argument which tries to suggest that the poor benefit from unsustainable resource use by the rich because this is what drives global growth, and that, as scarcities kick in, the market will trigger demand for more sustainable production and consumption systems. The alternative perspective sees sustainable resource use as a precondition for poverty eradication, not simply because of scarcities but also because sustainable resource use can be a driver of innovation and new value chains with implications for future (dematerialized) growth. This will mean dealing with inequality which is the root cause of poverty and, in particular, the economic and political power structures that reproduce these inequalities. Over-consumers will have to cut back and be satisfied with sufficient to meet their needs, and the savings this generates will be needed to ensure that poverty is entirely eradicated by making available infrastructures, services and goods that have been produced and consumed in accordance with efficient and sustainable resource use approaches. This idea was captured by the authors of an award-winning development plan for Goa (India) when they used the word 'sufficiency' to describe the twin goal of ensuring the poor get more while those with enough don't get too much, so that everyone can live within the limits of locally available resources (Revi *et al.* 2006). The South African Government's Department of Water Affairs and Forestry has a similar slogan – 'some for all forever'. This is very different from the current global consumerist culture which can be depicted as 'all for some for now'.

Developmental states and public value

The discussion about governance and public value that has taken place in Europe, North America, New Zealand and Australia in recent years has essentially been dominated by the tension between traditional Keynesian welfarist approaches and contemporary neo-liberalism. The discussions in this book are about finding, within this context, an alternative stimulated by the notion of public value that can point the way beyond these alternatives. However, since the reconstruction of Japan and Taiwan after World War Two, there has been a third governance model that was neither Keynesian welfarism nor neo-liberalism – the so-called developmental state, which is interventionist, productivist, ideologically opportunist, protectionist and quite often authoritarian. The decline of neo-liberalism in many developing countries, the rise of the unique Chinese alternative, the resurgence of nationalist economic policymaking (from Russia to Malaysia) and the re-appearance of socialist options (for example the Hugo Chavez regime in Venezuela, or the famous 'Kerala Option' which refers to what successive Communist Party Governments in India's state of Kerala have achieved since the

1950s) has triggered a rapid expansion of the developmental state literature (for early examples see Haggard and Kaufman 1992; Leftwich
2000). Informed by the new institutional economics, this literature
(cited in detailed below) poses a serious alternative to neo-liberal governance approaches. However, it also tends to be blind to the sustainability challenges. As will be argued, to resolve this problem, we need to
marry the new institutional economics with the insights of the rapidly
expanding field now known as ecological economics.

The new institutional economics has opened up some new and
exciting opportunities for debate within the development economics
community – in particular the work of writers like the Korean-born,
Cambridge-based economist Ha-Joon Chang (Chang 2002), University
of California sociologist Peter Evans (Evans 1995, 2005), the Indian
economist and Nobel prize-winner Amartya Sen (Sen 1999), Harvard's
Dani Rodrik[1] (Rodrik *et al.* 2004), World Bank Chief Economist
Joseph Stiglitz (Hoff and Stiglitz 2001), Vivek Chibber's seminal study
of the Indian phenomenon (Chibber 2002, 2003), and Ching Kwan
Lee's remarkable exposé of the China 'miracle' (Lee 2007). Examples
of active influence include Ha-Joon Chang's economic policy workshops in South Africa co-hosted by the South African Government's
Department of Trade and Industry; the distribution in many developing countries in Asia and Africa of academic publications by Peter
Evans; the backing of Sen's work by George Soros and his Open
Society Institute's Central European programme; and the writings of
the so-called Harvard Panel of economic advisers on South Africa's
economic policy options (Frankel *et al.* 2006).[2]

The significance of this academic ferment among development economists is that they confirm what many outside this exclusive club (particularly in the urban research and public management fields) have
been saying for nearly two decades, namely that it is the quality of
public institutions that matter crucially when it comes to development,
not just the quantities of capital in the financial circuits. Many public
management and urban policy researchers have gone beyond institutions, pointing also to the significance of social processes, power relations and culture (Mignolo 2000; Mbembe 2003; Swilling *et al.* 2003).
What is significant, though, about the new institutional economics is
the economic rationale provided for the centrality of institutions,
namely the recognition that value in today's globalized knowledge
economy is derived more from ideas than from the production of tangible assets, and that it is the quality of the institutional fabric of a
society that determines its capacity to generate useful ideas.
Institutional economists refer here, in the main, to the intellectual
regimes of commoditized intellectual property (from molecules to
machines), routinized corporate processes and the brands/symbols of
mass consumption goods that dominate the developed economies and,

indeed, the global economy. However, it can also refer to the micro-economics of development in the global South where it is now accepted wisdom that development only works when the experience and ideas that are deeply embedded in dense networks of lived social relations are directly tapped and mobilized to animate development processes.[3] In both cases, however, it is the quality and configuration of institutions that makes it possible – or impossible – to transform embedded or commoditized ideas into the drivers of economic growth and development. Once institutions, social processes and culture come to be valued because they are also economically significant, then this creates the much needed bridge between economics and public value management. Herein lies, in particular, the importance of Sen's notion of a deliberative democracy as the institutional context for expanding the 'capabilities for development' – a line of logic that runs somewhat contrary to the Asian 'developmental state' model where developmental priorities were bureaucratically determined in classic top-down ways. Peter Evans (2008) captured this recently by theorizing the notion of a 'capability enhancing developmental state'.

The origins of the developmental state at a global level go back to the 1960s when underdeveloped economies struggled to find ways of speeding up development to eliminate poverty via accelerated growth (for much longer-range historical treatment of this see Bagchi 2000). Although state socialism (Cuba), the national-democratic 'non-capitalist road' (Africa), authoritarian populism (Latin America) and the democratic socialist Kerala model were options, it was Hong Kong, Korea, Singapore, Taiwan and then Malaysia and Thailand that emerged as the archetypal developmental states – the so-called 'Asian Tigers', following quite closely the Japanese model (Leftwich 2000). The key elements of the 'developmental state' that emerged out of Asia were a capable, well-paid, rule-following, professional bureaucracy with sufficient policy 'autonomy' to set and drive national development strategies; and what institutional economists have called the 'embeddedness' of the state elite within the networks and circuits of influence of the nation's business class (Evans 1995; Chibber 2002). Autonomy and embeddedness must go together – the one without the other compromises the nature of the developmental state because autonomy without embeddedness means disconnection from the knowledge flows crucial to policy, and embeddedness without autonomy runs the danger of capture by special interests to the detriment of the general interest. Both were configured within the political project of the nation-state, including the full array of nationalist economic imperatives such as protectionism, inward investment, restrictions on capital flows and indigenization of ownership.

The core project of the twentieth-century developmental state was to massively accelerate the traditional Western pathway to industrialization, namely the transition from an agricultural to a manufacturing-based economy (Evans 1995; Leftwich 2000). The underlying economic theory that drove this was, of course, the notion that value derived from material and physical goods. It was this theory that consolidated GDP as the ultimate measure of economic success. One advantage of manufacturing-based industrialization is that it fits well with nation-building, because the state can simultaneously manage growth and limit excessive inequality via taxation and targeted interventions. The key to success was massive investments in education and human capital, within an urban hierarchy that was planned to absorb big investments in economic infrastructure to cope with high rates of urbanization. The other key, of course, was systematic exploitation of natural resources and ecosystem services – but it was the ecological economists who documented this (Fischer-Kowalski and Haberl 2007), not the development economists, who ignored this reality.

By the end of the twentieth century, growth theory was in turmoil because the emergence of the information technology revolution and the development of the globalized knowledge economy made it obvious that value (or more precisely profits) was being driven more by intangible assets, protected by intellectual property regimes, proprietary operating routines/systems, and brand marketing machines, than by tangible material goods and physical assets. At the international development level, capital did not flow from richer economies to poorer economies in search of higher returns as had been predicted by the neo-liberal economists that dominated thinking in the multilateral institutions. The rise of the services sector became the real motor of growth, and with it came new economic theories – 'endogenous growth theory' – that recognized returns on ideas as the new driver of growth (Aghion and Howitt 1999); 'institutional economics' that recognized the centrality of viable institutions and shared norms (North 1990); and Amartya Sen's theory that 'capabilities' are the real ends and means of development (Sen 1999). Taken together, these new perspectives, as argued by Evans, have effectively dethroned 'capital fundamentalism' as the self-appointed emperor of development theory and practice, because they all agree – for different reasons – that the state needs to be brought back into the development equation as the organizing agent of institutional reform. For Sen, in particular, expanding human capabilities to achieve the developmental goals of a particular group or nation is directly dependent on the creation of democratic spaces for public dialogues about what these goals should be, how best to achieve them and what roles different collectivities can play in the various development processes.[4] In other words, unlike the Asian developmental state that bureaucratically determined these goals, a democratic developmental state aims to facilitate the creation of a 'deliberative democracy' with institutionalized spaces to realize Sen's vision of development as freedom (Sen 1999; Evans 2006).

This provides the conceptual space for democratic developmental states overlapping to a large degree with the substance of the public value approach advocated from within a more developed country context. But is the twenty-first-century century developmental state the same as the twentieth-century developmental state? More specifically, are we still talking about an autonomous developmental leadership embedded in a patriotic business elite as the key condition of existence of a developmental state? Or have global economic conditions changed so drastically that we need more than this? For a start, we have a globalized economy where nation-states play very different roles from their twentieth-century forebears; they've become hustlers that mediate two-way global–national flows with significant discretion as to which local interests win and lose – much more discretion than anti-globalization critics often realize. More importantly, the global economy has bifurcated into two: highly profitable, Northern-controlled, IT-based flows of patented knowledge and symbols on the one hand, and millions of low-paid, people-centred services jobs (located overwhelmingly in the South) on the other. States in the South that get captured by powerful global business elites end up policing intellectual property regimes and low-wage export-processing zones to the detriment of their own local knowledge networks, businesses and working class. And, in so doing, they get cut off from civil society where the real knowledge about services that meets local needs exists. This clearly contradicts the public value approach, but it is a regime that is vigorously defended by many European Governments who must do the bidding for their multinational corporations via institutions such as the World Bank, IMF, WTO and the notoriously exploitative Economic Partnership Agreements advocated by the European Union.

The twenty-first-century developmental state has three basic tasks (Chang 2002; Evans 2006). First, if institutions are key to an environment that fosters innovation, networks and new value chains as the driver of growth, then the quality of governance to build effective institutions – and networks of institutions – across all sectors becomes the main challenge. This will mean striking a very delicate balance between regulation of shared norms and self-managed implementation. The growing consensus among those who think about 'corporate citizenship' is that this will not happen voluntarily (Hamann *et al.* 2005), while for Gelb the state must demonstrate it has the capacity to 'discipline' particular business interests to fit into the wider strategic direction (Gelb 2006). The other element of the consensus is that public leadership is critical: capable, relatively uncorrupted political leaders who can account for themselves without depending on media spin or shadowy thuggery are a necessary condition for building the institutions that foster trust, reciprocity, mutuality and creativity.

Second, no one disputes that knowledge and innovation matter, but these are, using complexity language, emergent properties that stem from dense networks of people working together across institutional boundaries, unconstrained by outdated (usually hierarchically organized) norms. The private sector will always underinvest in human capital, innovation and networks because the direct returns to the investor are impossible to predict. Without state-led investment in these sectors, via universities, NGOs and developmental partnerships/compacts, knowledge-based innovation-led economic development will be impossible. These are the alliances and processes that drove the Baltic economic miracle with a population similar in size to that of Southern Africa. It is what drives local economic development from the simplest agri-centre to the most complex global cities. It is what is driving the global organic farming revolution where advanced complexity theory, indigenous knowledge, agricultural science, ecological theory and everyday practice fuse into a completely new conception of production that is appropriate to a world characterized by food shortages caused by soil degradation (Pretty and Hine 2000; Madeley 2002).

Third, embeddedness for the twenty-first-century developmental state might mean partnering more with networks of civil society formations, trade unions and small entrepreneurial associations than with the business elites that are now fully consolidated in most places, especially in middle developing economies like South Africa. A weak national bourgeoisie is a good reason for the state to get involved in welding together local business elites. But in situations where the national bourgeoisie is fully consolidated (for example Brazil, India, Mexico, South Africa), the state has more freedom to integrate a wider set of class alliances. Herein lies the significance of Sen's notion of 'development as freedom'. If money on its own could resolve poverty, poverty eradication would not be so difficult to achieve. Effective solutions are context-specific, which means partnering with the requisite knowhow, and this is rooted within civil society – especially when it comes to the sprawling informal cities that dominate the rapidly expanding developing economies. What the trade unions, community-based organizations, NGOs, entrepreneur associations, faith institutions, science and research organizations, and the cultural arts community really need in developing economies is a state that knows how to engage, listen and co-create and partner with public, private and third-sector organizations within increasingly rich interrelationships that span the service networks that drive the services and manufacturing economy across the commercial, social, and public sectors. This entails a multiplicity of smallish interventions, rather than just a few massive physical infrastructure investments that satisfy the need for capital-deepening (that is, increasing investment in fixed assets), but achieve nothing to redefine the institutional context for the circulation of the benefits of these investments beyond the elites that make the investment decisions.

Since 2002 the ANC government in South Africa has shifted away from a neo-liberal discourse, favouring, rather, a developmental state discourse. Fortunately, the 1990s 'one-size-fits-all' neo-liberal state approach to development is dying, but this does not mean that the Asian model is the only alternative that is appropriate for the current context. Experimentation is the order of the day across the globe. From Chavez's Venezuela to the China boom, the Baltic miracle, India's unique road, the Kerala model, Cuban self-reliance, and the call for an 'African way' (Mkandawire 2001), now is the time for innovation and creativity if there ever was one. Public investments in skills, education and human capital were the key to success in every case. An open society that's free to deliberate and debate development goals is a necessity. Authentic empowerment of the poor is a precondition for success and a strong trade union movement is indispensable. And where developmental local governments think in these terms, remarkably creative initiatives are often the end result. Unfortunately, with some exceptions, it is the more limited pro-business Asian model that seems to be prevalent in contemporary South African policy discourse on the developmental state at present (Pillay 2007), this despite the fact that South Africa has a very consolidated national business class, a well-organized civil society, serious ecological challenges and a proven track record of limited returns on capital deepening.

These debates highlight the enormous difficulties that progressive political forces in the developing world face when it comes to building developmental alliances of the kinds that are required to realize substantive public value within a globalized economy that works to the advantage of the developed economies. Neo-liberalism has defended and deepened these inequalities. The interesting question is whether a public value approach in the developed world could result in more economically just approaches at the level of global economic policy? Joseph Stiglitz, former chief economist of the World Bank and Nobel prize-winner in economics, refers to precisely this when he talks about the need to rebuild 'global public goods'. What, for example, would a public value approach mean when it comes to the global lending policies of the World Bank and IMF, or strategies for reviving the Doha Round of global trade negotiations? Given that there is a 'new scramble for Africa' as France, the USA, India and China promote proxy wars to secure access to African resources, what would a public value approach mean for Africa's relations with the international economy? The litmus test, of course, will be whether agricultural subsidies for European farmers will continue to be coupled to measures that force developing economies to open up their markets to beneficiated EU agricultural products, in the name of 'free trade' – together these policies are driving rural impoverishment, soil degradation and mass famine.

How do we define public value in this context? And who does the defining? More specifically, what forums exist to globalize the notion of a 'deliberative democracy' about a new set of 'global public goods' in light of the refusal by the USA, Australia and Japan to approve the so-called 'global deal' proposed by the EU and developing countries at the World Summit on Sustainable Development in Johannesburg in 2002? Is this what the World Economic Forum provides? Or the World Social Forum? These questions bring into focus the global significance of a public value approach that emphasizes the need for a global deliberative democracy that creates the space for imagining and building a new set of global public goods and protects the rights of nations to build 'capability enhancing developmental states'. But will these global public goods and developmental states pay sufficient attention to the ecological crisis?

Towards sustainable public value

Although the new institutional economics opens up new and creative roles for democratic states and public managers, it does not go far enough because it does not provide political leaders and public managers with a conception of public value that responds to the consequences of the breakdown of the world's ecosystem services and depletion of natural resources. As already argued, many rapidly developing economies are already experiencing natural resource thresholds that threaten to undermine their modernization ambitions. China has adopted the 'circular economy' policy in response to these challenges (Yong 2007), and many others are following suit, especially at city level. In essence, China has recognized the resource limits of its growth path, in particular with reference to waste and pollution but also with respect to key resource inputs such as oil, water and soils. The 'circular economy' is seen by those advocating the approach in China as the start of a long-term process of increasing GDP per capita by decoupling this material growth from rising levels of primary resource use and also by decoupling resource extraction and use from environmental degradation. Global funds to incentivize low-carbon investments are playing a role here (but should not to be overestimated). Examples are varied and numerous: public transportation systems in Curitiba (Brazil), Japan's solar rooftops, Stockholm's methane made from sewage to fuel the bus fleet, Germany's sustainable housing designs, India's windfarms, South Africa's biodiversity conservation measures, sewage mining in Melbourne, waste recycling throughout the EU, ecovillages in Holland, solar-powered households from

Germany to Kenya, new production systems that increase efficiency with the same inputs by a factor of four (the so-called 'remanufacturing' movement), and the emergence of organic farming all over the world as the fastest-growing agricultural sector.

Much could be gained from a synthesis of Sen's concept of 'deliberative democracy' with the insights from the kind of ecological economics which has evolved into a rich literature, with seminal works appearing in the journal *Ecological Economics* (Daly 1996; Douthwaite 1999; Costanza 2000; Costanza 2003; Sneddon *et al.* 2006; Baumgartner *et al.* 2008; Ehrlich 2008). A deliberative democracy creates the space required for social actors to conceive and create the capabilities they require to take advantage of development processes. Ecological economics anticipates new kinds of ecologically sustainable development processes. The significance of the ecological economics literature is that it develops explanations of the varied histories of development by making society–nature relations the central driver of the analysis. To this extent, ecological economics is by definition a transdisciplinary endeavour that overcomes the disciplinary divide between the natural and social sciences that, as argued earlier in this chapter, is responsible for the failure to fully comprehend and prioritize the ecological determinants of global developmental challenges.

The most sophisticated empirically justified theorization of this approach has come out of the Institute for Social Ecology in Vienna. Fischer-Kowalski and her colleagues (Fischer-Kowalski and Haberl 2007) have proposed that the history of successive 'socioecological regimes' (hunter-gatherers, agrarian, industrial, sustainable) can be understood as the history of 'specific fundamental patterns of interaction between (human) society and natural systems' (p. 8). They go on to argue that

> [i]f we look upon society as reproducing its population, we note that it does so by interacting with natural systems, by organizing energetic and material flows from and to its environment, by means of particular technologies and by transforming natural systems through labour and technology in specific ways to make them more useful for society's purposes. This in turn triggers intended and unintended changes in the natural environment to which societies react. (p. 14)

Once we understand development in terms of the 'structural coupling' (Fischer-Kowalski and Haberl 2007) of social and natural systems, it creates the conceptual space for understanding sustainable development in terms of the decoupling of growth in GPD per capita from rising levels of resource consumption (in relative and absolute terms) (Gallopin 2003; Bringezu *et al.* 2004). This approach has now found its way into official global discourse (United Nations Environment Programme 2007) and the establishment of a new body called the International Panel for Sustainable Resource Management which aims to address this issue and provide policy advice (see www.unep.fr/scp/rpanel). What is missing in these discussions about decoupling, dematerialization and sustainable resource use is an institutional imagination[5] – a gap I have suggested can be filled by institutional economics and the public value approach.

By merging deliberative democracy, ecological economics and a public value approach rooted in the new institutional economics, we can start to make sense of the many transitions to more sustainable resource use already underway. These transitions have been achieved by reconfiguring institutions around a new set of ideas in response to ecosystem breakdown, and the result has often been the release of new investments as new value chains are created out of sources of value that were previously ignored or suppressed.[6] In most cases, the existence of well-networked stakeholders inspired by visionary leadership is what made the advances possible. These new value chains often undercut the constipated and constricted value chains that are so tightly controlled by the established (often monopolized) corporate sectors and the constraints they impose via their globally protected patent regimes. (Although 'big pharma' are the profit giants of the world, their record of innovation is pitifully poor precisely for this reason.) Alternatively, they create new flows of value where established corporate entities are absent because their costly systems could not access returns in these spaces; and, of course, there are the many emerging high-potential economic synergies between the old and new value chains predicated on the impact of new technologies as the costs of the old ones rise to critical thresholds (in particular in the energy, built environment, water and food production fields).

Interestingly, these newly configured value chains that tend to be more dependent on locally specific knowhow and contextually rooted knowledge networks of production tend to flourish in the new emerging secondary cities of the world and not the old smokestack megacities that currently define the spatial nodes of the global economy. Although there are important exceptions to this generalization (for example Ken Livingston's pro-environment leadership when he was mayor of London), it is certainly true at city level across many middle developing countries (for example under the regime of the architect Jaime Lerner when he became mayor of Curitiba, Brazil). This is unsurprising because it is in these 'new cities' that old compacts between corporate elites and traditional party machines are less significant, creating space for younger visionary leadership rooted in eclectic contextually idiosyncratic politico-economic networks and compacts. However, new 'green politics' alliances in some of the more compact

European cities have produced interesting results – Denmark, for example, grew by 70 per cent over the 25-year period up to 2005, but energy consumption remained at 1980 levels due to new investments in energy efficiency and renewable energy pioneered by Copenhagen-based initiatives (ASEM 2007).

These trends suggest that sustainability challenges could provide a new context for innovations that could lead to major new value chains, with significant positive implications for employment creation and market expansion within developing economies. Following the institutional economics advocated by the likes of, Chang, Evans, Rodrik, Sen and Stiglitz, this will not happen via private investment alone, because the returns on investments in social learning accumulate largely (and unpredictably) within the public sphere via open systems and knowledge networks, instead of in privately owned, tightly controlled intellectual property regimes that often lack the high-speed innovation capacity that open-source systems offer (Weber 2004). If environmental public goods are left to the private market, the result will be failure. This was empirically demonstrated by Harriss-White and Harriss who reveal that climate change mitigation in the UK is a government priority, but implementation is left to the private sector. As a result very little progress has been made (see Harriss-White and Hariss 2006). This may suggest that when it comes to measuring up to the task of cataclysmic ecological breakdown that could harm billions of people, private capital is rather weak and disorganized. Following the logic of the developmental state, this is a case for public sector intervention and/or (re-) regulation to prepare the conditions for an adequate response. In particular, it will mean substantial public investments in social learning for sustainable living both at the techno-infrastructural level and with respect to institutional arrangements and social behaviour.

The argument developed here is the logical outcome of a synthesis of the core logics of institutional and ecological economics, but it also overlaps with ideas about social learning, innovation and deliberative democracy that are so central to the public value approach. Probably the single most significant (and probably the cheapest) public value that could be fostered and promoted within the public sphere is new solution-oriented, open-source knowledge sets and well-networked social learning processes that equip developed and developing economies to deal with the transnational sustainability challenges that we all face. For many developing countries, however, this will mean following India's lead where handsome payoffs from substantial capital investments in high-speed information technology infrastructures are obvious. Without high-quality information technologies, high-impact knowledge networks cannot transform into locally rooted job-creating economic value chains capable of taking on the dollar-denominated extractive power of the corporate giants. This, however, is by no means to endorse the technological determinism that underpins naive notions driven by the IT companies that IT on its own will drive development – IT is simply another technology whose benefits are continuously contested as part of the wider struggles over resource control and distribution.

Conclusion

To conclude, I have argued that the search for alternatives that go beyond classical Keynesianism, contemporary neo-liberalism and (authoritarian) developmental statism could very well benefit from a public value approach that valorizes creativity as the energizing core of an expanded and reinvented public sphere. However, this will be unlikely as long as the content and scope of public value is limited to the socio-economic and political dimensions of the public sphere as traditionally defined. Outdated disciplinary divides reinforce this constrained notion of the public sphere. There is now sufficient scientific evidence that the ecosphere can no longer be assumed to be a stable state of fixed and predictable resource, climatic and energy flows. The result must be the enlargement of the deliberative boundaries of the public sphere to include the dynamics and logics of the ecosphere. This is what the global call for sustainable living is all about, and it is the essence of Edgar Morin's proposed shift into what he calls the 'planetary era' (Morin 1999). However, following Nicolescu (Nicolescu 2002) and Van Breda (Van Breda 2008), for this to happen we will need a multireferential, transdisciplinary epistemology capable of matching the demands on us to comprehend and transform the multidimensional realities of unsustainable development.

My attempt in this chapter to synthesize the new institutional economics, ecological economics and a public value approach to governance, in order to arrive at a tentative conception of sustainable public value that transcends the traditional 'triple bottom line' perspective, is an example of the kind of thinking that a transdisciplinary mindset can generate. From a developing-country perspective, this will mean democratizing our conception of the role and governmental modalities of developmental states and ensuring that these states realize that unsustainable resource use will prevent them from realizing their respective development ambitions to eradicate poverty. Decoupling rising resource use from economic growth and development may well hold the key to human wellbeing in an age threatened by oil peak, global warming, degrading soils and disintegrating ecosystem services. We may, however, need to go further and question whether economic growth is a worthwhile goal for development strategy at all. Following the core message of ecological economics, we might need to replace GDP with new measures that compute both the goods and the bads to generate qualitatively rather than quantitatively defined development goals. Until this happens, more sustainable dematerialized development aimed at the wellbeing of all will be an unlikely outcome. If we are going to equip the current and future generations of political and civil leaders and public managers with the conceptual wherewithal to take on the challenges of our times, we need a conception of public value that is appropriate for a public sphere confronted by the harsh realities of the planetary era. The notion of sustainable public value may provide the sustainability community and the public management community with a much-needed dialogical meeting-point for joint efforts to bring an understanding of governance and politics into the sustainability discussion, and an understanding of sustainability into discussions about the future of public management.

Chapter 6

Public Value, Deliberative Democracy and the Role of Public Managers

LOUISE HORNER AND WILL HUTTON

What is 'public value'? Public value is a not a new term, but nor is it well understood. We find that currently there are five sorts of answers to the question 'What is public value?'

First, there is an academic answer. Mark Moore (1995) suggests that his work has a very simple aim: 'to lay out a structure of practical reasoning to guide managers of public enterprises'. He begins by setting out a philosophy of public management, develops diagnostic frameworks to enable managers to analyse the settings in which they operate, and identifies the kind of interventions managers can make to exploit the potential of the circumstances in which they find themselves. Moore's conception of public value is therefore twofold: first, public value as the concept that defines the ultimate purpose of managerial action when using state-owned assets (which he describes as authority and money); and, second, public value as a system of practical reasoning to be relied upon by public managers in helping them to define and pursue public value in the domain in which they are operating. What makes public services distinctive, according to Moore, is that they involve claims of rights by citizens to services that are publicly provided because they are authorized and funded following the outcome of a democratic process. Moore's insistence (1995:48) on the centrality of 'the public' in public value requires that we distinguish between the user as consumer, who seeks what's good for her/himself, and the user as citizen, who seeks what's good for society.

Second, public value can be seen as part of a 'history of ideas'. As John Benington argues in Chapter 2, public value can be seen partly as a reaction to the ideas and practices of new public management (NPM). By reorienting public bodies to the doctrines and practices of the private sector NPM sought to address the supposed problems of the 'old public administration', notably the 'capture' of public sector bodies by those who worked in and controlled them, and the lack of responsiveness to users of public bodies, governed by upwardly accountable 'command and control' governance. Public value, with its ethos of co-production, emphasizes downward accountability to users, with recognition of users as citizens as well as recipients or consumers of services. Here public value challenges the risk within NPM of reducing what is valuable to what can be quantified. Public value, which is by no means hostile to the idea of performance measurement, reorientates public managers to question what constitutes the value of a particular service or policy intervention – that is, what is socially desirable or valuable, and then how this can best be measured. For example, public value informed broadcasting, instead of mainly measuring audience ratings, would foster cultured and knowledgeable viewers and listeners, whose judgements would be included in the assessment of performance and public value added.

More importantly, public value theory attempts to deal with the failure of NPM to see the need to construct an articulate collective of citizens' preferences and thereby redress the 'democratic deficit' between public services and 'citizens'. Public Value therefore emphasizes the importance of political and managerial processes that define the ends to be pursued by public leaders and managers, and argues that the resources deployed are collectively owned. Here, the body politic is not only the individuals who compose it but also the arbiter of public value. Given this, public value theory highlights some important distinctions for policymakers and public managers. The first distinction is between the individual as a private consumer or corporate entity, and the collective which is expressed through political and governmental decisions and debate. The second distinction relates to the individual as a citizen who pays taxes, or as a client who uses services or has obligations to society (for example undertaking jury service or taking responsibility for the disposal of household waste). Public value thus points to the fact that individuals will act differently depending on how they conceptualize what it means to be a citizen (for example, in the case of criminal justice, either as a victim, as an offender, or as a resident). Different groups will inevitably want the government to provide different services or services differently. Public value theory therefore acknowledges the plurality of the public and its preferences, and calls for adequate governance arrangements to allow for all these different voices to be heard.

Third, public value can be seen as a rhetorical device. 'Public value' has become a slogan and rallying cry for reinvigoration of public services and the effort to reconstitute a collective, deliberative process that decides how best to deploy publicly owned assets. Under the banner of public value, institutions mobilize those who work within them to respond to the public, involve the public and serve the public's (or publics') needs and aspirations rather than just promote institutional interests.

Fourth, public value can be treated as a classification of governance. As John Benington argues in Chapter 2, public value is associated with networked governance, in contrast to more traditional forms of hierarchical governance, or the new public management model of governance based on market purchase and exchange. Public value is a doctrine which orients those delivering services towards co-production between service-providers and users, rather than just as recipients of command and control public service provision, or as consumers of NPM marketized services. However, there is a further subtle distinction to be made here, and one which public value theory highlights rather than necessarily has to resolve. In one version of public value, the collective processes of representative politics are the primary arbiter of value, and public and private actors are then mobilized in a network of production to achieve the government's desired results. In a second version of public value, the various different actors in the distributed production system are given more room to define the purposes to be pursued as well as the obligations to help achieve the desired result. Often this right to define the purposes as well as to participate in the production comes as a consequence of the private actors having important contributions to make to the production processes.

The fifth answer to the question, 'What is public value?' is that it is the correlate of private, consumer value as expressed through the price mechanism. Here value is something to be quantified, measured and monetized. Though in the public sector this concept is not yet widely used, techniques are available to understand how much a product or service is worth relative to other things. We return to a discussion of the issue of measurement later in this chapter. (See also Chapter 13 by Mulgan.)

In the absence of a price mechanism for public services that would aggregate the public's preferences for a good or service and therefore determine its value, a number of approaches have been developed in economic theory to attach a monetary value to goods and services provided through the public purse. Key techniques include cost–benefit analysis, programme evaluation, analysis of revealed preferences and stated preferences, for example contingent valuation methods. Programme evaluation, by laying out the purposes that are publicly desirable and then evaluating the success of the programme in achieving those collectively defined purposes, has significant advantages as a method of assessing public value, over other approaches which rely on the quantification or aggregation of individual definitions of value or benefit – which may fail to capture what is valuable to society as a whole.

However, those wanting to understand the value of public services may also be interested in 'what the public values' – and their satisfaction with a particular service at a point in time. A host of methods can be used to determine public satisfaction with services, including attitudinal surveys and opinion-polling of both users and non-users. More sophisticated, participative approaches that attempt to refine the public's preferences and involve them in decision-making include citizens juries and deliberative polling – approaches which can help public managers to discern what the desirable social outcomes of publicly funded services ought to be. Once again the distinction needs to be made between, on the one hand, individuals acting as users or clients or consumers of public services who want to be satisfied with a public service they use, and, on the other hand, individuals as (different) citizens who need to be satisfied with the processes of decision-making, for example, by being consulted, involved and listened to. Finally, when it comes to understanding public values, surveys and discourse analysis can determine what values are currently held by the public, and which values they rank more highly – for example liberty or security. Here values can either emerge from individual and collective desire for something, or be seen to have intrinsic value which is independent from, or above, the ever changing preferences of the public.

Organizations are already using many of these approaches in order to understand the economic value of what they do, or what people think about their services or what values users and professionals hold in relation to a service or group. All of these approaches have their pros and cons. There is no single technique that gives a neat answer to the value of a public service, with a pound sign attached, nor is there a commonly held desire for one across the public sector. What public value means, and what different organizations want public value to do, varies significantly, for example in broadcasting, arts and culture, local government, health, policing and skills sectors.

Here, practice is becoming as important as theoretical developments in this area. Organizations such as the BBC have taken elements of some of the approaches mentioned above to develop a measure that incorporates citizen value, consumer value and economic impact.

Though it would make life simpler if there was one definition and one clear application of the term public value, it is perfectly legitimate for academic and public discourse to attempt to understand its possibilities, and limitations, for all 'five' of the above answers. In this respect, public value is as numinous as democracy, social capital, leadership or any other theoretical construct.

We now address the question of why public managers should be interested in public value at all. We propose two answers to this question – the need for public policymakers and managers to tackle the democratic deficit and, second, to overturn the perceived 'delivery paradox'.

Tackling the democratic deficit

Part of the democratic deficit is the gap between public demands to monitor and influence the activities of public institutions and the actual level of influence achieved. Public value encourages a renewed focus on the role of public policymakers and managers in reducing the democratic deficit and addressing the increasing perception that public services are losing their democratic legitimacy. This deficit is exacerbated when politicians and public managers fail to consider issues that citizens consider important, where citizens' voices repeatedly go unheard or where engagement and consultation fail to impact upon decision-making. The deficit is also evident in debates that polarize around professional judgement versus populist opinion, and in the worst cases even in outright disdain for the public. The growth of grass-roots community organizations, lobby and advocacy groups, is indicative of the lack of public satisfaction with the responses and information provided by public institutions, and of a desire for greater participation and influence.

The role public managers can play in reducing the democratic deficit is clearly not about addressing the failings of representative democracy, such as improving voter turnout or improving the role of parliamentary scrutiny – this is a task for politicians – but about placing individuals and groups as citizens centre stage in the decision-making process so that public resources best serve the needs of different publics, and are balanced against the wider public interest, and not mainly reflect the interests of public managers or professionals, or the interests of one particular group of citizens.

In this way, a public value framework and set of concepts encourages public managers to enact an ethos of service to the public and also encourages them to analyse and understand the variety and plurality of the publics they serve. A public value framework also encourages public managers to think about social outcomes, not just organizational outputs, within the context of the wishes of elected government.

The delivery paradox

The second reason why a public value approach to public service reform is useful is its ability to more fully understand and help public managers to overcome the so-called delivery paradox – where public satisfaction with services is not rising in line with the evidence of service improvement.

One explanation for this paradox may be the lack of belief or knowledge among the public about objective service improvements, but this cannot be overcome simply by communicating these facts better to an unknowing public. How the public evaluates a public service is determined by their existing knowledge, experience, perceptions and impressions of local and national services, and by the individuals delivering those services; as well as being shaped by an individual's own values and opinions about government in general.

But public policymakers and managers should also treat this paradox with some caution. First, 'satisfaction' is not entirely reliable as an indicator of improvement or as a driver of service responsiveness. For example, surveys often focus on how well a service is received rather than what that service should provide. The characteristics of a service can affect perceptions of that service. For example, increased satisfaction does not always correlate with improvement in services that are used frequently by the same users, such as public transport. The public can be ostensibly satisfied with an organization despite a large number of complaints about the kinds of services it provides.

Second, public or user satisfaction may be an inappropriate goal when service reforms are aimed at increasing safety, efficiency or redistribution, or simply when reforms are unpalatable or seek to dampen demand (for example, in the case of welfare benefit reform). It is more appropriate to use satisfaction data when an organization seeks to understand user priorities for improvement of a service, to benchmark performance and to help set targets. A more subtle, nuanced understanding of satisfaction is clearly required before public managers sit too comfortably (or rest uneasily) on satisfaction ratings with a service.

Managing public expectations

Satisfaction is not the only indicator of what the public value. Other indicators, such as public expectations of a service prior to it being delivered, could help public service providers to see where expectations of a service are likely to exceed available provision and may result in low levels of satisfaction, or indeed lead to an undersupply of that service.

Many factors shape an individual's expectation of what a service should provide, including need, previous experience, values and reputation of a service and government. These are similar to drivers of satisfaction. However, as indicators of public value, satisfaction and expectations tend to behave differently as well as having their own complex interrelationships.

As with satisfaction, managing the public's expectations of a service can become an agenda all on its own – for example the 'reassurance agenda' in UK policing, which seeks to reduce the fear of crime as much as the levels of actual crime. The context for each situation is crucial when considering the direction in which expectations need to be managed. If expectations are too low they can reinforce disillusion-ment with a service-provider; if they are too high they can be dashed by poor experiences. Service improvement, satisfaction and expecta-tions, and the story they tell between them, all require a public manager's attention if they are to be used more effectively to help reform services.

Mechanisms for increasing responsiveness

Choice and voice, alongside target-setting and contracting out services to the voluntary or private sector, are all mechanisms that are currently used to improve public services in the UK, with service improvement, satisfaction and expectations as potential indicators of their relative success.

In theory, choice in public services should allow users to exert an influence over who, what, when or how a service is provided and to 'exit' if it does not meet their needs. Examples of choice in practice include choice-based house lettings, direct payments to users of social care, and the 'choose and book' system for appointments in the National Health Service. In practice, people's choices are bound by money, location or information or even their physical or mental well-being, and scarce public resources are unable to meet unlimited public wants.

Improving the opportunities for users to have a greater voice in how services are delivered is a further mechanism for improving services, one that shifts accountability towards local service-providers. Improving voice also helps to reconnect people with the institutions providing services. Examples of enhanced voice for users of services include community safety forums that work with under-represented groups, local authorities and the police; consultations and workshops with local communities; and user/interest group campaigns, such as the 'Putting Breast Cancer on the Map' campaign that gave women suf-fering from breast cancer a voice on the relative neglect of research into the illness.

However, while voice may have democratic validity in its own right, it may also have limits as a mechanism for addressing poor perfor-mance in public services. Where voice accords no real power or weight to what users have to say, and does not lead to practical results, it can produce consultation fatigue. Equally, however, where voice mecha-nisms do accord such power and weight, it may result in unrepresenta-tive groups taking control of the decision-making process. Moreover, improved complaints systems often favour the well-educated and artic-ulate and not necessarily those whose complaints are more serious. Getting right the precise mechanisms that allows users' voices to be heard and acted upon can thus be a time-consuming challenge for public managers.

The delivery paradox therefore appears to derive from the fact that users are also citizens – not just consumers – who derive public value from a service because of how it is being provided and how it is used by others. A public value approach sees these as key sources of value upon which service reform should be based, signalling the need for a significant shift away from a narrow preoccupation with satisfaction ratings.

Having argued above that the theory of public value can help to overcome both the democratic deficit and the delivery paradox, we now turn to how public managers can create value through their activities. Here we outline the process as a dynamic, but it could also be conceptualized, as Mark Moore does, as a 'value chain'

How can public managers deliver public value?

Public value theory, as we articulate it, identifies three interdependent activities on which the production and delivery of public value depends: authorization, creation and measurement – a dynamic within which public managers have clear roles and responsibilities that can help to overcome the democratic deficit and the frustration with the delivery paradox. Our model builds explicitly on Mark Moore's (1995) concept of the strategic triangle (public value creation, the authorizing environment and operational capability) but differs in that it identifies the issue of *measurement* as critical to the production of public value, particularly within the UK policy context of performance management and upward accountability (see Figure 6.1).

- Conceptions and constructions of public value
- Methods of consultation and feedback
- Political mandate v. managerial imperatives?
- Processes of accountability

In order to produce public value the public must *authorize* – that is, confer legitimacy to spend public money and to allocate resources to relevant bodies to *create* public value; and they, and/or external assessors, then *measure* the effectiveness of these bodies in creating the authorized public value. This chapter now considers each of the three components of this dynamic in turn, the dilemmas each confronts, and the emerging principles that could underpin the actions of public managers. For each element, we propose a number of public value principles that can help guide activity in all public services.

Figure 6.1   *The public value dynamic*

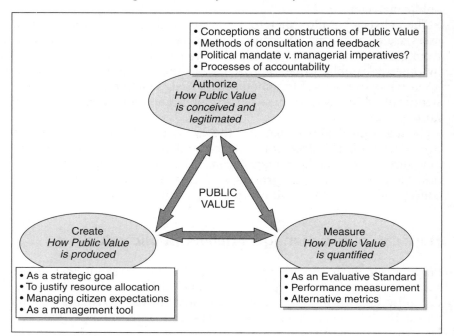

Authorization

Authorization for what is provided by the public sector traditionally results from what is seen as valuable by elected politicians, senior public managers, the media, professional associations, trades unions, social scientists, public intellectuals and other informed commentators. The question posed by our public value approach is whether the views of those who receive services – the public – are adequately taken into account in the construction and conception of public value.

We find a number of dilemmas facing public bodies with regard to securing authorization from the public for their activities. First, many an organization faces an extremely complex and confusing 'authorizing environment', due often to their current structure having evolved over several decades, with a tendency to focus on securing funding and the demonstration of accountability upwards to government and other funders, rather than focusing on what the public value. Legitimacy, whether for an organization's existence or for its subsequent actions, is not usually seen as being conferred on the organization by the public.

Second, the asymmetry of information that exists between the providers of public services and the public leads to dilemmas in how to balance professional judgement with citizen demands. Legitimacy for government action can arise from the need to provide a merit good – such as waste recycling or tobacco control – that would be underconsumed if provided for by the private market, because individual consumers would not know the wider public health benefits.

It can often be even harder (than for public health) for professionals to make the case to the public in relation to artistic and cultural activities funded through the public purse, where the issue looks like one of 'different tastes'. In these instances, the public is able to signal their lack of interest or displeasure by simply not attending performances or exhibitions. There are many examples of this within the arts and culture sector; for example the staging of the modern opera *Boulevard Solitude* by the Royal Opera House won critical acclaim but audience figures were poor.

Third, securing public authorization and legitimacy for the organization's goals is a process that some public organizations encounter at a distance. Some of the most concerted challenges to organizational legitimacy occur in local government and in public broadcasting. In the case of a local authority, elections seek legitimacy, for example, for how the streets should be kept clean, but not on whether or not to clean those streets. Similarly, while the BBC's process of charter renewal has involved the public extensively this happens only once every 10 years.

Fourth, as we have already seen, involving the public in the decision-making process is all too often viewed as costly, time-consuming and a waste of management time.

Understanding citizens' preferences and what the public value is unavoidable if legitimacy is to be maintained. Engaging the public is thus no more a waste of time than it would be for a business to seek greater understanding of their customers. Failure to involve the public in a collective search for needs and solutions not only can result in services failing to provide Public Value, but also allows organizational missions to drift, so that they at last come to serve the interests of politicians, public managers or even private organizations delivering services on behalf of government.

But two concerns remain. Discerning public preferences is notoriously difficult. Furthermore there are significant dangers in relying upon what an uninformed public claims it wants. Both politicians and managers have a clear role in shaping public preferences and in taking tough decisions about what the public need. The delivery of the MMR vaccine to children is a good example of justified intransigence by policymakers, on the basis of sound medical evidence about the benefits to public health, weighed against some vocal public debate about the risks to some individuals.

There is considerable evidence and experimentation, particularly in local government, with processes by which citizens can be more fully engaged, such as citizen's juries. It is difficult to make these participatory approaches meaningful. Yet the public value approach calls forcefully for the provision of better information and for more transparency in decision-making by public bodies. It is essential that service-providers continue to seek innovative ways to engage, consult and deliberate with the public. The public value approach would seek to add participatory methods to established accountability processes, and to make accountability a more democratic process in itself.

Public value creation

Public value is clarified and authorized by the public, but it is created by public service organizations in their decisions about what services to provide, and how to provide them. What activities, programmes and interventions a public body undertakes in order to generate public value will clearly vary considerably across organizations and sectors. Public value is not simply the summation of these activities but is an interrelated process of authorization, creation and measurement that determines what the public values through a process of consultation and deliberation.

Politicians and public managers must justify the allocation of resources towards specific outcomes, and develop management practices that are consistent with the generation of public value through the strategic planning process. A range of methods is used by public bodies for allocating resources, most of which are technical rather than democratic. In the health sector, one method used is the medical effectiveness analysis, which calculates benefit in terms of quality-adjusted-life-years (QUALYs). This is measured by asking hypothetical questions to a sample of the general population of potential patients, which then produces a ranking of health state utilities (different states of health are ranked in order of good to bad health). This is a utilitarian approach, which has various limitations. It assumes, at the outset, that moral benefit is additive – that is, that if the cost of resources used to save one life could instead save two then the latter choice is better. Such an approach also values younger people over older people, as it calculates that, all things being equal, the younger person would get more value from an intervention because they would have longer to benefit from an improved quality of life.

In contrast, public value creation focuses on outcomes not just on outputs or input/output ratios. At the organizational level, the creation of public value lies in the identification of specific outcomes that an organization wants to achieve – outcomes that are authorized by the public and other stakeholders, and that then guide activities towards the achievement of those outcomes. It is important to note that public value theory *per se* does not specify what these outcomes should be, because these are defined and redefined through an ongoing process of democratic deliberation between the public, politicians, service-providers and users.

Public value creation emphasizes the importance of understanding the values or qualities that inform the provision of public services, such as fairness and equality. Thus, the BBC is using a public value framework to help decide which new services will best support one of five core values they have identified as key to the organization's strategic mission as a public broadcaster. Their framework also highlights the potential use of public value as a strategic goal that is integral to being a public service broadcaster. The BBC's approach embraces individuals both as consumers of their services who derive personal enjoyment and education, and as citizens, who value the cultural, democratic or educational benefits of BBC services to society as a whole.

Measurement – the importance of democracy

There are two separate concerns about measuring public value. The first is whether an absolute measure can be derived, and whether this can be translated into a monetary value. This draws on economic as well as democratic theory. The second is the adequacy of performance management frameworks and whether they fully capture what public bodies do and to what extent they involve the public in decisions.

Economic theory has much to contribute to questions of value and social choice, yet economics does not adequately deal with how people arrive at the choices they make, as this covers a wider set of issues than simple monetary incentives. In regard to absolute measures of value, we are thus left with important yet unanswered questions. These relate to what can broadly be defined as intangibles, or values such as fairness that are not easily rendered through the price mechanism. It is thus the processes of democracy themselves that help ascertain what is valuable. As Moore puts it:

> We should evaluate the efforts of public sector managers not in the economic marketplace of individual consumers but in the political marketplace of citizens and the collective decisions of representative democratic institutions. (Moore 1995:31)

Public value creation, and its subsequent measurement, is not a property of particularly gifted individuals, nor of political parties, public service institutions, academic disciplines or professions. Public value is defined and redefined through political and social interaction. Creating a new 'currency' or system of metrics – an alternative to price – to measure that value is therefore both impossible and undesirable.

Though a single measure across different public bodies in different sectors would not capture the unique social outcomes that any particular organization promotes, public managers will play an important role in gauging whether that organization's activities are valuable. The political arena, like the marketplace, is imperfect. It is, therefore, susceptible to single interests or corruption, and relies on the aggregation of individual views (in the form of votes) without concern for how or why preferences were formed. As was argued earlier in this chapter, public managers need to increase the democratic legitimacy of their organization. In doing so, they can certainly utilize economic methods to inform decision-making, for example through the careful use of 'willingness to pay' methodologies. Yet this cannot exempt them from the distortions of existing performance management frameworks. Performance measurement criteria and methods are subject to a range of political, bureaucratic and professional interests that determine support for, resistance to and manipulation of measurement frameworks.

Public value points to certain principles for performance measurement. It does not cast aside existing performance management frameworks simply because they cannot find the holy grail of an absolute public value for all social outcomes. Performance measurement can fail to adequately capture what value is created, or, more seriously, it can actually help to destroy public value. For example in 2003 the UK House of Commons Public Accounts Select Committee found examples of patients inappropriately reclassified so that the ambulance service could meet its response time targets, and even of the removal of wheels from trolleys in an accident and emergency department so that they could be reclassified as beds in order to meet waiting time targets.

Alternative approaches to the use of performance measurement are therefore required if they are to help create public value. We argue that measurement regimes should better reflect how an organization is meeting national standards as well as how well they exploit their freedom to set their own targets, thus reflecting their responsiveness to their own unique circumstances. Whatever the metric, evaluative criteria require public authorization.

Even though there are comprehensive and elaborate systems for measuring performance, no organization in the UK has a single, comprehensive methodology for measuring the value it creates. The best example of such a plural approach is that currently being used by the BBC. The BBC has a very visible source of public funding – the licence fee – which lends itself to 'willingness to pay' methodologies. But even if a framework existed that could capture the value of every activity and outcome of a single public body, such as a police force, translating this into a framework that stretched across the public sector would be administratively unworkable and undermine the democratic process.

A wide variety of innovative measurement techniques have been used to address aspects of the democratic deficit and to restore organizational legitimacy in the eyes of the public. Techniques such as 'front-end evaluation' are carried out to discern what the public want, as for example in the case of the new Jameel Exhibition at the Victoria and Albert Museum. In another instance, Lancashire Constabulary's project to improve burglary victims' experience of the police service involved talking to burglary victims about the quality of service, and using this learning to inform the development of a revised approach to dealing with victims of burglary, including the redesign of a staff training programme. Following the project, there was a significant improvement in every aspect of public satisfaction.

Performance management frameworks can thus be sharpened to reflect key principles of 'public value measurement', as outlined below.

The argument from public value – responsiveness to refined preferences

There is clearly more to understanding the value of a public body and of public services than is conceived by 'new public management' models of value for money, with their emphasis on technical efficiency and the public as 'consumers' who need to be 'satisfied'. Public value must somehow articulate the distinctive type of value produced by a public-oriented service – one that reconnects public bodies with the public they are there to serve. It involves interacting with the public to design, plan, provide and evaluate service provision. Public value requires policy or services to be responsive to what is valued by the public but also to shape what the public need.

The orientation to greater engagement with the public means more than collecting consumer-like preferences or simply responding to uninformed public demand. It includes public deliberation and education. Public value thus entails responsiveness to refined (that is, considered, informed) public preferences. Responsiveness here relates to the quality of the processes for interaction with the authorizing environment. It includes deliberative engagements with the public in goal-setting, planning, decision-making and evaluation. It entails consultation initiatives to inform decision-making, satisfaction surveys and consumer feedback. Transparency and information-sharing are also key. Finally, it requires listening to the authorizing environment – that is, the public, other stakeholders, and so on.

Responsiveness to refined preferences – in effect, how you close the gap between policy and practice and what the public want – is about managing expectations, not just delivery of more or better services. It indicates an organization's capacity to do this, which, when faced with a tightening of the public money, is as important as being efficient. Finally, it gives public managers a clear role in this process, as the individuals who collect, analyse and act upon the information they receive and put it out to the public, in order to educate, inform or otherwise respond to public need.

In conclusion, we return briefly to our five definitions of public value. There remains a preoccupation in the UK with the issue of measurement. We conclude that, given the dynamic nature of political and social interaction that changes what the public value over time, any search for an absolute measure is to be actively avoided.

In outlining a series of public value principles around the inter-related dynamic between authorization, creation and measurement, we have emphasized the importance of the public as citizens – not just as an aggregation of individual consumers but as citizens thinking about the common good – in conferring legitimacy on public bodies to spend public money and to allocate resources. The power of public value lies ultimately in its advocacy of a greater role for the public in decision-making – and of public managers constantly seeking out, from the public they are there to serve, just what it is that citizens want.

Chapter 7

Choice and Marketing in Public Management: The Creation of Public Value?

ROBIN WENSLEY AND MARK H. MOORE

Introduction

We can interpret public value creation as the production of benefits which cannot be captured within the market-based pricing system. Broadly speaking, this is either because the benefit generated is not subject to charge – at least directly – or because what is happening is the reduction of costs which equally are not directly recognized. The two most obvious situations are, first, those in which there is an improvement in quality of the service concerned that cannot be reflected in increased prices; and, second, those in which there are significant changes to the unpriced externalities.

How does this approach to public value compare with the traditional mechanisms in the private sector to develop private value through a continual process of market-based consumer choice? At one level, public (rational) choice economists have given their answer to this question in terms of the need to develop more structures in which such (private) choices can genuinely be exercised. However, our experience and understanding of marketing would suggest that this is only a partial answer.

Marketing needs to be understood as the theories, tools, and techniques which support suppliers in developing and maintaining a sustainable economic position in the context of both competition and consumer choice. A marketing approach, whether its purposes are to be seen as benign or manipulative, starts properly with the consumer. Hence we start by trying to understand what they individually want and how they value and trade off various elements of the product or service concerned. We are also concerned however with how we can shape these attitudes or perceptions over time to generate the appropriate aggregate response within the competitive market place. In addition, we, as a supplier, will almost always wish to be selective about the consumers that we attract, for reasons of both affordability and the nature of their particular demands and requirements.

The idea of choice

The idea of choice – more specifically and importantly, individual choice – has long been at the centre of liberal thought. Choice is the emblem of freedom. It is the polestar whose preservation and protection guides the creation of liberal institutions. It is the dynamo that is seen to power both politics and markets. And it is the basis on which we assign legal and moral responsibility for the consequences of actions taken.

Given the central role of individual choice in liberal thought, it should not be surprising that enhancing individual choice has come to be seen as key to the improvement of public policy and the delivery of public services. Just as choice is central to the assumed efficiency of the market (both in directing productive activity towards products and services that individuals want, can use, and are willing to pay for, and in creating the inter-firm competition that stimulates firms to reduce their costs and deliver a larger share of the value they produce to consumers), so, it is argued, choice by users between providers can stimulate government agencies to provide services in a more responsive, cost-effective way.

While this line of thought may be both ideologically and practically appealing, some crucial conceptual and practical errors are revealed by thinking about the issues of choice and customers in the public domain. Further, the errors lead us to be confused about the important role that the ideas and techniques of marketing could conceivably play in the public sector once the translation from the private to the public has been successfully made. Indeed, once we think properly about marketing in the public sector, we might find a better way to understand different aspects of marketing in the private sector – particularly the role that marketing concepts and techniques play in creating and sustaining a licence to operate in the private sector, as well as developing a market of loyal customers who are prepared to pay a premium price for a given product or service. The aim of this chapter, then, is to reflect on the key ideas of choice, of customers, and of marketing in the public sector where the goal is to create public rather than private value.

A key definition: the role of the public manager

Central to this discussion is a recognition of the unique social position of a public manager, and the way in which it differs from that of a manager of a private enterprise. Of course, there are many ways public managers resemble private managers. They both occupy offices with control over assets. In most cases, the assets have been contributed by others who hope to see something valuable accomplished with them (investors in the case of private managers, citizens and taxpayers in the case of public managers). Those hopes become the purposes that managers seek to achieve with the assets entrusted to them. They have moral and practical reasons to want to do their job well. And their job consists of using their judgement and their administrative skills to see to it that the resources entrusted to them are well spent to achieve the desired purposes, given a particular set of technological possibilities, and environmental conditions. They use many of the same instruments for establishing, animating, guiding, and adapting the production processes, organizations and networks they lead. So we do not mean to suggest that managers in private and government organizations have nothing in common.

But there is an important way they differ from one another that has very important implications for the work they are supposed to do. That key difference is that, by definition, government managers have the sovereign authority of the state as an asset they can use to accomplish the purposes entrusted to them. Sometimes this authority is used pretty nakedly. Firms are regulated to reduce their pollution. Citizens are cited and fined for speeding or littering the streets. Young men and women are drafted into military service. Ordinary citizens are taken from their jobs to serve on juries. Those who refuse to pay their taxes are put in jail.

It is also worth noting that even when the government is spending money, it is implicitly using authority as well. Much of the money the government uses to provide services or to otherwise improve social conditions comes from the use of the taxing authority of the state. Thus, to the degree that special conditions attach to the use of authority, they might also attach to the use of money raised through the use of authority.

One could also note that many things which appear to be pure services come with certain kinds of obligations attached. This is entirely clear in the case of school, welfare, and drug treatment programmes. In each of these cases, the goal that society seeks to achieve through the actions of the public manager is not simply to satisfy the recipients of the service; it is also to encourage the recipients to behave in ways that are good for society as a whole. Schooling is not provided simply as a service. Children are required to go, and their parents charged with the responsibility of seeing that they do so. The goal is not only to make the kids or their parents happy; it is also to produce economically, socially, and politically educated and useful citizens. Welfare is not provided simply to meet the needs or increase the satisfaction of the recipients. It is also provided to make sure that their children are well cared for, and with the hope (and increasingly the legal requirement) that the recipients take steps to increase their autonomy and reduce their welfare dependence on welfare in the future. Drug treatment programmes are not publicly provided simply to protect the health and ease the strain on drug addicts; they are also sometimes required as a condition of civil or criminal proceedings, and are valued for the anticipated result that the user will stop using drugs, commit fewer crimes, become better employed, and give more care to his or her children.

It is less obvious but nonetheless true that even in the most extreme case in which government hands out vouchers to individuals to spend for particular services, the goal of the programme is not simply to satisfy the client/beneficiary. Even when we give individuals the right to choose the schools they attend, or the housing they will buy, or the job training programme they will enrol in, and use government money to pay for these services, the body politic lays its heavy hand on these choices. At least, those who receive vouchers are obligated to use them only for the services for which they were intended. If society has given out vouchers for schooling, for housing, for food, those vouchers must be spent for those broad purposes. They cannot be sold or transferred for other services. And in many cases, choices are further constrained (on the supply side) by requirements that the vouchers be spent only on certified providers. So, even in the case where government seems to be doing its utmost to privilege individual choice by paying for choices that individuals make, the hand of the collective is present to constrain those choices. The reason, presumably, is that the collective wants something out of the transaction, and seeks to satisfy itself as well as the individual who is ostensibly to be served.

So, there is a way in which the hand of the collective using its authority is always present in the actions of government managers. This is obvious when they are leading organizations whose primary job is to impose duties on citizens such as law enforcement agencies, regulatory agencies, or tax-collection agencies. But it is also present even for service-providing agencies. In all cases, the authority of the state is present, and makes those who decide how and for what state authority will be used important arbiters of value as well as those for whom the state services are provided.

The ubiquitous presence of state authority has a profound effect on how we think about choice, about customers, and about marketing in the public sector. Let's start with the idea of customers viewed from the point of view of the government manager, and those who would advise him or her about how to create public value.

Customers and intermediaries

There are many individuals who stand in a relationship to government operations that makes them appear to be analogous to customers in the private sector. They are the individuals that one sees engaged in individual transactions with the government organization at the delivery end of the organization: the teenager who is enrolled in a high school, the diabetic receiving treatment in a public hospital, the victim calling the police. They seem like customers since they are the ones who are seen on the other side of the counter. Further, they are engaged as individuals in a particular individual transaction. Moreover, in many cases, we imagine that these individuals are benefiting from their transactions in much the same way as private customers. Their lives are enriched and improved as a consequence of their encounter with a service-providing government.

But there are two problems with this image of a government customer. First, the client on the other side of the bureaucratic counter often does not pay for the service and benefits they receive. Or, if they do pay, they don't pay the full cost. The cost of establishing and continuing to produce a particular product or service is borne by society as a whole through its tax system.

If the individual person on the other side of the counter doesn't pay for their particular use of the service, then several important things we associate with customers in the private sector fall away. First, we can no longer use revenues voluntarily paid by the individual as a measure of the value that individual attaches to the good or service, because there is no such payment. Second, the threat to withhold one's custom does not focus the mind of the managers and owners, for there is no direct loss to the producer.

At the same time, something new is added to the equation. If we associate decisions to spend money with the right to define the value of what is produced with that money, then it is clear that the right to define what constitutes the value to be produced with tax dollars lies primarily with taxpayers and the body politic – not simply with the person on the other side of the counter. One could say that the taxpayer and body politic is just another customer of government services. But one must then ask what that customer wants from government.

We actually have an answer to that question. What the body politic wants from a government organization is the achievement of its authorized mission, or the social outcome which justified the use of public money and authority in the first place. One should note, however, that the idea of a public outcome is quite a bit different from the idea of customer satisfaction. They are similar – even identical – if the body politic says that its collective purpose is to satisfy a particular class of clients in particular ways that the clients choose for themselves. But this is rarely all that the collective says. It also says that it wants to achieve some social outcome that will be achieved by providing certain services to specific clients.

On top of this there is the question of the role of intermediaries between the customer and the supplier. In traditional consumer marketing, there is a need to distinguish between what might be seen as two forms of intermediation. In the first form, what might be called the 'buying unit' is actually a group rather than an individual; in the second form, the intermediate organization is acting much like a retailer in a supply chain. In Wroe Alderson's terms, it is sorting what is provided and matching it to user requirements (Alderson 1957, 1965). In a public service context, we find organizations that are fulfilling this particular commissioning role. However we should also recognize, as we will discuss later, that there are important ways a traditional marketing and customer approach does not fully engage with the nature of governance and accountability in the public sector.

There is an important sense in which the client also becomes part of the production process. This shouldn't be too surprising to marketers in the private sector. There has long been an understanding that commercial enterprises have to work with customers to generate value the firm wanted to create both for the customer and for itself. This is particularly true in service industries where the constant interaction of client with service is key to the success of the venture. But it is even true with products where we have had to recognize that the work done by the consumer in using the product is a crucial element in the achievement of customer satisfaction.

However, it is even more compelling to think this way in the public sector. There, the firm or agency is not just helping the customer get the benefit that the customer wants from the product; it is trying to get the customer/client to help produce the benefit that the body politic wants from the use of its publicly owned assets (see John Alford's Chapter 8). There is a socially established maxim (and public value) that differs from the simple summation of individual satisfactions (social welfare narrowly conceived).

This is particularly true in the case of those encounters in the public sector that involve obligations as well as services. Then the goal is not to make the client with whom the organization interacts happy. It is to achieve compliance. In addition, the body politic may be concerned about matters of justice in the way that the obligations are imposed. They are interested in this because we all have an interest in how collectively owned powers are brought to bear on individuals. We want them brought to bear when an individual has a duty to the collective. We want individuals to be protected from those burdens when they have a right not to be bothered. We count on the state to act in both these cases.

These characteristics (that the goal of a government agency is not simply to satisfy client beneficiaries, but also to achieve social outcomes; that among those who have to be satisfied by the government are the citizens in whose name the government acts, and that they are the actors who define the social outcome that is to be achieved; that government agencies deliver obligations to individuals as well as services, and that the point of these obligations is not to make the individual client happy) – suggest a rather radical shift in the way that we need to think about marketing in the public sector.

Marketing at both ends of the production process

First, it is important to think of marketing at 'both ends of the production system.' Like a private sector firm seeking a close relationship with customers, government managers have to figure out how they will structure their relations with those to whom they are delivering services. This is sometimes described as 'downstream marketing.' On the other hand, because most of the money to finance ongoing operations comes from citizens and their elected representatives, government agencies have to focus on managing their relationships with 'upstream' customers as well: those who provide the money and the authority the government needs to carry out its activities. We also need to recognize what might be termed 'midstream' marketing, that is marketing within the organization (or perhaps inter-organizational partnership) itself. In the private sector a number of commentators have dubbed this 'internal marketing'.

One can draw a reasonably close analogy between 'upstream' and 'downstream' customers, and the distinction made in the private sector between marketing to customers (whom the firm meets in individual sales transactions), and marketing to investors or to those who provide a private firm's 'licence to operate' (who provide the financial resources and authorization for the firm to launch itself and stay in business). Of course, in the aftermath of the Enron scandal, it might appear somewhat unseemly to think about 'marketing' firm performance to investors. Relationships with investors are supposed to be governed by accurate, consistent reporting on financial performance according to well-established rules and traditions, with little room for 'marketing'. But one doesn't have to observe too many conversations between CEOs, financial analysts, and shareholders to see that there is no small amount of 'spinning' involved. And, if one widens one's frame of reference to include stakeholders other than investors who are in a position to shape the prospects of a firm, such as government, the local community, or a firm's standing with the general public, it becomes clear that there is a lot of 'upstream marketing' going on in the private sector as well as the public. The fact that we call this 'corporate public affairs' rather than marketing *per se* should not blind us to the fact that something is being marketed to overseers as well as to clients.

In the public sector, what is here called upstream marketing is called 'public accountability.' It is the process through which public organizations report to taxpayers, citizens, and their elected representatives on their accomplishments. As in the private sector, much of this reporting is done in predefined financial and statistical terms with limited capacities for public sector managers to try to spin the data on their accomplishments. But in the public sector there is much more room for marketing an idea of public value creation to the wider public.

Part of the reason is that government organizations are answerable to many different individuals with quite different interests in the way the organization is performing. This means that when organizations talk about themselves, if they want to speak to their varied constituencies, they have to be ready to talk about different aspects and dimensions of their performance.

Another part of the reason is that government organizations have missions that are cast in broad terms and lend themselves to narratives and anecdotes as well as statistics. A third part of the reason is that the press plays a crucially important role in calling public agencies to account, and they are often more interested in stories than in numbers.

A fourth reason may be that there are important public purposes which are intangible, and hard to express in numbers. It may even be that citizens and taxpayers value the government's expressive efforts in a particular direction (for example, articulation of a sense of public purpose, such as eliminate child poverty) as much as the actual achievement of desired results.

For all of these reasons, there is more room for 'marketing efforts' to play an important role in mobilizing support from upstream customers in the public than in the private sector. Indeed, the narrative of public value creation that is sold to the authorizers, and then reflected in the performance numbers and reports filed by the organization, is a real product of the organization. Selling an ability to satisfy an aspiration that the community has as a whole, and that it hopes the government will be able to achieve, may in some cases be as important as delivering a service (or an obligation) to individual clients.

Having observed that there are many reasons for government organizations to focus marketing efforts on upstream 'authorizers' as well as downstream 'clients,' and that there are many opportunities for government agencies to 'spin' their performance in ways that are designed to curry favour with their authorizers, it is important to add that this should not be taken as advice to take advantage of the confusion, or gullibility of the citizens and their elected representatives. To the extent that 'marketing' is associated with what might be described as 'messing with people's minds and altering facts to persuade them to do something that they would otherwise not do', marketing seems particularly inappropriate when we are talking about the relationships between government managers, the agencies they lead, and the citizens and elected representatives they serve. To the extent, however, that marketing means, rather, 'finding out what really matters to people, and giving them accurate information about the performance characteristics of organizations in terms that matter to them', the marketing of public sector operations turns out to mean partly the same thing as making those organizations more responsive and more accountable. We will embrace the second idea of marketing for the purposes of this article, but note in passing that marketing academics have periodically debated the extent to which, in reality, it is more about what can be described as 'messing with consumers' minds' rather than 'responding to consumers' wishes' – for instance, see Wensley (1990). Viewed in this light, attention paid to marketing public sector organizations to their authorizers and overseers may result in increased responsiveness and accountability rather than obstruction and manipulation.

Marketing obligations and restrictions as well as services and opportunities

Downstream marketing in the private sector is concerned primarily with marketing services and opportunities to individuals, and with trying to find ways to attach desires that individuals have to concrete products and services so that they will voluntarily choose to do what the firm hopes they will do. In contrast, downstream marketing in the public sector is often trying to persuade individuals to do something that they would not ordinarily want to do, or to accept the necessity of an obligation that is being imposed on them, or to understand why a benefit that they would like is not available to them. In short, a lot of marketing by government agencies could be viewed as 'de-marketing' or 'negative marketing' – where we are given bad news rather than good news.

It is worth noting that this can occur in at least three different circumstances. One is the situation described above, where instead of delivering a service the government delivers an obligation. This occurs when government asks us to give up our driver's licence if we have driven while drunk, or to stand still for the orderly processes of justice to be visited upon us when we are suspected of crimes, or to pay the taxes we owe. A second is when governments deny us a service that we would like because the body politic has decided to ration the particular service to those who need it or more, or could make better use of it, or could not pay for it themselves, and we fell into none of these categories. This occurs when we are told we no longer qualify for disability payments, or that we aren't eligible for an expensive orthopaedic procedure that would be provided to someone younger than we are. A third is when the government seeks to engage large numbers of individuals in behavioural changes designed to save us from ourselves, to save the government money that it will have to pay over if we continue to behave foolishly, or to help the society and the government to achieve social purposes without having to pay staff for the production of those purposes, or to pass a law requiring individuals to contribute to the achievement of the social goal. This occurs when government asks us not to smoke, drink, or eat too many calories, or when they ask us not to drop litter or to participate in recycling programmes.

A number of these latter situations raise two interesting questions from a marketing policy perspective: on what basis is the policy of behavioural change justified? And how is the desired behavioural change promoted most effectively? In the former case we need to distinguish between situations in which, without intervention, individuals would be likely to act either individually or collectively against their own interest, and those situations in which, while such action conceivably may be in the individual's interest, it is not considered in the interests of society at large.

Having noted that there is marketing to be done on both sides of the production process – the upstream side and the downstream side – it is important to keep in mind that the ethical and normative obligations, and therefore the techniques, of marketing might differ a bit between upstream and downstream, and that there might be some special obligations that attach to marketing on the upstream side. The language of upstream and downstream marketing seems to suggest a flow, sequence, or stage in the process for distinguishing the actors to whom a firm is being marketed. Upstream marketing happens before a product or service is produced or delivered, when the idea of a particular product or service is being vetted by potential investors. Downstream marketing occurs after a product has been developed, and offered for sale. But the words upstream and downstream have an additional connotation. The upstream customers are the ones who are powerful, and to whom the firm manager owes an accounting. They articulate their desires for the firm through voice more than through exit, and their voice becomes powerful in the firm because of the obligations on the firm to report to them. The downstream customers in some ways seem less powerful, because they are encountered more as individuals than as institutional investors, and their influence is exercised more through the power of exit than through voice. In effect, relations with upstream customers are mediated by reports on the aggregate performance of the organization; relations with downstream customers are mediated by experiences with the product or service.

If a firm is accountable to, and has to provide reports to, a group of authorizers and overseers who constitute the upstream customers, then one might imagine that the marketing effort to engage the upstream customers in enthusiastic support for the firm would be different. The goal of the marketer might be to listen and respond even more than is the case with downstream customers. It might be to focus even more on relevant details of performance and tell the truth rather than distract with irrelevant issues, and give relentless focus on strong points while avoiding weaker points. One might even be interested in trying to assess the degree to which, in marketing to upstream customers, one had identified the appropriate range of overseers.

In traditional treatments related to the private sector, marketing activities are generally seen as distinct from those related to issues of accountability, since the two core groupings – actual or potential customers and shareholders – are treated as different. Of course in actual practice the distinction is sometimes less clear. In any mass market activity the customer base does in some sense overlap with the shareholder base, although a considerable amount of the overlap may be masked by intermediaries such as pension funds. What we might call spill-overs therefore occur in identifiable areas such as ethical behaviours where there is a degree of public scrutiny alongside visibility to consumers.

In the public sector such spillovers between responses to customers and responses to shareholders will often be a lot greater, particularly if various transparent measures of performance are adopted. In principle the very management systems that drive performance internally might also provide more public data for accountability. Here we might find that the ensuing public debate resulted not only in greater confidence in local accountability but also in improvements in the performance management system to ensure that it more closely reflected the genuine desires of the citizens. It is clearly the role of elected politicians in the public sector to perform many of these scrutiny functions, but it remains the case that there can be some significant confusion for those elected between the role of the executive itself and the processes of public scrutiny.

An example in community policing

The issue here can be clarified, perhaps, through the example of community policing. The basic idea of community policing was to increase the value of a police department to a community by making it more responsive to community concerns. This was judged to be important for two somewhat different reasons. First, if the police were focused on the problems that concern citizens, then the value of the police to the citizens would arguably increase. That would have been reason enough, perhaps, for the police to try to become more responsive. But they had a second reason as well. They thought that their primary goal was to reduce serious crime. They were startled to discover, however, that, while this was an important goal for most citizens, it was not the only, or the most urgent, thing that citizens wanted from the police. This created some tension between the idea of giving the citizens what they wanted and that of giving citizens what the police force thought they should want (and what they had indeed been established to provide). The tension was resolved when the police learned that their ability to deal with serious crime would go up, not down, if they paid attention to community disorder offences. One of the reasons was that when the citizens got what they wanted from the police, they were more likely to be willing to help the police in their inquiries. The success of the police in dealing with serious crime went up along with their ability to deliver services the citizens wanted.

In the interests of increasing their responsiveness to citizens, the police did several things. One was to increase the quality of service they offered in response to emergency calls. Individual citizens calling the police got a more supportive voice at the end of the line, a faster response, and more courteous treatment when the officers arrived. That was all part of improving customer service. But the police also began reaching out beyond those who called them, through the use of community surveys and other means, and so found out about crimes and concerns that they did not hear of through the reporting system, as well as about their own standing with the public, in the process gaining some insight into why individuals were not calling them even when they had been victimized in a crime.

First, they began holding meetings in which community representatives were invited to appear and share their concerns. These consultations with citizen groups were very effective, not only because they helped bolster the legitimacy of the police in the communities with which they consulted, but also because they mobilized on behalf of police objectives a significant amount of private, informal social control. At some stage, however, the police had to get concerned about just how representative were the individuals who were coming to the meetings, and how representative of the population of the city as a whole were the people with whom the police were in contact.

Once this issue gets raised, a new use for what might be viewed as an ordinary account management system is created. A police force can imagine itself enmeshed in a set of relationships with individual citizens and with groups of citizens to whom it is trying to be responsive. It wants to be responsive because that is good in itself, because it builds legitimacy and support for the police, and because it allows them to call on that community for help in achieving their goals. In short, the department thinks of these groups of upstream customers simultaneously as financiers, part of their production process, and customers. It wants to be sure that it is doing a good job with the principal stakeholders in its environment. And it sets up and uses an account management system to keep tabs on this. But it also wants to check to make sure that its network of contacts includes the entire community, and not just a part. The account management system can be used for that as well, by testing its comprehensiveness against the set of existing groups in the city. In effect, the account management system allows the organization not only to maintain the quality of its existing relationships, but also to see how strong those relationships are in the system as a whole, and perhaps even, although this is more difficult, who is being left out. Alongside account management systems come performance measurement systems. If managers respond in a proactive manners they can try to help democratic deliberation by giving the authorizers and other stakeholders something concrete to react to.

When marketing to the client side, there are lots of interesting things to be developed. In the field of social marketing itself there has been a long debate about the extent to which the approaches should focus on direct attempts to alter behaviour, or on a wider set of intentions including also influencing attitudes. The general conclusion seems to be that the former, more restricted, domain is the most suitable and effective. This suggests that in identifying the areas in which approaches based on mainstream marketing can contribute most effectively, we should perhaps exclude the promotion of obligations, norms, responsibilities and duties except where we have clear desired outcomes in terms of behaviour.

The reality of choice

Let's turn back to the question of choice. As we have already noted, choice is very important and very powerful, and much of the focus of traditional marketing approaches has been to inform, persuade and reinforce individuals in making particular choices between services or products.

But we have also already noted that an important part of a public manager's job is to constrain individual choice. This happens when individually held resources are collected for public purposes. It happens when those public purposes are achieved through activities that are tailored not only to satisfy individual clients, but to achieve social outcomes, and not only to provide services, but also to impose duties. In these cases, the collective is making claims on individuals, and constraining the free exercise of choice.

To use state authority in this way requires justification. This is the same as saying that the government needs to win consent from individuals. We have to agree that a purpose is important enough and special enough for us to be prepared to tax and regulate ourselves to produce the result. We have to agree that the means chosen are efficient and effective, and fairly distribute the burden of achieving the desired goal. We have to agree that the benefits and costs of the collective effort are fairly and justly distributed.

The techniques of marketing (but not necessarily the mindset of marketers) are important here, as we have discussed. Public sector markets want to inform and educate, not to manipulate. But who is to judge the difference between education on one hand and manipulation on the other?

Some of the most important justifications for government engagement in society turn on concerns about the capacities of individuals to make choices in their own interests, paying suitable attention to the interests of others. We have to be concerned about distortions of our ability to judge and act in our own self-interest (paternalism); inability to see and properly take account of the wider consequences of our action (externalities); and our insufficient commitment to principles of solidarity and justice which would bring a just world into existence (distributional objectives). Traditionally we have thought that democratic discourse was the best way to help with these problems. The state became both the agent for discussion as well as the instrument for achieving results that individuals could not achieve on their own.

Social marketing approaches can clearly be applied directly in the case of actions which should be in the individual's own self-interest. In areas such as health, food, and pension provision, it is clear that we face a collective tendency to discount too heavily either costs or benefits in the long term. The effects of such inaccurate discounting are to be found most clearly in the area of pensions where simple recourse to individual choice results in overall underprovision of services. The common policy response in such situations is a combination of legislation and persuasion through public information. Marketing approaches help us refine the specifics of the process of persuasion through information, while legislation can be used to introduce options which are more likely to result in appropriate choices. In many cases, we also move into an area where there are at least some elements of our second category – namely externalities, whether recognized or not. Recognized externalities include, for instance, the later costs of medical treatment in the case of poor dietary choice. These costs are at least to some degree already recognized but they are often not directly charged to the individual because there is either an insurance-based or a public-funded provision of healthcare. One of the most effective promotional devices is to try and reduce the apparent time delay between costs and benefits. A very good example of this was the anti-smoking campaign developed by the British Heart Foundation. There is reasonable evidence that the excessive discounting of long-term costs is itself particularly apparent among younger adults, and it is here that the public health concerns about smoking are at their most severe. Hence the Foundation developed an advertising approach which situated the negative health effects both in the present and in an identifiable social context.

The area of pension provision is another domain in which more detailed knowledge of customer behaviour can help design more effective interventions. The general tendency to over-discount future benefits against current costs is substantially moderated if these costs are not strictly in the present (and hence directly deductible from current income expectations and commitments) but in the near future in terms of additional income over and above existing income. It is likely that this effect is linked to the well-established 'money illusion', whereby decisions tend to get taken in terms of current nominal currency values rather than so-called real values which incorporate inflation. In this case, however, it seems that two 'wrongs' can make a 'right' – given that we tend not to fully incorporate future anticipated increases in earnings in our choices. We will make better and more rational provision of future benefits if we have the opportunity to use future income increases to fund such provision. Intervention and even sometimes legislation may be required to ensure that such contracts are made available as an option in the marketplace.

The debate about public choice has also had to recognize the contradictions surrounding redundant capacity. Within the provision of an essentially universal service (in terms of both individuals and geography) it is necessary, in terms of efficiency, to avoid excessive and redundant provision. However, in areas such as health and education, choice between providing organizations can only avoid defaulting to provider choice rather than user choice if there is redundant capacity in the system.

This has led to an interest in the so-called 'personalization' of public services, which can be seen as a way of providing choice within a particular process of service provision rather than between different providers of service. The basic idea is to provide choices at various stages during the process of service provision, based on each individual user's perspective. In principle, such an approach can indeed be applied when there are multiple provider organizations as well. However, we need to be aware of two important caveats. The first is that in many instances there will remain some requirement for the standardization of minimum service – particularly in the case of contractual arrangements between a number of organizations. Such problems have been noted by some of those who have advocated the analogous 'mass customization' approach in the private sector. The second is more directly related to our understanding of user choice processes. In many market-based choice processes, routines are developed to reduce the complexity of the choice process, particularly in what are called low-involvement, repeat purchase situations. In approaches to personalization however, particular emphasis is given to using a 'consumer script' approach to align user choices with the options provided. Besides the fact that a number of cases of 'choice' in areas such as education and health are very different from the archetypal low-involvement, repeat-purchase situations, we also know from empirical work in such areas both that there is considerable variation in individual scripts and that the user script on average differs from the supplier script.

A final question

This leads us back to the most important and difficult marketing challenge of all in a democracy – marketing the idea of being an active, engaged, and democratic citizen as both a duty and a consumption good. This is an area where, as we have noted above, advocates of social marketing have been cautious – not only because the whole process can be seen as wider than one focused on marketing a product or a service, but also because we have accumulated much evidence in both marketing and consumer psychology that, in many instances, attitude change follows behavioural change rather than the other way round. Much marketing activity is therefore about reinforcing existing behaviour rather than changing it.

However, winning the consent of individuals can also be seen as a marketing goal. This is manifest in elections, where candidates use the techniques of marketing to position themselves and their message to collect votes (without distorting their positions too much, and giving the voter a clear choice). A number of marketing commentators have commented on such activities. This marketing goal is less obvious but still present in advocacy campaigns. And, as noted above, it is particularly important when citizens are being asked to accept a burden (for example increased taxation or regulation). It may even be important when we bring the authority of the state to bear against particular individuals, and seek to earn, if not their happiness, at least their grudging agreement that they have been treated fairly.

In the end, we face a significant dilemma. A number of the tools and approaches from marketing can be used to make the provision of public services more responsive to the demands of users. This also often involves choice mechanisms even if there is also a requirement for regulation and accountability.

Chapter 8

Public Value from Co-production by Clients

JOHN ALFORD

Introduction

Public value is not 'public' because it is produced by government organizations, but rather because it is 'consumed' collectively by the citizenry. At a minimum, it includes value that citizens can obtain only through collective provision, such as law and order (which underpins markets), remedies to market failures of various types, and distributional equity. More broadly, public value embodies the goals or aspirations citizens have for the society as a whole, founded in social or normative commitments or purposes (see Alford 2002:339–40). An important implication of conceiving public value in this way is that it can be created not only by public sector organizations but also by a variety of entities, such as private firms, community organizations, other government agencies, volunteers, industry and professional associations and others. Many of them have typically been seen as suppliers, providing services on a contractual basis to government purchasers (Donahue 1989; Kettl 1993; Prager 1994). But to varying extents since the 1980s, some have also been conceived as co-producers, jointly producing services with government organizations through voluntary cooperation (see Sharp 1980; Whitaker 1980; Parks *et al.* 1981; Brudney and England 1983; Kiser 1984).

Here I consider one type of co-producer: the client of a government organization. Whereas contractors, community organizations, other government agencies and volunteers are more analogous to suppliers of services to a public sector organization, clients appear to be more like consumers, who receive services from it. The idea that they are also suppliers of co-productive effort is therefore counterintuitive at first sight.

This chapter defines and distinguishes the role of clients, then illustrates the necessity of client co-production in many public services, and its potential desirability in some others. It draws on research evidence

144

from Britain, America and Australia to offer some propositions about how client co-production is best elicited. Finally, it ponders the implications of some of these arguments for the creation of public value.

Defining public sector clients

What constitutes a 'client' in the public sector is a problematic issue, complicated by the fact that there are many terms dealing with the same phenomena, mostly derived from the private sector, such as customers, users, buyers or consumers, each with many contending definitions. In this chapter, the term 'clients' is employed to label those who deal with the agency at its 'business end' (Moore 1995), as its 'public-in-contact' (Blau and Scott 1963).[1] In so far as they have the role of clients, they receive private value from the agency's service – that is benefits that are consumed individually. Insofar as they have the role of citizens, they receive public value, which they 'consume' jointly with their fellow citizens.

The role of client is therefore different from that of the citizenry. Citizens' relationships to each other and to government are not the same as consumers' relationships to each other and to producers (Stewart and Ranson 1988; Alford 2002). In a democracy, citizens develop and express aspirations collectively, through processes of political deliberation such as voting, policy debate and other forms of political participation. Clients, on the other hand, signal their preferences as individuals, through market purchases or, especially in the case of government organizations, through surrogates such as client surveys, complaints departments or appeals processes.

To the extent that they receive private value, clients seem analogous to private sector customers. But they are quite dissimilar in important ways, which we can identify with different client roles (Alford 2002). Some of them may pay money in direct exchange for the services they receive, just like paying customers of the private sector. But most of them – for example social security recipients, pupils at government schools or public housing tenants – do not pay any money, or only pay a proportion of the actual cost.[2] In this capacity, they play the role of beneficiary. Many of them are unwilling clients: they are being compelled to 'receive' the service – for example, prisoners, taxpayers and many others subject to regulatory or other obligations. In this capacity, they play the role of obligatee (Moore 1995). Typically, an individual client embodies some mixture of these roles, in addition to being a citizen.

Although different from the private sector customer, the public sector client is similar in one important and perhaps surprising respect: that they are engaged in an exchange with the organization. Each receives something directly or indirectly from the other, and what they receive is linked to some degree with what they give to the other. However, in the public sector, the types of things being exchanged, the process by which it occurs and ultimately the range of parties involved are of a quite different character. They can be seen more usefully as what anthropologists call social exchanges, rather than the economic exchanges which characterize market transactions (Lévi-Strauss [1949] 1969; Homans 1961; Blau 1964; Ekeh 1974).

In social exchange, a broader set of things can be exchanged than tangible items such as money or goods or services. People may give each other intangibles such as respect, assistance, symbolic status, fairness or indeed anything the parties value. These exchanges entail more diffuse and more deferred reciprocity, with less precise and longer-term obligations than the immediate quid-pro-quo transactions that occur between buyers and sellers (Alford 2002).

Seen through this lens, the exchange between the public organization and the client is one in which the client 'pays' not with money but with behaviours, and does so at least in part to reciprocate the tangible or intangible 'gifts' they receive from the organization or from others prompted by the organization. The organization's aim is (or should be) to elicit behaviours from the clients which co-produce value for the public. It is more likely to do so to the extent that it understands and respects their needs.

The necessity of client co-production

In some cases, client co-production is a substitute for production by internal organizational staff. The issue for managers in these situations is whether the task would be better performed by the organization or the client. To inform these decisions, managers weigh up the relative cost-effectiveness of the two options, as is already well documented in decisions about whether or not to contract public services out to private providers (Donahue 1989; Kettl 1993; Prager 1994; Boyne 1998). They seek to ascertain, for instance, whether the co-producers have the requisite capabilities, and what it would cost to induce them to play that role usefully.

But there is another circumstance where it is not really a matter of choice as to whether client co-production should be utilized. This is where organizational and client co-production are interdependent – that is, where the task cannot be performed without some contribution from both parties. In these cases organizations must engage with client co-production whether they like it or not. The issue for them is not whether to utilize client co-production but how best to do so.

An example concerns long-term unemployed people – the clients of public employment agencies or of their contracted providers. At first sight, these agencies' clients could be seen as consumers of their services, such as job referrals. But to the extent that the purpose of the agency is to help the unemployed get work,[3] the clients are also necessarily co-producers. The agency cannot achieve that purpose unless the clients do certain things. Even if the agency finds a suitable job for an unemployed person, they have to secure and retain that job – something the agency cannot do for them. The client has to make a favourable impression on the employer, both at interview and after starting in the job. How well they do so will be a function of the person's knowledge, capabilities and attitudes. This in turn brings forth additional tasks in the process of getting the unemployed into work, in that they need to acquire skills and knowledge – either generic ones such as basic literacy and numeracy, or specific ones such as computer keyboarding. More particularly, they may need to learn interview techniques or other job search skills. Again, the agency can provide programmes such as basic education courses, skills training or job search training to assist unemployed people, but unless they engage with those programmes with some degree of commitment they will not gain much from them. Thus, the agency cannot achieve its purposes unless its unemployed clients contribute some time and effort into becoming 'job-ready', in skills and attitudes, and into securing jobs to which they are introduced.

The task becomes even more complex if we focus on the long-term unemployed, who may have become profoundly de-motivated by their experiences of failing to find work over a year or more, typically instilling a sense of hopelessness and resignation, fuelling a desire to avoid yet another rejection from a possible employer. The challenge for the agency is not only to find jobs and assist 'job-readiness', but also to prompt 'job-willingness'.

Since the 1970s, the ranks of both the unemployed and the long-term unemployed have swelled in many countries, and governments have been under political pressure to tackle the problem. Common to the strategies adopted in America, Britain and Australia has been a shift in emphasis, in which the unemployed must not only accept jobs offered to them, but also continuously demonstrate that they are 'actively seeking work' (King 1995).[4] This requirement has been imposed under the rubric of 'mutual obligation' (Mead 1986), in which an explicit link is drawn between welfare benefits and job search. The argument, based on a particular conception of who constitutes the 'deserving poor',[5] is that if the unemployed are to receive benefit payments then they should give something back in return – that is, they should genuinely and energetically seek work, or undertake valid substitutes for it, such as education, training, or work experience.

Supporting this philosophy has been a number of changes in service offerings and operations. First, the link between benefit payments and job search has been cemented by merging or strengthening the liaison between the employment agency and the benefit agency – as seen in Australia's creation of 'Centrelink' in 1996 (Husock and Scott 1999).

Second, an array of labour market programmes (LMPs) has been introduced, offering various kinds of support and assistance to the unemployed, including job matching, job search training, skills training, work experience, basic education, and supports such as child care and transport assistance. These have varied in approach. In the US, the increasing emphasis has been on what are called 'work first' (as opposed to 'education first') programmes, in which the focus has been on getting the unemployed into some kind of job (usually a casual, short-term one) as soon as possible, the theory being that this provides experience and confidence to progress to more stable employment.[6] The other two countries (Britain and Australia) have had a more mixed approach.

Third, an extensive system of sanctions has been introduced, in which clients who fail to meet either their 'activity' obligations (requirements to search for work) or their administrative obligations (for example requirements to attend agency interviews or notify changes of circumstances) are penalized by a reduction or suspension of benefits for a prescribed period, with subsequent 'breaches' incurring more severe penalties.

In each country, these changes have formalized a co-productive relationship between clients and employment agencies. However, in most cases the relationship is characterized by economic rather than social exchange, and backed by sanctions. Its success at its officially stated purpose – getting the unemployed into work – has been mixed. However its success in terms of another purpose – getting unemployed people off benefits – has been considerable (Grogger *et al.* 2002).

Another example concerns a group of people for whom at first sight the term 'client' seems inapposite – taxpayers.[7] However, as discussed above, as 'obligatees' they do have an exchange relationship with tax authorities alongside the coercive relationship that is also present. The exchange is one of behaviours rather than of 'money for services', in that the taxpayer 'pays' in compliance with tax laws.

One of the key tasks in tax administration – collecting the money – is performed not by taxpayers but by third parties, namely employers who withhold the tax out of employees' pay before they receive it, under a 'pay-as-you earn' (PAYE) system. However, the other key task is dependent on the individual taxpayer doing some work. This is the job of reconciling accounts at the end of each financial year, to ensure that the right amount of tax has been paid – operationalized through the annual submission of tax returns. What makes this necessary is that taxation has become an instrument of economic and social policy, applied through a variety of deductions, concessions, subsidies and allowances, which lead to variations in the annual tax owed (typically leading to a modest refund).

In America and Australia, all individual taxpayers submit annual tax returns. This requires them to perform a number of tasks: retaining receipts and other documents through the year (and for some years afterwards in case of audit); entering information accurately and honestly into a tax return form; and lodging the form together with whatever documentation is required. Given the circumstances, the tax system cannot function without this work. Long and Swingen (1991:642) report research which estimated that in the USA in 1988, the work done by taxpayers on individual federal income tax returns amounted to 25 times the work-hours expended by Internal Revenue Service (IRS) staff.

In Britain, many individual taxpayers are not required to submit annual returns. The reason is that the UK tax system is somewhat simpler, with fewer and more standardized deductions, and Her Majesty's Revenue and Customs (HMRC) is able more easily to tally taxpayers' obligations along the way.[8] However, some individual taxpayers have multiple sources of income, with differing incidences of tax obligation, each applied in isolation and calling for overall reconciliation at year-end. These taxpayers are present in all three countries. In each case the tax authority is unable to ensure the right amount of tax is being paid overall without taxpayers lodging returns.

Of course, in many cases these co-productive relationships are mediated by a third party: the tax agent or accountant. Tax authorities have sought to encourage the use of tax agents, with the aim of improving the accuracy of returns. However, even in these cases, some work is still required of the taxpayer, in retaining documents and giving information to the agent.

These examples could be generalized to many areas of public sector work, such as education, health, environmental protection, policing or community welfare. In all these cases, there is a degree of interdependency between organizational production and client co-production. This gives public managers good reason to take account of the role of their clients – they are necessarily contributors to the creation of value.

But the story does not end there. In many cases, while it may be possible for the organization to produce value without clients' involvement, it may nevertheless be able to do so better or at less cost if it does enlist client co-production. This is the situation where the respective contributions of the organization and the clients are substitutes for each other, and the latter is able to do the task better.

For example, a public housing department seeking to reduce antisocial behaviour, such as vandalism or petty crime, on high-rise estates ('projects' in the US) could presumably employ security staff to patrol the area and catch or warn off offenders. However, on large estates the cost-effectiveness of doing so may be substantial, and the resultant local atmosphere unacceptably repressive. Alternatively, the same problems might be tackled if the tenants were to adopt a sense of 'ownership' of the estate, and organize themselves as a more functioning community, as occurs under tenant management. Such communities can apply behavioural norms which discourage antisocial acts, as tenants develop greater respect for each other and become more solicitous of each other's security and of their physical environment and facilities. Effects of this type have been observable in tenant participation or neighbourhood renewal projects in each of the three countries. In this way, private value for individual clients can be enhanced by communal action to produce collective (public) value for groups of clients. (It is true that client co-production can be less cost-effective in some cases than organizational production, as government organizations tend to have advantages such as scale and expertise that enable them to do the work better or cheaper.)

The overall implication of this analysis, however, is that client co-production is not just a nice option but a hard-nosed imperative for many public sector organizations; they simply cannot produce public value without enlisting clients as co-producers. The question, therefore, is how they can better elicit that contribution.

What induces clients to co-produce?

Two kinds of factors affect whether clients will contribute time and effort to co-production. One is their willingness to do so, which is prompted by a complex mix of motivators, which I will consider in three groupings: (1) sanctions; (2) material rewards; and (3) non-material motivators. The other factor is clients' ability to co-produce, which is a function both of the relative complexity of the task and of their own capacities.

Willingness: sanctions

The evidence from the cases discussed in the previous section of this chapter indicates that both sanctions and material rewards are problematic motivators of client co-production. At best, sanctions are inadequate as motivators of client willingness, and at worst they tend to generate perverse behaviour, while material rewards only seem to have a motivational effect where the co-productive task is relatively simple.

The essential reason why sanctions are problematic is that they are not good generators of complex positive actions, which lie at the heart of client co-production. To act co-productively, as opposed to refraining from something prohibited, is to move from an inertial to an active state. This calls for 'consummate cooperation' rather than grudging compliance, one where judgement, forethought and discretion are required: to recall or compile an information input, to gain new skills or attributes, or to utilize an organizational output. By contrast, sanctions do not connect with these impulses, and indeed tend to de-motivate clients from contributing. Two of the cases illustrate this.

One is that of programmes for the long-term unemployed. The research on the impact of sanctions tends to focus more on intermediate effects on the motivations of the unemployed rather than on labour market outcomes (Riccio *et al.* 1994; Handler and Hasenfeld 1997; Finn *et al.* 1998; Millar 2000). On the latter, even the most positive verdict on sanctions, from the US Manpower Demonstration Research Corporation (MDRC), is somewhat qualified.[9] In a synthesis of the extant research on programme outcomes it declared:

> Programmes that actively enforced mandates by reducing the welfare grants of those who did not participate produced higher participation rates than did low-enforcement programmes. Beyond a threshold level, however, increases in sanctioning rates were not associated with higher participation rates. (MDRC 2002)

However, another synthesis by the RAND Corporation found that hardly any of the studies lending weight to this type of finding distinguished the impact of sanctions from that of other features of the programmes studied (Grogger *et al.* 2002:xxi). In particular, programmes emphasizing sanctions also tend to stress a 'work first' approach, which other research shows to be a little more effective than 'education first' (see below). Studies in the UK and Australia show a similarly unclear relationship between sanctioning and successful job placement (Considine 2001; Handler 2004).

Greater research has gone into how sanctions affect the unemployed themselves. First, it is clear, as the MDRC report acknowledged, that sanctions are applied most frequently in the US to the most disadvantaged jobseekers (for example least literate, addicts, having health problems or criminal records, or lacking social skills), who are also more often unclear about their obligations. The same applies in Britain and Australia (Vincent 1998; ACOSS 2001). This suggests that penalties fall more heavily on the very group which is least able to respond positively to them than on wilful non-compliers (Klerman et al 2000).

Second, as MDRC's synthesis puts it, 'aggressive enforcement of sanctions may be counterproductive' (2002). A number of studies report that sanctioning usually provokes non-compliant behaviour (Hasenfeld and Weaver 1996; Weaver and Hasenfeld 1997). However, other studies find that sanctions prompt more active job search, or at least exit from welfare (Dolton and O'Neill 1996; O'Neill and Hill

2001; Saunders *et al.* 2001). What may help make sense of these contending findings is a more finely grained approach, which acknowledges some segmentation in responses by the unemployed, based on differing attitudes. This is offered by several studies that show varying responses to sanctioning among the unemployed, in which some are prompted to search energetically for a job, whereas others become resentful or demoralized, and avoid or give up seeking work (Vincent 1998).

This raises a practical problem. If organizations apply sanctions to all their clients, some of them will be de-motivated from co-producing. On the other hand, if they refrain from applying sanctions to any of their clients, some may take advantage of the lax regime and withhold co-production. This issue turns out to be relevant to all clients, as will be discussed later.

One impact of sanctions is clear from the literature – while their impact on people's willingness to search for work is debatable, they are powerfully effective at getting people off the welfare rolls. That means, of course, that the need for co-production ceases!

In the case of taxation, the strong evidence is that, given an established compliance regime, increasing legal sanctions by itself does not encourage greater taxpayer willingness to complete their returns honestly, but in fact discourages it. Research indicates that the tightening of audits and penalties against taxpayers provokes resentment and gaming behaviour on the part of those to whom they have been applied (Schwartz and Orleans 1967; Schmolders 1970; Spicer and Lundstedt 1976; Levi 1988; Wallschutzky 1988; Roth *et al.* 1989; Kinsey 1992). Noting that the percentage of tax returns subject to detailed audit is quite small in most countries, and 'penalties seldom more than a fraction of unpaid taxes', Alm *et al.* (1992a:313) concluded that 'additional factors [besides sanctions] must play a role – perhaps a dominant one – in tax compliance' (see also Gray and Scholz 1991; Kinsey 1992; Sheffrin and Triest 1992; Gunningham and Grabosky 1998; May and Winter 1999; May 2002.)

Sanctions are deficient as motivators of positive behaviour for two reasons. One is that they signal that the required behaviour (co-productive work) is something unpleasant to be avoided. This may be true in some cases, but in others it arguably is not. For example, long-term jobless people may find intrinsic pleasure in the acquisition of skills in labour market programmes, but this intrinsic pleasure evaporates if they are told they must do these things. The other reason is that to apply enforcement – that is, to limit people's choices, monitor their behaviour, and threaten sanctions – is to imply that they are not to be trusted. Confronted with this message, the clients' likely response may not be one of increased willingness but of grudging compliance. Their behaviour may change in the short term, but not their long-term internalized attitudes (Bandura 1986; Ayres and Braithwaite 1992; Frey 1997). Instead of being willing to contribute, clients who are subject to sanctions are likely to engage in opportunistic behaviour to minimize their contributions of time and effort. This can set up a spiral which is increasingly destructive of clients' voluntary impulse to contribute, as clients find loopholes and the organization imposes more stringent rules to close the loopholes. The end result is that clients experience the organization's enforcement as arbitrary and rule-bound, and the organization finds it increasingly costly to secure compliance (Bardach and Kagan 1982; Braithwaite 1985).

If sanctions have these limitations, why do organizations such as employment and tax agencies use them, and persist in doing so? One reason is that sanctions elicit co-production by appealing to people's sense of fairness. The enforcement of sanctions against the non-compliant provides a guarantee to those more inclined to be cooperative that the process to which they are contributing is fair. It reassures them that all the other clients are being required to contribute their fair share of time and effort, and that they are not 'suckers' who are co-producing more than the rest (Levi 1988). In this context, sanctions appeal to an important non-material value – distributive justice. This is demonstrated every time a regulatory agency undertakes high-profile enforcement actions against corporate tax-evaders.

The other reason is that clients differ in their propensity to comply. In particular, some – usually a minority (Kagan and Scholz 1984; Braithwaite *et al.* 1994) – may be wilfully non-compliant, and will respond only to firm compulsion. This poses a problem for the agency, alluded to earlier in this chapter – treating all clients as if they deserve to be trusted will enable the non-compliant to take advantage of an 'easier' regime, but on the other hand treating them as if they are non-compliant will prompt resentment on the part of the compliant. A useful approach to dealing with this problem is to pursue a strategy of 'responsive regulation' or 'tit-for-tat', in which all clients are initially treated as cooperative, but then those who breach the trust are punished, while those who after breaching revert to cooperative behaviour are again treated as compliant (Scholz 1984; Ayres and Braithwaite 1992).

In summary, sanctions generally do not mobilize material self-interest to generate client willingness to co-produce. They are ineffective and sometimes counter-productive in stimulating the requisite voluntary impulse. To elicit voluntary impulses to contribute, organizations need to offer more positive rewards.

Willingness: material rewards

The most obvious positive incentives within the contractualist framework are material rewards, the basic idea being that if people are offered rewards proportionate to their performance then they will be motivated to perform better. But interestingly, to use Herzberg's terms, they turn out to be more like 'hygiene factors' (for example basic pre-conditions or enablers) than motivators (Herzberg *et al.* 1993). They are only motivators to the extent that the task is relatively simple.

In the case of unemployed people, material rewards have loomed large in both the literature and practice, starting with a recognition that, at least for some people (for example, those with large families), the level of income to be derived from working in a paid job is not much greater than that from unemployment benefits. Aside from being part of the rationale for applying sanctions, this has been one of the justifications for the introduction of time limits for benefits, introduced under the Temporary Aid for Needy Families (TANF) legislation in the US in 1996.[10] A more positive response, by contrast, has been to intro-duce some form of income supplement for long-term unemployed people who get a job, available either continuously or for some initial period of being employed – for instance the Earned Income Tax Credit in the US or the Working Families Tax Credit in the UK (Bloom and Michalopoulos 2001; Finn 2002). This has the effect not so much of adding an incentive to find work, but of removing a disincentive.

However, because these people are long-term unemployed, the prospect of additional income alone is not sufficient to prompt active job search, because of their deep demoralization in the face of repeated rejections from employers. Research to date indicates that such supple-ments by themselves have a modest effect on employment outcomes, but in concert with provision of positive assistance, such as job search training or work experience, they have a considerable impact (Bloom and Michalopoulos 2001; Finn 2002; Grogger *et al.* 2002). This is because positive assistance taps into other, non-material motivations.

More significantly, material rewards entail economic exchange, which 'stipulates the exact quantities to be exchanged', rather than social exchange, which entails 'unspecified obligations' (Blau 1964:93). This has implications for the relationship between the organization and the client. Blau points out that 'social exchange tends to engender feel-ings of personal obligation, gratitude and trust; purely economic exchange as such does not'. This is because the very diffuseness of the exchange, the lack of specifically defined reciprocity, 'requires trusting others to discharge their obligations' (1964:94). Thus social exchange fuels a spiral of rising trust: 'By discharging their obligations for ser-vices rendered, individuals demonstrate their trustworthiness, and the gradual expansion of mutual service is accompanied by a parallel growth of mutual trust' (Blau 1964:94, 315).

By contrast, economic exchange engenders a spirit of vigilance, 'with each party watching the other for infractions; jealously guarding con-cessions; and refusing any request for extra-contractual favours unless precisely defined reciprocation is guaranteed' (Fox 1974:72, emphasis added). This is unlikely to be a problem where the task is simple to prescribe and check, such as entering postcodes on letters. But where the task calls for 'extra-contractual favours', involving the exercise of discretion, tacit knowledge, or additional enthusiasm by the client, for example the long-term unemployed, the requisite level and intensity of willingness will not be elicited by precise calculation of reciprocity.

Contrary to the assumptions underlying the contractualist approach, eliciting contributions from clients requires more than the wielding of carrots and sticks. The more complex the task, the more it is likely to call for consummate cooperation rather than merely grudging compliance. This in turn calls for appeals to more complex, diffuse, non-material motivations.

Willingness: non-material motivators

Where co-production activities are complex, one or more of three types of motivators may play a role.

One is intrinsic motivation (Deci 1975) – the client's sense of self-determination and competence. This is most evident in programmes for the unemployed. First, to the extent that assistance is tailored to individuals' needs – as evidenced by client 'diagnostic' interviews and individualized intensive activity packages in all three countries – it shows respect for them as human beings, and enhances their sense of self-efficacy. A synthesis study of best practice in US programmes found 'personalized client attention' had a powerful impact on employment outcomes (Bloom *et al.* 2001:40).

Second, programme assistance which increases unemployed peoples' confidence, sense of competence and autonomy is more likely to motivate them to search actively for work. Interestingly, the debate about whether clients should be directed to 'work first' or 'education first' says little about this issue. It seems likely that both approaches can connect with clients' intrinsic motivations – 'work first' because it gives jobseekers renewed experience and a sense of competence in the world of work (Gottschalk 2005), and 'education first' because it enhances their skills. Indeed, one study found that the most successful programmes were those which offered a mix of both types of options (Bloom and Michalopoulos 2001).

Another motivator is sociality – the inherent benefits of associating with others, such as 'socializing, congeniality, the sense of group membership and identification, the status resulting from membership, fun and conviviality, [or] the maintenance of social distinctions' (Clark and Wilson 1961:134–5). To the extent that peers' approval of co-productive behaviour or disapproval of non-co-productive behaviour affects clients, it makes sense for agencies to seek to influence these peers or to establish collective interactions. 'Job clubs', in which groups of the unemployed jointly acquire and apply job search skills, is one example. Seeking to enlist tax agents in promoting compliant behaviour is another.

Finally, clients' propensity to co-produce is affected by their normative or expressive values – their norms and commitments about moral and social issues, such as saving the environment, exposing corruption, or supporting the needy. Contrary to the assumptions of contractualism, people may affirm these values even when it is against their material self-interest to do so. The research makes it clear that taxpayers are significantly more likely to comply if they feel that they receive satisfactory material or symbolic value from government and that other taxpayers are paying their fair share (Schwartz and Orleans 1967; Spicer and Becker 1980; Levi 1988; Roth et al. 1989; Alm et al. 1992; Scholz 1994). Thus their willingness to co-produce will be enhanced if they perceive that government is devoting their tax dollars to valuable purposes, and is applying enforcement firmly and visibly against tax-evaders. By doing these things, government is appealing to expressive values concerning collective purposes and distributive justice.

This seems to be most salient where an important part of the value enjoyed by the client is public value. By ensuring that the right amount of taxes is collected, tax authorities provide the means for resourcing the whole array of public value outputs delivered by government. It is therefore very telling that taxpayers' willingness to contribute to the tax office's work is enhanced by appeals to precisely the kinds of motivations that attach merit to public value – expressive values. Similarly, the military's ability to recruit for war is enhanced if there is a public perception that the war is justified.

Clients' willingness to co-produce is affected by a complex mix of factors. Moreover, different segments of clients are motivated by different factors. The efficacy of most of those such as non-material rewards is less immediate and targeted than the 'high-powered incentives' (Frant 1996) of managerialism, but significant nonetheless. The implication of the research is that if public organizations want to elicit co-productive activity, they must pay heed to these motivational complexities. They must 'give' their clients things they value – often non-material values – if they expect their clients to 'give' them co-productive effort.

Ability to co-produce public value

Of course, whether clients will co-produce depends on their ability as well as their willingness to do so. One way of fostering this ability is to make the co-production task easier, as exemplified by tax authorities taking steps to simplify the tax return process, by rationalizing the tax laws, simplifying the return forms, and making lodgement easier. In these cases, the use of technology seems to have been an important factor in reducing the complexity of the co-productive work.

The other method is to enhance the client's own capacities to perform it, for example by providing information, advice or training. Tax authorities have placed considerable emphasis on upgrading client service, information and assistance. In the unemployment case, clients' lack of job search skills has been addressed through job search training, and their lack of job-readiness through skills training and work experience.

Conclusion: the terms of the exchange

This analysis has posited co-production as a type of exchange between public sector organizations and their clients, and suggested how it might be optimized. At first sight, given the power imbalance between organizations and clients, this may seem an unrealistic, even naive idea. But this imbalance is no greater than that which exists between a private sector firm and its customers. In both the public and private cases, while the individual client/customer has little power, collectively clients can have significant power, because the organization needs certain things from them. Osborne and Gaebler fail to understand this when they argue that government organizations do not have any incentive to pay attention to their clients because, unlike their private sector counterparts, they don't earn any revenue from them (1993). In fact, a public agency can 'earn' something very valuable from their clients – their contribution to the achievement of the organization's outputs or outcomes. This will be all the more valuable to the extent that the organization cannot function without this contribution, as my examples illustrate. And as the examples also show, eliciting this contribution will entail offering some tangible or intangible benefits to clients. Thus, the process of delivering private value to clients can have the effect of creating public value for the citizenry.

Chapter 9

Framing the Production of Health in Terms of Public Value: Lessons from the UK National Health Service

JONATHAN Q. TRITTER[1]

Introduction

This chapter explores the complexity of the multiple responsibilities for health-related services and argues that these can be helpfully understood by framing the nature of the activity in terms of public value creation. It draws on a public value framework to explore examples of the collaborations and partnerships that exist at community level aimed at producing better health, and also to identify further opportunities. The chapter concludes with a discussion of the role of the individual and the potential contribution of patient and public involvement (citizen engagement) to the pursuit of 'good health' in a way that maximizes the production of public value.

A public value framework

A public value framework provides a useful way to understand how to promote entrepreneurial goals by public managers, or what Moore (1995) labels 'value mission'. Central to this approach is the identification of those who support and create the 'authorizing environment' for the 'value mission'; such support is central to justifying the aim as legitimate. In addition a public value approach clarifies the potential sources of operational capacity or resources to achieve the 'value mission'; importantly these resources may be outside the direct control of the lead organization. Both of these are interdependent and relate to the specifics of the 'value mission' (see Figure 9.1).

Thus the lead organization is given the opportunity to access resources from other organizations that share a common value

Figure 9.1 *The strategic triangle.*

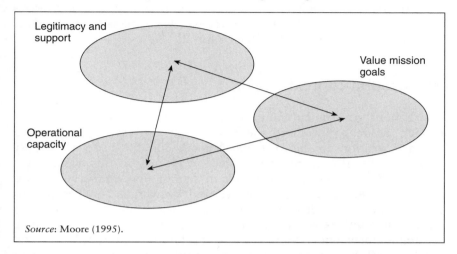

Legitimacy and support

Value mission goals

Operational capacity

Source: Moore (1995).

mission. This differentiation between leadership of the value mission and the provision of resources provides the basis for a distinctive form of collaboration between different organizations and actors and is central to a public value framework. The 'sharing' of a value mission that achieves the ends of multiple organizations creates scope for efficiency benefits through collaboration. In addition there are likely to be benefits associated with staff and organizational learning and capacity-building as a product of successful collaboration.

A second component of the public value framework that is essential to the argument in this chapter relates to the 'authorizing environment' to create public value. In order for the lead organization to successfully access (or annex) resources to achieve the agreed value mission its actions must be 'legitimated' by organizations that act in the same environment. The 'authorizing environment' brings together these legitimators to justify the value mission and attest to the validity of the lead organization's ability and position.

A further vital component of a public value framework is the process of co-production with partner organizations and also end users of the value mission. In the case of health, co-production at a basic level relates to people eating a healthy diet, taking exercise and not smoking or drinking to excess. The role of the individual in 'being healthy' and contributing to their own wellbeing is in tension with a traditional medical model that treats illness as a deficit that needs to be cured. Healthcare from this latter perspective often takes the form of a paternalistic approach and grants little agency to the individual. The assumptions on which this model is predicated are, as will be discussed, increasingly being challenged. A public value framework provides a conceptual tool for better understanding and framing the collaboration between public, private and voluntary sector organizations with users, citizens and communities, which is necessary to produce more and better health and wellbeing for all.

Background context

The Labour government came to power in the UK in 1997 with an explicit desire to promote the renewal of civil society through a changed relationship between government and the people; typically labelled under the rubric of the Third Way. Key to this agenda was greater participation by local people in determining what services they want, how they should be provided and by whom. Nowhere is this agenda more apparent than in the area of healthcare. The Third Way agenda in health is visible in a range of government policy including the requirement under Section 11 of the Health and Social Care Act 2001 for all NHS organizations to consult with users about current and planned services.

The reorganization of the NHS prompted by *Shifting the Balance of Power* and the creation of primary care trusts (PCTs) marked a sea change in the articulation of the relationship between local people and healthcare services. PCTs are patient-centred and adopt a public health perspective to work collaboratively with local authorities and other agencies:

> PCTs are now at the centre of the NHS and will get 75% of the NHS budget. As they are local organizations, they are in the best position to understand the needs of their community, so they can make sure that the organizations providing health and social care services are working effectively. (Department of Health 2004a)

The majority of NHS funding is being delivered through PCTs, which act as the main coordinators of primary and secondary care and directly provide community services. These changes resulted in five clear national priorities for the NHS: health improvement, chronic care management, promoting personal care, re-engineering waiting times and value for money.

Defining a value mission

For NHS organizations the central 'value mission' must be the production of better health for users. This aim benefits individual users, communities, industry the economy and society as a whole. For the

Figure 9.2   *The authorizing environment for the primary care trust*

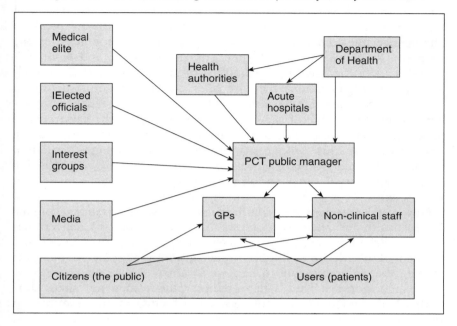

purposes of this chapter, I focus on how this 'value mission' can be accomplished within a local health economy. Within this context, the production of better health is legitimated and supported by a broad array of public sector organizations including local government (and local elected representatives), GP practices, primary and acute trusts (and local medical and other health professionals), local schools and other educational organizations (and educational managers and teachers) (see Figure 9.2). From a broader perspective, voluntary and community health organizations and local employers, as well as the Strategic Health Authorities and the Department of Health, support this aim. The lead organization for this value mission, however, is the PCT.

The different components of this diagram are direct and indirect beneficiaries of the value mission. At some level we, as users, benefit directly from better health. But families, employers and the state are key indirect beneficiaries, because ill health disrupts family life, lessens productivity, compromises the workforce and limits the tax base. It is also worth noting that there is likely to be significant overlap in the authorizing environment because, for example, some members of the medical elite may also be elected officials or employed within other parts of the health system (like the acute hospitals).

What is also apparent is that the degree of influence exercised by each of the parties on decisions made by the PCT manager varies in terms of their position and forms of authority and these are likely to change over the course of time; this is more difficult to indicate on the diagram. Influence varies with time, context, political (and 'Political') agendas and is mediated by the culture of the PCT. While PCTs are relatively new organizations they are built on the existing structure of general practice and all general practitioners are independent contractors to the NHS. One of the consequences has been the variations in style, leadership and culture within individual GP surgeries and the challenges that this produces in terms of developing a common purpose. The adoption of a relatively broad purpose – producing better health for all – may permit the signing-up of a heterogeneous set of GPs and GP surgeries to a common value mission.

However, agreement to a common value mission, a policy to pursue better health for all, does not establish the capacity to deliver that mission. Broad agreement grants legitimacy for a common policy and is essential in order to enable the organization to take responsibility for leading the 'value mission' to harness or annex resources overseen by other organizations. Thus, what a public value framework makes clear is that 'value missions' are not necessarily limited by the resources or operational capacity under the direct control of any single manager in a particular organization, but instead are a function of the resources which may be made available by other organizations which share and legitimate the value mission. This embeds co-production at the centre of the public value framework. In other words, for the achievement of the value mission, operational capacity $\neq$ organizational capacity, but instead operational capacity = organizational capacity (of leading organization) + partner resources + co-producer resources. It is also worth noting that users, families and local communities can be key partners in the production of health, and that the voluntary and community sectors are continuing to grow in importance as part of the co-production of health (Depeartment of Health 2004b).

The sources of good health are as likely to emerge from outside the publicly funded health system as within it. That is, good housing, a satisfying job, a clean environment are all essential to good health but none are the remit of the formal health system. Health, more than many aspects of the public sector, is dependent on boundary bridging and cooperation between different public, private and voluntary sector organizations. Cooperation and collaboration with the voluntary sector is made more complex by the diversity of organizational forms and the degree of segmentation. Even within health, very few voluntary sector organizations are oriented to communities as a whole but instead specify a particular category of patients or a specific condition.

The doctor–patient relationship: changing responsibilities

Historically, conceptual models of health were predicated on the sick patient. For these models good health was based on seeking medical attention and following medical advice (Parsons 1975). This paternalistic model has been challenged and a different relationship between patient and healthcare providers has emerged that embraces an active role in decision-making about treatment for the patient. Further evaluations of challenges to the health systems and population health in developed countries suggest that long-term and chronic conditions are likely to generate the greatest need for health resources (Wanless 2003). Expertise about a chronic condition at an individual level is likely to rest predominantly with the individual patient whose personal understanding of their condition is informed by day-to-day experience rather than episodic investigations.

This has spurred a reconfiguration of health services that seeks to shift responsibility for the management of long-term and chronic conditions on to the 'patient'. For the British NHS this is supported by the Expert Patients Programme. An import from the USA (Lorig *et al.* 1999, 2000), this programme consists of a free self-management course run over six weekly sessions. The aim of the course is to turn people's experience of their own condition into practical skills that can make a big difference to the quality of their lives (Kennedy *et al.* 2003). This change is presented as an aspect of increased patient and public participation in health and is now seen as a new touchstone for government health policy, not just in Britain but internationally (Tritter and McCallum 2006).

Such a shift reframes the nature and contribution of co-production to creating health. The increased recognition of patient and lay expertise in relation to the individual's own condition shifts more responsibility for 'staying well' from expert health providers (the PCT and the physician) to the individual patient (and their informal carers). Appreciation of this change has implications too for the authorizing environment, as greater significance may be placed on authorization from 'users'. There is little suggestion, however, in European health policy of this change being reflected in the relative resourcing of the different parts of the environment.

Patient and public involvement in health

Health policies across the OECD countries have sought to promote opportunities for users (patients and the public) to be involved in various aspects of healthcare from treatment decision-making to service evaluation and development (Vallgårda 2001; Vos 2002). A range of justifications for public and patient involvement exist, from the promotion of democratic and taxpayer accountability to ensuring more appropriately tailored services and fully informed consent. Even in healthcare systems with limited private sector involvement, market models of consumer choice are being used to promote reorganizations based on a rhetoric of strengthening patient choice. Involvement is presented as a mechanism for generating locally responsive higher quality healthcare systems and ensuring a model of accountability that is less reliant on medical self-regulation. But involvement also shifts some of the responsibility from managers of health systems to the users who have had a say in their design. The development of this relationship may also have the benefit of making the public (the users and potential users of the health services) more aware of the trade-offs that have to be made in resource allocation decisions. The growing recognition that increased health provision by itself has limited impact on the health of individuals or on the health of populations is further evidence of the importance of co-production of health with patients and potential patients.

Types of patient and public involvement

Patient participation in treatment decisions is one type of involvement but is perhaps a central aspect of patient-centred care. Similarly, involvement in service development, typically a consultation exercise with the local community, has a long history in the NHS (Baggott 2005). Attempts to ask users to prioritize services (for example, care for one condition over another) occur less frequently (Bryan *et al.* 2002), particularly in primary care (Crisp *et al.* 1996). The evaluation of services by users, however, has become common practice; simple satisfaction questionnaires, and more robust investigations, are now part of many audit exercises.

A final category of user involvement relates to participation in research. The promotion of randomized controlled trials as the gold-standard research methodology has increased calls for greater user involvement in research strategy (Bastian 1994; Johanson *et al.* 2002; Involve 2003). Recruitment of trial participants and a broader willingness of patients and the public to participate in research is related directly to the salience of research questions and agenda to their interests and illness experience. The advice on research governance in the NHS identifies the involvement of users in developing good practice (NHS R&D Forum Research Governance Working Group 2003). Users, as patients, have been involved in teaching medical students through testimonials about their own experience and, more recently, through participation in curriculum development (Greenfield *et al.* 2001).

Clearly, there are interactions and linkages between different categories of user involvement – service development may have a direct impact on the range of individual treatment options that exist, and service evaluation may identify inequities in access that affect individual participation in treatment. User participation in setting a research agenda may have an impact on shaping provision and service organization, and therefore options for treatment (Involve 2003). All of these categories are predicated on the co-production of health and therefore a degree of joint responsibility. Some types of involvement, however, relate more to individual patients while others are better framed as collective issues.

The policy background for patient and public involvement in the NHS

The NHS has long sought to demonstrate user involvement and patient-centred care; the potential has existed since Community Health Councils (CHCs) were established in 1974. Despite their achievements, criticisms of these organizations (ranging from geographical variations in working practices to an inability to reflect the diversity of local communities) led, at least indirectly, to their abolition in 2002 (Barnet Community Health Council 2001; Sang and Dabbs 2003). Other developments over the last decade have responded to the growing pressure to be proactive in seeking community views (Department of Health 1992), while the Patient's Charter focused on responsiveness to individual expectations by using the rhetoric of patient rights to clarify service aspirations nationally and locally (Department of Health 1991, 1996; Tritter 1994).

However, the perception of a centralist bureaucracy remained, reflecting a widespread view that patient-centred services require direct local democracy and demand-led care. In response to these criticisms, new legislation, particularly section 11 of the Health and Social Care Act 2001, mandated more direct forms of user involvement. This requires all NHS organizations to engage with users in service planning and evaluation, and facilitate participation in individual treatment decision-making. The NHS Reform and Healthcare Professionals Act 2002 established the bodies responsible for implementation, while *Shifting the Balance of Power* (Department of Health 2001a) set out the organizational changes needed to deliver *The NHS Plan* (Department of Health 2000), all of which set significant challenges for more effective and inclusive patient and public involvement.

Current policy shifts (Department of Health 2006) seek to locate patient and public involvement in local communities, as defined by local authority areas (municipal government), rather than linking them to a specific health organization. As local authorities have responsibility for social care services this sets the scene for greater integration between health and social care services: more explicit linking of NHS and local authority responsibilities in relation to services improving health.

Justifying patient and public involvement: voters, taxpayers and consumers

Rationales for, and definitions of, patient public involvement in health services occupy a continuum between democratic and consumerist models (Croft and Beresford 1993, 1995; Feldberg and Vipond 1999). Typically, the distinctions relate to rights inherent in citizenship versus those of individual choice in the marketplace. The diversity of approaches to patient and public involvement reflects different theoretical bases, but chief among these are distinctions in the question of accountability to patients and the public as voters, taxpayers, and consumers. These three aspects of accountability are highlighted in UK policy and are often used interchangeably. The aims of patient and public involvement, however, and the methods used to engage users can be understood only with regard to the relative primacy of one of these three justifications.

In relation to the first, involvement through voting, there are difficulties in recruiting and retaining involved users, and even once elected or appointed, user members may not participate. Most patient and public involvement initiatives require a critical mass of interested people who will stand for election, attend regular meetings and participate in training. In one North London area, during 1999–2000, more than half of the members attended less than two-thirds of the full Community Health Council meetings and only a third attended more than two-thirds of the meetings of project groups for which they had volunteered (Barnet CHC 2001). The results of the elections of the boards of governors of Foundation Trusts and the composition of Patient Forums in England reinforce this observation (Klein 2004).

A second justification for greater user involvement is based on users being seen as citizens and taxpayers, and relates to the public funding of national health services. Emerging from a decade of neo-liberal-inspired public sector reform (Osborne and Gaebler 1992), many Governments remain concerned with 'value for money' justifications for public spending and increasingly feel the need to strengthen the public's voice in decisions about the organization and delivery of health services. More recent reforms embrace this philosophy by seeking to empower staff to be responsive to the expressed needs of patients and the public (Department of Health 2001).

The third justification for greater patient and public involvement relates to the promotion of a patient choice agenda which has redefined the focus of health service provision and reframed healthcare providers as vendors and patients as consumers. Patient and public involvement is presented as *the* feedback mechanism for the expression of consumer views – an essential component of markets. However, to act as consumers, patients must have the necessary information to choose both between providers and between types of provision, and their choices must be able to change service provision.

Building a community-led Health Service

The public value framework not only provides concepts with explanatory power in relation to health systems; it also helps to illuminate some of the complex practical challenges facing health policymakers and managers. The following primary care examples illustrate the notion of leadership through collaborative working and co-production as a means of generating public value outcomes.

Health improvement

Primary care has a central role in health promotion and preventative care, but like the NHS in general can contribute only a small part to general health improvement. General practice must therefore change by linking to local government and the voluntary sector to create and promote health communities. GP practices sit at the heart of these communities and when joined up to local schools, early years and youth services can play a vital role in shaping how people learn and manage their own health. While directors of public health may be able to identify inequality trends in local populations, strategies to respond to such needs are far more likely to be effective if they come from within the community – that is, from a local surgery. A key aspect of health is the interaction with other forms of inequality.

Chronic care management

With the growing recognition of the role of the patient's expertise in the management of their own condition the role of the Health Service must shift to one of facilitating learning and collaboration; must change from chronic disease management to chronic care management. Instead of being based on a long-term epidemiological perspective, the approach to these issues must be grounded in the lived experience of patients. PCTs have a central role in promoting a whole-life approach to the management of care in a way that facilitates responses to issues of co-morbidity and the impact of age. While hospitals have an essential role in providing expert treatment and diagnosis, helping patients to learn to live with their conditions must be grounded in their local community, their local surgery and their family doctor.

Personalized care

Getting it right for the individual patient is the key to delivering high-quality healthcare. This requires an approach based on listening to people explain what they need and responding to it – an approach that challenges traditional forms of healthcare delivery. Consultations between health personnel and patients are decisions about care and treatment to be arrived at, based on expert advice. The need to tailor healthcare to the multiple and particular needs of patients based on their own understanding provides new challenges for the NHS but particularly for PCTs and other health commissioners. The evolution of public and patient involvement, at a systemic level, will help reshape the service to meet these new challenges.

The Brunswick Centre in Warwickshire provides an example of how these approaches can work in practice. A dilapidated local library and health clinic were replaced by a 'Healthy Living Centre'. The Centre provides library services, a computer cafe, a community hall that caters for a wide range of community groups and a coffee/snack bar. This all works alongside the health services that are delivered by the PCT. Members of the local community often visit with a social engagement in mind but are signposted to a variety of preventative health services.

A whole-system approach

What PCTs offer is a whole-system approach to the organization and delivery of healthcare which is structured around patient care pathways. Pathways must be anchored in the patient's GP surgery, and as the coherence and coordination of the process becomes clear the actual time for each phase of the process is less important. Such an approach places the GP at both the beginning and end of the pathway or care cycle and reaffirms a local GP as a central point of reference for their entire treatment. This reconceptualization also reinforces the need for NHS organizations, social services, and other organizations providing healthcare or information, to work together to clarify and specify care pathways. PCTs potentially have a central role, on behalf of the GPs and their local patient populations, to coordinate these pathways and make the patient experience as seamless and unproblematic as possible.

Despite the multiple organizations and actors within the authorizing environment, PCTs have a particular location that makes them best-placed to be the lead organization for a value mission that is focused on individuals within a community. The relationship between the target of the value mission – people in a community – and the members of the authorizing environment (stakeholders) and potential lead organizations is central to the decision on which organization should lead.

Key attributes of a community that make it attractive to live in or move to are good schools and good GP surgeries. Good-quality, accessible primary care and a long-term relationship with a surgery lie at the heart of every community. Primary care is the bedrock of the NHS and for people living in a community the most common and most appreciated aspect of the NHS is their local surgery and the professionals who work there. Lessening the health inequalities between communities and working to reduce the chronic illness and improve the health of the public requires a successful alliance between people and the public sector. As John Reid, the then health secretary reiterated, in announcing the consultation on the next stages to improving the health of the public, 'people and their communities are the core to the development of the health of the public' (Department of Health 2004a).

Conclusions: valuing health

A healthy population is essential for a country's future prosperity. The cost of ill health in lost working time, in particular the costs of long-term and chronic conditions, is significant. Further, the need for informal care by relatives of an ill person also has implications for their productivity. These issues, let alone those associated with quality of life, require more effective strategies for helping people to manage their health throughout their lifetime and stay healthy for longer. Historically this role has been a central aspect of primary care services. Hospital-based healthcare is hugely expensive. Evidence from managed care models in the US illustrate that it is possible to separate expert medicine from the hospital context. Forms of assertive outreach and innovative responses to decreasing accidents among the elderly reinforce this conclusion in the UK setting. Finding innovative ways to shift more care out of hospitals and in doing so freeing up resources for those who need it more is a challenge for the whole NHS but is the central responsibility of PCTs.

Such shifts cannot be accomplished without the legitimation of the role of PCTs as lead organizations for a common value mission. The common assumption by government is that policies that reform and restructure health systems can be effective mechanisms for relocating resources and leadership. One lesson from public value theory is that such an approach can do little to engineer a PCT-led NHS without the promotion of a common value mission and the authorization of the PCT as the lead organization. Shifts in health policy internationally that give greater responsibility to individual patients around the management of their own healthcare, and opportunities to influence the organization and delivery of services, can do little to shift the balance of power unless they engage with the definition of a public value mission and the authorization of a lead organization.

Chapter 10

Public Value Through Innovation and Improvement

JEAN HARTLEY

Introduction

This chapter examines why, how and under what circumstances innovation and improvement of public services may add value to the public sphere. It aims to contribute to the understanding of public value in two ways – first, by examining how innovation and improvement may contribute to the achievement of public value; and second, by using the prism of innovation and improvement to illuminate some aspects of the theory and practice of public value. The focus is on innovation and improvement at the organization and inter-organizational level of analysis (Hartley 2008).

The public value context of innovation and improvement

Under stable conditions (for example where the external and the internal environment of the organization remains much the same over time), public value may be achieved through consistent production processes, delivered steadily, reliably and efficiently with little expectation of change over time, except perhaps for small incremental improvements (Burns and Stalker 1961; Scott 1998). Under such conditions, innovation, seen as step-change, may not be necessary.

However, many industrialized societies have moved beyond the stable state, and others in developing countries have not yet achieved a stable state. The context for governance and public services in many countries is therefore one of profound, systemic political, economic, social and technological change (see Chapters 1 and 2). The definition of public value under such volatile conditions therefore has to be dynamic rather than static, and innovation and improvement become more prominent as a means to achieve public value.

Moore (1995) notes that societies may change their demands on governments, public organizations and public managers because the external environment changes, because citizens may change their needs and preferences, and/or because experience in implementing policies may lead to review or adjustment of those policies and practices. He argues that, therefore, public managers can be thought of as 'explorers commissioned by society to search for public value' (p. 299). The dynamic and changing context suggests the need for adaptation and change within and by public service organizations if they are to create public value on an ongoing basis.

Public value can be conceptualized within an open systems perspective (Scott 1998) which analyses interdependencies between the organization (as the open system) and its external environment (the political, economic, social and physical environment, for example). Open systems theory also predicts that the complexity of these interactions means that outputs and outcomes are bound to include emergent or unanticipated consequences as well as planned or intended ones. This suggests that any theory of public value will have to address unstable as well as stable contexts, and unplanned as well as planned outcomes. Public value theory would appear, therefore, to be receptive to the notion of innovation (as part of a necessary response to pressures for change within a dynamic and/or turbulent environment).

In some of the academic and policy literature innovation is treated as though it has inherent value – as though any innovation is, by definition, good for a firm, an organization or for society and essential as a means for firms to be competitive (for example Chesborough 2003; Tidd *et al.* 2005; Department for Innovation, Universities and Skills 2008). Government and public service organizations have also shown a growing interest in innovation in the last decade (for example Mulgan and Albury 2003; National Audit Office 2006; Audit Commission 2007) and this is not solely a UK phenomenon (for example Altschuler and Behn 1997). Albury argues that 'Innovation is essential to the improvement of public services: it is not an optional luxury but needs to be institutionalised as a deep value.' (2005:51). On the other hand, Moran (2003) comments that the British state suffers from hyper-innovation rather than a shortage of innovation, and he questions the extent to which the impact has been beneficial. Hartley (2005) has noted that innovation does not always lead to improvements in public service outcomes, and this will be examined further in the light of a public value perspective.

The concept of innovation has become popular in UK and US public policy discourse not so much because of any implied or demonstrated link with public value creation, but because of the recognition that the volatile environment facing public service organizations requires not only fine-tuning adjustments and improvements in existing policies, services and governance arrangements, but also disruptive change of the scale and scope that innovation can bring (for example Osborne and Brown 2005; Hartley 2006).

Organizations can use two broad managerial approaches to adapt their products, systems, structures and processes to anticipated and changing circumstances. The first is to fine-tune existing services and service delivery mechanisms in order to improve the quality, efficiency or reach of particular goods and services incrementally ('doing what we do better', according to Tidd *et al.* 2005). The range of 'continuous improvement' methods to undertake such fine-tuning includes, for example, total quality management, lean management, systems improvement, benchmarking and so forth. The second approach is to respond to the changing context more radically, by altering the nature and design of the goods and services offered, and the ways they are provided – and where the experiment is sufficiently different from previous approaches this is often labelled 'innovation'.

Defining innovation

There is a wide variety of meanings attached to innovation in the academic and policy literature, so it is helpful to begin this chapter by clarifying definitions. Bessant (2003) distinguishes between invention – having a bright new idea – and innovation, which is taking the new idea into implementation. Other writers concur that innovation is about ideas in practice (for example Osborne and Brown 2005; Audit Commission 2007). Most writers also suggest that innovation can be distinguished from continuous improvement, by emphasizing that innovation is defined through the degree of disjuncture or discontinuity with past practices – it is a step-change rather than continuous or fine-grained incremental improvement (Lynn 1997; Hartley 2006). This inevitably includes subjective as well as objective judgements of what constitutes step-change (Greenhalgh *et al.* 2004). Innovations may occur not only in products and services, but also in organizational and inter-organizational systems and processes, in strategic focus and in governance arrangements (Hartley 2005).

Innovation and 'continuous-improvement' approaches may both be important in achieving value for the public sphere. Yet innovation, by its nature (discontinuities with past practices) and its scale and scope (step-change in an open system, with unanticipated as well as planned outputs and outcomes) is inherently experimental, and so positive public value outcomes are not guaranteed, indeed are risky. It is therefore important to consider both those conditions under which innovation might lead to public value, and those where innovation might detract from public value. Continuous improvement, because it is based on fine-grain incremental change, is inherently less experimental and so is likely to be a more reliable and routine source of public value creation, except where the scale or pace of change in the external context requires a more fundamental response.

When does innovation contribute to or detract from public value?

There are important differences between the private and public sectors in terms of innovation. In the private sector, successful innovation is often seen to be a virtue in itself, as a means of ensuring competitive advantage either in new markets or to revive flagging markets (Schumpeter 1950; Hargadon and Sutton 2000). This is not always the case in the public service sector, where innovation is seen to be justifiable mainly to the extent that it increases public value in the quality, efficiency or fitness for purpose of services or where it improves the ways decisions about services are made.

Improvement in the public sector also needs to be analysed not only in terms of performance metrics (for example faster, cheaper, more reliable, higher quality, greater reach) but also in terms of the twin dimensions of public value (see Chapter 2 by Benington) – what the public values, and what adds value to the public sphere.

Many governments currently place a high policy priority on the overall improvement of public services, so it is easy to see how the concepts of innovation and improvement may become conflated. However, it is valuable to consider the range of possible relationships between innovation and improvement. These are shown in Figure 10.1. The analysis is based on organizations, but it is equally possible to apply this to service areas, business units, or inter-organizational networks and partnerships or the service sector.

There are two dimensions to the figure. The first (horizontal axis) indicates whether or not there is innovation in the sense of a step-change in the organization. The second shows whether or not there is improvement in organizational performance.

In Quadrant 1, an organization exhibits neither improvement nor innovation. This may occur where an organization is operating in a highly stable environment, where innovation is not needed because there is a close fit between that environment and the organizational processes, systems and stakeholder needs.

This is an important reminder that, despite the emphasis within public value theory on responding to dynamic contexts, in fact there may be situations where innovation may actually detract from the creation of public value because the risks of engaging in experimentation outweigh the benefits of continuity and routine in existing service or

Figure 10.1   *Relationships between innovation and improvement*

	Improvement but no innovation • Continuous improvement methodologies	**Innovation and improvement**
High		
	2	4
	1	3
Low	**No improvement and no innovation** • Stable environment • Organizational inertia	**Innovation but no improvement** • Increased choices but not desired by service users • Loss of performance due to learning curve and operational bugs • Innovation unsuccessful but useful organizational learning • Innovation not valuable

Improvement (vertical axis)

Low · High — Innovation (horizontal axis)

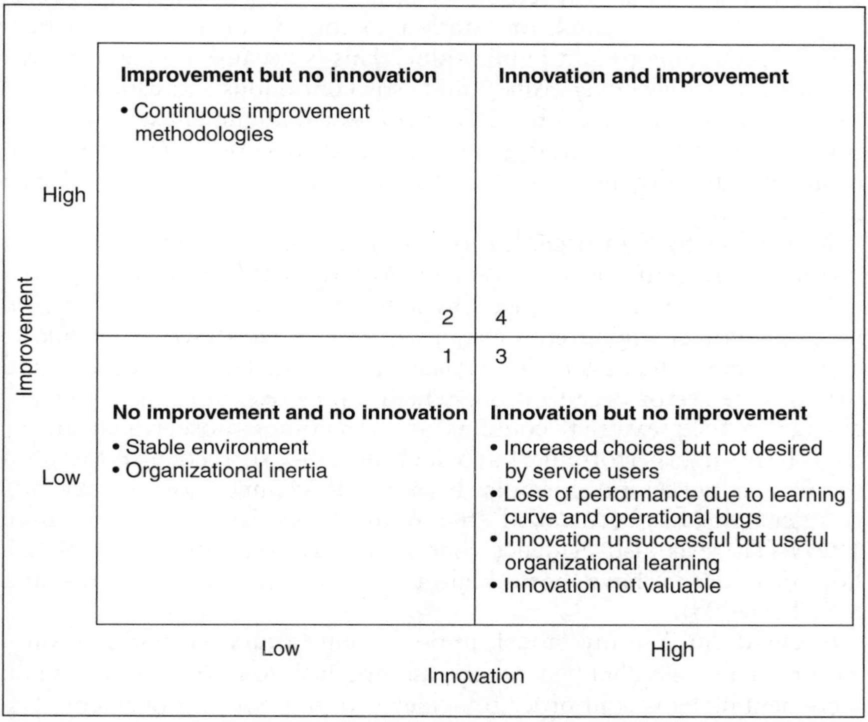

governance arrangements; or where a successful innovation does not improve the quality of service to the public or add sufficient value to the public sphere to justify the public expenditure. A careful analysis of the context and service may lead to a decision not to innovate. This mirrors some of the more informed literature about organizational change which urges careful analysis prior to action, and which counsels managers sometimes to decide not to stimulate change, rather than to go along with the fashion for change where it may not be required (for example Abrahamson 1991; Argyris 1993). We should not assume that public value is necessarily created by change rather than by continuity. Public value is created where there is close alignment between public provision and public need and/or aspiration. This is not an easy alignment to assess, but conceptually it is significant for public value theory.

However, while the proposition that the organization should be aligned and adapted to its environment is both theoretically and technically sound, in practice this is often not sustainable over the medium to longer term. An organization in Quadrant 1, in a relatively stable environment with a clear 'customer base' and constituency of citizens, would still need to search for continuous improvement in its practices if it is to continue to add public value. This is because no environment is entirely stable over time, and so continuous adjustment and improvement is necessary to achieve continued alignment with its environment. In addition, even if perfectly aligned with its external environment, an organization is still capable of internally driven improvement.

So the fact that an organization in Quadrant 1 is characterized by neither innovation nor improvement suggests that it may be in inertia, either not recognizing the need to innovate or improve to meet new needs and/or changing circumstances, or else paralysed from taking action to meet the new circumstances. Interestingly, it has been found that private sector organizations which fail to recognize the signals of change in their external contexts are sometimes those which are or have been high-performing but which now fail to recognize the need to alter a successful formula because of changes in the external context – this has been called "the innovator's dilemma" (Christensen 1997). There is also evidence that some UK local authorities which fall into inertia have been high performers in the past (Jas and Skelcher 2005).

In Quadrant 2 in my model, improvement occurs but without innovation. This may happen where an organization focuses on small, incremental changes in order to achieve continuous improvement. The changes, however, do not individually constitute innovation, in that they are insufficiently radical or disruptive to constitute a step-change. It is about 'doing better' rather than 'doing different' (Tidd *et al.* 2005). There is considerable evidence that employees have myriad ideas about how to improve the operational processes for which they are responsible or in which they are involved, and are able to help fine-tune and develop both products and services (Bessant 2003).

Continuous fine-grain improvement may increase value to the public sphere, because it can create better alignment between the needs of the public and the service offered (what the public values) or else because it may contribute to wider valuable outcomes. Within this scenario, experimentation is modest and so the risks of the changes are likely to be modest too; public value creation is therefore likely to be sustained but not radically enhanced. On the other hand, if the initial 'value proposition' of the service or governance arrangement is flawed, minor improvements may not create public value improvement. For example, improvements in customer care (for example a better reception area and customer-friendly receptionists) will not improve a service if the basic policy or programme is flawed, if the service is seriously under-resourced or if the professionals are underqualified.

This takes us back to the question of alignment between public need, public purpose and public provision and the three key features of the strategic triangle (the value proposition, the authorizing environment, and the operational capacity) which Moore (1995) argues can help public managers decide whether or not their organization is delivering maximum feasible public value.

Assuming there is alignment, however, then slow, steady continuous improvement can be a valuable means of building public value. The fine-tuning approach enables relatively low-risk improvements to operational performance. In addition, there is evidence that the implementation of many small-scale changes can, over time, have a cumulative effect such that, seen over the longer term, quite radical shifts in policies, strategies and practices and strategies can take place. The classic example from the private sector is the Toyota vehicle motor corporation, where the use of total quality approaches, systematic lean management procedures, and high-involvement personnel management enabled the suggestions and ideas of many employees to be used to improve production processes to a substantial degree (Schroeder and Robinson 1991; Womack and Jones 2003).

Quadrants 3 and 4 consider the varied relationships between innovation, improvement and public value. Innovation does not automatically create public value. Its experimental characteristics can mean that it sometimes innovation detracts from public value or that the outcomes are mixed. These are examined below.

In Quadrant 3 the organization engages in innovation but there is no resultant improvement in the quality of governance or public services. Indeed, there may even be a deterioration in performance. Several reasons or scenarios fit this pattern.

In the first scenario, innovations do not always lead to success – in any sector. Some of the rhetoric about innovation appears to be predicated on the assumption that improvement always follows, but the reality may be very different. Tidd *et al.* (2005) note that

> for most organizations the pattern is one of partial success but with problems. For example, studies of product innovation consistently point to a high level of 'failure' between initial idea and having a successful product in the market-place. Actual figures range from 30% to as high as 95%; an accepted average is 38%. (p. 39)

There may be several reasons for being even more pessimistic about failure rates in the case of innovation in the public service sector. First, given the range of stakeholders in the authorizing environment who may influence perceptions of 'success' (for example politicians, audit, inspection and regulatory bodies, the media, campaigning groups) – the criteria for 'success' may be contested. In addition, the democratic accountability frameworks of public service organizations often mean that the development of the innovation occurs in an open, even consultative, way, under the scrutiny of public debate, unlike the situation for many private sector firms, where innovations may be developed more secretively through patents, design rights and so on.

The second scenario within Quadrant 3 is where innovation occurs and proliferates alternative forms of provision but without any improvement in the actual service. This may increase the first sense of public value as 'what people value' (for example greater choice between alternatives) but if the choice is only wider but not better than previously, it will not necessarily increase the second sense of 'value added to the public sphere'.

Innovation without improvement may also occur through 'over-adoption', which can occur where an innovation is taken up through pressures of management or policy fashion, but where the innovation does not meet public needs, culture or context. Pressures on organizations to adopt 'innovative practices' for reasons of reputation management are common in both the private and public sectors (DiMaggio and Powell 1983; Abrahamson 1991).

The situations so far analysed for Quadrant 3 are ones where the innovation has not led to an increase in public value. However, there are situations where innovation occurs where there may initially be no improvement and yet the innovation is worth pursuing. Two examples can illustrate this. First, a situation may arise where innovation leads to a temporary performance decrease (for example as operational processes or bugs are ironed out, or as staff learn new ways of working). This is well recognized in the operations management and organizational psychology literatures but has perhaps been insufficiently acknowledged in the public service sector, where stakeholders often expect improved performance from the moment of introduction of the innovation.

A second situation is where the innovation is not ultimately successful (and has to be abandoned or killed off), but where sufficient learning takes place to justify the investment of time and resources, or to stimulate further attempts at innovation which benefit from the earlier attempt. There are many examples of this in both the private and public sectors (Hartley and Allison 2002; Newman, Raine and Skelcher 2000). Again there is insufficient recognition of this phenomenon of learning from 'failure' in the public sector literature (see also Albury 2005; Bessant 2005). Some research suggests that innovation failure, if well managed, can be beneficial to longer-term learning capacity and organizational improvement (Rashman and Hartley 2002), which itself may lead to added public value if there is an increase in organizational capacity or readiness to engage in further change and improvement.

Finally, Quadrant 4 indicates a situation where an innovation has been developed and turns out to be successful in that there is improvement which creates or strengthens public value. How this 'success' is assessed and evaluated is a question for later examination in this chapter.

This consideration of the varied relationships between innovation and improvement shows that general improvement may occur through two different means – continuous improvement and/or radical innovation. Each may contribute to or detract from public value, depending on the context and the degree of alignment between public needs and problems, and organizational solutions.

The above review of the relative contributions of continuous improvement and radical innovation to creating or adding public value suggests the importance of an alignment between the problem and the chosen solution or response. Alignment of this kind goes beyond a contingency perspective and implies active leadership by politicians and managers to assess both the external demands and choices, and the internal conditions, constraints and opportunities, and to judge whether the strategy for innovation and improvement should be based primarily upon continuous improvement or a step-change innovation. Dunphy and Stace (1988), using case-studies of banks, have argued that any general change strategy will require an analysis of the time to achieve the desired change, the scope and scale of the change and whether there is internal and external support for the change. This framework can also be usefully applied to the public service sector.

Some writers are interested in how organizations can become 'ambidextrous' – that is, how they can support both continuous improvement and innovation. In the private sector, research has shown that it is generally easier to do one or the other, because different structures and processes facilitate each activity, and few organizations manage to do both successfully (Utterback 1996; Christensen 1997; Tidd 2001). Among other things, the costs of the radical innovation are initially high and its outcomes uncertain.

The implications are clear for public service organizations, driven by tight targets for efficiency and short-term performance deadlines. Some rebalancing may be required, in Utterback's terms, if innovation is to compete with excellence for the longer-term public value prizes. The search for the ambidextrous organization and the difficulties in achieving this also highlight the tensions inherent within a public value framework: is improvement best achieved by 'doing better' (improvements in efficiency) or by 'doing different' (inventive leaps in approach or standards)? Each approach may have their place in the short-term and the longer-term.

Public value has to be created without the benefit of hindsight and it sometimes will require political and managerial judgement as to whether a particular policy or strategy will achieve the sought-after outcomes. Therefore, the question, 'How can public value be measured?' can never be fully and finally answered – there may be different assessments according to context and organizational capacity, according to short-term and longer-term perspectives, according to whether this reinforces particular strengths and weaknesses of the organization – quite apart from the different judgements, values and priorities that varied stakeholders may place on the innovation or improvement. Thus, right at the heart of public value theory is the existence of a tension, or even a paradox, about how public value is judged – in terms of incremental improvements in existing ways of offering services, or through innovation and step-change. While management theorists can point to research (albeit mainly from the private sector) which indicates the organizational features which most support continuous improvement or most support innovation, there remains, at heart, a political as well as a managerial judgement about the risks and rewards in these decisions.

Managing risk and reward in the pursuit of public value

Step-change innovation is a larger political and managerial risk than continuous incremental improvement but it can carry the prospect of considerable added public value, in that it can enable both large-scale improvement and also a significant change in direction, focus or strategy, in a way which can only be achieved by continuous improvement over a much longer timescale (see, for example, Toyota: Womack and Jones 2003). There are perhaps three main ways the risks of step-change innovation can be mitigated by public service organizations seeking to create added public value.

First, in the public services, there are pressures not only to develop innovations in specific organizations (for example a hospital or a school) but also to share them with other organizations (for example across the National Health Service or education system). Innovations in public services are therefore often spread between organizations, services and institutional fields through open, collaborative networks and communities of practice. This contrasts with the competitive environment within the private sector which often leads to secrecy and protection of knowledge and innovation from other organizations (except where the costs of innovation are so high that they need to be spread between several firms – for example joint ventures for new engine development within the auto industry). Sharing of knowledge within the private sector is often therefore limited either to strategic alliance partners or else to benchmarking across dissimilar firms and/or industries. For private sector organizations, the value of innovation is assessed largely in terms of competitive advantage to the specific firm, whereas in the public services, value needs to be evaluated at the level of the public sphere as a whole. For example, the value of an innovation in cancer treatment developed by one hospital within the UK National Health Service will be judged not primarily in terms of whether that hospital can maintain a competitive lead over other hospitals, but whether the innovation is adopted and further developed by other hospitals (and other organizations concerned with healthcare) and whether the innovation leads to improved prevention, detection and survival rates in the population. This highlights an important element of innovation for public value – it cannot be assessed solely at the level of 'customer' satisfaction or a single organization but needs to include the value to the wider population, and also prevention for future generations of citizens.

The diffusion of innovation between organizations and across services has traditionally been based on simple models of benchmarking and sharing good practice. This emphasizes a 'copy and paste' approach to new practices and focuses especially on using explicit knowledge transfer (Hartley and Benington 2006). However, our research with public service organizations shows that 'adaption' rather than simply 'adoption' is central to the sharing of good practices (where the model of knowledge transfer between the organizations is closer to 'graft and grow' than to 'copy and paste'), particularly where the political, social or organizational context of the organizations is dissimilar (Denis *et al.* 2002; Hartley and Benington 2006; Patel 2006; Hartley and Rashman 2007). The sharing of good practice between public organizations helps to mitigate risks as well as to spread the rewards of innovation. Co-creation of knowledge and its sharing is central to the diffusion of innovation, and might be explored further in public value theory.

A second approach to seeking public value through innovation is to pay close attention to the processes of innovation development as well as its outcomes. How services are provided has an impact on the public sphere as well as what is provided. Managerial interest in how innovations are developed (or extinguished) is important for public value creation, both to ensure that organizations are structured in ways to encourage innovation (Dougherty 2006) and to develop innovations in cost-effective ways, while ensuring that as much learning as possible is derived from all the phases from initial ideas-generation through to full implementation so that risks are reviewed and predicted as far as feasible (Albury 2005). Cooper (1988) has suggested a set of stage–gate decisions to inform choices at different phases of innovation (for example initial creative idea, prototyping, trialling, full-scale implementation). This can be valuable both in deciding whether or not to proceed with an innovation to the next stage, and also for taking stock of the emergent as well as the predicted aspects of innovation. It is a way to manage risk, and control resources by deciding whether the decision at this stage should be to proceed or to wait and gain more information, or whether the innovation is unlikely to be successful and so should be ended. Such an approach helps to analyse risk and increase learning by careful articulation of the processes which underlie innovation; identifying particular barriers and facilitators at particular stages; and examining how, where and why innovations fail (given that a significant proportion do). However, a number of writers have noted that innovation is often far from a rational process (Van de Ven *et al.* 1999; Osborne and Brown 2005) and that power, opportunity, mistakes and dead-ends are all found in innovation processes. This brings us to the third element of increasing public value through innovation.

Innovations in governance, democracy and public services are risky, ambiguous, multifaceted, complex and contested. They are subject to the views and opinions of a wide range of different stakeholders, from users, citizens, managers and staff, politicians and policy advisors, the media, lobby and advocacy groups among others. How then to decide whether an innovation contributes to improvement and public value? This is a much harder and more complex question in the public sector than in the private one, where innovation progression is largely a managerial decision, made with privacy protected and with innovation processes shared on a 'need to know' basis, and where the focus is largely about the benefit to the individual firm or strategic alliance, whereas public organizations have to consider the wider (and longer-term) public good.

The catalysts for innovation may be 'top-down' (the role of politicians and policy advisors can be as substantial as public managers, see Hartley 2005), 'bottom-up' (within the organization), 'lateral' (diffusion/sharing of good practice across organizations) or external (from users and those with a claim on the activities of the organization). Each implies a different configuration of actors and institutions, with different roles for policymakers, professionals, managers and citizens. Public value theory has emphasized the processes of 'co-production' in particular services and contexts (for example, Chapters 2 and 8) and this is an issue which innovation theory generally is also increasingly recognizing (for example, Von Hippel 1988, 2005; Von Hippel and von Krogh 2003). There is an increasing recognition both of the role that 'customers' may play in innovation development and also that members of the public may jointly develop innovations (such as open-source software) outside the ambit of the organization. Shaping and assessing the varied contributions of 'the public' (and groups within it) to innovation contains both possibilities and risks, given the unequal distribution of capacity and resources to create, lobby for and sustain innovations.

The politics of innovation to create public value

Given that improvement and innovation are concerned with impacts which may fall differentially on different groups in society and may have long-term and wide consequences for the public sphere, determining which innovations should be vigorously pursued and which should be dropped is not just a technical or managerial question but may often be an intensely political question. Therefore, finding the appropriate forums and processes for dialogue and debate may be a critical element of innovation where public services and governance arrangements are concerned.

Some innovations may be primarily technical, to which stage–gate decision processes can be relatively routinely applied. For example, deciding on the technical specification for street lighting in an urban area, or deciding to introduce innovations in surgical procedures in a hospital theatre may be largely based on the views of expert professionals. Professional information and values may predominate, not being primarily a concern to be reflected in public debate. Yet, even here there are examples of technical decisions with wider public value dimensions, where the interests of both users and citizens may need to be taken into account. For example, sodium street lighting has been chosen by a number of highways specialists in local authorities as efficient and effective, but more recent evidence (Raynham and Saksvikrønning 2003) has suggested that such lighting impedes human face recognition and contributes to lower levels of perceived safety in the street at night, compared with white lighting. Thus, even technical decisions may need to be reviewed in terms of their added public value.

Some decisions about innovations may appear to be primarily within the domain of the manager, in that they are about organizational and process changes with the intention of improving the flow, efficiency or effectiveness of existing services. An example would be the development of shared services (for instance information systems; payroll records) between local authorities, or the redesign of work processes into back-office and front-office functions. Again, stage–gate decision processes, based on management information from a variety of sources, may be important. Yet there may be a need also to consider the wider public value implications of a seemingly internal set of innovations. For example, shared services can be politically sensitive where the proposal involves jobs being moved from one locality to another, with consequences (or perceived consequences) for the economic well-being of the locality.

This is not to suggest that all technical and managerial innovations should be subjected to public or political debate or other forms of civic engagement before reaching a decision. However, it does suggest that a public value perspective on innovation should include an active searching-out of information and perspectives which are relevant to viewing the innovation in terms of its potential for wider impact on economic, social and environmental wellbeing. This may involve a range of stakeholders directly or may involve elected representatives. Also, technical, professional and managerial staff need to think in public value terms and not just in terms of immediate concerns, targets and outputs.

Some innovations are intensely political and have public value at their heart. The proposal by the mayor of London to introduce congestion charging was widely debated, and there was extensive consultation with civic, business and resident groups prior to its introduction. Elected representatives have an important role in orchestrating debate, articulating and exploring views, ensuring that those who are less articulate are able to express their views and in exploring tension and conflict over values, priorities, outputs and outcomes. Radical innovations in the public sphere may often require adaptive leadership (Heifetz 1994) where politicians, managers and informal leaders support and energize the deliberation of public value – the public valuing of public value. But renewing the political process through developing innovations in governance and democratic processes is also part of the challenge.

Chapter 11

Sustaining Public Value Through Microfinance

GUY STUART

Introduction

Managers create public value through two main processes: a production process and a legitimation process. The former concerns the delivery of services to the organization's clients. The latter concerns the policies and procedures which members of the organization follow, in terms of fairness and accountability (Moore 1995:53). In this scheme the manager of an organization that produces public value is in the centre of a strategic triangle, whose vertices are: the organization's value proposition; its authorizing environment; and its operational capacity (Figure 11.1). The organization's operational capacity enables it to engage in the production of value, conditional on its ability to gain legitimacy and support from its authorizing environment.

Microfinance institutions (MFIs) provide financial services to the poor – those who are at or below the poverty line in developing countries, with a majority living in households earning less than $2 per day. The services include credit, savings, insurance, and remittance services. Microfinance demonstrates the relevance of the public value framework: MFI managers must manage their operational capacity in the light of their authorizing environment, and vice versa, to produce public value. The chapter also argues that MFIs take the interrelationship between production, on the one hand, and policies and procedures that promote fairness and accountability, on the other hand, one step further because the latter are a key component of MFIs' competitive advantage in the provision of financial services. In other words, fairness and accountability promote the effective production of public value, as well as give it legitimacy in the eyes of the authorizing environment.

Finally, this chapter argues that the public value framework provides a useful way of understanding the hotly debated question over whether MFIs should focus on financial sustainability, defined as

Figure 11.1   *The strategic triangle*

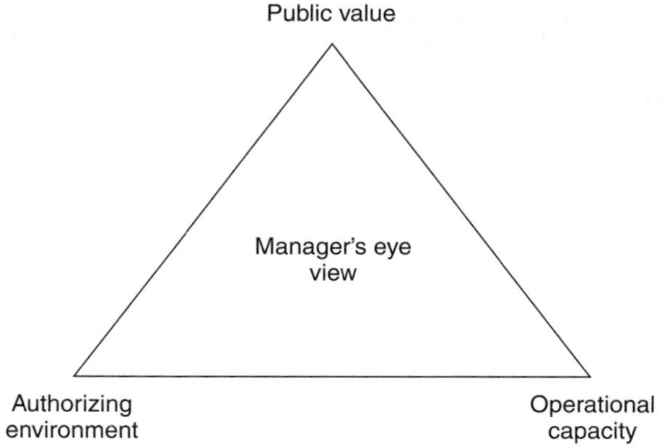

Public value

Manager's eye
view

Authorizing
environment

Operational
capacity

Source: Moore (1995).

revenue from customers exceeding the costs of service provision, or
make their primary goal to broaden their outreach to serve the
poorest of the poor. The Microcredit Summit Campaign defines the
'poorest' as those who are in the bottom half of those living below
their nation's poverty line, or any of the 1.2 billion who live on less
than $1 a day adjusted for purchasing power parity (PPP). There is
concern in the microfinance field that MFIs are only reaching the
better-off poor – those living below the poverty line but in the top
half of that group.

The public value framework makes two distinct but related contributions to this debate. One contribution is to broaden the definition of
sustainability to encompass revenues and benefits not generated
through direct service provision. The framework makes this contribution via the concept of public value in and of itself – that there is a
legitimate collectivity for whom an MFI manager can produce value.
The second contribution is to place the debate about whether MFIs
should be in the business of creating public value, in particular fulfilling a mandate to serve the poorest of the poor and not just the poor,
in the context of the strategic questions facing MFI managers. It gives
us a 'manager's eye view' of a thorny public policy question.

The chapter proceeds as follows. In the next section I identify the
public value which microfinance creates. Following that, I discuss,
from within the public value framework, the debate regarding the
financial sustainability of MFIs, and provide case-study examples from
three MFIs showing how they manage to be financially sustainable
while maintaining a commitment to serving the poorest of the poor. I
end the chapter with a summary of the argument.

The public value of microfinance

There has been considerable government, multilateral and philanthropic investment in microfinance over the past 30 years. That experience has revealed two strong justifications for the use of donor funds to support MFIs. First, funds from donors were crucial in supporting the development of MFIs as they sought to show that the poor are a market that can be served profitably by formal organizations (rather than purely by informal, indigenous ones as explained in more detail below). In other words, public and philanthropic subsidies jump-started a process that private investors were either unable or unwilling to support. As such, public support created public information (a crucial source and form of public value) that all formal MFIs, including private, for-profit ones, can now exploit. There are other justifications for public funding of microfinance, which are not as well supported by the evidence, but limited space precludes full discussion of these.

A second justification for donor funding was that there was a redistributive imperative that informed the initial development of MFIs and now informs the desire for them to reach the poorest of the poor today. For the most part, MFIs got into the business to help the poor, and the impact studies that evaluated whether they achieved their goal tend to suggest that they did (see for example Pitt and Khandker 1998; Snodgrass and Sebstad 2002). That they could serve the poor in a sustainable manner was an added benefit.

Beyond these basic value propositions, we see in MFIs today a more complex story. First, when we look at the capacity that MFIs have developed to deliver financial services to the poor, we see the development of policies and procedures that promote fairness and accountability as a way of doing business that gives MFIs a competitive advantage. This is true not only of the non-profit and member-owned organizations that pioneered microfinance, but also of the for-profit organizations that have since entered the market. Furthermore, this way of doing business is as much, if not more, relevant to the savings activities of MFIs as it is to their lending activities. And, finally, we see a complex and evolving authorizing environment composed of funders and regulators that is relevant to non-profit, for-profit and member-owned MFIs. I elaborate these points below, and Table 11.1 provides a summary of the argument.

Value and capacity

MFIs create value by providing financial services to the poor. They do so in a market already populated by a wide variety of indigenous, informal organizations, such as moneylenders, deposit collectors,

Table 11.1 *Microfinance, private value and public value*

	Credit only		Savings and Credit		
	Non-profit	*For-profit*	*Non-profit*	*For-profit*	*Member-owned*
PRIVATE VALUE	Access to credit	Access to credit	Access to savings and credit	Access to savings and credit	Access to savings and credit
PUBLIC VALUE *Production*	Social impact on clients and redistribution, public information ('it can be done')	n/a	Social impact on clients and redistribution, public trust (savings), public information ('it can be done')	Public trust (savings)	Community-based self-help, mutual trust (savings), public information ('it can be done')
Legitimation	Accounting, financial statements, impact reports	Accounting, financial statements	Accounting, financial statements, impact reports	Accounting, financial statements	Accounting, financial statements, member and board meetings
Capacity	Formalization: lending methodology, information and accounting systems	Formalization: lending methodology, information and accounting systems	Formalization: lending and savings methodology, information and accounting systems	Formalization: lending and savings methodology, information and accounting systems	Formalization: lending and savings methodology, information and accounting systems, member governance systems
Authorizing environment	Donors, social investors, charity regulator	Investors	Donors, social investors, prudential regulators, charity regulator	Investors, prudential regulator	Members, donors, prudential regulator, and/or regulator of cooperatives

various forms of savings and insurance clubs, and a wide variety of rotating savings and credit associations (ROSCAs) (Rutherford 2000:31). To understand how MFIs create value we have to understand how they are organizations that are distinct from the existing providers.

Existing providers offer rudimentary financial services to people that are part of their social network (see, for example, Ruthven 2002:267). This network gives them the information and accountability structures that allow them to extend services to their customers. This has a couple of consequences. First, the indigenous provider's market extends only so far as his social network reaches. Second, to gain access to indigenous providers, the poor must be able to tap into an existing social relationship with the provider or someone connected with the provider.

Furthermore, as the list of the providers given above implies, there is often a one-to-one match between service and organization – a moneylender offers credit only, a burial club offers burial insurance only, and a deposit collector offers savings services only. As a result, customers must engage in transactions with a wide variety of service-providers to meet their basic financial needs. (Robinson 2001:190–6). (Ostensibly ROSCAs are an exception to this rule because they have a savings and credit component, and are, by their very nature, an intermediary. But ROSCAs lack the product flexibility of a true intermediary and the 'savings' component is very closely tied to the credit component.)

Within this context microfinance brings the benefits of formalization to the market. Formal institutions have the ability to extend their services beyond the personal networks of an individual service-provider. In practice this manifests itself in the ability of MFIs to provide services to people that they initially do not know very well, but whom others in the community know. To manage their risk MFIs use various mechanisms to gain access to local knowledge. For example, they get their customers' knowledge of each other to work for the MFI through the use of the peer group, by which an MFI lends to individual members of a group but the group as a whole is liable for the loan. This puts the burden on the group, whose members have good local knowledge, to screen who receives a loan and who does not, and to enforce repayment. In addition, MFIs have developed techniques to build relationships with its customers. One such technique is 'step-lending.' The MFI makes small initial loans and then increases the loan amount as loans are repaid and the MFI gains knowledge about the borrower. On the savings side, the MFI goes to great pains to ensure that the customer knows how much money is in their account (the age-old practice of passbooks is an example of this) and how they can gain access to it.

A direct result of this approach to financial service provision is that the poor gain access to MFI services without the need for a personal relationship with someone in the MFI. They may have to have a personal relationship with other members of their community, but that is a much lower hurdle to participation. More generally, by not being confined by their social networks, MFIs can compete throughout the markets they enter.

Beyond this ability to cut across social networks, the formal qualities of an MFI allow it to offer a variety of products, because its organizational form is not dictated by its product offering. Rather, as a formal organization it is set up to develop products suited to its market. Furthermore, its formal status enables it to more easily intermediate funds, because it has the systems in place to account for the inflow and outflow of funds, and because it has the capacity to adapt its products to ensure that the intermediation works. This results in direct benefits to an MFI's customers. In addition to allowing an MFI the ability to offer savings services, the ability to intermediate funds also lowers the cost of credit because savings are a cheap source of funds. In addition, when necessary, the formal nature of MFIs allows them to gain access to external funds more easily, thus increasing the availability of funds to their customers. Finally, formalization increases the likelihood that an MFI will remain in the market, offering its customers the benefit of permanence. Permanence creates value for the customers because it allows them to plan for the future, knowing that the resources of the MFI will be available to them when they need them. The reputation for permanence also strengthens the MFI because it gives incentives for borrowers to repay their loans and for employees not to cheat it (Navajas *et al.* 2002:156).

In sum, effective MFIs bring the benefits of formalization to the markets they serve. A key component of this formalization is its ability to treat the clients of MFIs fairly – they are all subject to the same policies and procedures, from which the clients themselves benefit. Furthermore, MFIs are better able to provide benefits to their customers when they have good accountability mechanisms in place. This formalization succeeds, in part, because it takes advantage of the existing social relations in which MFIs' clients are embedded, and, as such, avoids one of the pitfalls of formalization – the inability to meet the particular needs of a diverse client basis. It is this combination that enhances the ability of the poor to gain access to the financial services on offer.

Authorizing environment

The authorizing environment of a financial institution includes at least two components: its source of funds; and the regulatory and supervisory rules under which it operates. These two are related in that a major determinant of a financial institution's regulatory regime is its source of funds – financial institutions that mobilize savings are highly likely to operate in a more regulated environment.

A for-profit, credit-only MFI on-lends to its customers funds that it has raised through equity and debt offerings. The MFI must satisfy the demand of its equity and debt investors in terms of rate of return, and their reporting requirements, with a particular focus on financial transparency. It is likely to have to comply with some government regulations regarding its lending practices, and, maybe, minimum capital requirements. A non-profit, credit-only MFI also on-lends to its customers funds it has raised, but these are likely to be grants that require no return (and essentially belong to the MFI itself), rather than equity investments, and credit that may be subsidized. MFIs that receive grant funding or concessionary credit are put in a position of having to justify the subsidies they are receiving. The funder is expecting a development return for their investment: are the subsidies doing any good? As such, the funder will require documented evidence of such an impact, as well as an accounting of the use of its funds.[1] In addition to such requirements, the MFI may also have to comply with the same regulatory requirements as the for-profit entity.

An MFI, whether for-profit or non-profit, that mobilizes savings is entering into a trust relationship with its depositors. Savings mobilization demands that customers deposit their funds in the MFI. To do so with confidence, they must believe that they can get their money back as and when they want, so long as they comply with the rules of the MFI for withdrawals. They must trust the MFI to hold their money securely and to remain in business so there will be an MFI from which to withdraw their savings in the future. This element of public trust places a deposit-taking MFI, whether it is for-profit or non-profit, in the public value space. It is not surprising that it is very common for the government to regulate such MFIs, to ensure their safety and soundness and to provide deposit insurance.

Despite these commonalities, there is a difference between the for-profit and non-profit deposit-taking MFIs. The former are still answerable to their equity investors, who are outside investors seeking a return commensurate with the demands of the international capital market. In contrast, the most likely ownership structure of a non-profit MFI is a member-owned institution, in which both savers and borrowers have a say in the governance structure of the organization.[2] To the extent to which savers and borrowers are different people, there is a division of interest within the MFI, between those who wish to maximize the earnings of the MFI, to maximize the return on their share deposits, and those who wish to have access to credit at the lowest price possible (Ferguson and McKillop 1997:133–5). But, this potential conflict of interest is mitigated by the fact that there is a mutual dependency between borrowers and savers in these organizations, and there are likely to be many members who are both borrowers and savers (ibid.:135).

In sum, MFIs face complex authorizing environments that vary in terms of the product they deliver and their ownership structure. A credit-only MFI faces a regulatory environment very different from that confronting a savings and credit MFI. For-profit entities must generate returns to their investors that are competitive with other demands for capital, while non-profit entities either must satisfy the demand of funders or, in the case of member-owned institutions, their own member-clients.

Sustainability and the creation of public value for all the poor

As noted above, there has been considerable public and philanthropic investment in MFIs over the past 30 years, because almost all MFIs had to start from scratch, and there was almost no interest from commercial investors or banks in financing the activities of MFIs. But today many MFIs have shown they are capable of covering their operational and financial costs with the revenues they earn from their customers. For the sake of convenience I will refer to the people who receive services from an MFI directly, and pay for them through interest and fee payments, as 'customers'.

This ability to cover costs with customer-generated revenues makes an important debate within the field of microfinance possible. That debate revolves around whether MFIs should make sustainability, defined in terms of revenues from customers exceeding costs, their priority, or whether they should make outreach to the poorest of the poor the priority.[3] Advocates of a strong emphasis on sustainability argue that the focus on sustainability itself improves the management of MFIs, because it forces the MFI to operate in a cost-effective, customer-focused manner. Furthermore, they argue that it is only through the self-sustainability of MFIs that we can be assured that the poor will continue to receive microfinance services in the long run. Those who focus on outreach to the poorest worry that a strong focus on financial sustainability causes MFIs to drift away from the poorest of the poor towards the more affluent poor, from whom they are able to earn more profits. The debate suggests an inherent trade-off between serving all segments of the poor population, while support for microfinance lasts, on the one hand, and serving the more affluent poor on a sustainable, permanent basis, on the other.

The idea of such a trade-off makes sense. The poorest of the poor have smaller-sized transactions with higher administrative costs relative to the income they generate. Furthermore, the poorest of the poor are more likely to have irregular income streams. As a result, they are not able to make regular payments of a fixed amount, which MFIs favour because they are administratively less costly to service and help them with risk mitigation (Rutherford 2004). Finally, the poorest are likely to live in more remote, rural areas, which are harder for an MFI to reach and raise the transactions costs associated with serving them. In sum, serving the poorest of the poor generates less revenue per transaction, and may involve higher relative and absolute costs.

The public value framework recasts the debate over sustainability and outreach to the poorest by rejecting the narrow definition of sustainability. The framework takes a broader view of sustainability: a public manager intent on creating public value can run a sustainable organization so long as she or he can secure revenues from a variety of sources, including non-customers. To do so, the manager must have the capacity to produce something of value for their authorizing environment – she or he must pay attention to the three vertices of the strategic triangle. In the context of microfinance, a manager of an MFI can run a sustainable MFI by generating revenues from its customers and receiving support from donors, who value the MFI's work. As a result, serving the poorest can be a sustainable enterprise even if the MFI loses money on each transaction with the poorest, because serving the poorest is something that donors value and for which they are willing to pay.

The purpose of recasting the debate in this way is not to rehabilitate subsidies for their own sake, but to use the broader definition of sustainability to raise questions about the inherent bias that the narrower definition brings to the debate about sustainability and outreach to the poorest, and explore fully the justifications for donor money in the sustenance of MFIs, especially for the purpose of reaching the poorest.

The narrow definition of sustainability brings both a normative and a practical bias to the debate about outreach to the poorest. The normative bias is that the satisfaction of the preferences of the customer is all that counts – private value is all that counts. In other words, customer-based sustainability is normatively superior because it is based on the satisfaction of customer demand, and nothing else. In contrast, the public value framework forces the debate to ask why anyone other than individual beneficiaries of MFI services should pay for them. A different way to ask this question is: what public value do MFIs create, for which anyone other than the direct recipients of MFIs' services are willing to pay? As discussed above, MFIs have created public value by creating public information about what is possible in delivering financial services to the poor, and by acting as a redistributive mechanism. But the normative bias inherent in the narrow definition of sustainability precludes even raising the question as to whether there are any donors in the microfinance field who are willing to pay for service to the poorest, despite the fact that service to the poorest has the potential to produce new public information about how to serve the poorest, and has clear redistributive intent. Donors have been willing to pay for these in the past – it is worth exploring more fully whether they will do so in the future, rather than assuming that they will not.

The practical bias inherent in the narrow definition of sustainability is that revenues generated from payments made by customers are more reliable than other sources of revenue; that it is only through an exclusive focus on the customer that MFIs will become more efficient and effective; and that service to the poorest of the poor can only be a by-product of this focus on the customer, not a goal in and of itself. The public value framework raises a number of practical points in this regard. First, with respect to their authorizing environment, it is rare in the world of microfinance, or in the world of retail financial services in general, to find a manager who is solely concerned with the value they create for the organization's individual customers. In particular, as noted above, many MFIs must manage their regulatory environment, and for-profit (financially sustainable) MFIs must deal with the capital markets. Furthermore, they must often manage their relationships with their customers as collectivities – as members of peer groups, village banks, or member-owners of the MFI. As such, if an MFI receives contributions from donors it is part and parcel of a broader set of relationships it must manage to survive. We cannot assume that having a relationship with a donor makes the MFI more vulnerable. It may make it less vulnerable, by supporting it in times when it has problems with other external agents, or when its customer base is in trouble, for reasons out of its control.

Second, with respect to their operational capacity, an assumption of those who argue that MFIs should put themselves on a sustainable footing, narrowly defined, is that it will force the MFIs to become more efficient entities. But they offer no empirical support for this proposition. In fact Hudon's (2006) analysis of 100 MFIs suggests that unsubsidized MFIs are no more efficient than their subsidized counterparts. Finally, also with respect to operational capacity, MFIs continue to experiment with different products and organizational techniques to reach out to the poorest of the poor, including techniques to protect the MFI against any disruptions created by problems resulting from serving the poorest. It may be premature to forestall this exploration by insisting on a push to sustainability, narrowly defined.

A good way to understand these practical considerations is to look at the situation facing two sets of MFIs operating in India, one a cooperative bank in Maharashtra and another a confederation of cooperatives in Andhra Pradesh. Their situation illustrates the complex strategic choices facing MFIs as they struggle with the imperative to reach the poorest while managing their authorizing environment. I conclude with a brief discussion of a strategic challenge facing the Grameen Bank in Bangladesh.

Subsidies through technical assistance: the Cooperative Development Foundation, Andhra Pradesh, India

The Women's Thrift Cooperatives (WTCs) are member-owned savings and credit cooperatives operating in the Karimnagar and Warangal districts of Andhra Pradesh, about 150 km north-east of Hyderabad. The WTCs are the product of efforts to promote independent, democratically governed cooperatives by the Cooperative Development Foundation (CDF). The first WTC was founded in 1990, and there are now about 250 WTCs with about 70,000 members (there are also about 180 Men's Thrift Cooperatives with about 40,000 members). The WTCs currently operate under Andhra Pradesh's liberal cooperative law, the Mutually Aided Cooperative Societies Act (MACS Act), passed in 1995 by the state legislature due to the efforts of the CDF. The act grants the WTCs a level of autonomy and freedom from political interference that is rare in the Indian cooperative sector.

The WTCs raise all their loan capital from their members, or through loans from other WTCs. The cooperatives hold annual elections for boards of directors, who serve 3-year terms and go up for election on a rolling basis. The board in turn elects the president. Each WTC is a member of an Association of WTCs, which holds monthly meetings at which the accounts of each WTC are reviewed and discussed. A WTC may borrow from its AWTC. Each AWTC has a president and they represent the association at the confederation level, where they set policies for the running of the WTCs. An individual member of a cooperative maintains her membership in good standing by paying her monthly thrift contribution of 20 or 30 rupees (depending on the cooperative; between $0.4 and $0.6).

The WTCs have a limited number of loan products. The most commonly used are products partly secured by the thrift, bonus, and insurance accounts of the members – they can borrow up to three times the amount they have in these accounts subject to the approval of their joint liability group and the board of directors. The amount in these accounts is almost solely determined by the number of months a woman has been a member: the thrift contribution is a fixed, monthly payment; the bonus is the dividend paid to each member at the end of the year out of the net earnings of the cooperative based on the amount they have in their thrift account; and the insurance account is a one-time premium payment. As a result, members of very different incomes but with the same membership history will have access to the same maximum loan amount (because they have the same amount in their thrift, bonus, and insurance accounts). Furthermore, data from Stuart and Kanneganti (2003:table 2) suggest that the cooperatives draw their membership from a representative cross-section of the community as measured by caste, suggesting that not only do members have the same access to services, but that women within a village have equal access to membership.

As a result, the trade-off between sustainability and depth of outreach is embedded within a set of institutional rules that determine who gets access to what loans. In many WTCs, the 'three times' loan limit has dampened the demand for loans because it has put a limit on the amount that the better-off members of the cooperative can borrow. In recent years the thrifts have developed new loan products, such as gold loans, that avoid this limit, but the constraint still exists. This, in turn, lowers the amount of funds the WTCs are able to lend out, thus lowering income, and lowering the 'bonus' each member receives at the end of the year.

If the WTCs change their policies and encourage wealthier members to borrow more from the WTCs, the income of the WTCs will rise from the additional loan demand. The poorest members of the cooperatives will benefit from the larger bonus they receive at the end of the year, because of the higher income earned by the cooperatives. But they are likely to suffer if the cooperatives' funds are used up by loans to the better-off and they cannot gain access to loan funds when they need them. Thus far, the cooperatives, through discussions organized by the Cooperative Development Foundation, have focused on an alternative strategy – increasing general demand for the WTCs' funds by promoting economic development. In particular, they created the Mulkanoor Women's Cooperative Milk Union, a dairy cooperative with its own collection, milk processing, packaging, and distribution system, in which many of the women who are members of the WTCs have bought share capital. The women members have also used loans from the WTCs to buy milk cows to increase the earnings they generate through the milk cooperative. As of this writing, a second milk-processing plant is under construction and a third one is planned. The realization of these plans hinges, nevertheless, on a legal challenge the Cooperative Development Foundation is mounting against changes made in the cooperative laws by the new government of Andhra Pradesh. The changes in the law would undermine the independence of the milk cooperatives, and open them up to political influence.

One way to think about this situation is that the CDF is operating as a technical and political resource for the WTCs; a subsidized technical and political resource. As such, the CDF has created public value by helping to promote the cooperatives through subsidized technical assistance and by helping to create a political and regulatory space in which they could grow. One could argue that in playing such a role it is 'crowding out' the evolution of the WTC confederation's own technical and political skills, and that they would be better off in the long run if they were left to fend for themselves. There may be some truth in this, but the CDF played an essential role in creating the WTCs and it remains a complex strategic question as to when, if ever, it should leave the confederation to fend for itself, and whether that will have any consequences for the WTCs' willingness and ability to serve the poorest.

In sum, the WTCs' institutional design promotes widespread access to their savings and lending services. But this comes at a price – lower earnings for the WTCs. The strategic response of the WTCs thus far has been to focus on ways to increase demand for their funds generally, rather than meet the demand of their wealthier members. It has adopted a cooperative solution to a cooperative problem. This cooperative solution is itself a replication of an organizational innovation in the dairy production and processing field, and was brought to the attention of the WTCs by the efforts of the CDF, which, unlike the WTCs, survives on grant funding. But the success of this solution rests as much on what happens in the authorizing environment of the dairy cooperatives as it does on the cooperative initiative of the women involved.

Creating a separate delivery channel: Mann Deshi Mahila Bank, Maharashtra, India

Mann Deshi Mahila Bank (Mann Deshi) is a rural, women-owned cooperative bank, licensed and regulated by the Reserve Bank of India (RBI), and the state of Maharashtra's cooperative department. It was founded in 1997 and is based in Mhaswad in the Satara District of Maharashtra. As of March 2005 it had 3,058 share depositors. Though its membership is women and 70 per cent of them are from the Backward Castes, Mann Deshi's strategy for reaching the poorest of the poor in its market extends beyond the financial services it offers directly through the bank to its members. In particular, it has founded a non-profit organization (Mann Vikas Samajik Sanstha), which among other activities promotes the development of self-help groups (SHGs) to extend the reach of its savings and loan services down the economic ladder.

Self-help groups (SHGs) are groups of 15 to 20 people, usually all women, who meet on a regular basis to provide support to each other. The government of India, at both the state and federal level, has promoted the formation of these groups through promotion activities and the provision of incentives. In particular, the National Bank for Agriculture and Rural Development (NABARD) has had a programme to promote SHG linkages with formal banks since 1992. As of March 2005, NABARD reported a *cumulative* total of over 1.6 million SHGs served through this linkage programme (National Bank for Agriculture and Rural Development 2005).

Mann Vikas is funded through a government programme designed to support the formation of self-help groups, private donations, and some foundation grants. The self-help groups are part of a federation (Mann Deshi Mahila Bachat Mandal). The SHGs meet regularly, at which time the members of the group make deposits with an agent of the bank, who receives a commission for collecting and depositing the funds. The bank also lends money to the SHG federation, which on-lends money to a group, which in turn on-lends money to an individual member of the group. As a result of these efforts, as of March 2005, Mann Deshi had 24,244 customers in total, far beyond the number of its members. Most of these customers are savers (Mann Deshi Mahila Sahakari Bank 2006). As of May 2006, 7,142 women had taken loans through the SHG federation channel (Gala-Sinha 2006).

One of the benefits of this strategy is that the core operations of the cooperative bank as a bank are less vulnerable to any sudden shifts in funding for the subsidized operations than they would be were the bank itself subsidized. Furthermore, the bank and the non-profit supporting the SHGs have separate accounts, allowing regulators and funders to assess the financial position of each independently. As a result, it would seem that Mann Deshi has created a sustainable, subsidized strategy for reaching the poorest of the poor.

But it is not as simple as that. From its inception Mann Deshi has tried to provide services to the poorer segments of its market through this strategy, but not always with the approval of its regulators, the Reserve Bank of India and the state cooperative department. Soon after starting the self-help group delivery channel Mann Deshi suspended it, because of concerns from the regulators, and did not start it again until 2001. At that time it started collecting savings again and disbursing loans through the federation. These activities took place in the context of the RBI's evolving policy towards microfinance and towards bank-SHG linkages in particular, which culminated in a January 2006 RBI circular. The circular established two types of agent through which banks can extend their services to rural areas – facilitators and correspondents (Reserve Bank of India 2006). The former play the role of facilitating and encouraging people in rural areas to interact with formal banks, without providing any banking services themselves, while the latter are allowed to provide small loans, collect deposits, offer micro-insurance, and handle remittances. Mann Deshi engaged in regular communication with the RBI about its own extension services through the federation since their re-inception in 2001. On 11 May

2006 it suspended its loan activities through this channel in order to seek formal RBI approval of this activity under the 25 January 2006 circular (Gala-Sinha 2006). At the time of writing Mann Deshi provides savings services through the federation, but not loan services.

In sum, Mann Deshi has established a subsidized service-delivery channel that is separate from, but complementary to, its regular, self-sustaining activities as a rural cooperative bank. It has done so within the context of an evolving regulatory framework, with which it has actively engaged, and which has become more favourable to the type of strategy Mann Deshi has been using, but which has ultimate control over whether it can continue to employ such a strategy.

Cross-subsidization: the Grameen Bank, Bangladesh

The stories of the WTCs and the Mann Deshi Bank are not unusual in the microfinance world in their strategic complexity. The story of the most famous MFI in the world, the Grameen Bank, includes a special law passed in 1983 to accommodate its operating as a bank while not being subject to Bangladesh's regular bank regulations. Today Grameen is extending its outreach to customers who are beggars, truly the poorest of the poor, with a loan product that has few rules for repayment except that it should, at some point, be repaid (Rutherford 2004:45). It is doing so in the context of the implementation of a revised lending strategy (Grameen II), and a branch strategy that requires that each bank branch reach profitability within 6 months to a year of its opening (Grameen Bank 2004). It is unclear how this will all play out, because the loan product for beggars is a new product that may or may not fit well with the Grameen II strategy, and may be undermined by the demands of branch profitability. Such a new product may be an ideal candidate for a subsidized investment – it is innovative and reaches the poorest of the poor, and without an external subsidy it is the less poor who are carrying the risks associated with it.

Summary of cases

These cases provide a 'manager's eye view,' that provides an alternative way of looking at the debate about financial sustainability and reaching the poorest of the poor. The manager's view is from the centre of the strategic triangle, and demonstrates the ability of the public value framework to shine a new and revealing light on the debate. In particular I wish to highlight three questions that arose from each case discussed in this section:

- MFIs operate in a complex environment in which their operations are often affected by external demands that may run counter to their efforts to meet their customers' needs over the long run. This includes demands by regulators and external funders. But it is unclear that the best way to manage an MFI is to shun external funders, if those funders provide the resources that help the MFI manage its regulatory environment more effectively, as in the case of the CDF and the women's' cooperatives. As in the case of any external funder, including private investors, the questions are: What, other than funding, does the external funder bring to the table? How reliable are they?

- As in the case of Grameen, it may be the case that an MFI is able to cover its costs of operation through customer-generated revenue, but is not required to maximize its profits or match equity returns in other sectors of the economy. Such an MFI is in a position to cross-subsidize financial services to the poorest with the revenues it generates through serving the poor. But this raises the question: why should the poor subsidize service to the poorest? Why not the better-off? Furthermore, if the MFI is taking a risk on a new product for the poorest, which may yield net income in the long run, why should the poor be the ones to carry that risk? In such a situation, the calls for sustainability, narrowly defined, internalize the subsidization process, placing it on the shoulders of the poor, and may undermine efforts to innovate new ways to serve the poorest.

- Finally, as in the case of Mann Deshi Bank, is the answer to the sustainability/outreach question as simple as creating two separate service delivery channels, one subsidized and one not, each providing appropriate products to their segmented markets, and each having their own separate accounts? Ostensibly this provides the separation that ensures that a sustainable, narrowly defined MFI can survive the vagaries of external funding cycles. But, if, for example, the subsidized channel is mobilizing deposits that are a cheap source of funds for the unsubsidized bank, at what point does the bank become reliant on that channel for its survival?

Conclusion

The concerns facing a manager of an MFI are the concerns facing the manager of any organization in the business of producing public value. As argued above, the work of MFIs highlights the relevance of the public value framework, even in an area of service delivery where some or all of the revenues are generated from the recipients of the service. Furthermore, microfinance extends the public value framework by tying more closely the production process to the legitimation process – MFIs gain competitive advantage through their adherence to fairness and accountability in delivering financial services.

The public value framework also makes two distinct but related contributions to the debate regarding the sustainability of MFIs and their ability to reach the poorest of the poor. One contribution is to broaden the definition of sustainability to encompass revenues not generated through direct service provision. The framework makes this contribution via the concept of public value in and of itself – that there is a legitimate collectivity for whom a manager produces value. In doing so, it reorients the debate towards the question: can MFIs create public value by serving the poorest of the poor? Implicit in that question is the idea that someone is willing to fund the creation of that value. This leads us to the second contribution the public value framework makes, which is to place the debate about whether MFIs should be in the business of creating such public value in the context of the strategic questions facing MFI managers. It gives us a 'manager's eye view' of a thorny public policy question. The debate regarding the trade-off between sustainability and outreach to the poorest in the microfinance field benefits from such a manager's eye view, because so much in the debate is contingent on what managers want to do, are capable of doing and are allowed to do. The cases from Andhra Pradesh, Maharashtra, and Bangladesh illustrate clearly that MFI managers are actively pursuing a variety of strategies to reach the poorest of the poor through the management of their operational capacity and authorizing environment, while remaining sustainable, as defined within the public value framework.

Chapter 12

Redefining 'Public Value' in New Zealand's Performance Management System: Managing for Outcomes while Accounting for Outputs

RICHARD NORMAN

During the past 20 years, the terms outputs and outcomes have changed from being analytical devices for accountants and economists (for example, Ramanathan 1985) to become everyday language for public officials. The outputs–outcomes distinction was adopted in New Zealand in 1989 as the central mechanism for forcing accountability and responsiveness on a public service system which was seen by political leaders to respond too slowly to a fiscal crisis. The New Zealand 'experiment' attracted international interest as a comprehensive example of New Public Management ideas. As a remote island nation of 4 million people, 2,000 kilometres from its nearest large neighbour, Australia, New Zealand was able to implement change more rapidly than other countries. The resulting public management model was variously seen as an example worth studying (Aucoin 1995), a radical outlier (Ferlie *et al.* 1996: 250), an experiment not to be recommended for most developing countries (Schick 1998), a system which is 'getting better but feeling worse' (Gregory 2000) and the 'world's most advanced performance system' (Kettl 2000:7).

The major changes were initiated by a small group of politicians and Treasury officials, who were frustrated by 'unresponsive and territorial behaviour by many senior public servants, especially in the commercial activities of government' and the impression from the public service that its response to a serious fiscal problem 'was business as usual' (Scott 2001:173).

One politician, Simon Upton, who made extensive use of an outputs framework as a cabinet minister in (conservative) National Party governments during the 1990s, recalled his first select committee meeting with the Department of Scientific and Industrial Research as a new opposition spokesman in 1985. The department's annual report provided

> acres of information on the resources deployed ... but no comprehensive account of exactly what research was being conducted with what end in view. That was assumed to be so self-evident that no elaboration was required.

Upton wrote that he would never forget the 'avuncular smile' with which the director general greeted his request for such information, when commenting that 'we don't gather information in that way':

> And yet what could have been of greater interest to someone concerned with making the case for publicly funded science? If politicians couldn't tell taxpayers what research their funds were supporting, why should taxpayers continue to support all that effort? (Upton 1995:2)

Drawing on concepts from new institutional economics (Boston *et al.* 1996), the designers of the New Zealand management system conceived of government as an owner of assets and as a purchaser of services. As an owner, government would want to ensure the value of its organizational assets was maintained; while as a purchaser, government would want efficient, effective services delivered as cheaply as possible. The concept of outputs was developed as the central device for implementing this model of government, with appropriations based on outputs instead of organizational inputs. Comprehensive reforms between 1988 and 1992 reshaped institution-based funding into more than 500 outputs, each specified in terms of quality, quantity and timing, and assessed through corporate plans, annual reports, and by the auditor general. Each output was defined sufficiently tightly to prevent an individual chief executive using a claim of 'factors beyond my control' as a reason for non-performance. Private sector accrual accounting was adopted so the cost of outputs would include the use of capital and be comparable with potential private or non-profit sector alternatives (Norman 1997).

The hard-edged nature of accountability for outputs was expressed in a technique used by Treasury officials engaged in changing the system, who posed this question to departments: 'Imagine your department is not here any more. It's gone. The government wants to buy those services in the private sector. What should they contract for? How would you write the contract?'

By 1992, all departments were gathering information in the way that Simon Upton had sought, with accounting systems developed to allocate all departmental costs against the 500 output targets A model of government as chief contractor, advised by policy ministries independent of delivery responsibilities, was established during the same period. As Scott (2001:70–1) put it, the aim was to create a

> degree of detachment from the legacy of what has been done in the past. It creates incentives for departments to produce services arising from an analysis of present and future policy requirements, rather than assuming that the past services will still be required. It promotes questioning about what is being produced and what it costs. Rather than ministers or central agencies having to argue that a service does not add value, from a position of less information than the department has, the burden of proof shifts towards the department.

Output specifications were the bottom line for government performance, and failure to deliver could be expected to result in restructuring or outsourcing of the service, overseen by policy ministries and central agencies. Buttressing the new accountability for delivering results, heads of government departments and ministries lost their job security as 'permanent heads' and instead were placed on performance based-contracts which were usually for no more than 8 years.

Outcomes as wish lists

In contrast to the above concern with outputs, outcome measures featured little in the late-1980s redesign of the New Zealand public sector. The Treasury head Graham Scott had a deep scepticism of outcomes as a performance device, based on his experience of programme budgeting, which had in his view degenerated into an easy budgeting solution for organizations. Budgeting for outcomes in his view provided 'a rich opportunity for plausible excuses' (Scott 2001:175–6), offering the same risk as programme definitions, of descending into 'a debate about evidence, causality and degree of control'. While definitions of outputs might at times be 'arbitrary', he argued that this technique was 'more reliable than would be any attempt to attribute input or output costs to outcomes.'

In contrast to the major effort involved in specifying outputs and creating cost systems to track them, outcome goals and targets were left as the responsibility of politicians to articulate. National Party-led governments of the 1990s grappled with defining government outcomes as strategic results areas (SRAs) such as 'reducing crime' or 'reducing income inequality'.[1] The aim was to guide ministers in developing their desired outcomes, and assist agencies in thinking about what outputs might be relevant to their achievement. The term 'key results areas'

(KRAs) was used to describe the contributions made by agencies to the SRAs and to encourage chief executives to collaborate across ministry and agency boundaries. National-Party-led coalition governments between 1994 and 1999 sought to make strategic priorities explicit through this framework and held strategic planning retreats for cabinet ministers at which cross-portfolio issues and inter-organizational outcomes could be debated.

A major flaw in this approach proved to be a profusion of KRAs from public service organizations, each claiming to be indispensable for achieving strategic results areas. The strategy process became overloaded with information, leading to a disillusion with the SRA/KRA approach which predated a change of government in 1999.

An assessment of government planning processes (Petrie 2001) concluded that information provided about outcomes was 'so general as to be virtually meaningless'. Disillusion with the strategy-setting process, and increasing concerns about a lack of balance from the focus on outputs, combined with a change of government to create the environment for change.

Overemphasizing output

The performance model developed in New Zealand in the late 1980s defined public value through the use of two dichotomies – government as purchaser and as owner, and public sector results as outputs and as outcomes. Schick (1996) in a major review of the system concluded that the 'purchase interest' had driven out the 'ownership interest.'

As a central agency control device, output measurement achieved the important result of creating an 'electric fence'[2] against overspending. While budget blowouts were a regular feature of the pre-1988 system, they have since been a rarity, as chief executives on performance contracts have been held accountable for staying within fixed output budgets. Such fiscal discipline has helped achieve a consistent run of budget surpluses since 1994.

However, concerns about the impact of a single-minded focus on outputs accumulated during the 1990s. Schick (1996) thought the reliance on contracts led to a checklist mentality where managers delivered only those things that were specified in the formal performance system. Stace and Norman (1997) and Norman (2001) found that public sector managers were increasingly uneasy about the extent of emphasis placed on results that were easy to measure and auditable.

Effectively, the focus on outputs benefited those public services that Wilson (1989) and Gregory (1995) categorize as 'production tasks', where the final output is also an outcome. Functions such as tax administration, passports, land titles, employment placements and company registration were able to use the reporting frameworks to demonstrate considerable gains in productivity, particularly through the use of information technology. Meanwhile, public services in areas such as health, social welfare and education tasks struggled to demonstrate progress. Their work tends to involve 'coping' or 'craft' tasks, to use Wilson's (1989) typology. Coping tasks involve persuasion and behaviour change with often-reluctant clients, such as those in the care of social workers or probation officers. Craft tasks have observable long-term outcomes such as educated children, but the outputs by which outcomes are achieved are much less visible professional processes. The fourth task, described as 'procedural', had clear outputs in the form of processes intended to maintain systems such as court processes.

Concerns about the effect of the purchase and output model as a definition of public value prompted the 1999 Labour-led government to review the public management systems, with one of the terms of reference focusing on the question:

> Whether the division of the state sector into a large number of departments and agencies, including the division between policy and delivery, is leading to an excessively narrow focus by managers and a loss of co-ordination across the public sector. (SSC 2001:29)

The effect of the dichotomy between outputs and outcomes was well captured for the author in an interview with a senior manager in the year 2000. The manager spoke of 'a disjuncture between committing psychologically to produce outcomes, but limiting formal paper contracting to outputs'. Outcomes were 'what we are really doing, what our heart is in and we are responsible for' but the accountability system required specification in terms of measurable outputs. That observation neatly captured the 'horns of the dilemma' of polarizing outputs and outcomes. In an outputs system, the manager who veers too far from the auditable and measurable can lose reputation and risk his or her job, even though outcome-oriented work is proceeding and may in the longer term be leading to more effective public value.

New efforts to focus on outcomes

Efforts to strengthen outcomes as a focus for public service work have been introduced incrementally, in contrast to the rapid and revolutionary changes of the late 1980s. After a series of pilot projects, the system-wide planning and reporting cycle was changed in 2003 to place more emphasis on outcomes, 'strategic intent' and organizational capability. By 2006 all public agencies had completed a full cycle of the new planning and reporting framework.

After nearly 15 years as deliverers of specified outputs, contributing to politically expressed 'outcomes,' chief executives and public sector organizations gained formal responsibility, in 2003, for managing for outcomes, while also being held accountable for efficiency measures related to outputs.

The significance of 'managing for' outcomes was highlighted in the official briefing for the new system: 'Outcomes are influenced by many factors. Some are in our control: others are not. Because of this chief executives are not accountable for achieving outcomes but are held accountable for "managing for outcomes"'(SSC 2005). Good information on results would help to decide what to start, what to stop and what to continue or expand.

Publicity for legislation for the new planning format (the Public Finance (State Sector Management) Act 2004) noted that the previous system had showed a 'strong bias toward financial matters and outputs, with little or no reference to other important aspects of performance, such as outcomes or organizational capability.' Previous reports had an 'almost exclusive focus on short-term (annual) intentions and results' (SSC 2003).

Managing for outcomes is envisaged as a cycle of continuous improvement, a self assessment tool, not an accountability mechanism, including:

- *Direction setting.* What do we intend to achieve over the next 3 to 5 years and why?
- *Planning.* What is the best way to achieve this and have we got the required capability?
- *Implementation and delivery.* Are we implementing and delivering as planned and managing out capability and risks effectively?
- *Review.* What impact have our interventions had and what improvements can we make?

Budget guidelines (Treasury 2006) now explicitly state that the role of a ministry or agency is to provide advice to ministers about outcomes they might want the ministry/agency to pursue, their relative priorities and whether the existing outputs are the most efficient and effective ones to achieve these outcomes.

The transition to a focus on outcomes is not straightforward. Budget specialists participating in a focus group established by the researcher[3] thought that in the first two years of the new system, outcomes were more of an overlay on outputs, rather than a fundamental change. In their view, outputs and fiscal control routines remained the essence of the performance budgeting and reporting system. Outcomes, in the view of the focus group, were taking an 'inordinately long time to reach maturity'. Agencies were on a spectrum in terms of the 'level of development and the robustness of outcomes and their measurement'.

The focus group agreed that requiring new budget bids to be clearly linked to outcomes was pushing the pace of change, but gathering appropriate data to prove links between outputs and outcomes was very difficult. The system required a 'high degree of understanding causality', which was difficult because in most public services a number of agencies had an impact on any single outcome.

The newness of the outcomes initiative in New Zealand means that this planning and reporting system is still largely untested rhetoric. It remains to be seen how effectively the 'manage for outcomes' distinction will result in a balance between the motivational power of outcome goals and the clear accountability provided by well-specified output targets.

Reconciling outputs and outcomes

Peter Hughes, chief executive of the Ministry of Social Development, which delivers employment and benefit services, has identified a way outputs and outcomes might be reconciled so the benefits of both can be retained. In his view, outputs are the equivalent of 'bottom line' accountabilities in the private sector, with outcomes being the 'top line'.

Outcomes can only be tackled effectively once 'core business', as defined by outputs, is under control. Achievement of outcomes relies on effective delivery of outputs, and the maintenance processes of equity, consistency and integrity, which are features of traditional bureaucracies. Outcomes are at the top of a staircase.

While accountability for outputs is the 'bottom line' of public sector management, the real gains are to be made by focusing on the 'top line' of outcomes. Such a change in approach is hard, in Peter Hughes' view, for people 'socialized in the '1990s straight-line accountability ideas' where the paradigm was 'you can only get performance if you can get accountability'.

Outcomes are a more 'organic' form of management which requires building relationships, rather than cascading performance agreements. Outcomes can work because 'most people are intrinsically motivated'. 'What we should focus on is the top line, which is the territory of outcomes.' The struggle should be with achievement of outcomes, not accountabilities, which should just be the bottom line, or the floor for the system.

In this chief executive's view, outcomes make immediate sense to frontline staff. Speaking about outcomes to field staff is like 'talking commonsense'. 'The client is in front of you. You know what the right

Table 12.1 *Strengths and weaknesses of outputs and outcomes*

	Outputs	Outcomes
Strengths	Clear, measurable statements of results, defined by quality, quantity and timeliness indicators. They can be clearly linked to the ability of a particular organization and chief executive to achieve and provide a 'no- excuses' approach to accountability for results rather than inputs.	Purpose-oriented descriptions of results, which take a broad and long-term perspective. They are potentially inspirational and motivational and sufficiently broad to incorporate contributions from a number of organizations.
Weaknesses	The focus of measurement can shift towards that which can be measured and easily audited. The output can become the goal in the process of goal displacement, at the expense of longer-term and more meaningful achievements.	An outcome can become so broad that it can mean all things to all people, with achievement being very difficult if not impossible to measure. An outcome statements can become window-dressing, which prevents outsiders from assessing how well an organization is doing.

thing to do is.' Resistance was more likely to come from middle managers and central agencies, 'the equivalent of middle managers in the government system'. 'The most remote bits of the system are the last to change. They don't face the client; they don't face the big picture. It's the same in central agencies where they don't face the client, and don't face the big picture.'

After 15 years of extreme focus on outputs, the New Zealand government's performance management system now expects public servants to 'manage for outcomes' while continuing to be accountable for outputs. The change is a result of outputs becoming too narrowly focused on the easily measurable and do-able, and the new system potentially offers a way of combining 'bottom line' accountability with the motivating power of less measurable outcomes.

The use of outputs as almost the only definition of public value, coupled with severe employment consequences for chief executives whose agencies failed to deliver on output indicators resulted in varying degrees of goal displacement (Merton 1957; Blau 1963). For example the Work and Income Department's single-minded pursuit of output indicators, as if the organization were a private sector bank operating independently of other public sector agencies, resulted in a political backlash, the removal of the chief executive and the subordination of the department within a larger ministry.

For designers of public sector performance systems there is a dilemma that both outputs and outcomes provide useful and important definitions of public value, and overemphasis on either can produce dysfunctional results. The strengths and weaknesses of each are summarized in Table 12.1. Too strong an emphasis on either outputs or outcomes risks setting in motion a cycle common to public administration reforms, identified by Kaufman (1956:1057). Exclusive emphasis on one value can create difficulties which then prompt calls for further change. Kaufman analysed values of representativeness, neutral competence and executive leadership, but the same cycle can be observed in the use of performance systems.

The current challenge of the New Zealand performance system is to reconcile the dilemma created by the contrasting values of outputs and outcomes. Hampden-Turner (1991) contends that a creative reconciling of dilemmas can lead to superior performance. Simons (1995) presents performance management as a craft of balancing yin and yang elements. The dark yin represents externally imposed controls such as measurable outputs and constraints on management action, while the lightness of the yang symbolizes the motivating power of self-driven initiative, such as that sought by outcomes.

Performance management in New Zealand in the late 1980s was driven by the pressure of a fiscal crisis, focused first on externally imposed controls. Since 2003, the planning and reporting processes have been changed to give agencies a mandate to 'manage for outcomes' while still being accountable to deliver outputs. This chapter describes the challenges involved in reconciling the outputs–outcomes dilemma, by reviewing the history of the New Zealand performance system and the reasons for recent change.

Conclusion

In seeking to break up a process-bound bureaucracy, New Zealand public management reformers in the late 1980s relied strongly on output targets and contracting to instil a new focus on results. As a technique for disturbing deep-seated organizational routines, funding for outputs has proved a powerful method of fiscal control and managerial accountability. But as Kaufman (1956) identified, overemphasis on one value of administration can create the conditions for a subsequent move to a different definition of value. Overemphasis on outputs has prompted the move to 'managing for outcomes,' a way of reconciling differing values that to date however remains largely untested.

The current challenge in New Zealand is to define 'public value' by reconciling two necessary but potentially conflicting features of a control system (Simons 1995). Outputs provide important 'diagnostic reporting', enabling managers to do the equivalent of setting a thermo-stat and being able to rely on preset standards to guide action, and change course when the need is clear from the variances. Outputs have also been found to narrow the definition of performance, resulting in 'goal displacement' and the creation of organizational silos focused on delivering measurable and auditable results.

Outputs provide the equivalent of the bottom line of private sector management. They channel effort and ensure a minimum threshold of performance, providing diagnostic clues about progress with results. Outcomes, as the chief executive quoted in this article suggests, add a 'top line' dimension to public sector performance, which potentially provides a motivational challenge to exceed the formally defined accountability targets and take into account the perspectives of clients and citizens in defining public value.

Public sectors have a long tradition of fashions and failures in the use of reporting systems (for example, Wildavksy's (1992) analysis of Planning, Programming and Budgeting System (PPBS) and zero-based budgeting initiatives). New Zealand's adoption of a radical approach to performance management in the late 1980s has been influential in the development of accounting and measurement systems in many other countries. The current effort to reconcile output-based account-ability with the broader picture provided by outcomes is less a sign of fashion or failure than an effort to reconcile tensions inherent in per-formance and control systems.

The challenge now is to reconcile the values inherent in the 'short-hand' descriptions of public value that outputs and outcomes repre-sent.

Chapter 13

Effective Supply and Demand and the Measurement of Public and Social Value

GEOFF MULGAN

All public strategies aim to turn the public's hard-earned money and freedoms into something more valuable: for example, security, better health or more education. Over the last decade much work has gone into trying to make sense of this value (see Kelly *et al.* 2002; Atkinson 2006; Mulgan *et al.* 2006), with metrics and targets that have shifted attention onto outcomes rather than outputs or activities. A recent survey by the Young Foundation discovered several hundred methods in use, many the offspring of the social impact assessment tools of the 1960s and 1970s.

Until the 1990s, international accounting conventions assumed that public sector productivity never improved. Yet in a period of greater public pressure for results, and value for money, that position became untenable, and considerable effort has gone into working out not just what public interventions cost, but also what value they create, and, just as important, what value civil society can provide for public commissioners and purchasers.[1]

Better metrics do not of themselves deliver better outcomes. You can't fatten a pig by weighing it. But if you don't have some means of weighing it you may find yourself unable to persuade others that it's as fat as you believe. Many methods try to put a price on value. The idea that the value to be gained from a new training programme can be directly compared with the value from a health screening programme or water conservation is immediately appealing to busy bureaucrats and ministers.

The methods which try to monetize public value usually draw either on what people say they would pay for a service or outcome ('stated preference methods') or on the choices people have made in related fields ('revealed preference'). There are also methods which try to adjust the cost of public services with reference to quality – for example comparing school exam results, or the success of operations.

Many methods attempt to add up disparate outcomes, from lower prison numbers to increased employment, and then to apply discount rates. Other methods compare public policy actions by estimating the extra income people would need to achieve an equivalent gain in life satisfaction. One imaginative study of a regeneration scheme, for example, showed that modest investments in home safety costing about 3 per cent as much as home repairs generated four times as much value in terms of life satisfaction (Dolan and Metcalfe 2008a). Analyses of this kind are at the very least instructive, particularly when they point to surprising results. [2]

But paying too much attention to monetary equivalence can lead to bad decisions. The different methods used to assess value can generate wildly different numbers, and they often miss out what people turn out to value most. Revealed preference and stated preference methods are notoriously unreliable; in the example above the urban regeneration project was found to have achieved an improvement equivalent to £19,000 per person of working age, yet 'willingness to pay' studies came up with a figure of only £230 per year (Dolan and Metcalfe 2008b).

As I will argue, all methods of this kind are useful only to the extent that they help inform the negotiations between providers of services and their users, or between public agencies and the citizens who pay for them. These conversations and negotiations are bound to involve qualities as well as quantities, values as well as value. As many commentators have pointed out, there is an analogy with the electromagnetic spectrum. Although radiation can take many forms, only a narrow range of frequencies are visible to the naked eye in the form of light. Similarly money focuses attention on only some of the features of the world around us and obscures others. Since many of the features it obscures matter a great deal to the voting public, it's not surprising that the simpler attempts to monetize public value have failed.

More sophisticated thinking about value tries to mitigate this common optical distortion by analysing what really matters to the public. In this chapter I set out an approach to value that tries to make the most of useful metrics without falling prey to the many pitfalls.[3]

I first became interested in the idea of public value when I read a remarkable book called *Relevance Lost* (Johnson 1991). A history of management accounting is not likely to be a gripping read. But this book tells in a very lively way the story of how over two centuries successive generations of business leaders, technicians and management accountants devised new ways to track value in everything from railways and steel to aerospace and software. It reveals that value is rarely easy to grasp and is never an objective fact. The economists' accounts of managers equating marginal costs and marginal returns turn out to be fanciful. Instead, even within firms, value is constantly being re-estimated and reallocated in the light of changing priorities and changing production technologies.

It seemed likely that the same would be true in the public sector where the dimensions of value are even more complex than in the world of business for which profit and loss provide at least a rough-and-ready measure of success. There are many methods for trying to make sense of value in the public sector and providing a bridge between the complex patterns of public demands and needs, as expressed through political and other processes, and the changing production systems that keep people healthy, educated or safe. Cost–benefit analysis has been the most widely used, mainly in transport (where in recent years it has been integrated with environmental appraisals) and for big projects (which are notorious for underestimating costs) (Flyvbjerg *et al.* 2003). There are also the many theories and applications of public sector welfare economics; the burgeoning field of environmental economics which has spawned methods for measuring everything from wetlands to emissions; and the lively thinking that has surrounded social accounting over the last 30 years. Social accounting matrices and satellite accounts supplement GDP with additional measures of activity and value. QALYS and DALYs (quality and disability adjusted life years) have become a common measure for judging health policies and clinical interventions. In education, 'value added' measures assess how much individual schools 'add' to the quality of pupils they take in – some schools might achieve very good exam results simply because of the quality of their intake. Social impact assessment methods have been in use since the 1960s, in trying to capture all the dimensions of value that are produced by a new policy or programme. All estimate numbers to guide the hunches and assumptions of politicians and officials who need to decide whether a new road, a hospital or protecting an endangered species will add or destroy value for the public they serve (Becker 1997; Barrow 2000; Becker and Vanclay 2003; Scholten *et al.* 2006).

The more ambitious methods try to be inclusive and exhaustive, capturing every direct and indirect impact of an intervention. In principle they and their equivalents can justify actions now that will save money in the future, showing how helping ex-offenders into work, investing in young children, or promoting health will lead in the long run to higher tax revenues or lower prison bills. Detailed methods have been in use for several decades to estimate the direct costs of an action (for example a drug treatment programme), the probability of it working, and the likely impact on future crime rates, hospital admissions or welfare payments. Analysis of this kind can be very powerful. In the USA, for example, researchers identified what they called 'million dollar blocks' where the costs associated with criminals topped the million dollar mark. In principle, good preventive actions targeted at the people living in these blocks might save far more than they cost if they diverted some people from a life of crime. A recent study in the UK found that using a mix of drug treatment, surveillance and behavioural interventions instead of prison could deliver cost savings per offender of as much as £88,000 for the taxpayer only and up to £200,000 if savings to victims were included (http://www.matrix-knowledge.co.uk/wp-content/uploads/economic-case-for-and-against-prison.pdf).

These analyses can be made highly sophisticated. They can, for example, be adapted to reflect income distribution, on the principle that an extra dollar, or an extra unit of utility, is worth more to a poor person than a rich one (since 2003 the UK Government's Green Book has required all appraisals to include distributional effects).

But all measurements of complex effects are inherently hard. The benefits tend to become more dispersed over time, affecting ever more agencies in ever more uncertain ways. Social science isn't robust enough to make any hard predictions about what causes will lead to what effects – there are usually far too many variables involved. Meanwhile standard cost–benefit models apply discount rates to these gains, usually based on prevailing commercial interest rates, which renders a benefit in a generation's time virtually worthless. An even more fundamental problem is that these analytic methods presume that everyone agrees on what counts as valuable. But in many of the most important fields for government action – like childcare, crime prevention or schooling – the public are divided over values as well as value. For most people, for example, there is an intrinsic virtue in punishing criminals regardless of the costs and benefits of alternatives to prison. This is why the economic models for thinking about public goods and externalities, though informative, are often inadequate to the real choices faced by policy-makers and out of sync with public attitudes and politics.

Developing a model of public value

At the beginning of the 2000s I commissioned a programme of work within the Cabinet Office Strategy Unit to flesh out the idea of public value. This section draws on that work which was published as 'Creating Public Value' by the Cabinet Office in 2002. We started with a few simple principles (see Moore 1995; Bozeman 2002; Jackson 2001). One was that something should be considered valuable only if citizens – either individually or collectively – are willing to give something up in return for it. Sacrifices can be monetary (for example paying taxes or charges); they can involve granting coercive powers to the state (for example in return for security), disclosing private information (for example in return for more personalized services), giving time (for example as a school governor) or other personal resources (for example donating blood). Some idea of 'opportunity cost' is essential for public value: if it is claimed that citizens would like government to produce something, but they are not willing to give anything up in return, then it is doubtful that the activity really is seen as valuable. For example an opinion poll that suggests that citizens would like government to spend more money on services but fails to indicate public willingness to pay for this course of action does not constitute evidence that higher spending will increase public value.

Another principle was that the different dimensions of value should not automatically be treated as commensurable. Economics has traditionally treated all values in this way: anything can be traded off against anything else, and turned into a monetary value. But many of the currencies governments deal with are not like this. Laws ensure that such things as votes, body parts and freedoms can't be sold, and the public turn out to have very clear views about which kinds of exchange or trade-off are legitimate and which ones are not. This is one reason why the many attempts to coerce different types of value into single numbers (as has happened with standard economic measures, as well as many environmental measures, cost–benefit analysis, and some methods used for estimating social returns on investment) have often destroyed relevant information rather than helping decision-makers. Useful methods of valuation need to cope with varied types of value, with differing degrees of certainty.

A more challenging principle is that any measures of value should be comprehensible and plausible to the public. It's not enough for a measure to make sense to specialists. If it doesn't help to educate the public about choices, and to enrich the democratic process, then it's likely at some point to be rendered irrelevant by raw politics.

Many things that governments do are valuable to the public, but they fall roughly into three main categories. The first is the value provided by services – like well-maintained roads, or hospitals. Services can be relatively easy to analyse in terms of value. In some cases there are private sector benchmarks, and in others people can be asked how much they would be willing to pay for different levels of service – for example, evening opening of a library, or retaining a very local post office.

The second category of value is outcomes – like lower crime, or security from invasion. Again, through democratic argument, or through surveys, people can place a rough value on these. One of the outcomes they often value highly is equity. In the UK 79 per cent of people (a figure that hardly varies across social groups) agree with the statement, 'Public services should be targeted at those with greatest need,' suggesting that they are not interested only in their own experience (Public

Management Foundation 1996). Whether people use privately funded alternatives to public provision has surprisingly little impact on their propensity to support higher state spending (there is a slight decrease in support for state spending on health and transport, but none in education – IFS 1997) and 66 per cent of people refer to their relationship with public services as being that of citizens or members of the public compared with only 30 per cent who think of themselves as customers or users (Public Management Foundation 1996).

A third category of value is trust in its widest sense, which includes whether the work of government is seen as just and fair. A recent study in Michigan, for example, found a significant link (a correlation of 0.26) between perceptions of procedural justice in government services, as distinct from outcomes, and trust in politicians (Miller and Listhaug 2002). There are many examples of reforms which apparently improved efficiency but ruptured this relationship and therefore damaged the legitimacy of government (Demery *et al.* 1993).

Social and public value: effective demand and effective supply

A critical conclusion of our work was that value is never an objective fact. Believing that it is has been the most consistent mistake of many of the methods used to assess social or public value. Instead these types of value can only be understood as arising from the interplay of supply and demand, and through processes of negotiation and argument. In consumer markets, value is determined by the shifting decisions of individual consumers and the interaction of supply and demand. In the public sector it's refracted through political argument, and more specifically from the interplay of what I call 'effective demand' and 'effective supply'. Effective demand means that someone is willing to pay for a service, an outcome or a change in trust. That someone may be a public agency, or it may be individual citizens. Effective supply means that there is a capacity to provide that service, outcome or trust: a public agency, NGO or business.

In some fields there are mature links between supply and demand: for example public willingness to pay through taxes for policing, or primary schools, connects to governments' ability to supply in familiar ways. In other fields the links are missing. There may be available supply but insufficient demand – because the public or politicians don't see the need as sufficiently pressing (in some countries drug treatment or sex education would fall into this category). In other cases there may be demand but inadequate supply at a reasonable cost (for example of methods for cities to cut carbon emissions).

Both sides of the equation may be complex or fragmented. In many areas of social policy demand for the results that come from more holistic approaches is split across many different public agencies, from welfare to prisons. Equally the supply may be equally fragmented, depending on the contribution of many different agencies, for example providing therapy, alcohol treatment, skills, and housing.

In these cases value has to be discovered, and a critical role will be played by a 'social market maker' who brings together supply and demand. This could be a local council or a national government (and in rare cases a foundation). To do this well they need to help both sides of the market clarify what they want and what they can provide. On the demand side public agencies need to work out what they are willing to pay for lower crime in 5 years' time or lower welfare payments. On the supply side, analysis needs to show what can plausibly be expected from different mixes of actions. For this, some of the existing social impact assessment or social return on investment methods can be used. Then a series of negotiations can take place to commission activities and services, with the 'social market maker' working to ensure that no agencies try to free ride on others. These processes are likely to work best when they can be disaggregated as well as aggregated, for example when commissioning agencies can directly specify what they want from provider agencies.

Horizons in time

To be strategic is to take the future seriously, and to resist the myopia that particularly affects institutions facing intense pressures to be accountable for present actions. Many institutions try to formalize their relationship to the future through devices to compare future values with present ones. Governments use discount rates to judge when to make investments, since a sum of money in 5 years' time is less useful, and less certain, than an equivalent sum of money now. Typically annual discount rates are around 5 per cent. These try to reflect both time preferences and also, in the more sophisticated versions, to take account of the fact that extra income in the future will be worth less than income today because future populations will be richer (the UK Treasury currently applies a 1.5 per cent rate to reflect time preferences, and 2 per cent to reflect these income effects).

A strict application of discount rates from the private sector radically reduces the attraction of investments in the future. A 5 per cent discount rate values $100 after 30 years at $35.85 today, and after 50 years at $7.69. Even the lower discount rates sometimes applied to health (like the 3 per cent usually applied to QALYs in the US) still render years saved in the distant future much less valuable than years saved now. But these 'exponential' discount rates are at odds with how people think and act.

Much of our behaviour reflects an implicit 'hyperbolic' discount rate that starts off high but declines, putting a higher value on distant outcomes than do exponential rates. In our own lives we generally regret past decisions that applied a high discount rate to future gains, and there is some evidence that people apply different 'mental accounts' to their choices (for example with a different way of accounting for investment in their own education, housing, pensions or their own children). Most governments also apply quite different discount rates to different phenomena, which is why they are willing to invest in future defence, education or infrastructures. Their behaviour is closer to that of a guardian or steward who is charged with sustaining or growing capital, rather than the strictly rational consumers of economic theory who always value present consumption more than future consumption.

Environmental economics has been riven by arguments over the appropriate discount rate to apply to issues like climate change. Nicholas Stern, author of an influential UK government review, argued that the 'inherent discounting' of economists such as William Nordhaus (who advocated a 3 per cent discount rate as a measure of future uncertainty in the costs and benefits of action on climate change) was ethically questionable because it devalued the future. His analysis applied a zero pure time preference and compared benefits today and in the future by comparing percentages of income (rather than cash), weighting income for the poor more than the rich, and for today's citizens more than future ones, since whereas current average global income is around $7000 his forecasts projected average world income in 2100 at around $100,000 (Quiggin 2006). But in all of these analyses economics has clearly reached its limits. It cannot explain some basic contradictions like the very wide gap between equity returns and returns for bonds (which calls into question the idea of a single market discount rate). And it cannot explain much of what's been observed in human behaviour in relation to the future.

Sociology may offer additional insights. If we dig deeper we find that attitudes to time generally reflect the intensity of social bonds and commitments. Very strong commitments eliminate the difference between the present and the future, even though there is still the same uncertainty as in commercial markets. Parents may commit all to their children's future; aristocratic landlords commit to passing on richer estate than they inherit; and for a committed NGO or social movement it is simply inappropriate to devalue future rewards – the cause is everything. Similarly where fundamental rights are involved it is inappropriate to devalue the future. Assessments of QALYs in a rights-based healthcare system might be expected to treat a year of life in

2050 as equal in value to an extra year of life in 2020: if they didn't they would build in a profound bias in favour of the old and against the young. The application of standard discount rates turns out to reflect the values of highly individualized market economies and sectors. It is, in fact, quite culturally specific.

These apparently arcane issues are very relevant to questions as diverse as climate change and childcare, both of which involve profound moral commitments. They suggest that assessments of social or public value need to explicitly take account of how public attitudes and morality affect time preferences. These attitudes are likely to show a very different view of time in those parts of the public realm which are most like private consumption (for example, air travel) as opposed to those which are touched with moral obligations of stewardship or mutuality (Price 1993; Offer 2006).

Public value in the built environment

The built environment of cities provides an example of how these ideas can be applied. Buildings are self-evidently things of value, and they can last for a very long time, far beyond the horizon of standard discount rates. They also provide a range of different kinds of value, to owners, users, residents and passers-by. There are many dozens of methods already in use to measure aspects of value in the built environment. These include 'multi-criteria' analysis methods such as VALID and DQI; 'stated-preference' models and an array of choice modelling and hedonic methods; quality-of-life metrics; environmental impact assessments; environmental footprints; placecheck; local environmental quality survey (LEQs); and landscape area characterization methods. These and others are described in Young Foundation and CABE (2006).

Some of these are relevant to thinking about public value in any field while others are very specific. Some of these are designed to guide investors, including income capitalization methods as well as methods focused on profits, residuals and replacement costs; methods using multiple regressions and stepwise regressions; methods using artificial neural networks and 'hedonic' price models (which attempt to define the various characteristics of a product or service); spatial analysis methods; fuzzy logic methods; and, for the eager, 'auto-regressive integrated moving averages methods' and 'triple bottom line property appraisal methods'. The different methods in use serve different interests – the developers concerned with asset values and income streams, other landlords and the public who may benefit from new parks or canals, municipalities which may benefit from growing tax revenues and the wider public who may benefit from lower crime. Each also has different strengths and weaknesses: hedonic methods, for example, ignore the values of buildings for which there is no market; multi-criteria analyses provide little help in allocating resources; and contingent choice methods reduce the value of the poor.

What none of these achieve is a method for handling the wide range of different types of value which are involved in urban developments, including not only the reasonably measurable world of asset values, rental streams and tax revenue streams, but also less tangible things like the value of good design or aesthetics, and the impact of design choices on crime, health and the environment. There is strong evidence that the urban environment affects health both directly and indirectly (for example through availability of leisure time); it also affects people's feelings of safety as well as objective levels of crime. Any major urban development can not only create private and public value but also damage value, whether through shutting off lines of sight, weakening the cohesion of communities, or cutting fitness levels if walking and cycling routes are replaced with roads for cars.

This field is a good one for thinking about value in that there are many tools in use around the world for capturing what's sometimes called 'planning gain' – the surplus which results from conferring planning consent on a developer. This means that there are often very overt negotiations trading off private values against public values, for example, requiring a developer to provide affordable housing or childcare facilities. Effective supply and effective demand come together in negotiations of this kind.

How they come together will depend on the underlying structure of value, which varies greatly in different fields. In the case of the built environment, value has a roughly four-level structure:

- The underlying value of land which is usually seen as a common good (since it is scarce, and socially defined, by planning decisions which can at a stroke increase land values a thousandfold, for example when agricultural land is redesignated for office development). Much of the theoretical work on development over the last century has focused on how to capture economic rents associated with land.
- The market value of buildings – including rental streams, property values as well as tax revenues – in proposed developments
- The other kinds of value that can be created or destroyed – including indirect effects on other property values but also various types of public value, including crime reductions, design and aesthetics, health effects (for example fitness), merit goods, environmental goods and so forth.

- The relationship between a development and the broader context for the city – its connectivity, contribution to economic growth potential, and so on.

Good planning processes ensure that economic rent on land is not captured by developers but directed to public good: in other words the surplus on level 1 is used to subsidize value at level 3. Local governments try to measure and capture this value through betterment levies, development land taxes and planning gain supplements (and a clutch of other potential devices), in order to finance public services or environmental improvements.

To put numbers on value there is a limited range of methods to use. As we've seen some ask people how much they would pay for a new service or a different kind of building. 'Stated preference' methods estimate what non-users might value, whether through 'altruistic use' (knowing someone else might like it); 'option use' (having the opportunity to do something if you want); 'bequest use (leaving something for the future), and 'existence use' (satisfaction that things exist even if you don't enjoy them personally). All methods of this kind are notoriously prone to distortions and have to be 'triangulated' with other methods. The most important of these look at real choices that people have made. These 'revealed preferences' are more reliable but gathering relevant data about how people respond to real choices is bound to be hard. 'Travel cost method' is one example which looks at the time and travel cost expenses that people incur to visit a site as a proxy for their valuation of that site. Because travel and time costs increase with distance it's possible to construct a 'marginal willingness to pay' curve for a particular site. Then there are methods which enable people to change their views through discussion, such as 'planning for real' exercises which enable the public to generate alternative options rather than being solely ex-post methods. In the future many more of these may be correlated with evidence on life satisfaction, using 'before and after' surveys to find out what exactly makes people happy.

These many methods provide insights into structures of value, and in all fields of public activity there are distinctive structures of value too. For example, in education, some value accrues directly to the learner (in the form of future earnings), while some accrues to the family or the wider community. Several decades of research has tried to distinguish individual and social returns from different types of education. In vocational education the structure is different from that in the imparting of generic skills. Some skills may be not only specific to an industry, but also to a location (for example particular language skills). A programme providing intensive support to a chaotic drug-user will have a more complicated structure of value, creating some value for the individual (both financial and in terms of wellbeing) as well as value for a wide range of public agencies (from hospitals whose emergency services will be less used, to police prisons and welfare agencies). To all of these can be added the complexities which come from data on life satisfaction, which tell us that it's not just absolute gains that matter, but also changed relative position. In other words, even if our position improves, if others around us improve more we may end up less happy. The general point here is that value is not one-dimensional, commensurate, quantifiable and comparable. Instead its specific character and context needs to be understood.

Any model of public or social value becomes useful only if it can inform processes for making decisions that bring effective supply and effective demand together. In the case of the physical environment this will include developers proposing plans through to approval, building and subsequent monitoring. In other fields the critical stages may include budget bids and planning, and subsequent allocations by finance ministries and cabinets. Using these methods earlier and upstream in decision-making helps to ensure that a range of options can be assessed rather than only one. Negotiations can then consider a rich range of options on the margins (for example everything from building heights to tenure mix to construction of childcare centres, street architecture and bicycle racks) as well as more basic trade-offs (for example between the interests of the elderly and families with children, or between cars and the environment).

Lessons for social and public value

These examples bring out some important general lessons which we have taken forward in the design of tools for measuring value in the National Health Service and in the social sector, in particular to guide spending decisions both in the commissioning of services and in the funding of specific innovations.[4]

First, measures of value are useful only to the extent that they support negotiations and arguments about what needs to be done. They are useful if they bring choices and trade-offs to the surface, useless if they disguise them. Second, more creative ways of handling value generally depend on a guardian or social market-maker who takes responsibility for bringing demand and supply together. In a democracy that has to involve democratically elected politicians whose constitutional role it is to distil and represent public preferences, even if sometimes they also have to challenge the public's beliefs. In relation to urban developments municipalities can play this role, and at least some of the time they can be reasonably neutral between the competing stakeholders (by contrast, the use of public value measures by public agencies primarily to legitimate themselves is inherently more problematic, and always risks being self-serving). Third, value is an aspect of the relationship between states and citizens rather than an objective fact. It is shaped by what each considers desirable and important and then becomes more precise through processes of conversation and negotiation.

In any real-world situation, trade-offs have to be struck between the costs and time involved in more detailed assessments of value and the need for urgency. But more systematic methods of mapping public and social value make assumptions more explicit and allow a more honest discussion between stakeholders about what they want and about what they can realistically get, helping technocrats avoid what Oscar Wilde described as the vice of knowing the price of everything and the value of nothing.

Chapter 14

Learning, Social Inequality and Risk: A Suitable Case for Public Value?

BOB FRYER

Personal troubles and public issues

Nearly 50 years ago, the celebrated radical American scholar C. Wright Mills (1959) described the principal intellectual challenge for the 'sociological imagination': to inquire into the complex links and subtle interplay between 'personal troubles' and 'public issues' exploring and thus understanding better the relationship between biography and history. In undertaking such a review, the role and skills of the scholar are to 'shuffle' back and forth between both persons and systems, on the one hand, and between empirical evidence and interpretive concepts and theories, on the other, in order to throw light on the main problems of the day.

Learning as 'public value'

The approach advocated by Mills, bringing burning personal concerns into direct relationship with a critical analysis of public policy and social provision, lends itself easily – automatically, you might even say – to the emerging field of 'public value', as an innovative framework for assessing the role, worth and impact of government and public services. Such a combination of perspectives can strengthen the analytical purchase of the public value framework. The case is strengthened further by focusing on a single major area of public policy and provision, namely learning, thus helping to refine and sharpen the developing concept of public value itself.

The application of this approach to a review of publicly provided learning will provide valuable insights into the rich variety of learning's multiple dimensions. It will also illuminate an especially challenging issue in the whole public value debate, namely the dogged persistence and deep influence upon both biography and history of social inequality in public provision. What the analysis will therefore seek to explore is the contradiction of how learning appears to serve simultaneously as the chief contemporary pathway to social mobility, yet also as a pervasive site and manifestation of wider social inequalities and as a key locale of their reinforcement and re-production.

Beyond unitary measures

Even the most cursory consideration of the range of personal troubles and public issues that figure in learning indicates that its value cannot, or rather should not, be reduced to a single, overriding criterion. Yet, more and more the 'performance' of both individuals and educational providers in the UK and elsewhere is measured against proportions of candidates reaching pre-defined 'levels' by a given age, passing tests or attaining particular formal qualifications. In those cases where learning is so assessed, perhaps for reasons of administrative convenience or of summary evaluation, then the otherwise promising richness and diversity of learning is of necessity seriously diminished and, even more serious, the persistence of marked inequalities in learning is not adequately addressed.

Similarly, any proposition to assess the value of learning simply, or even largely, in terms of its market outcomes is bound to overlook critical aspects of learning, from both a private and public point of view, not least the implications of its inequalities for individuals' life chances and for the social and economic fortunes of communities and whole societies. That does not mean that market evaluations of learning are either always wholly inappropriate or impossible (although admittedly difficult) to carry out, but that, standing alone, they are most likely to be partial, restricted and incomplete, especially in any exploration of the sources and consequences of inequality in learning.

Aspects of public value

As a starting-point, learning and its inequalities can benefit from analysis and action in accordance with Mark Moore's suggestion of the 'authorizing', 'operating' and 'task' environments. Similarly, a proper assessment of both the public and private impacts of learning and, especially, its serious implications for social inequality, would benefit from considering public value outcomes rather than depending largely on the standard, conventional measures of formal examination results and institutional 'league tables'. Benington in Chapter 2 proposes a focus on political economic and social value added outcomes and processes rather than just on inputs and activities; longer-term perspectives; creation by a range of public, private and third-sector organizations; a variable 'value chain' of production for different services; and scope for 'co-creation' of public value between service producers and users.

The Learning and Skills Development Agency has also suggested that the British further education and skills sector would benefit from the wider perspective on its various provision and functions that would follow from reviewing its performance from a public value point of view. Such an approach, say the paper's authors (Grigg and Mager 2005), could help to build a much-needed consensus on the core purposes of the sector, extend an appreciation of its contribution to a range of public policy priorities and broaden the criteria against which institutional success is measured. It would also, they claim, foster greater innovation in the sector, engender a more dynamic relationship with its main users, sharpen its focus and, incidentally, improve staff morale.

Evaluations of learning could also usefully explore the three core dimensions of 'outcomes, services and trust' that figure centrally in the analytical framework proposed by Kelly *et al.* (2002) for assessing public value as part of the reform of public services. Thus, learning might be reviewed in terms of its ethos, values, 'mood', public preferences, standards of equity, modes of public accountability and the scope for what the authors refer to as citizens' and users' involvement in 'co-development'.

An evaluation of learning that seriously followed this sort of framework would be very difficult to capture within a few simple, numerical indicators, but would enable the relationship between private problems and public issues to be more rigorously explored, in accordance with the challenge thrown down by Wright Mills. Of course, the whole business of making serious comparisons between different institutions and forms of learning and of 'benchmarking' would become much more complex and contentious, especially if such a review extended beyond formal learning into its equally significant informal, non-formal and tacit dimensions. It would certainly change the conduct and outcomes of the current 'inspection' regimes for UK public services, which would necessarily need to embrace a whole series of different conversations and be reported through extended and sensitive narratives, including one (seldom seen currently in such studies) addressing the scale and challenges of educational inequalities.

Quite rightly, Kelly *et al.* (2002) point out that, as well as operating independently, many of the different potential sources of the public value of learning they mention might also be expected to be mutually reinforcing or, on the other hand, subject to trade-offs or tensions. Unfortunately, the authors give no guidance as to who exactly should determine the eventual balance to be struck in such 'trade-offs' or how such 'tensions' might be resolved, let alone what might happen in any cases of complete contradiction or head-on conflict, such as occur quite frequently in the various fields of learning, especially where interest centres on inequality. In somewhat benign tones of reassurance, they merely state that

> recognizing these overlaps and tensions does not diminish the utility of the public value concept. Rather it clarifies the need for an integrated framework and associated decision-making techniques that will help policy makers and managers to think systematically about the various outcome benefits and costs that their actions can create (and how to weight them). (Kelly *et al.* 2002: 56)

Nevertheless, the public value framework is helpfully suggestive, and leads to a richer and more textured understanding of public provision. It promises to reveal a genuinely nuanced and multidimensional conception of the value of learning, not least by giving a serious voice to those whom learning is intended principally to benefit, especially those who manifestly gain little advantage from it, or even feel that they have been damaged by it. It also opens up many more potential lines of intervention and improvement by all those active in the many worlds of learning, as well as, more conventionally, by politicians and policy-makers.

In other words, taking an 'enhanced' public value perspective on learning seems to hold out an attractive promise, and appears to represent a domain of genuine hope for the various managers and funders of learning, as well as for teachers, mentors, advisers, learning administrators and, most importantly of all, learners themselves. That promise and hope are that the character and quality of learning, and its proper evaluation, should attest to the worth of their various contributions to, and judgements about, learning, as active agents in its organization, delivery, 'co-production' and achievements and not merely as either the impersonal instruments, largely passive beneficiaries or even victims of others' policies.

The personal problems and public issues of learning

In many respects, the different troubles and issues of learning are easy enough to summarize. On the one hand, in the sphere of private interests, it has become increasingly evident that individuals' particular life chances are more and more linked to their successes, or otherwise, in learning, both formal and informal. This mostly means, although not always, that there are discernible positive benefits apparently associated with individuals' involvement in successful learning and their (subsequent) employment and 'employability' generally, their level of authority and seniority at work and in society, their income, health, political engagement, opportunities to exercise choice, patterns of sociability, longevity and general wellbeing.[1] This appears to be the case particularly with respect to the level of that learning, its scope, the qualifications or credits gained and people's proclivity to continue learning both throughout life and across all aspects of their lifespan. If we want to thrive in the emergent 'knowledge-based' economy, we are told, we shall only do so by genuinely embracing lifelong learning. By the same token, those who do not so succeed appear mostly, but again not always, to suffer from a range of material, economic, social, political, psychological, and health disadvantages, exclusions and deprivations.

To the extent that this is true, it is scarcely surprising that, from all quarters (not least from governments), individuals are constantly urged to take ownership of their own learning, to cherish it and foster its continuous development. So far has this gone that, these days, it can very easily feel as if there is an absolute obligation on us all not just to learn successfully in the initial phases of our lives, but also to carry on learning, almost as a new moral and social duty. If we do not, we are told, we will largely have only ourselves to blame for any consequent limitations to our life chances. Not to succeed in learning and not to continue learning are thus regarded, at best, as cavalier and risky and, at worst, as both irresponsible and seriously damaging.

On the other hand, the whole business of learning is also clearly a major public concern. Education expenditure constitutes a large slice of GDP in most advanced industrial democracies, usually around 5 to 6 per cent or even more. Governments, and would-be governments, often make education and training a main plank of their political programmes and, in turn, their perceived performance in securing educational advancements frequently figure in the judgements made by electorates, press and political commentators on their relative degrees of success and failure. Politicians themselves often emphasize what they see as the public and collective interest in successful education and training policies and effective practices. They link them to such diverse matters as national prosperity, international competitiveness, skills enhancement, social inclusion, improved health, community coherence, reductions in crime, social mobility, citizenship and the prospects for thriving democracy.

In the realms of vocational training, skills for employment and preparation of young people for work, the UK is not alone is having developed extensive public policies and a range of initiatives to meet what successive governments have characterized as the various challenges of globalization, increased international competition, the 'knowledge economy', the requirements of innovation and the rise of

China. Over a period of some 20 years or so, British public policy has resulted in the creation of a 'national skills strategy', whose influence is to be discerned at every level of educational provision and qualification from schools, through further education, to universities, e-learning, workplace and adult learning.

By this token alone, the worlds of learning (and the plural is deliberate), and perhaps especially the roles and performances of those social institutions and processes specifically devoted to formal education and training – schools, colleges and universities – certainly merit serious and systematic investigation. So, too, do the various public and other bodies that are responsible for designing their policies, planning, controlling or overseeing their work, providing funding for or inspecting them, or receiving their 'products', as school-leavers, graduates and so on. Surveys of public opinion regularly demonstrate that education figures as one of the top concerns of people in Britain, while governments and international organizations as diverse as the European Union, UNESCO, the OECD and World Bank all argue that countries' future economic success and their chances of securing settled democracy are dependent upon their respective provision for learning.

Hence, inquiry into the 'personal troubles and public issues' in learning, as a key dimensions of its public value, is necessary not only in the United Kingdom but also for comparative purposes, at least, in all advanced industrial democracies, if not in every country of the world.

Learning and skills: some British evidence

The aims of British policy in the area of learning for employment were set out succinctly in the Government's White Paper, *21st Century Skills* (Department for Education and Skills 2003a). They were to 'ensure that employers have the right skills to support the success of their businesses, and individuals have the skills they need to be both employable and personally fulfilled.' British businesses and workers were seen to be far less productive than their principal oversees competitors and the country could not realistically expect to compete successfully on the basis of low wages. There was a particular shortage of technical and 'intermediate' skills, disturbingly large numbers of adults appeared to have difficulties with so-called 'basic skills' in literacy and numeracy, and there was a need to enhance the skills of management and leadership. Finally, too often, there was said to be a 'mismatch' between the skills that businesses required and the programmes of learning and levels of achievement on offer from education.

The British national skills strategy seems, in the policy documents at least, to recognize the key role and value of informal as well as formal learning, of tacit and implicit knowledge, and of learning on the job through participation, rather than being concerned simply with formal instruction. In practice, however, most of the indicators and proxies deployed to measure both individuals' educational attainment and educational institutions' effectiveness appear to depend upon using fairly simple empirical evidence of the various levels, rates and rates of improvement, numbers and proportions of learners obtaining particular qualifications or credits or reaching defined 'standards'. These are the data conventionally used in comparing the performance of different individuals, social groups and educational providers and in creating so-called 'league tables'.

It would not be fair to represent the UK government's skills strategy as being exclusively focused on jobs and the economy; social inclusion matters as well. As the 2003 White Paper (paragraphs 18–20) asserted:

> This is not only an economic challenge. It is just as much a social one. By increasing the skill level of all underrepresented groups, we will develop an inclusive society that promotes employability for all. When people are better educated and better trained, they have the chance to earn more and use their talents to the full, both in and out of work ... We are concerned that skills and learning initiatives are not reaching all of society. We want to increase the skills levels for all underrepresented groups and encourage all individuals to improve their employability. This is crucial for women workers who now constitute 44 per cent of the workforce, yet are typically locked in a narrow range of low-level manual occupations and in part-time work where training opportunities are limited. It is also an issue for ethnic minorities, agency workers and other disadvantaged groups who have low skill levels.

So, we see that governments and nations apparently need individuals to engage in relevant, successful and continuing learning to ensure their own success; individuals seem to need their governments to initiate and implement effective public policy to secure the right conditions to promote and support such learning. Of course, all of this begs the difficult and central question of what exactly constitutes 'successful learning', but more of that later.

As we also will see, this apparently straightforward reciprocity of private and public interests in learning is not quite so simple and mutually reinforcing as it might seem at first glance. Apart from anything else (and there is much else), even the most modest sociological curiosity would wonder what might be the effects on this relationship of the myriad of education and training organizations and processes that stand between aspirant individuals and expectant governments. It is not simply that there is bound to be many an empirical 'slip' between the 'cup' of strategic intent and the 'lip' of educational realities and outcomes. More importantly, social institutions and the webs of social relations, structures and systems of power in which they are embedded inevitably influence the experiences and priorities of different individuals and their chances of realizing them, as well as the likely fortunes and implications of public policy. This is especially true where learning is concerned, which is as much a distributional 'good' as a positional one.

Hence, if only as a precautionary move, it would be safest to allow for at least some differences, if not outright conflicts and struggles, in the various expectations, aims, values, preferences and interests and of the individuals and groups populating the many institutions and constituting the social relations that encompass learning. As Wright Mills wryly commented in *The Sociological Imagination*, when it comes to expectations, we should not be at all surprised if the expectations of some individuals and groups seem to count for very much more than do those of others! Nowhere is this truer than in the field of learning.

Social class, educational inequality and meritocracy

Shortly before Mills issued his inspirational challenge to the sociological imagination, two other significant publications about learning appeared in the UK. First, in 1956, came the results of the first systematic large-scale empirical research of its kind, carried out by the distinguished educational sociologists Floud, Halsey and Martin, demonstrating clearly the relationship between social class and educational attainment, and the systematic limitations on working-class educational opportunities. Second, just one year before Mills's book appeared, Michael Young published his devastatingly satirical dystopia *The Rise of the Meritocracy* (Young 1958). Young centred his gloomy critique on the contemporary world's growing replacement of the ascription of individuals' social status, largely through birth and family of origin, by the lifetime achievement of social position, through a combination of individual talent and hard work to obtain educational qualifications. For those who thus succeeded, there would, it seemed, be offered the added bonus of a new, and highly defensible, legitimacy for any resulting social inequality: any advantages accruing to the successful could be claimed to be largely 'deserved'.

The researches of Halsey and his colleagues revealed the damaging restrictions imposed upon the opportunities for working-class children of progressing through educational attainment, and the consequent squandering of their potential and the limitations experienced in their own adult lives, by the operation of the Eleven-Plus examination. This was reinforced by the subsequent segregation of children after 11 years of age, on the basis of that examination, into grammar, secondary modern or technical schools. With their work, Halsey and his colleagues opened up a greatly influential succession of 'action research' projects in the UK on the interrelated subjects of family and home background, parental attitudes, neighbourhood and peer-group influences, educational processes in schools, selection for and differentiation in secondary (post-11) education, teaching methods, assessment and the language and culture of learning. These sorts of 'educational and political arithmetic' studies have had a major impact on the policies and organization of so-called compulsory education in schools, especially on comprehensive secondary schooling, aimed at overcoming some of the worst aspects of both social and educational inequality.

Many of these kinds of deliberately policy-oriented, wide-ranging educational studies and interventions may also be seen, retrospectively to exhibit recognizable aspects of a 'public value' perspective, with a clear focus on reform and improvement and public and social outcomes. They resulted, for example, in the raising of the minimum school-leaving age to 16, changes to the public examination system for school-leavers, and the establishment in the late 1960s of educational priority areas (EPAs), led by a team headed by Halsey himself, that recognized the wider influences of home and the community on educational outcomes. EPAs were the forerunners of today's SureStart scheme, which also, in true 'public value' style, brings together a wide range of community-based services and professionals in order to support and enrich the early years' development of children from disadvantaged backgrounds.

Concerns with the persistence of educational disadvantage at school, and markedly differential levels of social class involvement and achievement in post-school learning, as revealed by research studies, also strengthened successive governments' determination to 'widen' participation in learning, to revise the schools' curriculum and examinations, to reform further education, to increase investment in skills development and to expand universities. As we shall see, despite these efforts, and notwithstanding some palpable improvements in levels of attainment amongst working-class learners, large disparities of formal attainment still stubbornly persist in what counts as 'educational success' for different social classes, for some black and minority ethnic groups and for people with disabilities. Moreover, as Helena Kennedy accurately remarked in her radical review of opportunities to widen participation in English further education, it still largely remains the case in the British educational system that, 'If at first you don't succeed, you don't succeed!' (Kennedy 1997).

The simple, raw data of educational attainment and continued involvement in learning in the UK, although admittedly showing some welcome reductions in absolute levels of inequality and some improvements in the formal attainments of the previously unqualified, are still remarkable for the sheer starkness of the social differences that they reveal. According to data collected by Anthony Heath and colleagues (2003), the overall proportion of the UK male adult population reportedly having no formal qualifications has fallen from 60 per cent among those born between 1930 and 1939 to just 15 per cent of those born between 1960 and 1969 and, commensurately, the proportions obtaining at least 'level 2' qualifications has increased from 41 per cent to 74 per cent. However, while 90 per cent of those born into professional and senior managerial families between 1960 and 1969 achieved at least 'level 2' equivalent qualifications, only 64 per cent of those from working-class backgrounds did so. Similarly, while 31 per cent of adults born into senior managerial and professional families in the same period have obtained degrees, only 5 per cent of those from working-class backgrounds have done so.

The most recent evidence from the Youth Cohort Study for England and Wales (DfES 2003), while again indicating some recent narrowing of social class differences, also demonstrates the dogged persistence of social inequality in formal educational outcomes. Whereas 77 per cent of young people from managerial and professional backgrounds obtained five or more 'good' grades at GCSE (level 2 equivalent), only 35 per cent of those from semi-skilled manual backgrounds and 32 per cent from unskilled manual backgrounds did so. The social composition of schools is also closely associated with rates of successful attainment of formal educational qualifications: research by Benn and Chitty (1996) in British comprehensive schools showed that children in schools largely composed of working-class pupils were only half as likely as those from mostly middle-class schools to obtain five or more good GCSE grades (level 2 equivalent). Young people aged 16–18 who are neither in work nor in continuing education or training are most likely to come

> from workless households, to have parents with low or no educational qualifications, and to live in social rented housing. They are also three times more likely to have been excluded from school and twice as likely to have caring responsibilities. (Fabian Society 2006)

These data confirm what other studies have revealed: despite some increases in social mobility, achieved partly through learning, people's achievements in education and beyond still closely reflect their families of origin and the neighbourhoods in which they are brought up. Those whose parents were unqualified are much more likely to be wholly unqualified or poorly qualified themselves and those with parents who possess higher levels of formal educational qualification are themselves highly likely to achieve similar or even higher levels of qualification.

Not surprisingly, then, these continuing and marked patterns of class difference are also evident in Britain's universities, despite their own often valiant attempts to widen access, where what a recent longitudinal study termed 'the long shadow of childhood' continues to be a principal influence on people's chances of getting a degree. The most recent data show that while 43 per cent of young people from classes 1 and 2 obtained higher education qualifications, still largely necessary in order to matriculate, only 14 per cent from classes 4 and 5 did so. Within an overall current participation rate in higher education in England of over 40 per cent among 18- to 21-year-olds, the comparative rates for those from the highest and lowest socio-economic groups are, respectively, almost 8 out of 10 and just over 1 in 10 (Whitson 2005). What university expansion in the UK over the past 40 years has mostly meant has been a huge increase in the opportunities for young people from already socially privileged backgrounds to gain a degree, with all of the subsequent material and other advantages. In other words, so far, the growth of British higher education has meant more of an increase in the levels of participation for certain social groups than a widening for all.

The situation in learning beyond formal education, in British workplaces and communities, confirms what has already been revealed by studies of schools, colleges and universities. Opportunities for participation in learning and the propensity to engage are closely associated with two main factors: first, one's relative position in the social hierarchies of class, status and power, and, second, one's previous record of formal educational attainment and age of leaving full-time study. At work, according to data collected regularly through the Labour Force Survey, it is senior managers, professionals and associate professionals who mostly report being involved in both job-related and other learning. Over one third of British workers report never having been offered any opportunities for learning at, for or through work. Where women workers are concerned, especially those working in lower-graded, lower-paid and part-time employment, they have fewer formal qualifications than men and less opportunity to access learning through work. According to the annual surveys of participation in adult learning undertaken by the National Institute of Adult Continuing Education, there is throughout a consistent association between social class and current, recent or likely future involvement in learning.

If these data are not sufficiently worrying for anyone concerned with ensuring that opportunity and achievement in learning outcomes are not seriously distorted by wider social inequalities, there is also evidence that some less tangible but still palpable aspects of social advantage both influence and are reinforced by learning. Thus, there are also deep divisions obtaining at the levels of both individuals and communities in the acquisition of, and resort to, the benefits of so-called 'social capital' – that cluster of relationships, skills, knowhow, networks and shared values that underpin people's ability to participate in and influence to their own advantage a wide range of institutions and processes. These include those centred on learning, skills, employment, resource allocation, political participation and decision-making, health and, crucially, the whole realm of public policy development.

At the same time, as recent research has begun to document systematically, the other side of this particular coin is understanding better the 'wider benefits' of learning. As the researchers report, existing quantitative studies of adult learning do not yet go much beyond using simple indicators of learning involvement. However, there is

> a growing body of qualitative and practitioner evidence across many types of provision [that] leads one to expect that there are general benefits of adult learning for which, so far, we have evidence in particular settings from case study, ethnographic and action research approaches. (Feinstein *et al.* 2003:12)

Again, these insights into the relationships and reciprocal benefits and other influences of learning and social capital further underline the need for a much wider, more inclusive and richer analysis of learning and its social context, as offered by a perspective on public value outcomes.

The rise of the new 'meritocratic' elite

For his part, Michael Young's great fear was that the use of education and formal qualifications to allocate people to their respective social stations in life would result merely in the replacement of one (undesirable) elite at the top of the social hierarchy by yet another. Moreover, he expected the new elite, true to form, eventually to pull up behind them the ladder that they had used to scramble to the top, in order to secure their own positions against future incursions. For those unable, for one reason or another, to succeed through this new, so-called 'meritocratic' route, life would be all the more grim, as they got increasingly left behind. This would occur, he feared, especially as some of the older and more varied ways of 'getting on' in life (particularly for working-class youngsters) – such as via apprenticeships, promotion through work or 'rising up through the ranks' – were sharply reduced or eliminated as a result of other, emerging historical changes in occupational, industrial and social structures.

Looking back on his bleak prognosis more than 40 years later, Michael Young expressed his 'sad disappointment' that a book that had been intended as a disturbing warning, had turned out to be an all too accurate forecast.

Ability of a conventional kind, which used to be distributed between the social classes more or less at random, has become much more highly concentrated by the engine of education. A social revolution has been accomplished by harnessing schools and universities to the task of sieving people according to education's narrow band of values. With an amazing battery of certificates and degrees at its disposal, education has put its seal of approval on a minority and its seal of disapproval on the many who fail to shine from the time they are relegated to the bottom streams at the age of seven or before ... It is hard indeed in a society that makes so much of merit to be judged as having none. No underclass has ever been left as morally naked as that. (Young 2001)

There could hardly be a bleaker or more chilling representation of the relationship between the personal troubles of the educationally excluded and the public issue of social advantage claimed and enjoyed on grounds of attainment and merit, and authorized, so to speak, by clear educational principles and policy. For all of the good intentions and strenuous efforts of those seeking to uncouple learning from the wider and pervasive influences of class, status and power, learning obstinately remains not simply a key site for the manifestation of inequality: it also persists in being a core mechanism for both reproducing and reinforcing it.

This stark issue not only sharply captures the critical intersection of people's personal troubles with a major public issue; it also represents one of the single most challenging problems for the emergent analytical framework of public value. It is not simply a question of whether the public value paradigm can fully capture these vital matters, but also of giving them the due weight they deserve, in terms both of analysis and the scope for corrective intervention, and how best this should occur.

John Goldthorpe has pointed out that, despite the obvious attractions to reformist politicians of the notion of creating a 'meritocratic' society based on educational attainment, it is nevertheless impossible, in the context of a liberal-capitalist society, for any one well-defined and objective conception of 'merit' to be established. This is especially true because those who have already demonstrated their deserts, and thus already joined the elite, are likely to define success strictly in their own terms:

Although 'merit' may be the criterion of selection and reward that is primarily invoked, it can be defined only in ways that are situationally specific, and thus quite variable, and that further involve an inevitable degree of subjective (and often incorrigible) judgement. (Goldthorpe 1996)

In other words, meritocracy's claim of legitimacy for what are mani-fest social and other inequalities (some of which flow from educational advantage) is itself likely to be merely a product of those very same inequalities.

What is more, this crucial issue, raised by Goldthorpe, of the signifi-cance of the specificity of any given situation for a proper analysis and understanding of it, also has implications for any thoroughgoing review of the public value of learning. To be fully valid, differential attitudes to learning, comparative opportunities to participate effec-tively, varieties of forms and types of learner engagement, formal levels of attainment and learner progression all need to be explored through in-depth studies of the specific context of local cultures.

Social change, risk and learning

In the half-century or so since the publication of the books by Mills, Young, Halsey, Goldthorpe and colleagues, the industrial, occupa-tional, cultural and social landscapes of the UK and other advanced industrial democracies have undergone remarkable change, all of which have both affected and have further implications for learning. Nowhere is this more obvious than in the world of work. In the mid-1950s, out of a working population totalling just over 24 millions, more than 12 million workers (over 50 per cent of the total UK work-force) were still employed in manufacturing, extraction, transport and construction industries, including the 'traditional' heavy industries of coal, iron and steel, engineering, shipbuilding, railways and docks.

After 50 years, while the workforce itself had grown by some 5 million (owing largely to increases in female paid labour), those working in heavy industry had dropped to fewer than 6 million, much less than a quarter of the country's workforce. The trades unions that had once powerfully organized a majority of the workers in those tra-ditional industries had dwindled to insignificance. When Wright Mills's *The Sociological Imagination* first appeared in Britain, the majority of the workforce was still engaged in manual labour, of one kind or another. Half a century later the labour market is dominated by white-collar, office-based, administrative, information- and knowl-edge-handling occupations, including managers, most of them employed in the service sector of the economy. Now almost 9 out of every 10 women in paid work are employed in services, compared with only three-quarters just 25 years ago, and more than two-thirds of men now work in services, by comparison with just over 40 per cent in 1980.

Gone from the UK, and other 'old' industrialized democracies, are the once-vast manufacturing plants, the dockside derricks, the huge fishing fleets and the distinctive pithead gear of the coal mines, many of which once provided a community-based form of social capital to local proletariats. Mass-production organized on strict Fordist principles has given way to 'just-in-time' forms of industrial organization and the alluring offer of increasingly customized products. Organizational structures are now flatter, layers of management have been hollowed out, and more work is scheduled through project management, outsourcing, subcontracting and consultancy. More and more of us, we are told, now work in an increasingly globalized, knowledge-driven economy, in which old-fashioned notions of a job for life, or even of some expectation of a reasonable period of employment security, have no place. The majority of British workers no longer belong to a trades union and unions themselves have had to diversify their 'offer' to members in order to retain such numbers as they have: without public sector membership, British unionism would now be virtually insignificant.

These dramatic shifts in the labour market have been paralleled by equally significant changes in other key social institutions. Similar rapid and profound changes can be discerned in patterns of demography, longevity and ethnicity; in the composition of families and household structures; in housing, home ownership and geographic mobility; and in the total volume and shape of consumption. Radical change over the past half century also figures in forms of transport and car ownership; in methods of communication; in leisure and travel; in the choice of food and drink; in the scale of personal borrowing and debt; and, not least, in educational participation, training and qualifications.

But this is not simply a story of change, however rapid, dramatic and ubiquitous. It signifies too a noticeable shift to quite different life worlds, underpinned by markedly different values, requiring from us different mental sets and increasingly characterized for many by uncertainty, insecurity and the sheer un-sustainability of traditional and well-established ways of thinking, living and being. Many different labels or descriptors have been proposed for this emergent and bewildering new world, with each epithet being followed by 'society': post-industrial, late- or post-capitalist, networked, information-based, knowledge-driven, and late- or post-modern. Whichever is preferred (and there are contested features of each), they all have in common an increasing tendency to substitute uncertainty for certainty, complexity for simplicity, ambiguity for clarity, unpredictability for predictability, change for continuity, unceasing flexibility for stability, unreliability for solidity, individualism for collectivity, unsustainability for adequacy, and contestation for agreement. These are the characteristics of what Ulrich Beck and others have usefully termed 'risk society'.

For some people, living and possibly thriving in this world of risk is

thrilling and exhilarating, surfing and enjoying the foaming and turbulent seas of the so-called 'new' economy. As Edward Luttwak has
rightly pointed out, there are bound to be some winners as well as
many losers in what he colourfully refers to as the 'turbo-capitalism' of
globalization:

> Everywhere it reaches, turbo-capitalism generates new wealth from
> all of the resources released by the competition-powered destruc-
> tion of inefficient practices, firms and entire industries ... Also
> destroyed, of course, are the secure jobs of the employees they once
> sheltered, while at the same time the architects and the beneficiaries
> of change enrich themselves at an unprecedented rate on an
> unprecedented scale. (Luttwak 1999:5)

However, for others, almost certainly the majority, it is hard to
know how best to prepare oneself, not least through learning, in order
to fend off the worst that turbo-capitalism can visit on us. How best
can we survive risk society and hope to navigate it with a modicum of
success, let alone thrive in it? For, as Zygmunt Bauman has so bril-
liantly portrayed it, this is a 'liquid' world of rapid use and even
quicker disposal; a fragmentary life lived increasingly as if in fragmentary time and in which, most puzzlingly:

> No jobs are guaranteed, no positions are foolproof, no skills are of
> lasting utility, experience and know-how turn into liability as soon
> as they become assets, seductive careers all too often prove to be
> suicide tracks. In their present rendering, human rights do not
> entail the acquisition of a right to a job, however well performed,
> or – more generally – the right to care and consideration for the
> sake of past merits. Livelihood, social position, acknowledgement
> of usefulness and the entitlement to self-dignity may all vanish
> together, overnight and without notice. (Bauman 1997: 22)

Confronted by such bleak possibilities, it is hard to define exactly
what sorts of learning might best equip individuals and communities to
be able not just to ward off the most damaging aspects of such a world
but also, and more importantly, to navigate with advantage, and even
with pleasure, the treacherous and constantly shifting waters of risk
society. If there is any validity in Bauman's depiction of the modern
condition, it is not immediately clear precisely what kinds of investment in which sorts and levels of skills, competences and capability
would be appropriate for individuals, communities or nation-states
and what types of strategy would manifest best public value.

No doubt, reference might be made to the overriding importance, in
such circumstances, of the lifelong updating of skills, of continuing

individual and workforce flexibility, of stimulating a more widespread development of entrepreneurial aptitudes and for greater commitment to sponsoring through learning people's inventiveness, ingenuity, innovation and creativity. Further, we might conclude that, if the disturbing scenarios depicted by Bauman or Beck are a real possibility, the best quality that learning could equip people with would be their ability to challenge, to think and act independently, and to be questioning and critical.

Without wishing to dismiss such strategies too lightly, the time, effort and costs involved in skills enhancement and increased competence may all prove to be in vain, in the circumstances of insecurity so vividly sketched by the likes of Beck and Bauman. Workers might feel they are moving (being moved?) from one dizzy, short-term treadmill to another, never finding a situation that offers some guarantee of continuity and self-fulfilment. Similarly, calls for yet more flexibility can easily amount to little more than merely endorsing the subordination of humanity and its needs to random market forces, regardless of the seriousness of the consequences.

Moreover, despite powerful and engaging arguments that creativity is not just the property of gifted and exceptional individuals, but can be taught and otherwise encouraged, there is nothing self-evident about the principal components of a curriculum designed to stimulate inventiveness and innovation at all levels. In any case, except at the level of rhetoric, advocating such a challenging way forward for learning would pose substantial problems of interpretation and implementation not just for public policymakers, but also for those charged with providing and assessing learning and, especially, for those individuals and communities who might reasonably be supposed to benefit most from such a reorientation.

Finally, the problem (especially for anyone in a position of authority) of advocating and engendering in those learners committed to their charge a genuinely critical consciousness, questioning intellect, and preparedness to act, is where to draw the line and how to determine the limits, as it were, of criticalness. In the end, that is precisely what those educationalists who see in a critically engaged learning the infinite possibilities of liberation and emancipation refuse to do. Only learners themselves, and those seeking liberation through their learning and actions, they say, can legitimately engage in such a task. As Raymond Williams rightly pointed out, in periods of rapid, profound and widespread social change, the real promise of adult learning is not simply to offer learners the important opportunity of better understanding and interpretation of that change. Nor yet is it to enable learners better to adapt those changes and turn them to their own improvement and advantage, vital though that is. The most valuable contribution of learning under such conditions is to enable people to become, in part, more the authors of such change, rather than its mere victims.

As far as Bauman is concerned, there is not much point in looking to conventional centres of learning, especially universities, for such a radical shift. The world in which men and women now need to live and struggle to shape their life strategies puts a premium on what he dubs 'tertiary learning'. This is

> a kind of learning which our inherited institutions, born and matured in the modern ordering bustle are ill prepared to handle; and one which educational theory, developed as a reflection of modern ambitions and their institutional embodiments, can only view with a mixture of bewilderment and horror. (Bauman 2001:127)

In any case, he argues, the sorts of systematic and rigorous learning that the best university education exemplifies

> cannot adopt the job market pace of flexible experiment, and even less can it accommodate the all-too-apparent normlessness and thus unpredictability of mutation which the drifting called flexibility cannot but spawn. (Bauman 2001:132)

Conclusion

This chapter has argued that, in the chronically precarious and, for some, runaway circumstances of contemporary life, there is an urgent need to investigate closely the relationship between the 'personal troubles' and 'public issues' of learning and its capacity to furnish people with the wherewithal to survive, if not prosper and thrive. In particular, attention should focus on the persistent and distorting influences of social class in Britain on learners' opportunities equitably to engage in learning and to succeed, especially for those people from family and neighbourhood backgrounds who might properly be seen to be most threatened by the exigencies and turbulence of 'risk society'.

In order to achieve this, a case has been made for adopting an 'enhanced' public value frame of reference so as to assess learning from a broader and deeper perspective than can readily be provided by attending only to conventional indicators of successful learning, although using proxy measures is, to some extent, unavoidable. What such an approach would need to exemplify would be a textured grasp of the subtle and pervasive ways learning opportunities are distorted and learners' potential is thwarted (or enhanced), including by the variously influential contexts and cultures in which learning is embedded, both immediate and global. This would mean inquiring into the mutual impact of learning and social capital in particular situations. It would require, too, sensitivity to the many dimensions of learning, including its informal, non-formal and tacit aspects, and not just to its admittedly important formal aspects and qualifications and the standard measures normally used to evaluate it.

Such a framework should also be designed to show how public value can be both better ascertained and more richly realized, by giving a clear and critical voice to learners, to potential learners and to those striving professionally and organizationally to serve them better. Finally, a full approach to public value in learning should recognize the key role that learning can continue to play, in the lives of both individuals and communities, in holding out the promise not just of improvement and progression, but also of emancipation and in underpinning a truly democratic and participative approach to social change.

In conclusion, the words of Zygmunt Bauman should serve as a sort of 'prospectus', both for learning itself and for the kind of evaluative public value framework which would do it justice:

> 'Preparing for life' – that perennial, invariable task of all education – must mean first and foremost cultivating the ability to live daily and at peace with uncertainty and ambivalence, with a variety of standpoints and the absence of unerring and trustworthy authorities; must mean instilling tolerance of difference and the will to respect the right to be different; must mean fortifying critical and self-critical faculties and the courage needed to assume responsibility for one's choices and their consequences; must mean training the capacity for 'changing the frames' and for resisting the temptation to escape from freedom, with the anxiety of indecision it brings alongside the joys of the new and the unexplored. (Bauman 2001:138)

Chapter 15

Public Value in Education: A Case-Study

DAVID WINKLEY

This is a study of the development over a period of years of a large primary school in inner-city Birmingham, which had, in the mid 1970s, major problems of disorder, in an area of multiple deprivation and multi-ethnic diversity at a time of high racial tension in the local community. Appointed as head teacher for an initial 2-year commitment (all I was prepared to offer at the time) I ended up staying for almost 25 years, working on building the school into an organization which would, we hoped, engage deeply, and creatively, with the local community.

First steps

The challenge was obvious – here was a complex and insecure multi-ethnic community with one of the highest unemployment levels in the UK, riddled with social and racial problems, on a knife-edge of explosive unrest. (The school had to survive a damaging attack from the National Front in the late 1970s and was at the epicentre of the Handsworth riots of 1981 and 1985.) This insecurity was reflected in the school in very unsettled pupil behaviour and in the unevenness and defensiveness of staff trying to survive the trauma of days of disruption and aggression.

As it turned out, a measure of stability was achieved relatively quickly. The school began to look more competent and in control, children no longer climbing on roofs, or running off home in foul tempers, the teachers more relaxed and confident, the parents reasonably reassured. Strategic planning was linked to clear, practical objectives, and a panoply of supports and constraints predictably underpinned improvements. With a more explicit understanding of expectation of standards there was less aggression, more civilized behaviour, and evidence of more productive teaching. Early inspection reports by Her Majesty's Inspectors (HMI) were positive, noting how much more 'settled' and 'orderly' the school was. This was the point at which I seemed to have largely delivered my contractual mandate, and could have decently left, as many heads do after a reasonable period of troubleshooting encumbrance.

But there are hidden dangers in the strategies of control which lie behind the rapid managed delivery of functional improvement. A philosophy of order-and-control may be good for establishing routines, but it tends to inhibit challenge and divergence. There is the potential of over-complacency, the danger of habitualizing practice on the assumption that as expectations have apparently been met – good enough to keep parents and governors happy, and inspectors satisfied, with the children more settled, disciplined and attentive – we can celebrate our newfound competence, and rest assured we've gone as far as we need.

But what if at this point we risk more challenging questions? What is this organization for? What does responsiveness mean in practice, for this school? What ought to be the basic principles and values which underpin the purposes of a school in this particular social and cultural environment? How can such values be assessed for their success and failure in the insecure arena of the lives of real individuals, as well as engaging us in the subtle, and sometimes difficult, reconciliation of differences between community expectations and political mandates? How can the school contribute to the community as well as serving it though its conventionally expected public service obligations? Given sufficient determination and a much more challenging, and possibly unrealistic, sense of vision what might be achieved?

Such questions seem to set us on the track of an entirely new narrative which enhances as well as unsettles the assumption that the end point of the high-reliability school has already been reached. And it is the progress of this second phase that I now explore further, within the framework of public value.

Knowledge-gathering

We started to dig deeper. We took the risk of testing out our achievements so far by formally canvassing the opinions of both parents and children, using questionnaires (designed and independently analysed by a university department) to identify emergent issues. In our first survey, for example, we discovered that a third of our parents claimed to be having trouble in dealing with their children at home. In responding to this the school appointed one of Birmingham's first home–school liaison teachers, and set up an on-call contact service for parents in difficulty, which from time to time involved me and other staff in evening home visits to sort out parental problems. (I have recollections of dealing with one particularly problematic family with four out-of-control young boys whose nightly caper was to toss Grandma out of bed!)

Such an interventional approach to community concerns seemed in itself to begin to open a whole new kind of relationship between the school and the community, with the families (even the vast majority whom didn't use the service) beginning to recognize that the school was unexpectedly there – almost as a psychological presence – open for business, as it were, beyond its normal institutional boundaries.

Questionnaire data, garnered over periods of time, became an increasingly important assessment tool, amplified in due course by far more face-to-face contact with families. We made a tenfold increase in evening meetings between teachers and parents for frank exchange of views, with an accompanying training programme for the teachers on how best to ask questions, how to balance advice with careful listening, how not to patronize parents from different cultural backgrounds. These regular contacts had the added virtue of opening up more general debates with the wider community about what the school was for, what it could provide, what was expected of it.

People's views were to be taken seriously, with translators on hand for non-English speaking parents. Opinions, problems, observations were registered and analysed. Any parents who failed to appear, or engage, were personally visited at home: these communal meetings were to be seen as mandatory and important. Community walkabouts involving all staff were now added to the annual programme, alongside a number of social events in the school itself. A strong, pro-active governing body, representing a wide range of local interests and ethnic groups was developed.

The children themselves mirrored their parents' views, requesting (surprisingly) tougher discipline, as well as more time spent in listening to and resolving personal problems. Children were encouraged to participate in their own way through a pupil-led school council with real influence, with teams of older children also trained as troubleshooting 'counsellors' taking on responsibilities for intervening in playground disputes. Personal problems could be reported at any time, including critical assessments of day-to-day teaching and curriculum programmes. There was discussion with pupils to explore the meanings of 'appropriateness' and 'professionalism' – on one occasion a class experiencing an abusive supply teacher impressively elected two girls as their representatives and made a formal complaint in a strikingly calm and mature way – a serious complaint, as it turned out, and duly taken seriously.

Discipline was strengthened, using clear (community-approved) sanctions, which individual miscreants were encouraged to choose, or reject. The aim was engagement and thoughtfulness. Why have I behaved in this way? What ought to be the appropriate consequences?

This was balanced by a deliberate attempt to build a positive, confidence-building culture with an emphasis on 'thinking well about yourself' in an atmosphere of good humour and calm. A carefully constructed external assessment of behavioural and mental health needs (by a medical psychiatric researcher) led to the setting up of a specialist in-school behavioural support unit, which eventually became a resource for the whole city, to support the significant minority of pupils unable to cope, some of whom had mental health problems.

External consultants, including a local GP as well as higher education specialists, were persuaded to carry out regular audits of progress and professional development for teachers in different subject areas, using the growing information base as a locus for discussion, working towards consensus on issues of quality, practice and outcomes. The unsatisfactory unevenness of teaching standards was addressed, in part, by opening up debate using real life examples, including video-analysis of the most effective teachers in action. Considerable pressures were put on some individuals to improve performance, and some staff left. The focus now was on the continuing learning of all who work in the organization (managers and professionals) and all for whom the organization had immediate consequence (pupils, parents and governors.)

Innovation and continuous improvement

This mushrooming bank of evidence now needed to be processed, made purposive and manageable, leading to operational objectives. At best it becomes a highly relevant, illuminating, diagnostic tool shaping a critique – and sometimes an articulated defence – both of existing and of innovatory practice. The school's sense of itself becomes linked to a dynamic sense of constant improvement – a vision of what might (in an ideal world), be possible.

Utopianism, however, is not a route-map to easy or obvious destinations. Final and fixed positions are hard to pin down in an evolving, adaptive culture where everything, potentially, is up for re-examination, with a flow of shifting critical judgements required as what best to preserve, what best to change. The process in practice is inherently exploratory and innovative, stakeholders committed to moving the ship forward. Task groups explored new ideas, which were trialled, piloted and evaluated. Proven successes began to enter the bloodstream, with the aim of generalizing and routinizing evidence of what seems to work well throughout the organization.

There seem to be tensions here. On the one hand there is the regular day-to-day business – the necessary flow of daily routines, the constraints of times, rules, curriculum, bureaucracy and the rest; on the other there's this contingent world of experiment and innovation.

These seem separate, distinct, even conflicting – the one dependent on certainties and tacit assumptions, the other leading us into the exploratory dangers of the yet-to-be realized. Yet there seems to be an advanced point in the life of the organization where the distinctiveness of these different worlds seems to begin to break down. The routinized (often thoughtless) and the experimental (invariably explicit) increasingly cross-fertilize, as innovations are absorbed into the bloodstream of the school. Habits become incrementally transformed, new practices are taken on board, and routines at every level become potentially open to explicit scrutiny and emendation – daily life taking on a new sense of unfolding energy and alertness.

Innovations worth generalizing now began to filter into many aspects of school life: new, narrative-based curriculum programmes, for example, were put in place anticipating the national curriculum by addressing issues of inadequate or unbalanced subject coverage – and beginning to grapple with concerns even now being raised by the Qualifications and Curriculum Authority, of how to deliver much more imaginative curriculum programmes through vastly better planned and resourced presentations to pupils. Major developments in the arts followed, with drama, music and the visual arts as priorities. Large-scale annual productions became regular features, and the work of local artists, as well as the work of our own pupils, was put on open display to the community. All children had the opportunity to take part in jazz dance sessions. Out-of-school clubs and programmes were greatly extended.

The school increasingly became a proactively participant enterprise to which governors, parents, the pupils themselves as well as the sometimes forgotten back-up staff could significantly contribute. Encouraging thoughtful participation needs persistence, with much time spent in discussion as the various players shape collectively understood frameworks for action. Mutual trust needs to underpin (and bind) the increasingly devolved decision-making. Networking with outsiders – drawing in the local community as well as external advice and expertise – also makes a contribution, as people work towards their increasingly shared interpretations of issues and practices.

Outcomes and evaluations

Awareness of outcomes and achievements becomes a critical factor in this evolution as the organization crucially focuses on performance. The school prioritizes tasks, with a weather-eye on the quality of experience as well as the achievement of pupils. It works at its own definitions of what is understood by excellence, actively responding to its own evidence base. It raises questions about the expectations of teaching and learning in the context of the climate and values of the organization as a whole. Where is the evidence? Key practical principles are kept in mind – with a determined eye on what might be achieved if the right support to each pupil can be arranged.

Assessment calls for a range of measures of manageable objectives tested against the wider principles of the organization – as important for music (say) as it is for maths. Ofsted identified the school as the first to develop detailed assessment criteria in literacy and numeracy in assessing pupil performance, the data computerized, used as a diagnostic tool by staff, and sent out in graph form to all parents. The aim was to get much better at identifying individual talent (and weaknesses) while holding on to principles of equal opportunity and entitlement. This requires a complex (and not always easily resolved) interrelation of awareness of the needs of individual pupils, with an across-school shaping of strategies and policies. To what extent should resources be given to special needs, or the particularly able, or the lone talent? How much diversification can the organization bear? What are the ethical questions of pupils removed from traditional classes into specialized environments?

It calls for considerable organizational flexibility in response to the diagnostic process. So when (as happened to me) an 8-year-old inner-city child is discovered, who can – unbeknown to anyone – play by ear the opening bars of Rachmaninov's Third Piano Concerto, or that a group of children show unusual ability in maths, and are already capable of achieving an A-C grade at GCSE at aged eleven, we have an obligation to respond as well as we can to such diagnosis (in the case of the musician, arrangements were made for personal tuition; for the mathematicians, programmes of advanced group teaching with a specialist teacher.) The outcomes – some impacting rapidly, others sustained over a number of years – paralleled a growing sense of trust and support from parents, based on a sense that the school was becoming an increasingly responsive base for their individual child.

Complaints from parents about their children had by now diminished almost to nothing, and the behaviour and attitude of the pupils had greatly improved. (Questionnaires now show that the children were really enjoying coming to school.) The school registered the largest proportionate turnout to the annual governors' meeting of any school in England and its performance data gathering process was now formally publicized to all schools by Ofsted as a national model, subsequently influencing government policy. One of the more unexpected developments was the influx of middle-class parents from outside the area, attracted by hard evidence of rising academic standards, the particularly high achievements of the upper third of the pupils, and the ability of the school culture to adapt its organizational arrangements to respond to the potential of individual talent.

Such an evolutionary process commits the organization to becoming unreservedly self-critical. It remorselessly attends to slackness, incompetence, insensitivity, poor team work, inefficient use of resources, unfocused or unsatisfactory work at all levels. A strong sense of internal accountability becomes the basis for a constructive response (and use of) external accountability. A focus on cost-benefit assessment might seem a function of basic service competence, but there is an added need to assess for resource-value at every level. A scrutinizing organization unearths inadequacies which are often unforeseen. It exposes lack of energy, defensiveness, the stasis and debilitating psychology of 'good enough' performance (which in this new, dynamic cultural mode is never good enough.) Such critical toughness is a corporate process, not to be confused with aggressive top-down management – it arises out of persistent questioning by all participants. 'I'm sorry sir', said one pupil to me as I was teaching a class, 'Sahid is messing about and we need to do something about him.' Exactly right; Sahid's behaviour is a corporate class responsibility and this critic is adding value to the class as a whole.

The evolution of culture

It is important to note that that the six components that underpin this story – visioning, knowledge-gathering, innovation, democratic involvement, outcome focus and self-criticism – need to function together like different timbres of organ stops creating the full complexity of the music, each in its way potentially discomforting. The factors that emerge from this process of 'adding value' tend, if anything, to destabilize and disconcertingly challenge a conventional sense of the expectation of a 'competent public service'.

The organization is, by now, plainly shifting from acceptance of the status quo to investigation of what is possible, moving from 'assuring continuity and efficiency in current tasks to one of improvising the translation from current to future performance'. It is taking us beyond satisfaction with basic competence, to the prospect of innovation, and to a new and more sophisticated sense of the meaning of response to the individual requirements of its clients.

This investigative prospectus creates a context or culture with many dimensions, deeply rooted in real-life events and experiences, searched out, negotiated, discussed and accomplished by various authors – and paradoxically, what emerges is a kind of stability – a security of style and intention, a secure base, that lays the necessary confidence-building foundation for further exploration and calculated risk-taking.

Such a culture is instantly recognizable even to casual outsiders, with all the signs of intellectual restlessness, and quality of outcome shown in the open-minded, confident way people engage with each other. It creates a 'text' mirrored in every aspect of relationships – and ultimately in the classroom, the teachers' interaction with pupils, the way pupils question, respond and interrelate and in the pupils' sense of themselves. It is the language used (body language, styles of communication, attitudes as well as word-exchange), the 'continuous and interactive dialogue,' to use Mark Moore's phrase, that is the glue that draws our six factors together. It is language exchange that creates and brings alive the textual identity that creates and defines the quality of learning at all levels. It matters how we communicate, how we talk, converse, argue, interact. 'The nature and strength of the patterns of interaction', writes Jennifer O'Day, 'are . . . key to understanding the relationship between individual and organizational behaviour and change' (O'Day 2002).

The ways communication takes place will be complex and varied, ranging from more relaxed exchanges to the sensitivities of group decision-making, to formal explanations (publishing data for inside and outside scrutiny) and this multifaceted 'language world' creates interconnections that mirror and refract from one situation to another – ultimately, and most importantly, impacting on the way the teacher uses language exchange – such as higher-order questioning – in the classroom.

'Language', says Richard Hoggart, writing about literature,

> is one way to seize a particular kind of reality ... the way of talking to people – in this society, at this time – reveals a great deal about a culture ... about frames of assumption, about the assumed orders that underpin a work. (Hoggart 1957)

What is true here about a text is, I would argue, also true about a context. It is in the subtleties of discourse that we ultimately discover the values and intentions of an organizational culture – which is why the 'reading' of an organization – any organization – is so subtle and complex and value-laden an exercise.

In this more dynamic sense of 'public value' – the growth of opportunity, the improved motivation, the multiplicity of opportunity – we foster the deepening of relationships, the understanding of consensus and civility, the attention to individual entitlement, the enjoyment of being part of a creative community. Such a culture is part planned, part free-flowing, part – to use Raymond Williams's word – 'unrealized'. It is, as Terry Eagleton, says, 'a network of shared meanings and activities never self-conscious as a whole, but growing towards 'the advance in consciousness' and this in full humanity of a whole society'.

This notion of such a culture challenges us to redefine public service in terms of purpose and function as well as measurable outcome. The new sense of 'value created' is not easily captured in conventional forms of data (however useful that may be), but becomes connected to evolving cultures whose outcomes can only be assessed over longer periods of time. It takes the view, moreover, that not everything is yet known: improvements are always possible.

Leadership

Developing such cultures requires leadership skills which are themselves adaptive to different stages in the development of the organization. Achieving competence (which may, for a while, involve a centralist, directive style of leadership) is different from the advanced stage in which the cultural force of an innovative participant organization draws many people into the enterprise and the role of the leader correspondently becomes lighter, less determining, more democratically orientated, adapting a management style to the state of progress of the evolution as a whole, though the shifts of response to the different phrases of context which are themselves complex and continually open to review.

This is not a simple task. There are numerous inbuilt tensions in the enterprise which call for a personal leadership style that has the confidence to interpret and translate the various counter-forces that can easily constrain progress, as well as an ability pro-actively to carve out opportunities from prevailing circumstances. Fulfilling the potential and aspirations of individual pupils is a challenging proposition. How do we best generalize practices in a culture that applauds a focus on individual needs and constantly presses us to diversify and adapt to the particularities of circumstances? How do we encourage personal initiative and divergent thinking in an atmosphere working towards corporate common goals? Conversely, how do we deal with counter-forces of resistance, reactionary opinions and destructive behaviour? (I found it useful to assess individual staff on their performance in group meetings and discuss at length attitudes which seemed to be constraining, or undermining discussion and development, negative behaviours which people often don't recognize in themselves.) To be constructively critical without being negative or destructive is a real skill in itself – which raises the question of how best to create an atmosphere of confidence sufficient to encourage participants to engage in positively focused self-criticism.

It is for the leadership to work on the reconciliation of these challenges – and many others – which often means holding opposites in mind, in compromising, in repositioning themselves in the team, sometimes as director, sometimes as a participant observer, judgements which depend on a continuous assessment of the social maturity of the group. Above all the leader needs to 'hold' the emotional tone of the culture, to make people feel safe and confident, which requires the ability to contain tension, tolerate divergence, know exactly when to remain firm, and when to withdraw. This can be a lonely and difficult challenge, calling for calm in stormy seas.

Advanced cultures do not evolve overnight. It's possible to impact on an organization quite quickly by making a variety of immediate changes – in say, 2 to 4 years, but there is usually not enough time, here, for the deeper evolution of the kinds of cultures that sustain to the point where they move beyond the leadership to create a texture, a way of working, a set of absorbed and accepted attitudes and approaches that will survive even when the formative leader leaves.

The wider challenge

There is unquestionably a sense in which the identity – the authenticity – of the school as an organizational culture is shaped in this continuing process through the ground base of what Charles Taylor usefully calls 'dialogical relationships'. Healthy organizational cultures, both in terms of their sense of responsibility to others, and their determination to achieve for them the best possible outcomes, benefit from permeable boundaries that access the views and influence of outsiders. External forces of policy, in contributing to this dialogue, can either strengthen or constrain the particular progress of the institution. It is hard to avoid the view that some of the political attempts from the 1970s onwards to create reform by edict, quality by blueprint – with approving nods in the direction of the smoke-and-mirrors of markets and choices – have made advanced phases of organizational development in the public services by no means impossible, but much more difficult to achieve. High levels of bureaucracy, limiting frames of reference, and an atmosphere of threat constrain and distract. The tutelary power of the state has helped to ensure competence and to standardize quality differences, but has, equally discouraged institutions from engaging in the more advanced self-determining and often radical processes required to address questions of what we might become.

Politics, above all, needs to reconnect public value with commitment to public services. Where participants are co-creators of value, driven by initiative, intelligence, and a confident sense of self-worth we are less likely to suppose that existing institutional arrangements can't be constantly incrementally improved. There are new connections to be made between private and public, commercial and state, individual and social, personal and technical – the politics of adding public value engaged in planned collaboration across sectors. None of this implies less tolerance of the second-rate: but it does require a more empirical and complex approach to analysis of the kind schools need to take on themselves.

One question asked by my own school, late in the day, was whether the traditional institution of schooling is the best and only vehicle for delivering the best of all possible supports to its clients in a high technology world of distance learning, increasing choice, improving out-of-school opportunities, expectations of equity and individual aspiration. There is plenty of evidence that the family is the principal educator of the child, and determinant of its future. We know, too, that health issues have significant consequences for educational achievement. Rothstein, among others, has argued that non-educational interventions might in the end be more effective than direct educational strategies in improving the life chances of many children. We know that the first 5 years are overwhelmingly important in the mental and emotional development of the children, a recognition still not adequately accounted for in funding allocations. The school needs to respond to such evidence through its own diagnosis of local family need – to reassess the meanings of education-in-service and open its doors to much wider community resources. Our home support service policies were a start; but there was obvious potential to go further – looking, for example, at the possibilities of weekend and holiday learning programmes, internet and distance learning support, much more structured and intensive home-based work with parents, the school extending even further beyond its traditional boundaries – without losing a sense of its own internal priorities to offer the best possible deal to its pupils. The school needs increasingly to work collaboratively alongside other professions and disciplines, driven by a flexible and focused determination, particularly – for us – in addressing fundamentals of underachievement and disadvantage. Our school now opened at weekends to set up a range of voluntary out-of-school learning programmes – some for children with obvious talents – which eventually developed through into cross-city and national networks of similar initiatives across the country.

The school's various initiatives now began to be recognized by the political centre, first by Gillian Shepherd, Conservative Secretary of State for Education in the mid 1990s, and then by Tony Blair in the late 1990s, both describing different features of the school in public speeches – which led in due course to extensive media interest, and a full page profile in the main section of *The Times* newspaper. The school could now claim some influence on policy thinking – particularly on inspection, pupil assessment, and the teaching of gifted pupils – though we have also seen, as the years have gone by, how centrally driven policies, implemented nationally, tend to distort and greatly reconceptualize their origins.

Montaigne succinctly described what a citizen might aspire to gain from an education: 'Let us judge how the child profited from it not from the evidence of his memory, but from that of his life.'

Such aspiration – translated into the twenty-first century – implies the identification and exploration of needs and talents, the assurance that each individual child develops a sense of self-worth in the profound challenge to enhance – as far as is possible – the growth of minds and sensibilities in the context of diverse home backgrounds. Despite all pressures to focus on the examinable mass, none of us is one kind of person. The notion of public value in addressing these complex ambitions is in a sense an aspirational abstraction – abstract rather in the way that the notion of the 'fulfilled person' is abstract. Beyond a certain point it can neither be prescribed nor blueprinted – it is too local, and subtle and unpredictable for that. But it is not so abstract that ways of breaking the mould cannot be envisioned and enacted in the particularities of the real world of practice through the aspirations of public workers who have a sense, given a fair wind, of just what might be achieved.

Chapter 16

Conclusions: Looking Ahead

MARK H. MOORE AND JOHN BENINGTON

The chapters in this book have boldly taken up the challenge of developing the concepts surrounding public value and applying them to different substantive domains, in different institutional contexts, and different political cultures. In doing so, they have tested the generality and robustness of the ideas, but also transformed them, and rendered them more practically useful. In *The Savage Mind*, Lévi-Strauss noted that all practical tools become enriched with use. As a tool, originally constructed for some particular use in some particular context, is used to solve a different problem in a different context, the tool itself changes. So it is with the tools associated with creating public value.

Our aim in this chapter is not to summarize the themes and arguments running through the book. It is, instead, to look ahead to two key concerns that will continue to challenge theorists and practitioners.

First, to what extent are the concepts and principles of public value still relevant to the world we now inhabit and seek to improve?

Second, what are the important conceptual and practical difficulties that continue to frustrate those who would like to apply the principles of public value creation to particular concrete tasks?

We begin with some broad observations about how the world of public management and leadership seems to have changed in the decades since *Creating Public Value* was first published. We then argue for the continued – indeed increased – relevance of the central ideas contained in the public value concept. Finally, we turn our attention to the frontiers of public value theory, and the particular theoretical and practical issues that need to be addressed if the concepts of public value are to be useful in guiding the efforts of government officials and other public leaders in the future.

Changes in the context of governance and public service

Much has changed in the world in the decades since *Creating Public Value* was first published. Three trends seem particularly important:

the rehabilitation of the idea of government as a value-creating social institution, the increased recognition of our interdependence, and the understanding that government is but one part of the overall process of social governance.

The revival of government as a value-creating institution

First, the political attack on government has abated, and, more importantly, shifted its focus. Most citizens have come to a renewed understanding that government is, in fact, a value-creating enterprise that helps create the conditions for economic prosperity, civility in social relationships, and the advancement of justice. They continue to debate the particulars about how big the government should be, the purposes government should pursue, and the methods it should use in pursuit of collectively defined goals. But the wholesale assault on government as a socially unproductive institution seems to be over. The attack on government had reached its limits before the recent financial crisis. But the financial crisis has made it abundantly clear to many that unbridled market forces are unable on their own to produce the kind of prosperity, civility, and social justice that human beings want for themselves, their communities and their children. We know that we need government to do its part as a regulatory and service delivery operation to create the material conditions under which we as individuals and a communities would like to live.

Many citizens are also beginning to understand that government is not only valuable as society's agent in acting to create the conditions that society deems good and just, but also as an occasion for building a public sphere. It is because we have a government, and we have to figure out how to use it, that we have to sometimes leave our private lives aside, and enter into a public realm where we can talk collectively about what we would like to achieve, and what we owe to one another. In such gatherings, we can continue to conclude that we would like to keep the public sphere small to provide for the maximum of individual liberty, but we cannot do without a public sphere where we share our individual ideas about what our society as a whole should be like, and how we should use the collectively owned powers of the state to help us approximate those desired conditions. This means not only improving the practice of traditional representative democracy but also creating wider and deeper channels of consultation between citizens and government about the ends and means of government action. The 2010 coalition government in the UK calls this 'creating the Big Society'.

So, the pressure on government has shifted quite a lot. The demand for smaller government has given way to a new demand for better government. Moreover, the idea of better government includes not only more efficiency and effectiveness in the pursuit of collectively desired ends, but also better processes of public deliberation about what the ends and means should be.

Operational challenges to government

On the operational side of government, citizens no longer want or tolerate a 'one-size-fits-all' government. They want a government that can see its citizens as individuals and respond to their particular status and condition and as communities and respond to their diversity.

Citizens have also lost patience with government agencies that excel only in performing their narrowly defined missions. They want instead a 'networked government' in which different levels of government, and different government agencies, deliver 'joined-up' services to individuals, families, and neighbourhoods in a coordinated way.

And when citizens call their governments to account, they want more than reassurances that organizations have complied with existing policies and procedures and not stolen the money. They want to be sure that the government has actually achieved the outcomes they promised to produce when they asked for tax income and public authority to pursue collectively defined public purposes.

Political/legitimacy challenges to government

On the political legitimacy side of government, citizens have also become more demanding. Formal elections remain the core of democratic politics. But we are increasingly aware of the limits of this process in legitimating all subsequent acts of government.

Fresh electoral mandates go stale very quickly as time passes from the point of election. Many important issues which governments are called upon to face are never addressed in the political campaigns that precede the election. And there are thousands of issues that do not rise to the level of a national debate, but are of extraordinary importance to individuals and groups who will be affected by policy decisions.

Understanding all this, governments have begun to develop new forums and processes for consultation with citizens. There has been a world-wide push to decentralize governance, and to give more autonomy and influence to local authorities and communities.

Increasingly, administrative rule-making agencies have opened up their decision-making processes and sought wider consultations with those likely to be affected by the decisions. Service delivery agencies have created forums in which clients have the opportunity to discuss and define what they value, and what constitutes quality in the delivery of services. And public agencies are making more extensive use of different kinds of surveys to learn the degree to which government seems to be meeting the expectations and demands of its citizens. In these respects, then, politics – understood as all of those processes through which citizens make claims on government – has opened up, in a bid to improve the responsiveness and democratic legitimacy of the state.

The re-emergence of the social consciousness of interdependence

Second, one of the forces that has led to the re-evaluation of government as an important, value-creating social institution is the re-emergent sense of our social interdependence. The politics of Ronald Reagan and Margaret Thatcher insisted on the fundamental independence of individuals. The symbol and instrument of that independence was the right of individuals to choose for themselves. The triumph of individual choice was reflected in the economic sphere by the importance accorded to private market mechanisms. It was reflected in the political sphere by the commitment to shrink the size both of the public sphere and of government.

The neo-liberal emphasis on the fundamental independence of individuals went hand in hand with the attack on government because it implied not only that individuals had a right to decide important matters for themselves, but also that the consequences of individual choices for other individuals, or society at large, would best be orchestrated by the hidden hand of the private market. If this were true, there would be no need for any higher authority to regulate those choices. This was the preferred state of things to the proponents of individualism, because they believed it was nigh on impossible for any kind of collective to decide whether and how it should restrain individual choices to achieve a good and just society.

The ideologies and institutions that give primacy to individuals – liberal democracy in politics and market capitalism in economics – continue their powerful advance throughout the world. But their promise of individual independence masks the real material, social, and political conditions in which people live.

The fact is that our individual lives are becoming much more deeply intertwined rather than less connected. Each individual is now much more dependent on what others in the world are doing than has ever been true in the past. In today's interconnected global world we have many more opportunities to help and hurt one another than in the past. The emergence of a truly global economy has made each of us vulnerable to competition from others throughout the world, but also given each of us a chance to find others in the world who might value what we can produce. The growth of international travel has brought with it the threat of world pandemics, but also the possibility of far-flung but intimate social networks in which the individuals we call our friends stretch across geographic and cultural boundaries. Ethnic and religious conflict and global terrorism have made us feel vulnerable to the intolerant views of our fellow humans, but also forced us to reconsider our own fixed ideas and search for the empathy and common purpose that would allow us to live in a highly diverse but tolerant world. The internet has made us vulnerable to new forms of theft and exploitation, but also spawned a global consciousness of one another as people sharing a physical, economic, and social world without sharp national, political, or cultural boundaries.

The fact of our interdependence forces us to be aware of one another. Consciousness of our effects on others creates some kind of responsibility for taking account of those effects, minimizing them if they are harmful, and finding ways to mutually benefit from the effects if they are positive. Much of this social co-ordinating work can be done naturally as individuals encounter one another and seek both to avoid harm and to find useful means of cooperation on their own.

The necessity of social institutions that constrain individuals

While we might hope that this consciousness of others, and the kind of restraint that this consciousness implies, would arise naturally in the society, and that we could manage our interdependence through voluntarily embraced self-discipline, civility and empathy alone, the reality is that to manage our thick, penetrating interdependence reliably, society has to develop social institutions that do not allow individuals to do whatever they want, but requires them to act with attention to the interests, wellbeing and expectations of others. And that puts independent, choice-making individuals in relationships of duty and obligation to one another, and to the social institutions that both restrain and enable the conduct of individuals and groups as well as protects their rights. One important implication of this line of thought is to understand that individual citizens interact with government not only as customers who receive services and benefits, but also as obligatees who will have to accept their fair share of the responsibility for accomplishing important collective goals. If they want to renegotiate these obligations, they have to participate as citizens in designing the 'architecture of their own restraint' (Hannah Arendt 1958). Government, in turn, has to learn how to manage relations with individuals. It has to become as expert in the management of 'obligation encounters' as it is in the management of 'service encounters.' And it has to become expert in creating the occasions for individuals to come together as a public and become both informed and articulate about what they would like to accomplish together through their social institutions.

From government to governance

In the past, prior to the neo-liberal attack on government, we have relied on governments to do much of this important work. But the neo-liberal attack on government increased our awareness that government was not the only institution involved in managing the social interdependence of individuals.

The recognition that government is only one part of the institutional apparatus that societies rely on to govern themselves is the third major trend in contemporary understandings of government. We now see – not only in advanced industrial societies, but also across the globe – the invention and emergence of new institutions of governance for managing the increasingly complex interdependences that operate with and alongside government, and sometimes quite independently of it. This is happening at the international level as individuals and nations across the world search for the means to combat global threats such as terrorism, infectious disease and climate change without the benefit of a global government. But it is also happening at the local and grass-roots levels as small communities discover the degree to which their neighbours influence their welfare and find ways to come together to solve local problems through the combined efforts of government, voluntary associations and non-profit organizations. And, as noted above, governments are learning to supplement their legitimacy and capacity through new working relationships with one another, and with private and voluntary organizations at national, state, and local levels.

The enduring relevance of public value theory

These three key changes in our social context – the rehabilitation of the idea of government as a value-creating social institution, the increased recognition of our interdependence, and the understanding that government is but one part of the overall process of social governance – seem to have, if anything, increased the importance of public value as a theoretical concept and a practical framework for public leadership. The authors of the chapters in this volume find ways to use the ideas associated with public value not only to deal more effectively with problems that have been around for a long time, but also to tackle the complex new problems facing governments, citizens and communities. They find ways to use these concepts not only when they are focusing on how to create new programmes within existing organizations to deal with new problems, and not only when they are trying to reposition a particular government organization in a changing environment to make better use of the assets held within that particular organization, but also when they are searching for an improved overall system response to a social problem that is not now being well handled by any single government organization. And, they find ways to use the concepts of public value to talk about improving the processes of public deliberation and community mobilization that are necessary to create both the legitimacy and support needed to achieve large social outcomes, as well as to mobilize the networks of capacity that are distributed across many organizations, and sometimes millions of decentralized individuals. Indeed, if anything, the concepts of public value creation seem even more important in the brave new world of interdependence and networked governance than they were in the old world either of big government on one hand or small government on the other.

One of the most important implications of the above trends shaping our individual and collective lives is that many different individuals, standing on different social platforms, can make contributions to the overall quality of our collective lives. Government officials remain crucially important, of course, as organizers of collective efforts, as deployers of public assets, and as convenors of public deliberations about what we would like to accomplish together. But in the new world of governance, they are joined by individuals in the voluntary, non-profit sector, and even those in the commercial, for-profit sector. Each can offer certain kinds of public leadership in identifying and dealing with public problems.

To do so, however, they have to think and act differently in these roles. And the concepts of public value creation and the strategic triangle give them some useful guidance about how to think and act in these roles, in this new world:

- The concept of public value acts as a guide to search out conditions that need to be improved, and problems that need to be addressed, but are not necessarily the responsibility of any single agency.
- The concept of operational capacity highlights the importance of actions taken by 'partners' and 'co-producers' drawn from the voluntary and for-profit sectors.
- The concept of authorization acts as a reminder that political mobilization is essential to creating social contexts in which government-imposed obligations feel legitimate, and lead to acceptable changes in thinking and behaviour within society.

The idea that politics ought to help the public deliberate about what it should be trying to do with government and other public assets is becoming an urgent issue as citizens increasingly find the contemporary political discourse lacking in substance, and disconnected from their key concerns.

While the concepts are useful in general, it is worth giving close attention to some which need to be developed further to be particularly useful – first to government officials acting in their role as government managers, second to individuals seeking to offer leadership from other platforms in society.

Public value as a guiding concept for government officials and other public leaders

In thinking particularly about public value as an idea to guide the diagnoses, judgments, and actions of government officials (whether in elected, appointed or career positions), five key issues seem to arise.

- Whether and how politics and administration might be more effectively integrated with each other in the development of legitimacy and support for governmental action
- How the performance of government agencies might best be measured and evaluated – that is, how we might recognize the creation of public value when it occurs
- How best to analyse the production processes of government and to orchestrate the contributions made to government and public purposes by partners and clients
- How much room there is for innovation in government, and how to create conditions to stimulate increased innovation
- What government leaders and managers can and should do to help bring a public into existence that can understand and act on its own interests

Increasing legitimacy by linking politics and administration

There is still a lot of work to do in understanding what public managers can and should do to support and strengthen legitimacy and authorization for governmental decisions and operations. The old debate about the dividing line between policymaking and administration goes on, and traditionalists continue to emphasize the primacy of elected politicians in defining the ends of government and restricting career civil servants to the search for efficient means to achieve those ends.

But this approach seems to ignore a deeper problem: namely, that democratic government has a legitimacy deficit which is only partly closed by ensuring that the elected government of the day has the necessary authority to implement its policies. Perhaps it would add something to the old debate to recognize that one of the key goals of a democratic government (in addition to developing policies and delivering services) is to deepen democracy, and to maximize the legitimacy of the choices made by government. The legitimacy of these choices depends not only on the imprimatur of an elected or appointed government official, but also more broadly on the public's acceptance of the decisions made and of the way those decisions were made (for example the adequacy of the consultative and deliberative processes that informed the decision). The debate should also make room for the idea that the legitimacy of a political choice depends not only on the process by which it was made, but also on its perceived legality and fairness, and the likelihood that it will produce the results that were claimed for it.

If one of the key goals of the elected, appointed and career public officials who share executive responsibility in government is to maximize public legitimacy and support for the government's choices and actions, then the individuals who occupy these positions might do well to think of themselves as a team, jointly aiming to create specific public value outcomes, and with legitimating these choices as one of their common goals. After all, they each bring different assets to that task. Elected politicians bring the authorization that comes from having stood for and won election. Politically appointed advisers and executives bring not only their close relationship to the victors in the election, but also (ideally) some significant expertise and knowledge of their own. And career civil and public servants bring both a detailed knowledge of the laws that guide the actions of government, and substantive expertise in analysing and dealing with particular policy problems.

If we transform the debate about the relative powers held by elected politicians on the one hand and career civil servants on the other into a discussion which focuses on their joint responsibility for producing and implementing policy decisions and government operations that are legitimated and supported by a combination of political consent, law and expertise, then we need theories and practices that can take account of this emerging reality. This cannot be helped by thinking and acting as though electoral legitimacy is the only kind of legitimacy that is engaged when a public choice is made by a democratic government; nor that the only source of political legitimacy is the judgment of an individual politician acting in isolation from other sources of advice and action within the whole system of governance.

It is also important to note that as democratic governments seek to deepen democracy and close legitimacy gaps by developing new processes of consultation with citizens and users, some political work shifts from national governments to local and community governments and organizations. As local government officials (and leaders of local partnerships between public, private and voluntary sector agencies) take responsibility for orchestrating public deliberations to legitimate the choices they make, and develop new methods of consulting with citizens and client groups, the frontline officials (many of them public servants) become engaged in a particular kind of politics – the politics of how to use administrative discretion to achieve purposes that smaller but more continuously engaged political communities want to achieve.

The old preoccupation with the powers of elected officials over career civil servants remains important in so far as it reminds us that we have to be concerned about enhancing the democratic legitimacy and accountability of government – to be sure that it becomes a 'government of, by and for the people.' But the chances for advancing that goal seem much larger once we understand that the process of endowing decisions with democratic legitimacy can be something more than simply ensuring that elected officials have full and final power over government agencies. Indeed, elected politicians themselves know this is true, and rarely act as though they had the powers that some would like to give them. They understand all too well that legitimacy is a hard thing to achieve, and that it takes a complex blend of wide political consultation, understanding of the law, and technical expertise to achieve.

The concept of public value and the strategic triangle help to make sense of these complex processes – not only by focusing the joint effort of both elected and appointed government officials on producing outcomes that the public values but also by focusing attention on the processes that build legitimacy and support for specific purposes being pursued by government officials using the powers of government. In effect, the strategic triangle makes the creation of a vital public sphere one of the important ends and means of public officials – whether elected, appointed or career.

Recognizing public value: measuring government performance

There is also much work to be done in developing the concept of public value outcomes and deploying the performance measures necessary to recognize when and how much public value is being created by government and other organizations. Once again the strategic triangle provides some guidance about how that work should be done.

The choice to give 'public value creation' priority standing in the strategic triangle points to the crucial importance of offering a clear account of the value to be produced by a particular government organization or programme. Neither society nor government managers can be sure they are headed in the right direction if no strategic direction or outcomes have been specified. Nor can the conditions necessary for continuous improvement be created if there is no way to measure incremental improvements. So, government organizations cannot function rationally and intentionally without some concept of the public value they seek to create, and some means of measuring the degree to which they are successful in creating it. But there are philosophical, technical and political impediments to developing useful measures of public value.

The philosophical problem arises because the question of what constitutes public value is, at its core, a normative question. Those attempting to answer the public value question have to consider and respond to the utilitarian idea that social welfare consists of nothing more than the maximization of individual desires. They have to consider the more socially oriented but still utilitarian idea that public value consists of achieving some collectively defined social outcomes. And they also have to consider where and how deontological ideas, such as individual human rights, social justice and fairness in government operations, fit into their conceptions of public value as a whole. When we reflect on these questions about value as citizens or public servants, we enter the realm of political philosophy – engaging in discourse about both the good and the just.

The technical problem arises because those charged with creating and measuring public value must be able to construct a reliable bridge from a philosophical concept of value to an empirically observable reality. If they want to talk about the degree to which a policy satisfies individual values, needs and desires, they have to have some way of measuring that satisfaction. If they want to talk about the degree to which a public policy achieves desired social outcomes, they have to be able to name the outcomes that society values and find the means of measuring the degree to which they were achieved. If citizens and public servants want to talk about the degree to which a policy advances the cause of justice, or the degree to which the policy distributes its benefits and burdens across the population in a fair way, they have to be able to give an operational as well as a conceptual definition of justice and fairness. In each case, it is necessary to construct and test particular instruments to measure progress in achieving the abstract concepts that define public value. The measures have to align closely with the concept, behave consistently over time, and allow for efficient and inexpensive data collection.

It is easy to lose oneself in the philosophical and technical challenges described above in a quixotic effort to construct a simple objective ideal that could do for public sector organizations what financial measures do for private sector organizations. Yet, there is a danger in focusing on the public value question alone, independent of the parallel questions about legitimacy and support and operational capacity.

A far greater danger, however, is that thinking about public value purely as an abstract philosophical and technical concept tempts one to think that public value is an absolute that can be decided once and for all time, and exists independently of public debate or organizational experience. Viewed alone, one could make the grave error of thinking that the problem of measuring public value is only philosophical and technical – not also political and managerial.

The strategic triangle deliberately and determinedly binds the concept of public value to the idea of political legitimacy and authorization on the one hand and to the idea of operational capacity on the other. The framework insists that the idea of public value can live somewhat apart from and in partial tension with the idea of political legitimacy. It creates a sphere in which new conceptions of public value can be offered to challenge the old, and weaknesses in political processes that cause some important public values and interests to be neglected can be probed. But a satisfactory conception of public value can never be wholly distinct from the democratic political process that confers legitimacy on a particular conception of public value.

Our conception of public value then has not only to stand alone as a philosophical ideal (made concrete and practically useful with the technical construction of a measurement system); it must also be linked closely to the messy and dynamic world of competing and changing political aspirations on one hand, and organizational activity and production on the other. These linkages are among the main benefits of using the strategic triangle as a guide to managerial thinking and action.

Co-production with partners and clients

While much of the controversy about public value has focused on whether and how public managers of different stripes should participate in the political processes that define public value, public value theory has also contributed to some radical claims about the core production processes of government as well. One of the most important of these is that the successful achievement of socially desired outcomes often depends on the active assistance of actors and stakeholders who operate outside the boundaries of government agencies – that public value is typically 'co-produced.' The success of schools often depends on contributions from parents. The success of police departments sometimes depends on neighbourhood watch groups. The success of solid waste management systems depends on the voluntary actions of thousands of home recyclers. And so on.

The role that co-production could play in the achievement of socially desired outcomes was initially heralded by the contracting-out of some government services to private for profit and non profit agencies. The idea that government did not necessarily have to directly produce everything it authorized or financed gave government the opportunity to reach out for and use private and/or voluntary sector capacities when those seemed better able to achieve the desired objectives at lower costs. It also increased the importance of the contracting function in government, and made government procurement managers more central to the managerial task. Critical to the success of these managers, however, was their ability to define and recognize public value. Only when those managing public assets could specify with some precision and objectivity what they wanted to buy (including hard-to-quantify factors like quality, culture, and fairness) could a contract management system be made to produce public value outcomes.

Beyond the relatively narrow idea that government could contract out some of its work lay the larger and more subtle point that virtually all social outcomes sought by government are co-produced, at least in part, by actors who are not being paid or directly supervised by government agencies to produce those results. The performance of schools can be improved in part by strong socio-cultural supports for higher educational attainment. The performance of the police can be improved by communities that are prepared to support the police in their efforts to prevent and control crime and to reduce fear. And so on. Thus, government success depends a great deal on a supportive (and demanding) civic and political culture that can throw its weight behind government's efforts to produce desired social results.

For public managers, this observation about the dependence of government organizations on the contributions of partners and co-producers raises several important practical questions. The first is how much time and effort they should spend on trying to mobilize and deploy the latent capacity of potential partners as against improving the operations of the organizations they directly control. Perhaps, for example, a school superintendent could boost student achievement more by strengthening connections with parents than she could by overseeing operations within the schools?

A second question is whether and how operational managers could adjust the operations of the organizations they lead to build and strengthen working relationships with potentially important partners. For example, a police commissioner paradoxically might improve the performance of the police department she led by focusing more time on responding to citizens' demands for emergency services of various kinds, in the hope of building a stronger working relationship with communities that would pay later dividends when the police needed individuals to report serious crimes and act as witnesses in court.

A third question is the degree to which public managers could afford to adjust their methods and goals to take advantage of the particular interests and/or the particular capacities of partner organizations. Perhaps the manager charged with finding more foster homes for children might be able to tap into networks of faith-based organizations, or community-based organizations who are in close contact with potential foster parents if they accommodate their bureaucratic procedures to the methods that these organizations want to use to recruit and support a new group of foster parents?

A fourth question is how government managers ought to respond to the fact that the private and voluntary capacities which are so important to their success in co-delivering desired social outcomes are unevenly distributed in society. Some neighbourhoods have more, or better aligned, capacity to support government operations than others. Consequently, government managers have to decide whether to compensate for the weaknesses of weaker communities in order to pursue greater equality of provision, or to play to the strengths of the stronger communities in the interests of achieving the greatest overall return on their effort, at the price of exacerbating inequalities between communities.

A related question is whether they should take the surrounding civic and political culture as they find it or whether, in the pursuit of increased legitimacy and improved public value, they should search for methods to challenge and engage the civic culture in a shared effort to define and achieve social outcomes. It is not only private and voluntary organizations that act as co-producers of public value. The clients of government organizations, as well as those who stand alongside government organizations trying to affect the behaviour of clients in ways that are closely aligned with government goals, are also essential to the co-production of public value. This is certainly true when services such as drug abuse treatment or job training are provided to individuals at public expense, at least in part in hope that these services might help the individuals transform their own lives and, in doing so, improve the overall quality of life in the society. The public value outcomes of these programmes depend critically on whether the clients move in the direction the services seek to lead them. (See Chapter 8 by Alford; also Alford 2009.)

Clients play a crucial role in 'co-production' whether they are accepting public services or public obligations. When a government agency pressures individuals to pay their taxes, or recycle their cans and bottles, or lose weight, or use condoms, its success depends ultimately on millions of individuals accepting the obligation and doing their duty. Some of these obligation encounters are direct, with government agents sanctioning individuals for the failure to do their duty, but others are more indirect – relying on public information campaigns or political mobilizations to remind individuals of their duties and promote changes in thinking and behaviours.

Several public services are exploring this kind of co-creation through open-source innovation, in which users contribute their knowledge and preferences into the design, production and monitoring of services (for example the UK National Health Service programmes for patient and public involvement).

Innovation in programmes and institutional design

The emphasis that public value theory places on innovation (what it is, how it is created, who initiates it, who legitimates and evaluates it, and under what conditions it adds to, or subtracts from, improvement in public service and increases in public value) also seems even more important for the future than in the past. (See Chapter 10 by Hartley.)

Creating Public Value was written at a time when it was generally assumed that government was operating in a fairly simple, stable, and homogeneous environment – in terms of both its managerial 'task environment' and its political 'authorizing environment'. If the scope of government was fixed, and the tasks to be accomplished well known, then there was little need or room for innovation. In this context, the credit that *Creating Public Value* gave to the innovative, value-creating imagination of public executives seemed suspicious to some traditionalists.

Yet, since 1995, these assumptions about the political and task environments in which government works have changed dramatically. Profound changes in the ecological, political, economic and social context have fundamentally altered the roles of government and the meanings of public service. We can no longer assume that the tasks of government agencies are clear, straightforward, homogeneous or static. Those overseeing public schools are no longer satisfied with a one-size-fits-all solution for a highly diverse student population. Police departments now reach out for problem-solving approaches designed to predict and prevent as well as to respond to crime. Courts have developed specialized problem-solving arenas to deal with complex issues like domestic violence, child abuse and neglect.

Not only are the tasks complex and heterogeneous, but the overall character of those tasks is changing over time. New problems show up, such as the integration of new immigrant populations into schools, or finding the best means to engage local communities in efforts to prevent school shootings or terrorist attacks. And the relative importance of different kinds of tasks changes over time, with problems that were once minor becoming major, and vice versa. It takes innovation to respond to the variety and fluidity of the task environment.

Experience has shown that the political authorizing environment is also highly complex, heterogeneous and dynamic – and certainly not restricted to the formal cycles of 3- or 4-year elections. The political authorizing environment is composed of many different actors, each with their own interests, priorities and values, and each with their own platform to use in making claims on government operations. The variety of clamouring voices is only partially controlled by elected officials struggling to hold a governing coalition together. Much of it remains uncontrolled, and overflows the political channels that the elected politicians seek to contain.

To deal with this, many governments have opened up new political channels by creating more powerful roles for partners and stakeholders, or developing new procedures for consultation or engagement with users and local communities. All this tends to increase rather than reduce the heterogeneity of the demands made on government managers, and send them looking for ways to adapt their operations to accommodate the new political and public aspirations.

As public executives – elected, appointed, and career – seek to respond to these diverse and rapidly changing environments, they have to increase the range and rate of innovation. Some of these innovations take the form that is familiar in private business – innovations in products and services designed to meet new needs and demands or solve new problems; or innovations in production processes that allow government managers to achieve higher levels of performance at lower costs.

But many of the innovations take the form of altered institutional arrangements that redistribute rights and responsibilities with respect to particular social conditions, and how collective efforts to deal with socially defined problems will be organized, financed, and governed. In effect, they are innovations in governance arrangements rather than in government operations.

And many of these new governance arrangements are taking the form of public/private/third-sector partnerships in which government is not always the dominant partner, setting the purposes, and then using its authority or money to engage others in the doing of the work. Civic or private sector actors increasingly take the initiative in calling attention to and acting on public problems, and co-opt the government as a partner. Just as often, the government, lacking the knowledge, the powers, the money or the legitimacy to achieve its purposes on its own, reaches out to private and not-for-profit actors for help and practical support. In exchange for their assistance, these actors may seek some special 'partnership' role in co-defining and co-creating the proper ends and best means for government to use in trying to achieve these purposes.

If the demand for innovation is high, and if the form that innovation takes is not only product and process innovation but also innovation in governance arrangements, then the question of who can initiate and legitimate innovations becomes an important issue for government. In the past, the implicit answer has been that government should not do much innovation, and when it does, the innovations should be authorized through elections, or by elected officials, and only at the initiative of the government, not in response to the aims and ambitions of other social actors. But that system may produce adaptation that is too slow and/or innovation that is too limited for a period of increased complexity and rapid change. And it may fail to take advantage of the knowledge held by those at the front lines of public organizations, and by those social actors who are in touch with social conditions about which government may be ignorant, or those who have ideas about how to deal with problems that government has not yet fully considered.

In this context some public organizations are decentralizing the authorization to innovate to the front line where producers and users ('pro-sumers') know the problems first hand and can jointly generate innovative solutions or improvements. In some cases this also involves reaching out to those beyond the boundaries of government organizations who seem to have something to contribute to the solution of social problems that may or may not have been assigned to government.

Calling a public into existence: administrative politics and community consultation

The single most important contribution of public value theory in the future may be its potential to redirect attention to the critical role that democratic politics and public management can play in helping to shape a sense of communal identity and public purpose. (See Chapter 2 by Benington.)

Implicit in the concept of public value is the notion that there is a public (a collective consisting of individual citizens) that can be a reliable arbiter of public value. The core question of public value theory is how such a public can be brought into existence – a public that can articulate the value it wants to produce through the assets it has turned over to its government. That public is different from the mere aggregation of individual client or consumer interests, and different even from the electorate that expressed its views in the most recent elections. It is a broader more actively engaged public that has a stake in how the society and economy develop, what values inform its culture, how its civil society is strengthened, how government uses public assets, and how government is held to account for its performance in achieving these wider societal goals.

The creation of a public that can be articulate about the values it wants to promote in its society and culture, the goals it wants its government to pursue, and the values that ought to be reflected in the way its government operates is, therefore, a central task for successful public leadership and management – both normatively, and practically.

It is at the core normatively because it is only an articulate and engaged public that can act as the appropriate arbiter of public value. It is at the core practically because only when public leaders and managers enjoy the legitimacy and support that comes from having such a public behind them can they expect to achieve their objectives. Only when they have this legitimacy and support can they count on a continuing flow of public money and authority to do their work. It is only when they have legitimacy and support that they can call upon partners and co-producers to help them achieve public goals. It is only when they have legitimacy and support that they can bring the weight of society's expectations on clients who receive services and obligations from them. And it is only when they and their programmes have legitimacy and support that they can mobilize networks of citizens to co-create public value. In this sense, enlisting a public to provide legitimacy and support for a particular conception of public value lies at the moral and practical centre of creating public value.

John Dewey, in his remarkable book *The Public and Its Problems* (Dewey 1927), argued that the challenge that democratic societies face when they choose to use the powers of government to act on a problem is how to 'call into existence a public that can understand and act on its own best interests'. What is compelling about this idea is its suggestion that a public does not naturally exist in society; it has to be created, to be called into existence. Moreover, the challenge in calling a public into existence is to do so in a way that can allow that public to think and act as a collective entity that recognizes the diversity of its individual constituents, but strives to build within each individual in the group a kind of empathy, and a sense of the whole interdependent system as well as its separate constituent parts. This encourages each individual to rise a bit above his or her particular situation and to ask government for what is valuable not just for themselves in their own particular role but also for those who have different interests, and for realizing a shared idea of a good and just society.

In this respect, Dewey is talking about an ideal of the public that is similar to ideals the Greeks once held (at least according to Hannah Arendt). It is also close to John Rawls's idea that a public should consist of individuals who, in making decisions about what would be good or just for all, act from behind a 'veil of ignorance'. Rawls's ideal citizens do not know what particular position they will occupy in society, and so cannot privilege their individual interests within collective decisions. None of these ancient or modern philosophers thought we could routinely and reliably create an ideal public. But they all understood that the quality of a democracy would depend to no small degree on how well we could approximate that ideal.

One of the core challenges that public value theory confronts is this normative and practical question of how those who hold executive power in governments might help to call into existence a public that can understand and act on its own interests. It seems clear that we cannot do that all at once and forever. It will have to be done repeatedly for each of a variety of issues, some large some small, some substantively important, some more symbolically important. And it is here that some of the most important innovations in public leadership and management are likely to come: in the invention of improved ways of engaging the public actively in deliberations about what constitutes public value, and how it might be best produced.

Citizens, political theorists, and public leaders and managers all have to grapple with the challenge of how democratic politics and democratic government can be part of a transformative process in which individuals become conscious of themselves also as citizens as they encounter other individuals and take one another's interests and concerns seriously. The primary challenge facing governments in the developed countries may be to engage individuals in ways that cause them to think and act as citizens. If governments can meet this challenge, they stand to gain both the guidance necessary to define public value and a vital partner in creating it.

Conclusion

The future of public value is bright. It is bright for the same reason that the dream of democracy has always been a beacon for human societies. The idea of public value creation calls on individuals to pursue the good and right, and to do so with respect to principles of democratic governance – to use their own capacities to do what they can to understand and realize a valued public purpose in the world. The specific ideas and diagnostic frameworks are less important than the call to make oneself of use in creating public value. It is only as individuals heed this call, listen and respond to the initiatives of others, and learn how to deliberate together as well as merely exchange goods and services, that we will find out how to create public value more reliably, more ably and more respectfully. We trust that this book has contributed something to that goal.

Notes

Chapter 3

COLIN CROUCH – Privates, Publics and Values

1. It is also the idea at the root of one of the everyday words for 'public' in modern Germanic, Scandinavian and Slav languages (for example, German *öffentlich*, Dutch *openlijk*, Swedish *offentlig*, Russian открытый).
2. This was embodied in the Latin language in the word *publicum*, which was derived from that for 'people', *populus*. This has become the root of the standard word for public in Latin-based languages, including here of course English. Interestingly, it also found its way into the other European language groups (for example Dutch *publiek*, Swedish *publik*, Russian публичный), though not into German.
3. To avoid clumsiness of expression, I shall henceforth use the word 'church' instead of 'religious organization', acknowledging at the outset that strictly speaking this has until recently referred only to Christian organizations.
4. 'Bourgeois' after all means city-dweller; 'politics' comes from the Greek word for a city (always implying city state), and 'civil', 'civic' and 'citizen' all come from the Latin word (*civis*) for the same.
5. In practice also medieval bourgeois traditions survived into the nineteenth and twentieth centuries through the concept of urban philanthropy by local businesses, and into the late twentieth and twenty-first through corporate social responsibility.
6. In common-law systems this may also happen as a result of the ability of those who have secured riches in the market to be able to deploy them to hire better lawyers, enabling them to win cases, with the state's enforcement arm supporting their successful claims.
7. Interestingly, the USA and many parts of the Islamic world stand at opposite ends of the spectrum in terms of the relationship between state and religious organization, the former being an example of extreme separation, the latter frequently of fusion – though there are currently pressures in the USA for a closer relationship between state and religious faith.
8. This partly explains the hostility of the church towards the extension of the state's role in these areas in the nineteenth and early twentieth centuries (Van Kersbergen 1995).
9. Literally, 'compassion', or 'pity felt for a state of wretchedness'. In Christian usage it came to denote Christ's compassion for humans sunk in the wretchedness of sin and separation from God; but the church has long combined this with the original Roman secular meaning to imply works of compassion for all kinds of wretchedness, in particular poverty, surrounding mundane activities of welfare provision with the halo of a connection to Christlike action.

10. There is some debate whether the French and Italian words might not descend instead from *ministerium*, implying service under constraint. Even then, the term has a clear religious origin in the sense of 'ministry' – a religious concept later appropriated by the polity.

11. There are also important tensions between professionals and volunteers, which often surface within voluntary organizations and between these organizations and public-service professionals. This is the clash between *caritas* and *mysterium*. It is unfortunately beyond the scope of this chapter to explore it.

12. The debate over the role of private firms within the formation of public policy and the delivery of public services is central to the relationship between public and private in early twenty-first century society. For present purposes this issue has to be neglected as we are pursuing the issue of values and the public realm. A full account of the subject would include the way these two themes become entwined.

13. For an excellent survey of the long historical development of the term, its lengthy disappearances, changing meanings, and eventual rediscovery in the late twentieth century, see Wagner (2006).

14. It may be significant that the modern discipline of economics took its name, not from the public institution, the market – in practice its central object of study – but from οικοζ, the household being a private structure, outside the public realm of civil society.

Chapter 4

NOEL WHITESIDE – Creating Public Value: The Theory of the Convention

1. For a more detailed account of this section see Whiteside (2003).

Chapter 5

MARK SWILLING – Greening Public Value: The Sustainability Challenge

1. Dani Rodrik is one of the so-called 'Harvard Economists' who has advised the Presidency.

2. This chapter and its argument have been influenced by a masters thesis by Kate Rivett-Carnac (2007), project-supervised by the author.

3. This is not to suggest that these ideas can be extracted from these networks – they are only accessed by working with the networks themselves.

4. Sen does not, in fact, have a notion of collectivities as social actors – this is an interpretive elaboration of his logic.

5. In this regard I am grateful to the work of, and communications with, Rob Lichtman (see Lichtman 2003).

6. This is the conceptual space that explains the rise of social entrepreneurship.

Chapter 8

JOHN ALFORD – Public Value from Co-production by Clients

1. There is no ideal term to describe these entities. Other terms such as those cited could as well be employed, but 'clients' seems to have the benefit of referring to people who receive services without having so much of a private sector connotation. What matters is not the precise term but rather its substantive content as defined here.
2. They may pay taxes which fund these services; but unlike the private customer exchange there is no direct nexus in that case between the money and the service, which is instead collectively funded.
3. Some would argue, with some justification, that the aim of some governments is not so much to find jobs for the unemployed as to get them off the welfare rolls. But the argument here is that *if* the purpose is to get them into jobs, then government organizations face certain imperatives.
4. There has been considerable policy transfer in this area among industrialized nations.
5. Generally, the accepted norm is that those who are able-bodied and unencumbered should not receive welfare payments, whereas the elderly, the disabled and sole parents of young children are 'deserving'. More recently, however, even the claims of the latter two are being challenged, especially in the US.
6. A fierce debate has occurred in the US about the relative merits of these two approaches, with republicans and conservative democrats supporting a 'work first' approach. For discussion of the issues, see Bloom and Michalopoulos (2001).
7. Here the specific focus is on individual rather than corporate or other taxpayers.
8. In the UK, employees' entitlements to deductions and allowances are determined by Her Majesty's Revenue and Customs (HMRC) on the basis of information provided by each employee (and updated as required from time to time). HMRC then notifies the employer of the employee's allowance category, which is factored into the amount of tax withheld by the employer. In most cases, tax paid and tax owing tally at year-end, but if the HMRC finds that there is still a mismatch, a tax return form is sent to the employee to complete and lodge. Just under 90 per cent of individual income taxpayers do not have to lodge returns (Gale 1997).
9. MDRC has been the organization most extensively researching the impact of welfare-to-work programmes in the US, partly contracted by federal or state governments, partly with foundation funding.
10. TANF was set up under the 1996 Personal Responsibility and Work Opportunity Reconciliation Act, and embodied President Clinton's promise to 'end welfare as we know it' (Handler 2004).

Chapter 9

JONATHAN Q. TRITTER – Framing The Production of Health in Terms of Public Value: Lessons from the UK National Health Service

1. This chapter is the product of an evolution of a University of Warwick Health Service Partnership Discussion Paper (2005). I am grateful to the other contributors and the editors for their useful comments.

Chapter 11

GUY STUART – Sustaining Public Value Through Microfinance

1. For example, in June 2003 the US passed a law (HR 192, Microenterprise for Self-Reliance Act of 2000 Amendments) to ensure that at least 50 percent of all microenterprise assistance is targeted to the very poor. It required that USAID's Fiscal 2006 Reports must document: (1) the percentage of its resources that were allocated to the very poor; and (2) the absolute number of the very poor reached.
2. There are some prominent non-profit, non-member MFIs that mobilize savings. BRAC and ASA are traditional non-profits, each with a self-perpetuating board of directors, operating in Bangladesh.

Chapter 12

RICHARD NORMAN – Redefining 'Public Value' in New Zealand's Performance Management System: Managing for Outcomes while Accounting for Outputs

1. A detailed account of this phase of strategic planning is contained in Matheson (1998).
2. The metaphor comes from a comment by the associate minister of finance, Maurice McTigue, *The Press*, Christchurch, 6 June 1992. Electric fences play an important role in New Zealand agriculture and are a significant export industry.
3. A group of thirteen budget specialists were invited in November 2005 to use the electronic meeting software, WebIQ (described at www.webiq.net). The specialists were invited to comment on their experiences with the relatively new outcomes system among other aspects of performance budgeting, after which statements of individuals were voted on by the group. The views presented above were agreed by the whole group.
4. Interviewed 15 December 2005.

Chapter 14

BOB FRYER – Learning, Social Inequality and Risk: A Suitable Case for Public Value?

1. For evidence of this, see for example the excellent research from the Centre for Research on the Wider Benefits of Learning (WBL), Institute of Education, London: www.learningbenefits.net.

Bibliography

Aberbach, J. and Christensen, T. (2005) 'Citizens and Consumers: An NPM Dilemma', *Public Management Review*, 7(2) 225–45.

Abrahamson, E. (1991) 'Managerial Fads and Fashion: The Diffusion and Rejection of Innovations', *Academy of Management Review*, 16(3) 586–612.

ACOSS (Australian Council of Social Service) (2001) *Breaching the Safety Net: The Harsh Impact of Social Security Penalties*. Strawberry Hills, NSW.

Aghion, A. and Howitt, P. (1999) *Endogenous Growth Theory*. Cambridge, MA: MIT Press.

Albury, D. (2005) 'Fostering Innovation in Public Services', *Public Money and Management*, 25(1) 51–6.

Alderson, W. (1957) *Marketing Behavior and Executive Action*. Homewood, IL: Irwin.

Alderson, W. (1965) *Dynamic Marketing Behavior*. Homewood, IL: Irwin.

Alford, J. (2002) 'Defining the Client in the Public Sector: A Social Exchange Perspective', *Public Administration Review*, 62(3) 337–46.

Alford, J. (2008) 'The Limits to Traditional Public Administration, or Rescuing Public Value from Misrepresentation', *Australian Journal of Public Administration, 67(3)* 357–66.

Alford, J. (2009) *Engaging Public Sector Clients: From Service Delivery to Co-Production*. Basingstoke: Palgrave Macmillan.

Alford, J. and Hughes, O. (2008) 'Public Value Pragmatism As the Next Phase of Public Management', *American Review of Public Administration, 38(2)*, 130–48.

Alford, J. and O'Flynn, J. (2009) 'Making Sense of Public Value: Concepts, Critiques and Emergent Meanings', *International Journal of Public Administration, 32*, 171–91.

Allison, G. (1979) 'Public and Private Management: Are They Fundamentally Alike in All Unimportant Respects?', in J. Shafritz and A. Hyde (eds) *Classics of Public Administration*. Belmont, CA: Wadsworth.

Alm, J., Jackson, B. and McKee, M. (1992a) 'Deterrence and Beyond: Toward a Kinder, Gentler IRS', in J. Slemrod (ed.) *Why People Pay Taxes: Tax Compliance and Enforcement*. Ann Arbor: University of Michigan Press.

Alm, J., McClelland, G. and Schultze, W. (1992b) 'Why Do People Pay Taxes?', *Journal of Public Economics*, 48(1) 21–38.

Altshuler, A. and Behn, R. (1997) *Innovation in American Government: Challenges and Dilemmas*. Washington, DC: Brookings.

Andreasen, A. (1994) 'Social Marketing: Its Definition and Domain', *Journal of Public Policy and Marketing, 13(1)* 108–14.

Andreasen, A. (2002) 'Marketing Social Marketing in the Social Change Marketplace', *Journal of Public Policy and Marketing*, 21(1) 3–13.

Arendt, H. (1958) *The Human Condition*. New York: Doubleday.

280

Argyris, C. (1993) *Knowledge for Action: A Guide To Overcoming Barriers To Organizational Change*. San Francisco, CA: Jossey Bass.

ASEM (2007) *Danish Ministry of Environment: Decoupling*. Copenhagen: Government of Denmark. Department of Environment. http://asem.mim.dk/Topics/Documents/ [3 June 2008]

Ashby, W. (1956) *An Introduction to Cybernetics*. London: Chapman & Hall.

Ashby, W. (1958) 'Requisite Variety and Its Implications for the Control of Complex Systems', *Cybernetica (Namur)* 1(2) 83–99. Oxford University Press.

Atkinson, T. (2006) *Measurement of Government Output and Productivity for the National Accounts*; at www.statistics.gov.uk/about/data/methodology/specific/PublicSector/Atkinson/final_report.asp

Aucoin, P. (1995) *The New Public Management: Canada in Comparative Perspective*. Montreal: Institute for Research on Public Policy.

Audit Commission (2007) *Innovation in Local Government*. London.

Ayres, I. and Braithwaite, J. (1992) *Responsive Regulation: Transcending the Deregulation Debate*. New York: Oxford University Press.

Badgley, C. and Perfecto, I. (2007) 'Can Organic Agriculture Feed The World?', *Renewable Agriculture and Food Systems*, 22(2) 80–5.

Bagchi, A. (2000) 'The Past and the Future of the Developmental State', *Journal of World-Systems Research*, 1(2) 398–442.

Baggott, R. (2005) 'A Funny Thing Happened on the Way to the Forum', *Public Administration*, 83(3) 533–51.

Bandura, A. (1986) *Social Foundations of Thought and Action: A Social Cognitive Theory*. Englewood Cliffs, NJ: Prentice-Hall.

Bardach, E. and Kagan, R. (1982) *Going by the Book: The Problem of Regulatory Unreasonableness*. Philadelphia, PA: Temple University Press.

Barnet Community Health Council. (2001) *Annual Report 1999/2000*. Barnet, Herts.

Barrow, C. (2000) *Social Impact Assessment: An Introduction*. London: Arnold.

Bastian, H. (1994) *The Power of Sharing Knowledge: Consumer Participation in the Cochrane Collaboration*; at www.informedhealthonline.org/item.aspx?tabid=37 [8 February 2006].

Bauman, Z. (1997) *Postmodernity and Its Discontents*. Oxford: Polity.

Bauman, Z. (2001) *The Individualized Society*. Oxford: Polity.

Baumgartner, S. *et al.* (2008) 'Relating the Philosophy and Practice of Ecological Economics: The Role of Concepts, Models and Case Studies in Inter- and Transdisciplinary Sustainability Research', *Ecological Economics*, 67(3) 384–93. University of Luneburg, Working Paper Series in Economics, 75; at www.leuphana.de/vwl/papers

Baxter, V. (1994) *Labor and Politics in the U.S. Postal Service*. New York: Plenum.

BBC (2004) *Building Public Value: Renewing the BBC for a Digital World*; at http://www.bbc.co.uk/pressoffice/pressreleases/stories/2004/06_june/29/bpv.shtml.

Beck U., Giddens, A. and Lasch, C. (eds) (1994) *Reflexive Modernization: Politics, Tradition and Aesthetics. The Modern Social Order*. Cambridge: Polity.

Beck, U. (1992) *Risk Society: Towards a New Modernity*. London: Sage.

Becker, H. and Vanclay, F. (eds) (2003) *International Handbook of Social Impact Assessment*. Cheltenham: Edward Elgar.

Becker, H. (1997) *Social Impact Assessment: Method and Experience in Europe, North America and the Developing World*. London: UCL Press.

Beezley, T. and Ghatak, M. (2003) 'Incentives, Choice and Accountability in the Provision of Public Services', *Oxford Review of Economic Policy*, 19(2) 235–49.

Benington, J. (1986) 'Local Economic Strategies: Paradigms for a Planned Economy', *Local Economy*, 1(1) 7–24.

Benington, J. (1997) 'New Paradigms and Practices for Local Government: Capacity Building Within Civil Society', in S. Kraemer and J. Roberts (eds), *The Politics of Attachment*. London: Free Association Books.

Benington, J. (1998) 'Risk and Reciprocity: Local Governance Rooted within Civil Society', in A. Coulson (ed.) *Trust and Contracts: Relationships in Local Government, Health and Public Services*. Bristol: Policy Press.

Benington, J. (2000) 'The Modernization and Improvement of Government and Public Services', *Public Money and Management*, 20(2) 3–8.

Benington, J. (2001) 'Partnerships as Networked Governance? Legitimation, Innovation, Problem Solving and Co-Ordination', in Geddes, M. and Benington, J. (eds) *Local Partnerships and Social Exclusion in the European Union*. London: Routledge.

Benington, J. (2006a) *Reforming Public Services*. Sunningdale: National School of Government, and The Stationery Office (TSO).

Benington, J. (2006b) *From Private Choice to Public Value*; at www.publicnet.co.uk

Benington, J. (2007) *Reforming Public Services*. London: National School of Government and The Stationery Office (TSO).

Benington, J. (2009) 'Creating the Public in Order to Create Public Value', *International Journal of Public Administration*, 32(3–4), 232–49.

Benington, J. and Hartley, J. (2009) *Whole Systems Go!: Improving Leadership Across the Whole Public Service System*. Sunningdale: National School of Government.

Benington, J. and Turbitt, I. (2007) 'Adaptive Leadership and the Policing of Drumcree Demonstrations in Northern Ireland', *Leadership, 3(4)*, 371–95.

Benn, C. and Chitty, C. (1996) *Thirty Years On: Is Comprehensive Education Alive and Well or Struggling to Survive?* London: David Fulton.

Bentley, T. and Wilsden, J. (2003) *The Adaptive State*. London: Demos.

Berger, C., Möslein, K., Piller, F. and Reichwald, R. (2005) 'Co-designing the Customer Interface', *European Management Review*, 2(1) 70–87.

Berkes, F. and Folke, C. (2000) *Linking Social and Ecological Systems: Management Practices and Social Mechanisms for Building Resilience*. Cambridge University Press.

Bessant, J. (2003) *High-Involvement Management: Building and Sustaining Competitive Advantage Through Continuous Change*. Chichester: Wiley.

Bessant, J. (2005) 'Enabling Continuous and Discontinuous Innovation: Learning from the Private Sector', *Public Money and Management*, 25(1) 35–42.

Black, A. (1984) *Guilds and Civil Society in European Political Thought from the 12th Century to the Present*. London: Methuen.

Blackburn, R. (2002) *Banking On Death*. London: Verso.

Blake, D. (2003) *Pension Schemes and Pension Funds in the United Kingdom*. Oxford University Press.

Blau, M. (1964) *Exchange and Power in Social Life*. New York: Wiley.

Blau, P. and Scott, W. (1963) *Formal Organizations: A Comparative Approach*. London: Routledge & Kegan Paul.

Blau, P. (1963) *The Dynamics of Bureaucracy: A Study of Interpersonal Relations in Two Government Agencies*. University of Chicago Press.

Blinder, A.S. (1988) 'Why Is the Government in the Pension Business?', in S. M. Wachter (ed.) *Social Security and Private Pensions*. Lexington, MA: Lexington Books.

Blond, P. (2010) *Red Tory: How Left and Right Have Broken Britain, And How We Can Fix It*. London: Faber.

Bloom, D. and Michalopoulos, C. (2001) *How Welfare and Work Policies Affect Employment and Income: A Synthesis of Research*. New York: Manpower Demonstration Research Corporation.

Bloom, H., Hill, C. and Riccio, J. (2001) *Modeling the Performance of Welfare-to-Work Programs: The Effects of Program Management and Services, Economic Environment, and Client Characteristics*. New York: Manpower Demonstration Research Corporation.

Boltanski, L. and Thevenot, L. (1991) *De la Justification: Les Economies de la grandeur*. Paris: Gallimard. Tr. C. Porter (2006) as *On Justification: Economies of Worth*. Princeton University Press.

Boltanski, L. and Thevenot, L. (1999) 'The Sociology of Critical Capacity', *European Journal of Social Theory*, 2(3) 359–77.

Bonoli, G. (2000) *The Politics of Pension Reform:. Institutions and Policy Change in Western Europe*. Cambridge University Press.

Boston, J., Martin, J., Pallot, J. and Walsh, P. (1996) *Public Management: The New Zealand Model*. Auckland: Oxford University Press.

Bourdieu, P, (1990) *The Logic of Practice*, Cambridge: Polity.

Boyne, G. (1998) 'Competitive Tendering in Local Government: A Review of Theory and Evidence', *Public Administration*, 76(4) 695–712.

Boyne, G. (2002) 'Public and Private Management: What's the Difference?', *Journal of Management Studies*, 39(1) 97–122.

Bozeman, B. (1987) *All Organizations Are Public: Bridging Public and Private Organizational Theories*. San Francisco, CA: Jossey-Bass.

Bozeman, B. (2002) 'Public Value Failure: When Efficient Markets May Not Work', *Public Administration Review*, 62(5) 447–54.

Bozeman, B. (2007) *Public Values and Public Interest: Counterbalancing Economic Individualism*. Washington, DC: Georgetown University Press.

Bozeman, B. and Sarewitz, D. (2005) 'Public Values and Public Failure in US Science Policy', *Science and Public Policy*, 32(2), 119–36.

Braithwaite, V., Braithwaite, J., Gibson, D. and Makkai, T. (1994) 'Regulatory Styles, Motivational Postures and Nursing Home Compliance', *Law and Policy*, 16(4) 363–94.

Braithwaite, J. (1985) *To Punish or Persuade: Enforcement of Coal Mine Safety*. Albany, NY: State University of New York Press.

Bringezu, S., Schutz, H., Steger, S. and Baudisch, J. (2004) 'International Comparison of Resource Use and Its Relation to Economic Growth', *Ecological Economics*, 51(1–2) 97–124.

Brinkerhoo, M. and Jacob, J. (1999) 'Thoughts on Mindfulness and Quasi-Religious Meaning Systems: An Empirical Exploration Within the Context of Ecological Sustainability and Deep Ecology', *Journal for the Scientific Study of Religion*, 38(4), 524–42.

Brook, L. (1997) *What Drives Support for Higher Public Spending?* Institute for Fiscal Studies, Working Paper Series No. W97/16. London.

Brookes, M. (2004) *Watching Alone: Social Capital and Public Service Broadcasting*. London: Work Foundation and BBC.

Brown, L. and Moore, M. (2001) 'Accountability, Strategy, and International Nongovernmental Organizations', *Nonprofit and Voluntary Sector Quarterly*, 30(3) 569–87.

Brown, S. and Eisenhardt, K. (1998) *Competing On the Edge: Strategy as Structured Chaos*, Boston, MA: Harvard Business School Press.

Brudney, J. and England, R. (1983) 'Toward a Definition of the Co-production Concept', *Public Administration Review*, 43(1) 59–65.

Bryan, S., Roberts, T., Heginbotham, C. and McCallum, A. (2002) 'QALY-Maximisation and Public Preferences: Results from a General Population Survey', *Health Economics* ,11(8) 679–93.

Burns, T. and Stalker, G. (1961) *The Management of Innovation*. London: Routledge & Kegan Paul.

Buxton, J., Clarke, L., Grundy, E. and Marshall, C.E. (1995) 'The Long Shadow of Childhood: Associations Between Parental Social Class, Educational Attainment and Timing of First Birth; Results from the ONS Longitudinal Study', *Population Trends*, 121(Autumn) 17–26.

Capra, F. (1996) *The Web of Life*. New York: Anchor.

Castells, M. (1996) *The Rise of The Network Society*. New York: Blackwell.

Centre for Urban Policy Research. (2000) *Towards a Comprehensive Geographical Perspective on Urban Sustainability: Final Report of the 1998 National Science Foundation Workshop on Urban Sustainability*. New Brunswick, NJ: Centre for Urban Policy Research, Rutgers University.

Chang, H. (2002) *Kicking Away the Ladder*: Policies and Institutions for Development in Historical Perspective. London: Anthem.

Chen, S. and Revallion, M. (2004) *How Have the World's Poorest Fared Since the Early 1980s?* World Bank, Policy Research Working Paper WPS 3341. Washington, DC.

Chesbrough, H. (2003) *Open Innovation*. Boston, MA: Harvard Business School Press.

Chibber, V. (2002) 'Bureaucratic Rationality and the Developmental State', *American Journal of Sociology*, 107(4) 951–89.

Chibber, V. (2003) *Locked in Place: State-Building and Late Industrialization in India*. Princeton, NJ: Princeton University Press.

Christensen, C. (1997) *The Innovator's Dilemma*. Boston, MA: Harvard Business School Press.

Clark, G. (2000) *Pension Fund Capitalism*. Oxford University Press.

Clark, G. (2006) 'The UK Occupational Pension System in Crisis', in H. Pemberton, P. Thane and N. Whiteside (eds) *Britain's Pensions Crisis: History and Policy*. Oxford University Press.

Clark, P. and Wilson, J. (1961) 'Incentive Systems: A Theory of Organizations', *Administrative Science Quarterly*, 6(2) 129–66.

CM 5810 (2003) *21st Century Skills: Realising our Potential*. London: Stationery Office.

Cohen, J. and Arato, A. (1992) *Civil Society and Political Theory*. Cambridge, MA: MIT Press.

Considine, M. (2001) *Enterprising States: The Public Management of Welfare-to-Work*. Oakleigh, Victoria: Cambridge University Press.

Consultative Group to Assist the Poorest (2000) *The Rush to Regulate: Legal Frameworks for Microfinance*. CGAP, Occasional Paper No. 4. Washington, DC.

Cooley, M. (1982) *Architect or Bee? The Human/Technology Relationship*. Boston, MA: South End Press.

Cooper, A. and Lousada, J. (2005) *Borderline Welfare: Feeling and Fear of Feeling in Modern Welfare*. Tavistock Clinic Series. London: Karnac.

Cooper, D. (2004) *Challenging Diversity: Rethinking Equality and the Value of Difference*. Cambridge University Press.

Cooper, R. (1988) 'The New Product Process: A Decision-Making Guide for Management', *Journal of Marketing Management*. 3(3) 238–55.

Costanza, R. (2000) 'The Dynamics of the Ecological Footprint Concept', *Ecological Economics,* 32(3) 341–5.

Costanza, R. (2003) 'A Vision of the Future of Science: Reintegrating the Study of Humans and the Rest of Nature', *Futures,* 35(6) 651–71.

Crisp, R., Hope, T. and Ebbs, D. (1996) 'The Asbury Draft Policy on Ethical Use of Resources', *British Medical Journal,* 312(7045) 1528–31.

Croft, S. and Beresford, P. (1993) 'User Involvement, Citizenship and Social Policy', *Critical Social Policy,* 9(26) 5–18.

Croft, S. and Beresford, P. (1995) 'Whose Empowerment? Equalising the Competing Discourses in Community Care', in R. Jack (ed.) *Empowerment in Community Care*. London: Chapman & Hall.

Daly, H. (1996) *Beyond Growth: The Economics of Sustainable Development*. Boston, MA: Beacon.

Davis, G. (1997) 'Implications, Consequences and Futures', in G. Davis, B. Sullivan and A. Yeatman (eds) *The New Contractualism*? Melbourne: Macmillan.

Davis, P. and West, K. (2008) 'What Do Public Values Mean for Public Action? Putting Public Values in Their Plural Place', *American Review of Public Administration,* 38(1) 62–79.

De Montaigne, M. (1991) *The Complete Essays*. London:, Penguin.

Deakin, N. (2001) *In Search of Civil Society*. Basingstoke: Palgrave Macmillan.

Deci, E. (1975) *Intrinsic Motivation*. New York: Plenum.

Demery, L., Ferroni, M., Grootaert, C. and Wong-Valle, J. (eds) (1993) *Understanding the Social Effects of Policy Reform*. Washington, DC: World Bank.

Denis, J. *et al.* (2002) 'Explaining Diffusion Patterns for Complex Health Care Innovations', *Health Care Management Review,* 27(3) 60–73.

Department for Communities and Local Government (2006) *Strong and Prosperous Communities: The Local Government White Paper (Cm 6939)*. London: Stationery Office.

Department for Education and Skills (2003) *21st Century Skills: Realising Our Potential. Individuals, Employers, Nation*. Norwich: TSO.

Department for Education and Science (2003) *Youth Cohort Study*. London.

Department for Innovation, Universities and Skills (2008) *Innovation Nation* London: Stationery Office.

Department of Health (1991) *The Patient's Charter*. London.

Department of Health (1992) *Local Voices*. London: NHS Management Executive.

Department of Health (1996) *The Patient's Charter and You: A Charter for England*. London.

Department of Health (2000) *The NHS Plan* (Cm 4818-I). London.

Department of Health (2003a) *Building on the Best: Choice, Responsiveness and Equity in the NHS* (Cm 6079). London: HMSO.

Department of Health (2003b) *Response to Reforming NHS Financial Flows*. London: Department of Health.

Department of Health (2004a) *Speech by John Reid MP, Secretary of State for Health, 3 February 2003: NHS Chief Executives Conference*. Available at http://webarchive.nationalarchives.gov.uk/20040223040136/http://dh.gov.uk /NewsHome/Speeches/SpeechesList/SpeechesArticle/fs/en?CONTENT_ID= 4071448&chk=tV3Hgy

Department of Health (2004b) *Making Partnership Work for Patients, Carers and Service Users: A Strategic Agreement Between the Department of Health, the NHS and the Voluntary and Community Sector*. London.

Department of Health (2006) *A Stronger Local Voice: A Framework for Creating a Stronger Local Voice in the Development of Health and Social Care Services*. London.

Dewey, J. (1987) *The Public and Its Problems*. New York: Holt.

Diamond, J. (2005) *Collapse*. New York: Viking.

DiMaggio, P. and Powell, W. (1983) 'The Iron Cage Revisited: Institutional Isomorphism and Collective Rationality in Organizational Fields', *American Sociological Review*, 48(2) 147–60.

Dobereiner, D. (2006) *The End of the Street: Sustainable Growth Within Natural Limits*. Montreal: Black Rose.

Dolan, P. and Metcalfe, R. (2008a) *Comparing willingness to pay and subjective well-being in the context of non-market goods*, CEP Discussion Paper, No. 890. Centre for Economic Performance, London School of Economics and Political Science, London.

Dolan, P. and Metcalfe, R. (2008b) *Valuing Non-Market Goods: A Comparison of Preference-Based and Experience-Based Approaches*. Imperial College London.

Dolton, P. and O'Neill, D. (1996) 'Unemployment Duration and the Restart Effect: Some Experimental Evidence', *Economic Journal*, 106(435) 387–400.

Donahue, J. (1989) *The Privatization Decision: Public Ends, Private Means*. New York, Basic.

Dore, R. (2000) *Stock Market Capitalism: Welfare Capitalism. Japan and Germany versus the Anglo-Saxons*. Oxford University Press.

Dougherty, D. (2006) 'Innovation in the Twenty-First Century', in S. Clegg, C. Hardy, T. Lawrence and W. Nord (eds) *The Sage Handbook of Organization Studies*. London: Sage.

Douthwaite, R. (1999) *The Growth Illusion*. Gabriola Island, BC: New Society.

Doyal, L. and Gough, I. (1991) *A Theory of Human Need*. Basingstoke: Macmillan.

Dresner, S. (2002) *The Principles of Sustainability*. London: Earthscan.

Du Gay, P. (2000) *In Praise of Bureaucracy: Weber, Organizaton, Ethics*. London: Sage.

Dunphy, D. and Stace, D. (1998) 'Transformational and Coercive Strategies for Planned Organizational Change: Beyond the O.D. Model', *Journal of Organization Studies*, 9(3) 317–34.

Dupuy, J.-P. (1989) 'Convention et Common Knowledge', *Revue Economique*, 40(2) 361–400.

Durkheim, E. (1897) *La Division du travail*. Paris: Alcan.

Eagleton, T. (2000) *The Idea of Culture*. Oxford: Blackwell, 119.

Ehrlich, P. (2008) 'Key Issues for Attention from Ecological Economists', *Environment and Development Economics*, 13(1) 1–20.

Ekeh, P. (1974) *Social Exchange Theory: The Two Traditions*. London: Heinemann.

Eliot, T.S. (1923) 'The Function of Criticism', *Criterion* (London), October.

Englestrom, M. (1999) *Activity Theory and Individual and Social Transformation*. Cambridge University Press.

Erhlich, P. (2002) *Human Natures: Genes, Cultures and the Human Prospect*. London: Penguin.

Evans, P. (1995) *Embedded Autonomy: States and Industrial Transformation*. Princeton University Press.

Evans, P. (2002) 'Collective Capabilities, Culture and Amartya Sen's "Development as Freedom"', *Studies in Comparative International Development*, 37(2) 54–60.

Evans, P. (2005) 'The Challenges of the Institutional Turn: New Interdisciplinary Opportunities in Development Theory', in V. Nee, and R. Swedberg (eds) *The Economic Sociology of Capitalist Institutions*. Princeton University Press, 90–116.

Evans, P. (2006) *What Will the 21st Century Developmental State Look Like?* Implications of Contemporary Development Theory for the State's Role. Conference on 'The Changed Role of the Government in Hong Kong' at the Chinese University of Hong Kong. Hong Kong, Unpublished.

Evans, P. (2008) 'Is an Alternative Globalization Possible?' *Politics and Society*, 36(2) 271–305.

Fabian Society (Great Britain), 'Commission on Life Chances and Child Poverty' (2006) *Narrowing the Gap*. London.

Feinstein, L., Hammond, C., Woods, L., Preston, J. and Bynner, J. (2003) *The Contribution of Adult Learning to Health and Social Capita*. Centre for Research on the Wider Benefits of Learning, Research Report No. 8. London: Institute of Education.

Feldberg, G. and Vipond, R. (1999) 'The Virus of Consumerism', in D. Drache and T. Sullivan (eds) *Health Reform: Public Success, Private Failure*. London: Routledge.

Ferguson, C. and McKillop, D. (1997) *The Strategic Development of Credit Unions*. New York: Wiley.

Ferlie, E., Ashburner, L., Fitzgerald, L. and Pettigrew, A. (1996) *The New Public Management in Action.* Oxford University Press.

Ferrera, M. (2006) 'Pension Reforms in Southern Europe: The Italian Experience', in H. Pemberton, P. Thane and N. Whiteside (eds) *Britain's Pensions Crisis: History and Policy.* Oxford University Press.

Finn, D., Blackmore, M. and Nimmo, M. (1998) *Welfare-to-Work and the Long-Term Unemployed: "They're Very Cynical".* London: Unemployment Unit.

Finn, D. (2002) 'Getting Welfare to Work: Lessons from Britain's "New Deal"', *Australian Journal of Labour Economics,* 5(4) 471–87.

Fischer-Kowalski, M. and Amann, C. (2001) 'Beyond IPAT and Kuznets Curves: Globalization as a Vital Factor in Analyzing the Environmental Impact of Socio-Economic Metabolism', *Population and Environment.* 23(1) 7–47.

Fischer-Kowalski, M. and Haberl, H. (eds) (2007) *Socioecological Transitions and Global Change: Trajectories of Social Metabolism and Land Use.* Cheltenham: Elgar.

Floud, J.E., Halsey, A.H. and Scott, F.M. (1956) *Social Class and Educational Opportunity.* London: Heinemann.

Flyvbjerg, B., Bruzelius, B. and Rothengatter, E. (2003) *Megaprojects and Risk: An Anatomy of Ambition.* Cambridge University Press.

Fox, A. (1974) *Beyond Contract: Work, Power and Trust Relations.* London: Faber.

Frances, J., Levacic, R., Mitchell, J., and Thompson, G. (1991) *Markets, Hierarchies and Networks.* Milton Keynes: Open University Press.

Frankel, J., Smit, B. and Sturzenegger, F. (2006) *South Africa: Macroeconomic Challenges after a Decade of Success.* Centre for International Development, Working Paper 133; at www.cid.harvard.edu/cidwp/pdf/133.pdf [28 June 2008].

Frant, H. (1996) 'High Powered and Low Powered Incentives in the Public Sector', *Journal of Public Administration Research and Theory,* 6(3) 365–81.

Frey, B. (1997) *Not Just for the Money: An Economic Theory of Personal Motivation.* Cheltenham: Elgar.

Fung, A. and Wright, O. (2000) *Deepening Democracy: Institutional Innovations in Empowered Participatory Governance.* London: Verso.

Gains, F. and Stoker, G. (2009) 'Delivering Public Value: The Implications for Accountability and Legitimacy', *Parliamentary Affairs,* 62(3) 438–55.

Gala-Sinha, C. (2006) Personal communication to the author.

Gale, W. (1997) 'What Can America Learn from the British Tax System?', *National Tax Journal,* 50(4) 753–77.

Gallopin, G. (2003) *A Systems Approach to Sustainability and Sustainable Development.* Project NET/00/063. Santiago: Economic Commission for Latin America.

Gelb, S. (2006) 'A South African Developmental State: What Is Possible?' Paper presented at the Harold Wolpe Memorial Trust's Tenth Anniversary Colloquium "Engaging Silences and Unresolved Issues in the Political Economy of South Africa", 21–23 September 2006, Cape Town.

Giddens, A. (1998) *The Third Way.* Cambridge: Polity.

Giddens, A. (2000) *The Third Way and Its Critics.* Cambridge: Polity.

Goldthorpe, J. (1996) 'Problems with Meritocracy ', in R. Erikson and J. Jonnson (eds), *Can Education Be Equalized?* Boulder, CO: Westview. Reprinted in A.H. Halsey, H. Lauder, P. Brown and A.S. Wells (eds) (1997) *Education: Culture, Economy, Society.* Oxford University Press.

Gonzalez-Vega, C. *et al.* (1996) 'BancoSol: The Challenge of Growth for Microfinance Organizations', Economics and Sociology, Occasional Paper No. 2332. Rural Finance Program, Department of Agricultural Economics, Ohio State University, Columbus.

Gottschalk, P. (2005) 'Can Work Alter Welfare Recipients' Beliefs?', *Journal of Policy Analysis and Management*, 24(3) 485–98.

Grameen Bank (2004) *Annual Report.* Dhaka, Bangladesh.

Gramsci, A. (1971) *Selections from the Prison Notebooks*, ed. and tr. Q. Hoare and G. Nowell Smith. London: Lawrence & Wishart.

Granovetter, M. (1985) 'Economic Action and Social Structure', *American Journal of Sociology*, 91(3) 481–510.

Gray, W. and Scholz, J. (1991) 'Analyzing the Equity and Efficiency of OSHA Enforcement', *Law and Policy,* 13(3) 185–214.

Greener, I. (2003) 'Patient Choice in the NHS: The View from Economic Sociology', *Social Theory and Health*, 1(1) 72 –89.

Greenfield, S. *et al.* (2001) 'Community Voices: Views on the Training of Future Doctors in Birmingham, UK', *Patient Education & Counseling*, 45(1) 43–50.

Greenhalgh, T. *et al.* (2004) *How to Spread Good Ideas.* Report for the National Coordinating Centre for NHS Service Delivery and Organization. London.

Gregory, R. (1995) 'The Peculiar Tasks of Public Management: Toward Conceptual Discrimination', *Australian Journal of Public Administration,* 54(2) 171–83.

Gregory, R. (2000) 'Getting Better But Feeling Worse? Public Sector Reform in New Zealand', *International Public Management Journal*, 1(3) 107–23.

Grigg, P. and Mager, C. (2005) *Public Value and Learning and Skills: A Stimulus Paper.* London: Learning and Skills Development Agency.

Grint, K. (2005) 'Problems, Problems, Problems: The Social Construction of "Leadership"', *Human Relations*, 58, 1467–94.

Grogger, J., Karoly, L. and Klerman, J. (2002) *Consequences of Welfare Reform: A Research Synthesis.* Santa Monica, CA: RAND Corporation.

Guiltinan, J. (2002) 'Choice and Variety in Antitrust Law: A Marketing Perspective', *Journal of Public Policy and Marketing*, 21(2) 260–68.

Gunningham, N. and Grabosky, P. (1998) *Smart Regulation: Designing Environmental Policy.* Oxford University Press.

Habermas, J. ([1962] 1989)) *The Structural Transformation of the Public Sphere,* tr. T. Burger. Cambridge: Polity.

Haggard, S. and Kaufman, R. (eds) (1992) *The Politics of Economic Adjustment: International Constraints, Distributive Politics, and the State.* Princeton University Press.

Halder, S. (2003) 'Poverty Outreach and BRAC's Microfinance Interventions: Programme Impact and Sustainability', *IDS* [Institute of Development Studies] *Bulletin*, 34(4) 44–53.

Hall, P. and Soskice, D. (2001) *The Varieties of Capitalism: The Institutional Foundations of Comparative Advantage.* Oxford UniversityPress.

Hallberg, P. and Wittrock, B. (2006) 'From Koinonia Politikè to Societas Civilis: Birth, Disappearance and First Renaissance of the Concept', in P. Wagner (ed.) *The Languages of Civil Society*. Oxford: Berghahn.

Hamann, R., Agbazue, T., Kapelus, P. and Hein, A. (2005) 'Universalizing Corporate Social Responsibility? South African Challenges to the International Organization for Standardization's New Social Responsibility Standard', *Business and Society Review*, 110, 1–19.

Hampden-Turner, C. (1990) *Charting the Corporate Mind*. New York: Free Press.

Handler, J. and Hasenfeld, Y. (1997) *We the Poor People: Work, Poverty and Welfare*. New Haven, CT: Yale University Press.

Handler, J. (2004) *Social Citizenship and Workfare in the United States and Western Europe: The Paradox of Inclusion*. Cambridge University Press.

Hargadon, A. and Sutton, R. (2000) 'Building an Innovation Factory', *Harvard Business Review*, 78(3) 157–66

Harriss-White, B. and Harriss, E. (2006) 'Unsustainable Capitalism: The Politics of Renewable Energy in the UK', in C. Leys and L. Panitch *Coming to Terms With Nature*. London: Merlin.

Hartley, J. (2002) 'Organizational Change and Development', in P. Warr (ed.) *Psychology at Work*, 5th edn. Harmondsworth: Penguin, 399–425.

Hartley, J. (2005) 'Innovation in Governance and Public Services: Past and Present', *Public Money and Management*, 25(1) 27–34.

Hartley, J. (2006) *Innovation and Its Contribution to Improvement: A Literature Review for Policy-Makers, Policy Advisers, Managers and Academics*. London: Department of Communities and Local Government.

Hartley, J. (2008) 'The Innovation Landscape for Public Service Organizations', in J. Hartley, C. Donaldson, C. Skelcher and M. Wallace (eds) *Managing to Improve Public Services*. Cambridge University Press.

Hartley, J. and Allison, M. (2002) 'Good, Better, Best? Inter-Organizational Learning in a Network of Local Authorities', *Public Management Review*, 4(1) 101–18.

Hartley, J. and Benington, J. (2006) 'Copy and Paste, or Graft and Transplant? Knowledge Sharing in Inter-Organizational Networks', *Public Money and Management*, 26(2) 101–08.

Hartley, J. and Rashman, L. (2007) 'How Is Knowledge Transferred Between Organizations Involved in Change?', in M. Wallace, M. Fertig and E. Schneller (eds) *Managing Change in the Public Services*. Oxford: Blackwell.

Hasenfeld, Y. and Weaver, D. (1996) 'Enforcement, Compliance and Disputes in Welfare-to-Work Programs', *Social Service Review*, 70(2) 235–56.

Hattingh, J. (2001) *Conceptualising Ecological Sustainability and Ecologically Sustainable Development in Ethical Terms: Issues and Challenges*. Annals of the University of Stellenbosch. Stellenbosch: University Printers.

Havel, V. (1985) *The Power of the Powerless*. London: Hutchinson.

Hayden, C. and Boaz, A. (2000) *Making A Difference: The Better Government for Older People Programme Evaluation Report*. Coventry: University of Warwick Local Government Centre.

Hayek, F. (1960) *The Constitution of Liberty*. University of Chicago Press.

Hayek, F. (1963) *Capitalism and the Historians*. University of Chicago Press.

Heath, A. (2003) 'Education Since 1945 in Britain', in J. Hollowell (ed.) *Britain Since 1945*. Oxford: Blackwell, 296–312.

Heath, S., (1983) *Ways with Words*. New York: Cambridge University Press.

Hegel, G. (1821) *Grundlinien der Philosophie des Rechts*. Berlin.

Heifetz, R. (1994) *Leadership Without Easy Answers*. Cambridge, MA: Belknap.

Herzberg, F., Mausner, B. and Snyderman, B. (1993) *The Motivation to Work*. New Brunswick, NJ: Transaction.

Higgins, M. and Smith, W. (2202) 'Babies Cost Less at Tesco', *Journal of Marketing Management*, 18(9–10) 833–56.

Hinrichs, K., (2006) 'Reforming Pensions in Germany and Sweden: New Pathways to a Better Future?', in H. Pemberton, P. Thane and N. Whiteside (eds) *Britain's Pension Crisis: History and Policy*. Oxford University Press.

Hirsch-Hadorn, G. *et al.* (2006) 'Implications of Transdisciplinarity for Sustainability Research', *Ecological Economics*, 60(1) 119–28.

Hirschman, A. (1970) *Exit, Voice and Loyalty*, Cambridge MA: Harvard University Press.

Hoff, K. and Stiglitz, J. (2001) *Modern Economic Theory and Development. Frontiers of Development Economics: The Future in Perspective*. New York: Oxford University Press for World Bank.

Hoggart, R. (1983) *An English Temper*. London: Chatto & Windus.

Hoggett, P. (2000) *Emotional Life and the Politics of Welfare*. New York: Routledge.

Hoggett, P. (2006) 'Conflict, Ambivalence, and the Contested Purpose of Public Organizations', *Human Relations,* 59, 175–94.

Homans, G. (1961) *Social Behaviour: Its Elementary Forms*. New York: Harcourt, Brace & World.

Hood, C. (1991) 'A Public Management for All Seasons?', *Public Administration*, 69(1) 3–19.

Horner, L., Lekhi, R. and Blaug, R. (2006) *Deliberative Democracy and the Role of Public Managers*. London: Work Foundation

Hoxby, C. (2001) 'If Families Matter Most, Where Do Schools Come In?', in T. Moe (ed.) *A Primer on America's Schools*. Stanford, CA: Hoover Institute Press.

Hudon, M. (2006) *Financial Performance, Management and Ratings of the Microfinance Institutions: Do Subsidies Matter?* Working Paper, Solvay Business School, University of Brussels.

Husock, H. and Scott, E. (1999) *Centrelink: A Service Delivery Agency in Australia*. Kennedy School of Government, Case Study 1524.0. Cambridge, MA.

Hutton, W., Clements, J. and Sang, B. (2007) 'Public Leadership for the 21st Century: Delivering "Public Value" through Entrepreneurship, Engagement and Rigour', *International Journal of Leadership in Public Services,* 3(1), 47–51.

Institute of Public Policy Research, (2001) *Building Better Partnerships*, London.

Intergovernmental Panel on Climate Change (2001) *Climate Change 2001 (IPCC Third Assessment Report)*. Geneva.

Intergovernmental Panel on Climate Change (2007) *Climate Change 2007 (IPCC Fourth Assessment Report.* Geneva.

Involve [previously Consumers in NHS Research] (2003) *Strategic Plan 2003–2006: Creating the Expert Resource.* Eastleigh, Hampshire.

Jackson, P. (2001) 'Public Sector Added Value: Can Bureaucracy Deliver?', *Public Administration,* 79(1) 5–28.

Jas, P. and Skelcher, C. (2005) 'Performance Decline and Turnaround in Public Organizations: A Theoretical and Empirical Analysis', *British Journal of Management,* 16(3) 195–210.

Johanson, R. *et al.* (2002) 'Suggestions in Maternal and Child Health for the National Technology Assessment Programme: A Consideration of Consumer and Professional Priorities', *Journal of the Royal Society of Health,* 122(1) 50–4.

Johnson, T. (1991) *Relevance Lost.* Boston, MA: Harvard Business School Press.

Jørgensen, T. and Bozeman, B. (2007) 'Public Values: An Inventory', *Administration and Society,* 39(3), 354–81.

Kagan, R. and Scholz, J. (1984) 'The "Criminology of the Corporation" and Regulatory Enforcement Strategies', in K. Hawkins and J. Thomas (eds) *Enforcing Regulation.* Boston: Kluwer-Nijhoff.

Kaufman, H. (1956) 'Emerging Conflicts in the Doctrines of Public Administration', *American Political Science Review,* 50(4) 1057–73.

Keane, J. (1988) *Civil Society and the State.* London: Verso.

Kelly, G., Mulgan, G. and Muers, S. (2002) *Creating Public Value: An Analytical Framework for Public Service Reform.* London: Cabinet Office.

Kennedy, A., Gately, C., Rogers, A. and the EPP Evaluation Team (2003) *Assessing the Process of Embedding EPP in the NHS.* Manchester: National Primary Care Research and Development Centre.

Kennedy, H. (1997) *Learning Works:* Coventry University: School of Natural and Environmental Sciences.

Kernaghan, K. (2003) 'Integrating Values into Public Service: The Values Statement as Centrepiece', *Public Administration Review,* 63(6) 711–19.

Kettl, D. (1993) *Sharing Power: Public Governance and Private Markets.* Washington, DC: Brookings.

Kettl, D. (2000) 'Performance Management: The State of the Field,' paper presented at Association for Public Policy and Management, 22nd Annual Research Conference, 2–4 November, Seattle, WA.

King, D. (1995) *Actively Seeking Work: The Politics of Unemployment and Welfare Policy in the United States and Great Britain.* University of Chicago Press.

King, D. (1999) *New Forms of Local Social Governance.* London: Routledge.

Kinsey, K. (1992) 'Deterrence and Alienation Effects of IRS Enforcement: An Analysis of Survey Data', in J. Slemrod (ed.) *Why People Pay Taxes: Tax Compliance and Enforcement.* Ann Arbor: University of Michigan Press.

Kiser, L. (1984) 'Toward an Institutional Theory of Citizen Co-production', *Urban Affairs Quarterly,* 19(4) 485–510.

Klein, R. (2004) 'The First Wave of NHS Foundation Trusts', *British Medical Journal,* 328(7452) 1332.

Klerman, J. *et al.* (2000) *Welfare Reform in California: State and County Implementation of CalWorks in the Second Year.* Santa Monica, CA: RAND Corporation.

Knight, F.H. (1921) *Risk, Uncertainty and Profit.* New York: Houghton Mifflin.

Kotler, P. and Zaltman, G. (1971) 'Social Marketing: An Approach to Planned Social Change', *Journal of Marketing*, 35(3) 3–12.

Lasch, C. (1984) *The Minimal Self: Psychic Survival in Troubled Times.* NY: Norton.

Le Grand, J. (2003) *Motivation, Agency and Public Policy.* Oxford University Press.

Leadbetter, C. (2004) *Personalisation Through Participation: A New Script For Public Services.* London: Demos.

Leavis, F.R. (1952) *The Common Pursuit: Critical Essays.* London: Chatto & Windus.

Lee, C. (2007) *Against the Law: Labor Protests in China's Rustbelt and Sunbelt.* Berkeley: University of California Press.

Leftwich, A. (2000) *States of Development: On the Primacy of Politics in Development.* Cambridge: Polity.

Levi, M. (1988) *Of Rule and Revenue.* Berkeley: University of California Press.

Lévi-Strauss, C. ([1949]1969) *The Elementary Structures of Kinship.* Boston, MA: Beacon.

Lichtman, R. (2003) *Sustainable Development: From Concept to Action.* Amsterdam: E-Systems Foundation.

Long, S. and Swingen, J. (1991) 'Taxpayer Compliance: Setting New Agendas for Research', *Law and Society Review*, 25(3) 637–83.

Lorig, K. *et al.* (1999) 'Evidence Suggesting that a Chronic Disease Self-Management Program Can Improve Health Status While Reducing Utilization and Costs: A Randomized Trial', *Medical Care*, 37(1) 5–14.

Lorig, K. *et al.* (2000) *Living a Healthy Life with Chronic Conditions*, 2nd edn. Boulder, CO: Bull.

Lovelock, J. (2006) *The Revenge of Gaia.* New York: Basic.

Luttwak, E. (1999) *Turbo-Capitalism: Winners and Losers In the World Economy.* London: Orion.

Lynch, J.G. Jr and Wood, W. (2006) 'Special Issue Editors' Statement: Helping Consumers Help Themselves', *Journal of Public Policy and Marketing*, 25(1) 1–7.

Lynch, J.G. Jr and Zauberman, G. (2006) 'When Do You Want It? Time, Decisions, and Public Policy', *Journal of Public Policy and Marketing*, 25(1) 67–78.

Lynn, L. (1997) 'Innovation and the Public Interest: Insights From the Private Sector', in A. Altshuler and R. Behn (eds) *Innovation in American Government.* Washington, DC: Brookings.

Lyons, M. (2007) *Place-Shaping: A Shared Ambition for the Future of Local Government.* Lyons Inquiry into Local Government, Final Report and Recommendations. London: Stationery Office.

Madeley, J. (2002) *Food for All: The Need for a New Agriculture.* London: Zed.

Mann Deshi Mahila Sahakari Bank Ltd (2006) *MDMSB Statistics*. Maharashtra, India.

Marquand, D. (2004) *Decline of the Public*. Cambridge: Polity.

Matheson, A. (1998) 'Governing Strategically: The New Zealand Experience', *Public Administration and Development*, 18(4) 349–63.

May, P. (2002) 'Social Regulation', in L. Salamon (ed.) *The Tools of Government: A Guide to the New Governance*. New York: Oxford University Press.

May, P. and Winter, S. (1999) 'Regulatory Enforcement and Compliance: Examining Danish Agro-Environmental Policy', *Journal of Policy Analysis and Management*, 18(4) 625–51.

Mbembe, A. (2003) 'Necropolitics' (tr. L Meintjes), *Public Culture*, 15(1) 11–40.

McFayden, L., Hastings, G. and MacKintosh, A. (2001) 'Cross Sectional Study of Young People's Awareness of and Involvement with Tobacco Marketing', *British Medical Journal*, 322(7285) 513–17.

MDRC (Manpower Demonstration Research Corporation) (2002) *What Works in Welfare Reform?: Evidence and Lessons to Guide TANF Reauthorization*; at www.mdrc.org/Reports2002/TANF

Mead, L. (1986) *Beyond Entitlement: The Social Obligations of Citizenship*. New York: Free Press.

Mebratu, D. (1998) 'Sustainability and Sustainable Development: Historical and Conceptual Review', *Environment Impact Assessment Review*, 18(6) 493–520.

Merton, R. (1957) *Social Theory and Social Structure*, rev. edn. Glencoe, IL: Free Press.

Meynhardt T. (2009) 'Public Value Inside: What Is Public Value Creation?', *International Journal of Public Administration*, 32(3–4) 192–219.

Mignolo, W. (2000) *Local Histories/Global Designs: Coloniality, Subaltern Knowledges, and Border Thinking*. Princeton University Press.

Millar, J. (2000) *Keeping Track of Welfare Reform: The New Deal Programmes*. York: Joseph Rowntree Foundation.

Miller, A. and Listhaug, O. (1999) 'Political Performance and Institutional Trust', in P. Norris (ed.), *Critical Citizens: Global Support for Democratic Government*. Oxford University Press.

Mills, C.W. (1959) *The Sociological Imagination*. Oxford University Press.

Mkandawire, T. (2001) 'Thinking About Developmental States in Africa', *Cambridge Journal of Economics*, 25 289–313.

Monbiot, G. (2006) *Heat: How to Stop the Planet Burning*. London: Allen Lane.

Moore, M. (1995) *Creating Public Value: Strategic Management in Government*. Cambridge, MA: Harvard University Press.

Moore, M. (2000) 'Managing for Value: Organizational Strategy in For-Profit, Nonprofit, and Governmental Organizations', *Nonprofit and Voluntary Sector Quarterly*, 29(1) 183–204.

Moore, M. and Hartley, J. (2008) 'Innovations in Governance', *Public Management Review*, 10(1) 3–20.

Moran, M. (2003) *The British Regulatory State: High Modernism and Hyper-Innovation*. Oxford University Press.

Morduch, J. (1999) 'The Role of Subsidies in Microfinance: Evidence from The Grameen Bank', *Journal of Development Economics*, 60(1) 229–48.

Morduch, J. (2000) 'The Microfinance Schism', *World Development,* 28(4) 617–29.

Morin, E. (1992) *Method: Towards the Study of Humankind, Volume 1: The Nature of Nature.* New York: Peter Lang.

Morin, E. (1999) *Homeland Earth.* Cresskill, NJ: Hampton.

Morrell, K. (2009) 'Governance and the Public Good: A Virtue/Narrative Approach', *Public Administration,* 87(3) 538–656.

Mosley, P. (2001) 'Microfinance and Poverty in Bolivia', *Journal of Development Studies* 37(4) 101–32.

Mosley, P. and Hulme, D. (1998) 'Microenterprise Finance: Is There A Conflict Between Growth and Poverty Alleviation?', *World Development,* 26(5) 783–90.

Mulgan, G. (2009) *The Art of Public Strategy.* Oxford University Press.

Mulgan, G. and Albury, D. (2003) *Innovations in the Public Sector.* London: Cabinet Office.

Mulgan, G. *et al.* (2006) *Parties for the Public Good.* London: The Young Foundation.

Mulgan, G., Kelly, G. and Muers, S. (2002) *Creating Public Value: An Analytical Framework for Public Service Reform.* London: Cabinet Office.

National Audit Office (2006) *Achieving Innovation In Central Government Organizations.* London.

National Bank for Agriculture and Rural Development (2005) 'SHG: Bank Linkage: Agency-Wise Cumulative Participation up to 31 March 2005. 2006.' at http://www.nabard.org/pdf/introduction05–06.pdf.

Navajas, S. *et al.* (2000) 'Microcredit and the Poorest of the Poor: Theory and Evidence from Bolivia', *World Development,* 28(2) 333–46.

Newman, J., Raine, J. and Skelcher, C. (2000) *Innovation and Best Practice in Local Government: A Good Practice Guide.* London: Department of the Environment, Transport and the Regions.

NHS R&D Forum Research Governance Working Group. (2003) *Examples of Good Practice: Peer Review*; at www.rdforum.nhs.uk/workgroups/governance.htm [14 February 2006].

Nicolescu, B. (2002) *Manifesto of Transdisciplinarity.* Albany: State University of New York Press.

Norman, R. (1997) *Accounting for Government: How New Zealand Built an Accounting System That Tells the Full Story About a Government's Financial Performance.* Wellington: VictoriaLink Ltd, Victoria University Press.

Norman, R. (2001) 'Letting and Making Managers Manage: The Effect of Control Systems on Management Action in New Zealand's Central Government', *International Public Management Journal,* 4(1) 65–89.

Norman, R. (2003) *Obedient Servants? Management Freedoms and Accountabilities in the New Zealand Public Sector.* Wellington: Victoria University Press.

North, D. (1990) *Institutions, Institutional Change and Economic Performance.* Cambridge University Press.

O'Day, J. (2002) 'Complexity, Accountability and School Improvement', *Harvard Education Review,* 72(3) 293–308.

Offer, A. (2006) *The Challenge of Affluence.* Oxford University Press.

O'Neill, J. and Hill, M. (2001) *Gaining Ground?: Measuring the Impact of Welfare Reform on Welfare and Work*. New York: Center for Civic Innovation, Manhattan Institute.

Orenstein, M. (2008) *Privatizing Pensions: The Transnational Campaign for Social Security Reform*. Princeton, NY: Princeton University Press.

Osborne, D. and Gaebler, T. (1993) *Reinventing Government: How the Entrepreneurial Spirit is Transforming the Public Sector*. New York: Plume.

Osborne, S. and Brown, K. (2005) *Managing Change and Innovation in Public Service Organizations*. London: Routledge.

Parks, R. *et al.* (1981) 'Consumers as Co-producers of Public Services: Some Economic and Institutional Considerations', *Policy Studies Journal*, 9(7) 1001–11.

Parsons, T. (1949) *The Structure of Social Action*. Glencoe, IL: Free Press.

Parsons, T. (1975) 'The Sick Role and the Role of The Physician Reconsidered', *Milbank Memorial Fund Quarterly*, 53(3) 257–78.

Patel, I. (2006) 'Understanding Innovations and Best Practices', in United Nations (ed.) *Innovations in Governance and Public Administration*. New York: United Nations Department of Economic and Social Affairs.

Pemberton, H., Thane, P. and Whiteside, N. (eds) (2006) *Britain's Pension Crisis: History and Policy*. London: British Academy/Oxford University Press.

Pensions Commission (2005b) *A New Pension Settlement for the Twenty First Century: The Second Report of the Pensions Commission*. London.

Petrie, M. (2001) 'Transparency and Accountability in New Zealand: An Assessment', *Public Sector* 24(1) 14–19.

Petty, R. (2002) 'Limiting Product Choice: Innovation, Market Evolution and Antitrust', *Journal of Public Policy and Marketing*, 21(2) 268–74.

Pezzoli, K. (1997) 'Sustainable Development: A Transdisciplinary Overview of the Literature', *Journal of Environmental Planning and Management*. 40(5) 549–74.

Pillay, D. (2007) 'Transcending Two Economies: Renewed Debates in South African Political Economy', *Africanus*, 37(2) 198–215.

Pitt, M. and Khandker, S. (1998) 'The Impact of Group-Based Credit Programs on Poor Households in Bangladesh: Does the Gender of Participants Matter?', *Journal of Policy Economics*, 106(5) 958–96.

Prager, J. (1994) 'Contracting Out Government Services: Lessons From The Private Sector', *Public Administration Review*, 54(2) 176–84.

Prahalad, C. and Ramaswamy, V. (2008) *The Future of Competition: Co-Creating Unique Value with Customers*. Cambridge MA: Harvard Business School Press.

Pretty, J. and Hine, R. (2000) *Feeding the World with Sustainable Agriculture: A Summary of New Evidence*. Colchester: University of Essex.

Price, C. (1993) *Time Discounting and Value*. Oxford University Press.

Public Management Foundation (1996) *The Glue That Binds: Public Value of Public Services*. London: Public Management Foundation and MORI.

Putnam, R.D. (1993) *Making Democracy Work*. Princeton University Press.

Putnam, R.D. (2000) *Bowling Alone: The Collapse and Revival of American Community*. New York: Simon & Schuster.

Quiggin, J. (2006) *Stern and the Critics on Discounting*; at http://john-quiggin.com/wp-content/uploads/2006/12/sternreviewed06121.pdf

Ramanathan, K. (1985) 'A Proposed Framework for Designing Management Control Systems in Not-For-Profit Organizations', *Financial Accountability and Management,* 1(1) 75–92.

Rashman, L. and Hartley, J. (2002) 'Leading and Learning? Knowledge Transfer in The Beacon Scheme', *Public Administration,* 80(3) 523–42.

Raynham, P. and Saksvikrønning, T. (2003) 'White Light and Facial Rrecognition', *Lighting Journal,* 68(1) 29–33.

Reserve Bank of India (2006) *Financial Inclusion by Extension of Banking Services: Use of Business Facilitators and Correspondents*; DBOD.No.BL.BC. 58/22.01.001/2005–2006.

Revi, A. *et al.* (2006) 'Goa 2100: The Transition to a Sustainable Rurban Design', *Environment and Urbanization,* 18(1) 51:65.

Rhodes R. and Wanna J. (2007) 'The Limits to Public Value, or Rescuing Responsible Government from the Platonic Guardians', *Australian Journal of Public Administration,* 66 (4) 406–21.

Rhodes, R. and Wanna, J. (2009) 'Bringing the Politics Back In: Public Value in Westminster Parliamentary Government', *Public Administration,* 87(2), 161–83.

Riccio, J., Friedlander, D. and Freedman, S. (1994) *GAIN: Benefits, Costs, and Three-Year Impacts of a Welfare-to-Work Program.* New York: Manpower Demonstration Research Corporation.

Riccio, J. and Hasebfeld, Y. (1996) 'Enforcing a Participation Mandate in a Welfare-to-Work Program', *Social Service Review,* 70(4) 516–42.

Rivett-Carnac, K. (2007) 'Local Economic Development, Industrial Policy and Sustainable Development in South Africa: A Critical Reflection on Three New Policy Frameworks.' MPhil thesis, School of Public Management and Planning, Stellenbosch University.

Robinson, M. (2001) *The Microfinance Revolution: Sustainable Finance for the Poor.* Washington, DC: World Bank.

Rodrik, D., Subramanian, A. and Trebbi, F. (2004) 'Institutions Rule: The Primacy of Institutions over Geography and Integration in Economic Development', *Journal of Economic Growth,* 9(2) 131–65.

Rogers, E. (2003) *Diffusion of Innovations,* 5th edn. New York: Free Press.

Rosa Luxemburg Foundation (2008) Talk presented at the Conference on Democracy and Developmental State in the 21st Century, Johannesburg, 25–27 May 2008.

Roth, J., Scholz, J. and Witte, A. (eds) (1989) *Taxpayer Compliance, Volume 1: An Agenda for Research.* Philadelphia: University of Pennsylvania Press.

Rothstein, R. (2002) *Out of Balance: Our Understanding of How Schools Effect Society and How Society Effects Schools.* Chicago: Spencer Foundation.

Rutherford, S. (2000) *The Poor and Their Money.* New Delhi: Oxford India Paperbacks.

Rutherford, S. (2004) *GRAMEEN II At the End of 2003: A 'Grounded View' of How Grameen's New Initiative Is Progressing in the Villages.* Dhaka, Bangladesh: MicroSave.

Ruthven, O. (2002) 'Money Mosaics: Financial Choice and Strategy in West Delhi Squatter Settlement', *Journal of International Development,* 14(2) 249–71.

Salais, R. (1999) 'A la Recherche du fondement conventionnel des insititutions', in R. Salais, E. Chatel and D. Rivaud-Danset (dirs) *Institutions et conventions: La Réflexivité de l'action économique*. Raisons Pratiques no. 9. Paris: EHSS.

Salais, R. and Whiteside, N. (1998) *Governance, Industry and Labour Markets in Britain and France: The Modernizing State in the Mid-Twentieth Century*. London: Routledge.

Samuelson, P. (1954) 'A Pure Theory of Public Expenditure', *Review of Economics and Statistics*, 36(4), 387–9.

Sang, B. and Dabbs, C. (2003) 'Will CPPIH be Democratically Diverse?', *British Journal of Healthcare Management*, 9(6) 210.

Saunders, T., Stone, V. and Candy, S. (2001) *The Impact of the 26 Week Sanctioning Regime*. Working Age Research and Analysis Publications, Report No. 100. London: Department for Work and Pensions.

Schatzki, T., Knorr Cetina, K. and von Savigny, E. (2001) *The Practice Turn in Contemporary Theory*. London: Routledge.

Schick, A. (1996) *The Spirit of Reform*. Wellington: State Services Commission.

Schick, A. (1998) 'Why Most Developing Countries Should Not Try New Zealand's Reforms', *World Bank Research Observer*, 13(1) 123–31.

Schmahl, W. (1992) 'Transformation and Integration of Public Pension Schemes: Lessons from the Process of the German Unification', *Public Finance*, 47, Supplement, 34-56.

Schmolders, G. (1970) 'Survey Research in Public Finance: A Behavioural Approach to Fiscal Theory', *Public Finance*, 25(2) 300–06.

Scholten, P., Nicholls, J., Olsen, S. and Galimidi, B. (2006) *SROI: A Guide to Social Return on Investment*. Den Haag: Lenthe.

Scholz, J. (1984) 'Voluntary Compliance and Regulatory Enforcement', *Law and Policy*, 6(4) 385–404.

Scholz, J. (1994) *The Adaptive Intelligence of Citizens: Tax Compliance as Contingent Consent*. Administration, Compliance and Governability Program Working Paper No. 21. Canberra: Australian National University.

Schroeder, D. and Robinson, A. (1991) 'America's Most Successful Export to Japan: Continuous Improvement Programs', *Sloan Management Review*, 32(3) 67–81.

Schumpeter, J. (1950) *Capitalism, Socialism and Democracy*. New York: Harper & Row.

Schwartz, R. and Orleans, S. (1967) 'On Legal Sanctions', *University of Chicago Law Review*, 34(Winter) 274–300.

Scott, G. (2001) *Public Management in New Zealand: Lessons and Challenges*. Wellington: New Zealand Business Roundtable.

Scott, W. (1998) *Organizations: Rational, Natural and Open Systems*, 4th edn. Upper Saddle River, NJ: Prentice-Hall.

Sen, A. (1999) *Development as Freedom*. New York: Knopf.

Sennett, R. (1977) *The Fall of Public Man*. Cambridge University Press.

Sharp, E. (1980) 'Toward a New Understanding of Urban Services and Citizen Participation: The Co-production Concept', *Midwest Review of Public Administration*, 14(2) 105–18.

Sheffrin, S. and Triest, R. (1992) 'Can Brute Deterrence Backfire? Perceptions and Attitudes in Taxpayer Compliance', in J. Slemrod (ed.) *Why People Pay Taxes: Tax Compliance and Enforcement*. Ann Arbor: University of Michigan Press.

Simons, R. (1995) *Levers of Control: How Managers Use Innovative Control Systems to Drive Strategic Renewal*. Cambridge MA: Harvard Business School Press.

Smith, A. (1759) *The Theory of Moral Sentiments*. London.

Smith, A. (1776) *The Wealth of Nations*. London.

Sneddon, C., Howarth, R. and Norgaard, R. (2006) 'Sustainable Development in a Post-Brundtland World', *Ecological Economics, 57*(2) 253–68.

Snodgrass, D. and Sebstad, J. (2002) *Clients in Context: The Impacts of Microfinance in Three Countries*. Washington, DC: Management Systems International.

Snow, C. (1993) *The Two Cultures*. Cambridge University Press.

Solomon, L. and Collins, K. (1987) 'Humanistic Economics: A New Model For the Corporate Social Responsibility Debate', *Journal of Corporation Law*, 12(2) 331–53.

Southall, R. (2006) 'Introduction', *Can South Africa Be a Developmental State? State of the Nation, 2005–2006*. Cape Town: HSRC Press.

Spicer, M. and Becker, L. (1980) 'Fiscal Inequity and Tax Evasion: An Experimental Approach', *National Tax Journal*, 33(2) 171–5.

Spicer, M. and Lundstedt, S. (1976) 'Understanding Tax Evasion', *Public Finance*, 31(2) 295–305.

SSC (State Services Commission) (2001). *Report of the Advisory Group on the Review of the Centre*. Wellington, State Services Commission.

SSC (State Services Commission) (2003) *Parliament Briefing Document on the Public Finance (State Sector Management) Bill*. http://www.beehive.govt.nz/mallard/public-finance/02.cfm#2 [11 January 2007].

SSC (State Services Commission) (2005). *Getting Better at Managing for Outcomes*. http://www.ssc.govt.nz/display/document.asp?NavID=208&DocID=4727 [11 January 2007].

Stace, D. and Norman, R. (1997) 'Re-invented Government: The New Zealand Experience', *Asia Pacific Journal of Human Resources, 35*(1) 21–36.

Stewart, J. (2001) *Modernizing Government*. Basingstoke: Palgrave Macmillan.

Stewart, J. and Ranson, S. (1988) 'Management in The Public Domain', *Public Money and Management*, 8(2) 13–19.

Stoker, G. (2006) 'Public Value Management: A New Narrative for Networked Governance', *American Review of Public Administration*, 36(2) 41–57.

Storper, M. and Salais, R. (1997) *Worlds of Production: The Action Frameworks of the Economy*. Cambridge MA: Harvard University Press.

Stuart, G. and Kanneganti, S. (2003) *Embedded Cooperation: Women's Thrift Cooperatives in Andhra Pradesh*. Kennedy School of Government, Working Paper RWP03-026. Cambridge, MA.

Swilling, M. (2007) *Growth, Dematerialisation and Sustainability*: Resource Options for 2019. Stellenbosch: Paper Commissioned by the Presidency, South African Government.

Swilling, M., Khan, F. and Simone, A. (2003) 'My Soul I Can See: The Limits of Governing African Cities in a Context of Globalization and Complexity', in R. Stren and P. McCarney (eds.) *Governance on the Ground: Innovations and Discontinuities in Cities of the Developing World.* Baltimore, MD: Johns Hopkins University Press, 220–50.

Talbot, C. (2009) 'Public Value: The Next Big Thing in Public Management?', *International Journal of Public Administration,* 32(3–4) 167–70.

Taylor, C. (1991) *The Ethics of Authenticity.* Cambridge, MA: Harvard University Press.

Thevenot, L. (1987) 'Pragmatic Regimes Governing Engagement With the World', in T. Schatzki, K. Knorr Cetina and E. Von Savigny (eds) *The Practice Turn in Contemporary Theory.* London: Routledge.

Thevenot, L. (2001) 'Organized Complexity: Conventions of Coordination and Composition of Economic Arrangements', *European Journal of Social Theory,* 4(4) 405–25.

Thompson, G., Frances, J., Levacic, R. and Mitchell, J. (eds) (1991) *Markets, Hierarchies and Networks.* London: Sage.

Tidd, J., (2001) 'Innovation Management in Context: Environment, Organization and Performance', *International Journal of Management Reviews,* 3(3) 169–83.

Tidd, J., Bessant, J. and Pavitt, K. (2005) 'Managing Innovation: Integrating Technological', *Market and Organizational Change,* 3rd edn. Chichester: Wiley.

Timmins, N. (2001) 'Squaring Circles? Funding the Provision of the Public Services', *Political Quarterly,* 72(4) 493–7.

Trades Union Congress (2008) *Rethinking Public Service Reform: The Public Value Alternative.* London.

Treasury [New Zealand] (1987) *Government Management: A Report to the Incoming Government.* Wellington.

Treasury [New Zealand] (2006) *Budget Process Guide for Departments and Ministerial Offices*; at www.treasury.govt.nz/budgetprocessguide/ [11 January 2007].

Tritter, J. (1994) 'The Citizen's Charter: Opportunities for Users' Perspectives', *Political Quarterly,* 65(4) 397–414.

Tritter, J. and McCallum, A. (2006) 'The Snakes and Ladders of User Involvement: Moving Beyond Arnstein', *Health Policy* 76(2) 156–68.

Unger, R. (1998) *Democracy Realized.* London: Verso.

United Nations (2004) *World Population Prospects: The 2004 Revision.* New York: United Nations; at www.un.org/esa/population/publications/publications.htm [12 August 2006]

United Nations (2005) *Millennium Ecosystem Assessment.* New York: United Nations; at www.maweb.org/en [12 August 2006]

United Nations Development Programme (RSA) (2004) *Ten Days in Johannesburg.* Pretoria: Department of Environmental Affairs and Tourism and United Nations Development Programme.

United Nations Development Programme (1998) *Human Development Report 1998.* New York, at http://hdr.undp.org/reports/global/1998/en/ [5 November 2006]

United Nations Environment Programme (2007) *Introducing the Concept of*

Decoupling. Unpublished background paper in preparation for the launch of the International Panel on Sustainable Resource Management. Paris.

Upton, S. (1995) 'Contracting in the Science Sector', *Public Sector*, 18(4) 2–5.

Utterback, J. (1996) *Mastering the Dynamics Of Innovation*. Cambridge, MA: Harvard Business School Press.

Vallgårda, S., Krasnick, A. and Vrangbæk, K. (2001) *Denmark: Healthcare Systems in Transition*. Copenhagen: European Observatory on Healthcare Systems.

Van Breda, J. (2008) *Overcoming the Disciplinary Divide: A Necessary Prerequisite for the Establishment of Sustainability Science: Towards the Possibility of a Transdisciplinary Hermeneutics*. Stellenbosch: African Sun Media.

Van de Ven, A., Polley, D., Garud, R. and Venkataraman, S. (1999) *Innovation Journey*. New York: Oxford University Press.

Van der Wal, Z. and Van Hout, E. (2009) 'Is Public Value Pluralism Paramount? The Intrinsic Multiplicity and Hybridity of Public Values', *International Journal of Public Administration*, 32, 220–31.

Van Kersbergen, K. (1995) *Social Capitalism: A Study of Christian Democracy and the Welfare State*. London: Routledge.

Vincent, J. (1998) *Jobseeker's Allowance Evaluation: Qualitative Research on Disallowed and Sanctioned Claimants. Phase Two: After Jobseeker's Allowance*. Norwich: Department for Education and Employment/HMSO.

Von Hippel, E. (1988) *The Sources of Innovation*. New York: Oxford University Press.

Von Hippel, E. (2005) *Democratizing Innovation*. Cambridge, MA: MIT Press.

Von Hippel, E. and Von Krogh, G. (2003) 'Open-Source Software and the "Private-Collective" Innovation Model: Issues for Organizational Science', *Organization Science*, 14(2) 209–23.

Vos, P. (2002) *Health and Healthcare in the Netherlands*. Maarssen: Elsevier Gezonheidszorg.

Wackernagle, M. and Rees, W. (2004) *Our Ecological Footprint*. Gabriola, BC: New Society.

Wagner, P. (ed.) (2006) *The Languages of Civil Society*. Oxford: Berghahn.

Wallschutzky, I. (1988) *The Effects of Tax Reform on Tax Evasion*. Australian Tax Research Foundation, Research Study No. 8. Sydney: Australian Tax Research Foundation.

Walras, L. (1874) *Éléments d'économie politique pure; ou, théorie de la richesse sociale*. Lausanne: Corbaz.

Wanless, D. (2003) *Securing Good Health for the Whole Population: Population Health Trends*. London: HMSO.

Watson, R., Wakhungu, J. and Herren, H. (2008) *International Assessment of Agricultural Knowledge, Science and Technology for Development (IAASTD)*; at www.agassessment.org/ [21 April 2008]

Weaver, D. and Hasenfeld, Y. (1997) 'Case Management Practices, Participants' Responses, and Compliance in Welfare-to-Work Programs', *Social Work Research*, 21(2) 92–100.

Weber, M. (1925) *Wirtschaft und Gesellschaft*. Tübingen: Mohr.

Weber, S. (2004) *The Success of Open Source*. Cambridge, MA: Harvard University Press.

Wensley, R. (1990) 'The Voice of the Consumer?: Speculations on the Limits to the Marketing Analogy', *European Journal of Marketing*, 24(7) 49–60.

West, K. and Davis, P. (2010) 'What Is the Public Value of Government Action? Towards a (New) Pragmatic Approach to Values Questions in Public Endeavours', *Public Administration*, online, July 2010.

Whitaker, G. (1980) 'Co-production: Citizen Participation in Service Delivery', *Public Administration Review*, 40 240–6.

White Paper (2006) *Security in Retirement: Towards a New Pensions System*. London: Pensions Policy Institute.

Whiteside, N. (1997) 'Regulating Markets', *Public Administration*, 75(3) 467–87.

Whiteside, N. (2003) 'Historical Perspectives on the Politics of Pension Reform', in G. Clark and N. Whiteside (eds) *Pension Security in the 21st Century*. Oxford University Press.

Whiteside, N. (2005) 'Conventions, Institutions and Political Frameworks of Welfare Policy Comparison', in J.-C. Barbier and M.-T. Letablier (eds) *Politiques sociales: enjeux methodologiques et epistemologiques des comparaisons internationales*. Brussels: Laing.

Whiteside, N. and Salais, R. (1998) 'Comparing Welfare States: Social Protection and Industrial Politics in France and Britain', *Journal of European Social Policy*, 8(2) 139–55.

Whitson, K. (2005) 'HEIs and Widening Participation' in C. Duke and G. Layer (eds), *Widening Participation: Which Way Forward For English Higher Education?* Leicester: National Institute of Adult Continuing Education.

Wildavsky, A. (1992) *The New Politics of the Budgetary Process*. New York: HarperCollins.

Williams, I. and Shearer, H. (2010) *Public Value and the Englsih NHS: A Review of the Literature*. Warwick Business School and the NHS Business School and the NHS Institute for Innovative and Improvement.

Williams, I. and Shearer, H. (2011 forthcoming) 'Appraising Public Value: Past, Present and Futures', *Public Administration*.

Williams, R. (1958) *Culture and Society*. Harmondsworth: Penguin.

Williams, R. (1976) *Keywords:* London, Fontana/Collins.

Williams, R. (1989) 'Adult Education and Social Change', *What I Came to Say*. London: Hutchinson.

Wilson, J. (1989) *Bureaucracy: What Government Agencies Do and Why They Do It*. New York: Basic.

Winkley, D. (1983) 'An Analytical View of School Leadership', *School Organization*, 3(1) 1–6.

Winkley, D. (2002) *Handsworth Revolution: The Odyssey of a School*. London: de la Mare .

Womack, J. and Jones, D. (2003) *Lean Thinking*, 2nd edn. New York: Free Press.

World Bank (1994) *Averting the Old Age Crisis*. Oxford University Press.

World Bank (2002) *Globalization, Growth and Poverty*. Washington, DC.

World Bank (2002) *The Development Effectiveness Record: Learning from Experience*. Washington, DC.

World Commission on Environment and Development (1987) *Our Common Future*. Oxford University Press.

World Wildlife Fund, Zoological Society of London and Global Footprint Network (2006) *Living Planet Report 2006*. Gland, Switzerland: WWF.

Yong, R. (2007) 'The Circular Economy in China', *Journal of Material Cycles and Waste Management*. 9(2) 121–9.

Young, M. (1958) *The Rise of the Meritocracy*. Harmondsworth: Penguin.

Young Foundation and CABE (Commission for Architecture and the Built Environment) (2006) *Mapping Value in the Built Urban Environment*. At http://www.youngfoundation.org/files/images/CABE_Final_April_7_2006.pdf

Zeller, M. and Meyer, R. (2002) 'Improving the Performance of Microfinance: Financial Sustainability, Outreach, and Impact', in M. Zeller and R. Meyer (eds) *The Triangle of Microfinance: Financial Sustainability, Outreach, and Impact*. Baltimore, MD: Johns Hopkins University Press.

Index